ABORIGINAL AMERICAN INDIAN BASKETRY

ABORIGINAL AMERICAN INDIAN BASKETRY

STUDIES IN A TEXTILE ART WITHOUT MACHINERY

OTIS TUFTON MASON

Peregrine Smith, Inc.
SANTA BARBARA AND SALT LAKE CITY
1976

Mason, Otis Tufton, 1838-1908.
  Aboriginal American basketry.

  Reprint of the 1904 ed. published by Govt. Print.
Off., Washington, which was issued as Annual report
of the Board of Regents of the Smithsonian Institution
for the year ending June 30, 1902 and also as Document
no. 484 of House of Representatives, 57th Congress,
2d session.
  Bibliography: p.
  1. Indians—Basket making. I. Title. II. Series:
Smithsonian Institution. Annual report of the Board of
regents. III. Series: United States. 57th Congress, 2d
session, 1902-1903. House. Document; no. 484.
[E59.B3M3 1976]   746.4'1   76-11828
ISBN 0-87905-034-9

PREFACE

Aboriginal American Basketry was originally published in 1904 as a report to the U.S. National Museum under the direction of the Smithsonian Institution. As such, it was one of the papers included in a massive volume of the reports of the National Museum for that year. In respect for the origins of this study and because of bibliographic citations and references to existing pagination elsewhere in the text, we have retained the original pagination. Thus, this book commences with page 173.

We are very happy to be able to take a part in making this magnificent book available to the thousands who would otherwise be unable to know and study the finest work ever written on American Indian basketry. To keep the book from becoming prohibitively expensive, the forty-six hand painted color plates in the original have been reproduced in black and white. Two of these can be seen on the front and back covers.

PREFACE

FOREWORD

Of all the indigenous crafts of Pre-Columbian North America, none is generally regarded as so typically "Indian" as basketry. Rightly or wrongly, basketry and American Indians have become synonymous not only for modern Americans but also for much of the world. While not wholly accurate, this equation or association does have considerable basis in hard fact.

The production of basketry, which presently extends back at least 11,000 years (cf. Adovasio 1974, 1975, 1976), is one of the oldest aboriginal crafts in North America. The antiquity of basketry manufacture is probably second only to the making of cordage and netting among the so-called "perishable fiber arts." The origins of North American basketry manufacture are so remote that the craft may have been part and parcel of the technological milieu of the first migrants to this hemisphere.

More impressive in some ways than its great antiquity is the enormous technological and stylistic diversity as well as the broad geographical distribution of North American basketry manufacture. In almost all of the major cultural sub-areas – from the cold and windswept Arctic and Sub-Arctic to the arid Southwest – basketry was widely used both prehistorically and ethnographically. Not surprisingly, basketry served a multiplicity of functions and assumed stunningly myriad forms in the many and varied environments of the northern hemisphere of the New World. Indeed, so great is the technical and stylistic variety of North American basketry that few have ever attempted to describe, classify, or systematize it on a regional, not to mention continental, basis.

In this light, it is therefore both astonishing and fitting that the *first* meaningful attempt at describing and classifying North American basketry was also the greatest of its kind ever produced to date. I am, of course, referring to this volume, *Aboriginal American Basketry*, and I choose the terms astonishing and fitting with care, not unmixed with admiration. The book is astonishing because the extraordinary task of synthesizing the basketwork of a thousand plus Indian populations is precisely that; I elect to say fitting because the author, Otis Tufton Mason, was extraordinarily well endowed to initiate and execute a work of this magnitude.

The span of Mason's life from 1838 to 1908 effectively encompassed two profound and not wholly unrelated episodes in the history of the United States. The first was the rapid and explosive development of

American industry and science, while the other was the extinction of aboriginal American culture, at least as it once was.

Drawn to and ultimately trained in the humanities, Mason joined the still fledgling Smithsonian Institution in 1872 as a collaborator in ethnology. For the next twelve years he devoted the great bulk of his considerable energy and talent to classifying and arranging the oftentimes chaotic ethnology collections. In so doing, he contributed heavily to the development of the system and order which are among the hallmarks of the National Museum today.

During the same period, Mason produced an edited version of Klemm's *Kulturgeschichte* (1875) and also prepared short pamphlets and manuals for the guidance of archaeologists and ethnologists in the field.

After assuming the curatorship of the National Museum's Department of Ethnology in 1884, Mason continued and expanded his work in classification and systematics. In fact, for the next 25 years, these interests were the cornerstones of his life. A stream of generally short publications reporting the results of his classificatory/descriptive efforts appeared at more or less regular intervals. Among them were a series of articles (1884a, 1884b, 1893, 1900a, 1900b) in which he propounded and subsequently refined a classificatory system or approach for the treatment of material cultural assemblages.

Basically, Mason believed that every human "invention" or artifact assumes "tribal" (i.e. culturally bound or determined) modifications, the sum total of which defines the range of variation of that particular item. He believed that by precisely delineating the range of variation of items of material culture he could establish a useful typology for virtually any class of objects. As noted by Hough (1908: 662), any specimens thus worked up become "types" and Mason firmly believed that by arranging these types, "like with like," a coherent, ordered and culturally meaningful taxonomy would result. His basic approach was geocultural and his descriptions were formulated according to the prevailing practices in natural historical studies.

Mason's taxonomic and descriptive efforts culminated in his massive compendium of North American basketry which was completed in 1902 and published in 1904. This work was not only the longest he ever produced but also, without question, the greatest. Using all of his considerable experience and expertise in handling individual collections, Mason tackled the problem of ordering and describing the basketry production of a whole continent.

The success of his undertaking should be apparent to any who have or will read this volume. While modern scholars can find many flaws in Mason's approach to basketry, particularly on the same taxonomic/descriptive levels which were his chosen forte, the work itself has justifiably become a classic of its genre.

Not only did Mason succeed in presenting to scholars and laymen alike the bewildering panorama which is or was aboriginal American basketry, he also accomplished his task with true literary style and flair.

In retrospect, Mason's work epitomized and underscored the great socio-cultural processes of his time. *Through* his work and writings he contributed greatly to the development of American science, and *in* his writings, particularly this work, he preserved for posterity a craft, often elevated to the level of true art, which was passing away forever along with its makers.

J. M. Adovasio, Ph.D.
Department of Anthropology
University of Pittsburgh

References Cited

ADOVASIO, J. M.

    1974   "Prehistoric North American Basketry". *Nevada State Museum Anthropological Papers*, No. 16.

    1975   "Basketry and Netting in North America". In *The Handbook of North American Indians*, Volume XIV, *Technology and Visual Arts*, edited by W. C. Sturtevant. (In press).

    1976   *Basketry Technology*. Aldine.

HOUGH, WALTER

    1908   Otis Tufton Mason. *American Anthropologist*, N.S. Volume 10:661-667.

MASON, OTIS T.

    1875   *Ethnological Directions Relative to the Indian Tribes of the United States*. Prepared under the direction of the Office of Indian Affairs. Washington.

    1884a   "Basketwork of the North American Aborigines". *Report of the U. S. National Museum*. Washington.

    1884b   "Throwing-Sticks in the National Museum". *Report of the U. S. National Museum*. Washington.

    1893   "North American Bows, Arrows, and Quivers". *Smithsonian Report*. Washington.

    1900a   "Traps of the Amerinds: A Study in Psychology and Invention". *American Anthropologist*, N.S. Volume 11: 657-675.

    1900b   "Aboriginal American Harpoons: A Study in Ethnic Distribution and Invention". *Report of the U. S. National Museum*. Washington.

ANNUAL REPORT

OF THE

BOARD OF REGENTS

OF THE

SMITHSONIAN INSTITUTION,

SHOWING

THE OPERATIONS, EXPENDITURES, AND CONDITION OF THE INSTITUTION

FOR THE

YEAR ENDING JUNE 30, 1902.

REPORT

OF THE

U. S. NATIONAL MUSEUM.

WASHINGTON:
GOVERNMENT PRINTING OFFICE.
1904.

ABORIGINAL AMERICAN BASKETRY:
STUDIES IN A TEXTILE ART WITHOUT MACHINERY.

BY

OTIS TUFTON MASON,

Curator, Division of Ethnology.

TABLE OF CONTENTS.

LIST OF ILLUSTRATIONS.

PLATES.

TEXT FIGURES.

Page.

ABORIGINAL AMERICAN BASKETRY:
STUDIES IN A TEXTILE ART WITHOUT MACHINERY.

By Otis Tufton Mason,
Curator, Division of Ethnology.

Adde et *bascuada* et mille escaria.
Terence, 12:46.
Barbara de pictis veni *bascuada* Britannis
Sed me jam mavult dicere Roma suum.
Martial, XIV: 99.

INTRODUCTION

Aboriginal British or Pictish baskets and a thousand receptacles, says Terence, were carried to Rome by the successors of Julius Cæsar, and Martial adds that the word "basket" is Pictish, [a] though the Romans would have us believe it to have been indigenous.

Remnants of basketry are gathered from the Swiss lake dwellings, made in several of the technical processes well known to the American Indians and to be described later.

In the second volume of Keller's Lake Dwellings (pls. 134–137) are startlingly interesting groups of such basketry. You have, first of all, the methods of treating the bark of trees and flax to form the fiber in various stages of preparation. Network and frame weaving are also there illustrated, but in this place attention is drawn only to the basketry. On his Plate 134 may be seen plain checkerwork and twined work in 2-strand and 3-stand varieties, also coiled work in the following varieties: (*a*) Foundation of two rods, sewing done with bark strips so as to inclose both rods below, the stitches interlocking; (*b*) foundation of two rods, sewing inclosing them both, but not one of the rods underneath; the stitches interlock and split the upper portion of the one just below, as in many American baskets. The twined work of Robenhausen and Wangen is in a great number of varieties. There is solid, plain weaving; also open work twined weaving, the body being stems of plants; borders are held together with twined weaving. In some specimens of open work the warp of twined weaving is in pairs;

---

[a] On the derivation of the word, however, consult the New English Dictionary and the Century Dictionary.

but there are not shown in any of Keller's plates the types of twined work in which the warp plays any part for ornamentation; and in the remains, so far as examined, no attempts are made at embroidery, or overlaying, or any of the species of fine decoration, to be seen in the Alaskan or Californian weaving.[a]

In the Arabian Nights, the story of the lady who was murdered by her husband mentions a very large basket, by its size reminding one of the granary baskets of California, but this was evidently in coiled work, very much in the style of the Hopi plaques.   The Caliph, Haroun Alraschid—

came to the bank of the river, and the fisherman, having thrown in his net, when he drew it out again brought up a trunk, close shut and very heavy. The Caliph made the vizier pay him 100 sequins immediately and sent him away. Mesrour, by his master's orders, carried the trunk on his shoulders, and the Caliph, eager to know what it contained, returned to the palace with all speed. When the trunk was opened, they found in it a large basket made of palm leaves, shut up, and the covering sewed with red thread. To satisfy the Caliph's impatience, they cut the thread with a knife and took out of the basket a package wrapped in a sorry piece of hanging and bound about with rope, in which, when untied, they found, to their amazement, the dead body of a young lady cut in small pieces.

The Ute Indians in ancient times used basketry for mortuary purposes, but by them made of the rarest material and with faultless workmanship, adorned with symbols of their religion.   The dead man or woman was covered with a large carrying basket, and all around were laid with loving care the finest specimens of the craft.

It is interesting to know that the first mention of baskets in the Bible is in connection with dreams.   Joseph was a prisoner in Egypt. He had interpreted the butler's dream so favorably that Pharaoh's baker came also to him.

When the chief baker saw that the interpretation was good, he said unto Joseph, I also was in my dream, and, behold, I had three white baskets on my head; and in the uppermost basket [sal] there was of all manner of baked meats [sweetmeats] for Pharaoh; and the birds did eat them out of the basket upon my head. And Joseph answered and said, This is the interpretation thereof: The three baskets are three days; yet within three days shall Pharaoh lift up thy head from off thee, and shall hang thee on a tree; and the birds shall eat thy flesh from off thee.

It may in general be assumed that the baskets used by the Israelites were not unlike those of the Egyptians.   If the ancient baskets of Egypt resembled the modern, those mentioned were of the coiled type, made from palm leaf, resembling thick bread plaques of the Hopi pueblos of Arizona.   They were doubtless in use throughout North Africa long before the days of Joseph.

Specimens of this type of ancient coiled basketry were dug up by Randall-MacIver and Wilkin at El Armah, 6 miles south of the site of

---

[a] Ferdinand Keller, The Lake Dwellings of Switzerland and other parts of Europe, 2 vols., London, 1878.

Abydos, in middle Egypt.   They are the oldest that have yet been found in the world.   El Armah dates back to the earliest "new race," through the entire middle period down to the late prehistoric in Egypt.   Far up the Nile the type persists.   It will be seen in abundance at Aden, and it exists in much more elegant material in Hindustan.   This proves the persistence of a single type through six thousand years.   Long ago caravans took it into the heart of Africa, and the reader must not be surprised further on in discovering at least a limited sphere of influence for it in America, where the descendants of the Moors who invaded Spain left them.

The Greek word for basket is kaneon, or kanastron, from kanna, a reed, whence our cannister, through the Latin canistra.   Or, to come closer to our theme, basketry was made long ago in the warmer countries of the Old World, as they are now in the New, from cane.   In the time of Homer this word was applied frequently to receptacles of clay, bronze, and gold.   Doubtless, in earlier ages the Greek women were nimble-fingered basket makers, but the forms are not preserved.

Wherever civilization has come in contact with lower races, whether in Britain, Africa, Polynesia, or America, it has found the woman enjoying the most friendly acquaintance with textile plants and skillful in weaving their roots, stems, and leaves into basketry, matting, and other similar products without machinery.   Basketry was wellnigh universal throughout the Western Hemisphere before the discovery, while at least one-half of the area was devoid of pottery.

Ancient cemeteries, mounds, caves, ruins, and lake dwellings gave evidence of the high antiquity of the art in both continents.   The researches of Holmes and Willoughby on mound pottery; of Yarrow and Schumacher in southwestern California; of Cushing, Fewkes, and Hough in ancient pueblos; of Nordenskjöld and Pepper in the cliff dwellings of the southwest; of G. O. Dorsey, of the Field Columbian Museum, and many European explorers in Peru, demonstrate that no changes have taken place in this respect, either in the variety of the technical processes or the fineness of the workmanship.   There is an unbroken genealogy of basket making on the Continent, running back to the most ancient times.

For a time cheap patented ware made from veneering threatened to obliterate the ancient plicated basket, but at the same time the latter became exalted to a pastime and a fine art, and there were never so many genuine lovers of the handicraft as at present.

In the past few years a sympathetic spirit has been awakened in the United States to keep alive this charming aboriginal art and to preserve its precious relics.   In every State in the Union will be found rich collections, both in public and private museums.   People of wealth vie with one another in owning them.   It almost amounts to a disease, which might be called "canastromania."   They resemble the "merchantman seeking goodly pearls, who, when he had found one pearl of great price, went and sold all that he had and bought it." The genuine enthusiasm kindled in the search, the pride of success in the acquisition, the care bestowed upon them, witness that the basket is a worthy object of study. The story is told of a distinguished collector who walked many weary miles to the shelter of a celebrated old weaver. He spent the day admiring her work, but still asking for something better. He knew that she had made finer pieces. At last flattery and gold won. She tore out the back of her hut, and there, hid from mortal eyes, was the basket that was to be burned at her death. Nothing could be more beautiful, and it will be her monument.

I. DEFINITION OF BASKETRY

A place for everything.—FRANKLIN.

Basketry is the mother of all loom work and beadwork. In that elaboration of industries, through which they pass from naturism to artificialism, from handwork to machine work, from human power to beast power, wind power, water power, steam or fire power, and electric power, the loom is no exception. The first and most versatile shuttles were women's fingers. Machinery has added speed. But there are many niceties of technic to which the machine device can not yet aspire.

Over and above the sympathetic spirit engendered and the kind encouragement given to exquisite and most worthy artists by the collection of basketry, the study is a very important one from the side of culture. It is the alpha of an art in which billions of capital are invested, millions of human beings are employed, whose materials and products are transported to earth's remotest limits, whose textures are sought by every tribe of mankind. It is from this last point of view that the present work is written.

The praises of men who invented the cotton gin, the power loom, and the tapestry loom will be repeated, and monuments erected to memorialize those who harnessed the forces of nature to do their bidding. Here a good word is said for the earlier, more primitive, women who made the others possible. It is true that pride in the ownership of an exquisite piece of work may be joined with frigid indifference toward the maker. It is to be hoped that with admiration of American basketry may be coupled a humane feeling for Indian women themselves, who have made so much genuine pleasure possible.

American basketry, ancient and modern, may be studied under the following subdivisions:

I. Definition of the art, its materials, tools, processes, and products.
II. Materials for basketry, with lists of plants, animals, minerals, including the Indian name, common names, scientific names.

III. Basket making or construction.
   Harvesting materials, with account of tools and apparatus.
   Preparing materials, including the tools and processes, peeling, splitting, making splints, shredding, soaking, cleaning, yarning or twisting, twining, braiding, gauging, coloring (dyeing).
   Processes of manufacture—tools, apparatus, and patterns.
   Braiding, checkerwork, wicker, twilled, wrapped woof, twined, and coiled, and checks, decussations, meshes, stitches.   Women at work.
 IV. Ornamentation on basketry.
   1. Forms and structure in baskets.
   2. Mosaic elements in decoration.
   3. Design in technic and color.
  V. Symbolism, also absence of, and meanings.
 VI. Uses of basketry.
VII. Ethnic varieties and culture provinces, ancient and modern.   Indian names.
VIII. Collections, public and private.
 IX. Bibliography.

For convenience, basketry may be compared in the following-named regions:

1. Eastern region: Canada, Eastern States, Southern States, Western States.

2. Alaskan region: Interior Alaska, Arctic Alaska, Aleutian Chain, Southeastern Alaska, Queen Charlotte Archipelago.

3. Fraser-Columbia region: Fraser drainage, Columbia drainage.

4. Oregon-California region: Southern Oregon, California.

5. Interior Basin region: Between Rocky Mountains and the Sierras.

6. Middle and South American region: Mexico, Central America, eastern and western South America.

These regions must be regarded only as convenient divisions for reference.   The last named is a measure of ignorance, rather, for it could easily be divided into half a dozen regions.   Again, before the balance of savagery had been violently disturbed by the discovery of the hemisphere there were migrations of native blood and speech and arts.   Basketry further on will be witness to many of these.

Basketry is differentiated from network by the fact that the meshes of the latter are not formed by decussations, but by knots; and from loom products, not only by the material, which is usually less rigid, but by the workmanship, which is done by machinery.   Needlework is approached in coiled basketry and beadwork borrows from all weaves. No wide gulf separates the different varieties of textiles, however, beginning with such coarse products as brush fences and fish weirs and ending with the finest lace and needlework.

In form basketry varies through the following classes of objects:

1. Flat mats or wallets, generally flexible.

2. Plaques or food plates, which are slightly concave.   These occur in quality of the coarsest sieve to that of the sacred meal tray.

3. Bowls for mush and other foods and for ceremonial purposes, hemispherical in general outline.

4. Pots for cooking, with cylindrical sides and rounded or flat bottoms. These vary into cones, truncated cones, and trough-shaped baskets.

5. Jars and fanciful shapes, in which the mouth is constricted, frequently very small, and now and then supplied with cover. They are spindle shaped, pyriform, napiform, and, indeed, imitate fruits known to the natives. The influence of civilization in giving modern shapes to basketry has not always been beneficial to this class of forms.

W. H. Holmes, writing of the transition from service to decoration, speaks of form in and on basketry as (1) functional and essential only, (2) functional and æsthetic combined, and (3) as suprafunctional and wholly æsthetic.

There are two distinct types of technic in basketry, namely, (1) hand-*woven* basketry, which is built on a warp foundation, and (2) sewed or *coiled* basketry, which is built on a foundation of rods, splints, or straws.

KINDS OF WOVEN BASKETRY

A. Checkerwork: The warp and the weft having the same width, thickness, and pliability.

B. Diagonal or twilled basketry: Two or more weft strands over two or more warp strands.

C. Wickerwork: Inflexible warp; slender, flexible weft.

D. Wrapped weft, or single weft wrapped: The weft strand is wrapped, or makes a bight about the warp at each decussation, as in the Mohave *Kiho*.

E. Twined or wattled basketry: Weft of two or more elements.

KINDS OF COILED BASKETRY

A. Coiled work without foundation.

B. Simple interlocking coils.

C. Single-rod foundation.

D. Two-rod foundation.

E. Rod and welt foundation.

F. Two-rod and splint foundation.

G. Three-rod foundation.

H. Splint foundation.

I. Grass-coil foundation.

K. Fuegian coiled basketry.

These will be described at length in the proper place.

In basket-making there are several characteristics to be observed which will enable one to classify the objects and to refer them to their several tribal manufacturers. These characteristics are the material, the framework, the methods of weaving, the coiling or sewing, the border, the decoration, the use, etc.

The tool almost universally employed in the manufacture of coiled ware is a bone awl or pricker. Of the manipulation of the material previously to the weaving little is known.

In the technical drawings accompanying this paper the actual size of the specimens is generally indicated by a series of inch marks in the margin. The inches on the standard line are shown by spaces between dots. In order to indicate exactly the manner of weaving, a square, usually an inch in dimension, is taken from a portion of the surface wherein all the methods of manipulation occur. This square is enlarged sufficiently to make the structure comprehensible. This plan enables one to show form and ornamentation in the whole figure, as well as the method of treatment in the enlarged inch.

The writer is indebted to a large number of friends in various parts of the United States, especially on the Pacific slope, who have given him access to their valuable collections, furnished information, and sent photographs. Especial thanks are due to F. V. Coville for writing the chapter on plants, to William H. Holmes for advice in matters of ornamentation, and to Dr. C. Hart Merriam for privilege of studying the precious collection made by him. Many friends who have generously given their special knowledge and supplied photographs and illustrations will be mentioned in the proper place. At the same time he would express his admiration of their zeal and generosity, through which the Sybilline leaves of an almost lost chapter in human industrial history has been rescued from oblivion.

With a few exceptions the makers of baskets are women. In the division of labor belonging to the lowest stages of culture the industrial arts were fostered by women, the military and aggressive arts by men. It is a well-known rule in these first stages of progress that, with few exceptions, the user of an implement or utensil was the maker of it There are people on the earth among whom the men are the basket makers. Indeed, for ceremonial purposes our own Indian priests or medicine men are frequently the makers of their own basket drums, etc.

As soon as the products of this art entered into the world's commerce, and uncanny machinery was necessary for the manufacture, the art of basket weaving passed from the hands of its foster mothers and became man's work, but in the Western Hemisphere almost exclusively the basket makers have been women.

It is a matter of profound regret that already over much of the United States the art has degenerated, or at least has been modified. In methods, forms, and colors truly old things have passed away, and, behold, all things have become new. But proof is forthcoming that the contrary is true in some places. The Hyde Expedition and other associations have made determined efforts to resist the demoralizing influences of trade.

This process of extinction has gone on with differing rapidity in the several areas. Nothing ancient in mechanical processes, in form, and design can be predicated of the basketry sold at summer resorts. The trees are felled by the white man and the trunks divided into ribbons by his latest machinery. The Indian woman uses a steel gauge to regulate the width of her weft, steel awls for sewing. Even in Western ware the demand and influence of mercenary motives drown the cry of the ancient spirit in the lowly artist. Plate 1 will show the conflict for preeminence between the old and the new. Dogs and horses are mingled with designs older than the Discovery. (See also Plates 42, 168.)

But it is not alone the unrefined public who eliminate the delightful classic from the decoration of basketry; men and women with the most exalted motives have for centuries substituted European and Asiatic forms for aboriginal in basketry.

Plate 2 is worthy of notice in this regard. Eliminate the human figures altogether as pictorial and realistic and without standing in an art whose designs are preeminently symbolical. The others are divided into two series, those bearing some suggestion of old patterns and those covered with classical fretwork as the underlying motive and then run wild with savage freehand. (See also Plates 50, 58, 233.)

The reason for the genuine unspoiled art of the tribes in northwestern California is given by Carl Purdy. The Franciscan fathers who built the missions in the central and southern portions of the State never penetrated these wilds; the traders of the Hudson's Bay Company, whose presence and traffic changed the arts of other Indians so profoundly, did not come so far south, and Mexican soldiers were driven out of the country. It was not until settlers in the middle of the last century began to maltreat the Indians that bloody conflicts arose which resulted in their present status, but, fortunately, these pioneers had no interest in baskets and probably did not notice them. There are in possession of old families in the Eastern States baskets sent home by the Forty-niners that now are worth their weight in gold. The forms and designs on these are similar to many still made. This indicates that the art has kept its old-time purity.

It must be distinctly understood that many basket-making Indians are not now in their priscan homes. Besides the migration occasioned by the ordinary motives operating on the minds of savages, the rapid intrusion of white settlers and the strong arm of the Government have hastened these movements. For our purposes these compulsory migrations must be noted specially in the case of basket makers. For example, on the Round Valley reservations in northern California are the Concow (Pujunan); and from the eastern side of the Sacramento Valley, the Nomelakki and Wailaki (Copehan), Little Lakes (Kulanapan), Ukie (Yukian), and Pit rivers (Palaihnahan), belonging to five absolutely different linguistic families. Now, in a collection of baskets from Round Valley one must not be surprised to find shapes, uses, decorations, and names for the same form or part or design extremely varied and mixed.

The author is aware that he has come far short of doing justice to his theme. Omissions will be noticed, and it is feared that some references of work to the wrong band or tribe have been made. This is unavoidable in a great museum. It is only in such rare collections as have been gathered with one's own hands that such errors can be avoided.

VOCABULARY OF BASKETRY

So much is said and written on the subject of Indian basketry that a vocabulary is desirable. On some terms all are even now agreed. All things considered, words in common use should be adopted. There are, as before mentioned, two absolutely different kinds of technic employed, dividing basketry into *woven* and *coiled*. The former leads to the loom, the latter to the needle. It is not correct to speak of warp and weft in the latter, only in the former; the parts of coiled basketry are the *foundation* and the *sewing*. The following terms and definitions are suggested, not arbitrarily, but subject always to amendment and common consent. Words from Indian languages are purposely omitted. A few of them, however, ought to be retained, such as "tee," for the Pomo twined weaving:

Basket.—A vessel or receptacle in textile material; a technic product resembling this.

Basketry.—A general term including (1) basket making, the process or art; (2) basket work, the technic or stitches, any textile motive resembling work in baskets; (3) basket ware, a collection of finished products.

Beading.—A strip of bark or a splint run in and out through the spaces in woven or among the stitches in coiled basketry.

Braidwork.—Fabric in which three or more elements are braided, as in some three-strand twined basketry. See *False braid.* Preferred to the word plaited. There may be flat, round, or square braid. The term sennit is also allowable.

Buttonhole stitch.—A series of half hitches, as in Fuegian coiled basketry.

Check.—Where warp and weft cross.

Checkerwork.—Basket work in which the warp and weft are equally flexible and the checks are square, or at least rectangular.

Chevron.—V-shaped ornament, in which two or more colored lines meet at an angle; for example, the device on the sleeve of a non-commissioned officer. (See *Herringbone* and *Zigzag.*)

Chinking.—Soft materials between hard stems in the foundation of coiled basketry.

Coil.—An element in basketry ornamentation. The varieties are plain coil, reversed coil, loop coil, continuous loop coil.

Coiled basketry.—Type of basket work in which a foundation of hard or soft material, arranged in a spiral, is held together by means of over-and-over sewing.

Crossed warp.—Type of basket work in which two sets of warp cross each other at an angle—for interlacing weft, for seizing or wrapping (Makah), or for twined weaving, common in Attu wallets.

Decussations.—Crossing of warp at acute angles.

Diagonal weaving.—Passing weft over two or more warp elements, but not the same in adjoining rows. Used here chiefly of twined weaving to distinguish it from twilled weaving with single weft element; also running the weft at an angle, as in matting.

Diaper.—A surface decoration which shows a pattern by the relief or direction of warp and weft.

Designs.—Figures and patterns used in the ornamentation of basketry. Must not be confounded with *Symbol.*

Embroidery.—Ornamentation added after the basket is finished. (See *False embroidery.*)

Fagotting.—Same as *Hemstitch.*

False braid.—An appearance of braid work on the margin of a basket made with a single splint in ball stitch or "racking-seizing."

False embroidery.—An appearance of embroidery made on Tlinkit and other twined ware by wrapping the strands on the outside with colored material in the process of weaving.

Fiber.—A flexible substance composed of filaments such as cedar bark, wild hemp, etc.

Frap.—To bind one element about another.

Fret.—The Greek ornament occurring in endless variety on basketry.

Furcate.—Said of stitches in coiled sewing intentionally and symmetrically split—bifurcate, trifurcate, etc.

Fylfot.—Ornament imitating a Greek cross with arms extended at right angles, all in the same direction; called also Swastika.

Gorrita.—The shallow basket bowl of the Pimas and other southwestern tribes.

Hemstitch.—Drawing warps together in groups of two or more and holding them by twined weavings. Seen in Aleutian openwork wallets. Called also fagotting.

Herringbone.—Basketry designs in which chevron patterns are in parallel series.

Herringbone border.—On coiled basketry a finish in which with a single splint the appearance of 3-ply braid is given. (See *False braid.*)

Hitched weft.—Basket work in which the weft makes a half hitch about each warp element. In coiled work it would be hitched sewing, same as buttonhole stitch.

Hurdle.—A coarse form of basket work in brush and trees for hunting and fishing purposes.

Imbricated ornament.—Coiled basketry in which a strip of soft material is folded back and forth over the stitches, overlapping like shingles on a roof or the folds in knife plaiting. Klikitat and Fraser River basketry are imbricated.

Impacted.—Driven close together, as the weft or stitches in basketry.

Inset.—A pattern worked separately into a basket. The Chilcat blankets are thus woven.

Interlacing.—The crossing and intertwining of parts, as in woven baskets and borders.

Interstices.—Open spaces left in weaving.

Knife plaiting.—See *Imbricated ornament.*

Lattice weaving.—Basket work in which a frame of rods crossing at right angles is held together by wrapping the intersections with a single splint or ribbon, as in Makah basketry, or by a twined weft, as in the Pomo Tee weaving.

Multiple coil.—The foundation of coiled basketry made up of filaments, grass stems, or splints.

Muskemoot.—Loucheux netted bags of babiche. Coiled work without foundation.

Meander.—Crossed frets in basketry ornament.

Oblique weaving.—Chiefly in matting, where the weaving begins at one corner.

Osier.—Basket materials prepared from small stems of willow or similar plants. Shoots of dogwood (*Cornus stolonifera*) are called red osier.

Overlaying.—Laying a split straw or other colored material on a tough weft splint or sewing material in basket making, to take the place of colored bark. If the two are not twisted on each other, the figure does not show inside the basket.

Padding.—Soft material in the foundation of coiled basketry, helping to make the structure water-tight. (See *Chinking.*)

Pentacle.—In basket ornament a 5-pointed star, whose lines inclose a pentagon.

Pierced warp.—The form of weaving in cat-tail and other soft material when the weft strings pass through the warp. The warp stems are strung on the weft strings.

Radial warp.—The arrangement of warp elements or spokes in the bottom of a cylindrical basket. They may be (1) crossed, (2) cut away, or (3) inserted. Radial patterns or designs are such as proceed from the central portion of a bowl-shaped basket outward to the border.

Scroll work.—Imitation of art scroll on basketry. It is usually angular.

Sewing.—The joining of parts with an awl and splint. Coiled basketry is sewed, not woven.

Shoots.—The young and pliable growth of plants in the first year. Rough shoots, prepared shoots, and split shoots are used.

Shreds.—Irregular strips of plants used in foundations of coiled baskets.

Spiral.—Term applied in basket making and decoration: (1) To the whorled coil, wound about a center and receding, as in Hopi plaques, *flat spiral;* (2) to the helical coil, winding on a cylinder, *cylindrical spiral*, as in coiled jars; (3) to the conical coil, rising in a cone, *conical spiral*.

Splint.—In basketry, a long strip of split wood, uniform in width and thickness for weaving or sewing materials. Often the term is more loosely applied to the split pieces that make up the foundation of coiled work.

Spoke.—Term sometimes applied to each of the elements in radiating basket warp.

Stalk.—The stems of reeds, grass, cattails, etc., for basket materials.

Stitches.—The separate elements in sewing coiled basketry. They may be close or open, whole or split (furcate), and interlocked.

Strand.—One of the elements of the weft in twined basketry, which may be two-strand, three-strand, etc.

Strip.—A narrow ribbon of leaf or other thin basket material answers in function to the harder splints.

String.—Two or more small yarns twisted together. The warp of twined wallets is of strings.

Symbol.—The meaning of a design on a basket. Care must be exercised in the use of this word. Only the maker of the design knows the symbol or meaning.

Tesselate.—Inlaid, as in checkered mosaic. The checks and stitches as well as the designs in baskets have a tesselate appearance.

Twine.—To bend something around another object. In basketry, to make twined ware in any of its varieties, plain, twilled, wrapped, latticed, three-strand, etc.

Warp.—The elements of woven basketry on which the fabric is built up; may be parallel, decussated, latticed, radiated, zigzag, etc.; also a single one of these. Each element may be called a warp. (See *Spoke*.)

Wattling.—Coarse fence or fish weir in wicker or twined basketry.

Weft.—The filling of woven basketry, same as woof.

Weftage.—The texture of woven basketry.

Whip or *whipstitch*.—To sew with an overcast stitch, with long wrapping stitches. The sewing of coiled basketry may be so called. Borders of baskets are often whipped on.

Wickerwork.—Weaving in which the warp is rigid and the weft flexible.

Wind.—To wrap one element about another. Same as *Frap*. In Thompson River wallets the twined weft is wound or frapped with corn husk.

Wrapped weft.—Basket work in which the plain or twined weft is wrapped with soft decorative material.

Waterproofing.—Resin of the pine and mesquite for covering and lining basket jars, rendering them waterproof.

Woof.—See *Weft.*

Yarn.—Fibers twisted together, as in receptacles made from native hemp.

Zigzag.—A broken line of equal angular portions applied to structure or decoration in basketry.

II. MATERIALS FOR BASKETRY

Man is one world, and hath another to attend him.—EMERSON.

In the manufacture of their baskets the Indians have ransacked the three kingdoms of nature—mineral, animal, and vegetal. For the first named Cushing has shown how the Havasupai Indians line the inside of a basket with clay in order to render it fireproof. A great many of the paints or dyes with which the baskets are colored are drawn from the mineral kingdom. In the decoration of basketry beautiful stones and the mineral shells of mollusks are employed, either whole or cut into beads and pendants. (See Plate 3.)

Besides the beautiful shells, teeth, wings of insects, and other hard animal substances used for added ornament, softer parts enter into the very texture of basket work. In a few localities the tribes have relied on them largely. It will be seen that wool of goat, sheep, and llama are treated in precisely the same manner as splints of wood. The undressed skins of smaller mammals, notably the rabbit, are cut into strings and twisted; and dressed hides into babiche to serve as weft in woven baskets and bags. Sinew thread was employed in making coiled basketry about the Great Lakes and farther north. But the most serviceable animal substance for basketry was the feather, its plume for decoration and its quill for hard work as well as ornament. Porcupine quills were likewise split and worked into coiled basketry, in addition to their embellishment of birch-bark utensils. The multitude of uses for feathers in this art will be described later.

The chief dependence, however, of the basket maker is upon the vegetal kingdom. Nearly all parts of plants have been used by one tribe or another for this purpose—roots, stems, bark, leaves, fruits, seeds, and gums. It would seem as though in each area for purposes intended the vegetal kingdom had been thoroughly explored and exhausted above ground and under ground. Is it not marvelous to think that unlettered savages should know so much botany? Mr. Chesnut, in his Plants used by Indians of Mendocino County, California, calls attention to the fact that in our advanced state we are yet behind these savages, not having caught up with them in the discovery and uses of some of their best textile materials.

How did the savages find out that the roots of certain plants hid away under the earth were the best possible material for this function? And for another use the stem of a plant had to be found, perhaps miles away, so that in the makeup of a single example leagues would have to be traveled and much discrimination used. Unless the utmost care is exercised the fact will be overlooked that often three or four kinds of wood will be used in the monotonous work of the weft. One is best for the bottom, another is light and tough for the body, a third is best for the flexible top. This in addition to the employment of half a dozen others for designs, for warp or foundation, or for decorative purposes.

Among the basket maker's materials must not be forgotten the demand for water-tight vessels. Besides the widely spread faculty of securing this result by texture, there were present in certain areas natural substances such as the gum of the pinyon (*Pinus edulis*), the resin of various pines, and even the mineral asphalt.

The making of canteens and other water vessels, in lieu of pottery, in this way was most prevalent among the Shoshonean tribes of the Interior Basin and the migratory Apache farther south. Barrows[a] calls attention to Humboldt's Essay on New Spain,[b] in which the Indians around Santa Barbara are spoken of as "presenting the Spaniards with vases very curiously wrought of stalks of rushes" and "covered within with a very thin layer of asphaltum that renders them impenetrable to water."

The author is greatly indebted to Mr. Frederick V. Coville, Botanist of the Department of Agriculture, for the identification of plants used in basketry by the Indians of America north of Mexico. This list contains those that have been certainly identified. There are other plants alleged to be used in basketry, but of which no scientific determination has been made as yet. A complete discussion of this part of the subject would demand that for each tribe making baskets there should be a list of the plants employed by them, and for each plant used a list of the tribes by whom it is used. Such a discussion requires a long and tedious investigation by a number of talented workers cooperating. It is hoped that the chapter here given by Mr. Coville will be a starting point for a complete study of Indian phytotechny.

---

[a] The Ethno-botany of the Coahuilla Indians of Southern California, Chicago, 1900, p. 41.

[b] Vol. II, p. 297.

PLANTS USED IN BASKETRY

By Frederick V. Coville.

While some of the materials used by American Indian tribes in their basketry have long been known, by far the larger number had not been identified with precision prior to the beginning of the past decade.   Most students of Indian plants had been satisfied with casual names applied by themselves or given to them by botanists after the examination of fragmentary specimens.   Since the year 1890 a few botanists, notably Mr. V. K. Chesnut, of the Department of Agriculture, have turned their attention to the plants used by the aborigines and have made new records with definite identifications of the plants concerned, covering among other subjects of Indian activity that of basketry.   When, therefore, after Professor Mason's invitation to prepare a chapter on the subject, the compilation of existing records was begun it was found that the earlier publications contained much that was indefinite, considerable that was incorrect, and a little that was both correct and exact.   The notable exception to the general rule was the publications of Dr. Edward Palmer, whose work as a botanical collector in the western United States and Mexico extended from the late sixties of the last century to the present time.   Under the circumstances it was determined to admit only such matter as was capable of verification, based, first, on the writer's own observation; second, on published records that seemed to come under the last of the categories mentioned above; and, third, on the collections of the United States National Museum.   A few unverified statements have been admitted for the purpose of bringing them to the attention of those who may be in a position to verify them.   In the case of statements which did not originate with the writer a parenthetic reference indicates the source of the information and, if published, the year of its publication.   The work as here presented is recognized as by no means complete, but it is offered as a substantial basis for future investigation.

Acer macrophyllum.   Oregon Maple.

Päl-gun'-shi (Yuki).

The Indians of Mendocino County, California, particularly the Concows, who now occupy a reservation there, use the white inner bark, preferably gathered in spring, in making baskets.   (V. K. Chesnut, 1902.)   From its inner bark the Indians of the Pacific slope make baskets so closely woven as to hold water.   (J. T. Rothrock, 1867.)

Adiantum pedatum.   Maidenhair Fern.

The slender, black or dark-brown, shining stems, after splitting, are used by the Indians of Mendocino County, California, in the ornamentation of some of their baskets, particularly those worn as hats. (V. K. Chesnut, 1902.)   The Hupa Indians of Humboldt County, California, and other nearby tribes use the stems in the same way.   The practice extends also to the Snohomish Indians of western Washington (C. M. Buchanan, letter) and to the Tlinkit Indians of southern Alaska. (G. T. Emmons, letter).

Agave deserti.   Desert Agave.

In the coiled basket bowls of the Coahuilla Indians of southern California the cleaned fiber from the leaves is used to form the first few turns of the coil, which is then continued with grass stems.   Evidently the grass is not sufficiently flexible to make these first turns without breaking, but the Agave fiber answers the purpose admirably. (Cat. Nos. 207580 and 207581, U.S.N.M.)   Some of the basket hats of the Diegueño Indians of San Diego County, California, are woven from cords made of the cleaned and twisted fiber, and from their great strength must be almost indestructible by any ordinary wear.   (Cat. No. 19751, U.S.N.M.)

Alnus oregana.   Red Alder.

Among the Hupa Indians of northern California the roots are sometimes used as weft at the beginning of a basket and in a round between the bottom and the sides (P. E. Goddard, notes).

Alnus rhombifolia.   White Alder.

Various species of alder have been used by the American aborigines to produce an orange or red-brown dye, but the only authenticated use of alder in dyeing basket materials seems to be that of *Alnus rhombifolia* among the Hupa, Yuki, and other Indians of northern California.   The dye is obtained from the bark by infusion in water, or sometimes the bark is chewed and the material to be dyed is drawn through the mouth.

Amaranthus palmeri.   Amaranth.

Ko'-mo (Moki).

This is the source of a pink to purple dye used in the coiled and wicker plaques of the Moki Indians of northern Arizona.   (W. Hough, notes.)   The identification is by C. F. Millspaugh.

Amelanchier alnifolia.   Sarviceberry.

Ĭ-ta'-gĕ (Apache).
Chak (Klamath).

The small, straight, peeled branches of this and other species of Amelanchier are used by the Apaches of the White Mountain Indian Reservation, Arizona, to form the uprights in their large carrying baskets, a use for which the very tough wood is well adapted.   The

Klamath Indians of Oregon often weave a stout branch, peeled or not peeled, into the rims of their large coarse baskets to stiffen and strengthen them.

Apocynum cannabinum.   Indian Hemp.

The well-known Indian hemp, including a number of plant forms once referred to *Apocynum cannabinum*, but now treated as belonging to several species, occurs from the Atlantic to the Pacific coast and was and still is widely used by the aborigines in the making of many kinds of cordage articles. It is commonly cited as an Indian basket material, and although it has not been possible to secure a verifiable record of its use in a basket, it is altogether probable that some of the strings and cords so frequently used in beginning a basket, or in making the carrying loops, are twisted from the inner bark of this plant. (See illustration in Chesnut's Plants used by the Indians of Mendocino County, California.[a])

Artemisia ludoviciana.   Wormwood.
                    Hang-al (Coahuilla).

In that portion of the Colorado Desert of California known as the Cabeson Valley the Coahuilla Indians make from the stems of this plant the large granary baskets in which they store seeds and other dried vegetable foods. (D. P. Barrows, 1900.) The plant was identified by W. L. Jepson.

Arundinaria tecta.   Cane.

The split outer portion of the stems of the cane was the favorite basket material of the Southern Indians, including the Choctaws, Chickasaws, Cherokees, Creeks, Seminoles, and other tribes from Texas and Arkansas to the Carolinas, and it is still in use among the remnants of these peoples. The handsome baskets of the Chetimacha and Attakapa Indians of Louisiana are made from split cane.

Berberis nervosa.   Oregon Grape.

Among the Hupa Indians of northern California a yellow dye is obtained by steeping the twigs and bark of one of the species of evergreen barberry, or Oregon grape. (Mary H. Manning, letter.) Leaves of squaw grass (*Xerophyllum tenax*) dyed with this are sometimes used in the yellow patterns occasionally seen in the Hupa hat baskets. The same material and dye are used in the huckleberry baskets of the Snohomish (C. M. Buchanan, letter) and Klikitat Indians of western Washington. The particular species used has been definitely identified in one instance as *Berberis nervosa*. Another species, *B. aquifolium*, is undoubtedly used also.

---

[a] U. S. National Herbarium, VII, p. 379, fig. 75.

Betula populifolia.   White Birch.

The soft wood of this tree is still employed in the northeastern
United States and Canada by the descendants of the Algonkin and
Iroquois in the making of baskets. (V. Havard, 1890.) These baskets are thoroughly modernized and doubtless give little idea of the
aboriginal methods of using this material.

Bromus sitchensis.   Bromegrass.

The split stems are sometimes used by the Tlinkit Indians of the
south Alaskan coast as an overlaying material for the white patterns
of spruce-root baskets.   (G. T. Emmons, notes.)

Butneria occidentalis.   Calycanthus.

Sai ka-le′ (Pomo).

Both the wood and the bark from young shoots of this shrub are
used in basketry by the Indians of Mendocino County, California.
(V. K. Chesnut, 1902.)

Calamagrostis langsdorffii.   Bluejoint.

Chu′-kan shark ki-kark-tush′ (Tlinkit).

The split stem is sometimes used for overlaying material in the
spruce-root baskets of the Tlinkit Indians of the south Alaskan coast.
(G. T. Emmons, notes.)

Carex barbarae.   Sedge.

Ka-hum′ (Pomo).

The long, tough, woody, interior portion of the rootstocks of this
sedge is used to form the white sewing strands in the fine coiled baskets of the Pomo Indians of northern California.   Among the neighboring Wailakis the roots of another unidentified species of Carex are
used in the same way, and the leaves are made into hats and crude,
somewhat flexible baskets.   (V. K. Chesnut, 1902.)

Carthamus tinctorius.   False Saffron.

A-sap-zran′-Ɩ (Moki, from the Spanish).

This plant, introduced by the Spanish, produces a bright yellow
dye, used in basketry by the Moki Indians of northern Arizona.
(W. Hough, notes; Cat. Nos. 11724 and 11726, U.S.N.M.)

Ceanothus integerrimus.   California Lilac.

Hi′-bi (Concow).

The long, flexible shoots are used in basket making by the Concows
of northern California.   (V. K. Chesnut, 1902.)

Cercis occidentalis. Redbud.

Ché-e (Yuki).

The wood of the branches, with or without the bark, is used in basketry by many California tribes, notably by the Round Valley Indians of northern California. (V. K. Chesnut, 1902). Among the Nishinam Indians of Bear Valley, Placer County, the willow foundations in certain coiled baskets are sewed together with a thread of redbud wood. (Stephen Powers, 1877.) The dark red patterns in the baskets of the Pit River Indians and the Tulare Indians are formed from split branches with the bark left on.

Ceropteris triangularis. Goldenback.

This little fern, known usually as *Gymnogramma triangularis*, has a black stipe or stem which is sometimes used by the Round Valley Indians (V. K. Chesnut, 1902) and the Hupa Indians (Mary H. Manning, letter) of northern California as a substitute for maidenhair stems, when these are not available, in black basket patterns.

Chrysothamnus laricinus. Rabbitbrush.

Ma'-i-bi (Moki).

The branches are sometimes used by the Moki Indians of northeastern Arizona for the weft of their finer wicker plaques. (W. Hough, notes.)

Chrysothamnus moquianus. Rabbitbrush.

Ha'-no shi'-va-pi (Moki).

The twigs are used at Oraibi, Arizona, to form the weft in the wicker plaques of the Moki Indians. (W. Hough, notes.) The identification of the plant (U. S. Nat. Herb. 274057) is by E. L. Greene, the species being one closely related to the widely distributed *Chrysothamnus [Bigelovia] graveolens*.

Cinna latifolia. Wood Reedgrass.

Chu'-kan shark (Tlinkit).

Among the grasses employed by the Tlinkit Indians of the south Alaskan coast for the white patterns in their spruce-root baskets this species is the commonest. The part used is the stem, from which sections are split to be applied as an overlay on the spruce-root strands. (G. T. Emmons, notes.)

Cladium mariscus. Cladium.

From the root, coiled baskets of excellent quality are made by tribes on the lower Sierra from Fresno River to Kern River, California. (C. Hart Merriam, 1903.) Identified by Miss Alice Eastwood.

Corylus californica. Hazelnut.

Ol mam (Yuki).

The shoots of the hazelnut are used by many of the Indian tribes from northern California to Washington, west of the Cascade Mountains, in the making of baskets, especially as radials or uprights. (Mary H. Manning, letter.) The burden basket, baby basket, and salmon plate of the Hupas are made entirely of the shoots of hazelnut. (P. E. Goddard, notes.) (See Plate 4.)

Covillea tridentata.   Creosote Bush.

A gum-lac found upon the branches of this desert bush has a wide application among the southwestern Indians as a cement and among the Cocopas of northern Lower California it is used for pitching baskets. (E. Palmer, notes.) The gum, which occurs in conspicuous nodules of a reddish amber color, is not a direct exudation from the plant, but is deposited by a minute scale insect, *Carteria larreae*.

Dasylirion wheeleri.   Sotol.

The leaves, split into strands about a quarter of an inch wide and the coarse marginal teeth removed, are used among the Pima Indians of southern Arizona in coarse twilled baskets. (Cat. No. 218027, U.S.N.M.)

Delphinium scaposum.   Larkspur.

So-ro′-si (Moki).

The flowers are the source of a light-blue dye used by the Moki Indians of northern Arizona in their coiled and wicker plaques. (W. Hough, notes.)

Deschampsia caespitosa.   Tufted Hairgrass.

Kût-kûk-kli′-te shark (Tlinkit).

This is one of the grasses the split stems of which are used among the Tlinkit Indians of the south Alaskan coast to form the white patterns on their spruce-root baskets. (G. T. Emmons, notes.)

Dondia suffrutescens.   Sea Blite.

The Coahuilla Indians of the Colorado desert in southern California, blacken the stems of their basketry rush (*Juncus acutus*) by steeping them for several hours in a decoction of this plant. (E. Palmer, 1878.) The identification of the species is by W. L. Jepson.

Elymus mollis.   Beach Rye.

The split stems of this grass are sometimes used for the white patterns in the spruce-root baskets of the Tlinkit Indians on the south Alaskan coast. This material is employed only for coarse work, and when other grasses better adapted for the purpose are not available. (G. T. Emmons, notes.)

Epicampes rigens.   Epicampes.

In the region of the Mohave and Colorado deserts of southeastern California the Panamint, Coahuilla (D. P. Barrows, 1900), and other tribes use this grass for the packing of their coiled baskets. The part used, at least in the better baskets, is that portion of the stem above the uppermost joint, which sometimes reaches a length of 45 centimeters (18 inches).

Equisetum palustre.   Horsetail.
>   Dabts (Snohomish).
>   Hin mûn-Y′ (Tlinkit).

The rootstocks of this plant, which sometimes reach a diameter of 1.5 centimeters (⅔ inch) and a length of 20 centimeters (8 inches) between the joints, were used in the early days, though rarely now, in the patterns on spruce-root Tlinkit baskets of the south Alaskan coast. Strips are split from the surface of the rootstock and used as an overlaying material. The color is a rich, very dark purple, which appears as a black. (G. T Emmons, notes.) A similar use was made of the plant, in their cedar-root baskets, by the Snohomish Indians, of Puget Sound, Washington. (C. M. Buchanan, notes.)

Equisetum robustum.   Scouring Rush.

The coal-black surface of the rootstock is sometimes used by the Cowlitz Indians of southwestern Washington as a substitute for the rootstock of *Equisetum palustre* in the black overlay patterns on cedar-root baskets.

Evernia vulpina.   Wolf Moss.
>   Se′-ho-lĭ (Tlinkit).
>   Swä′-u-sam (Klamath).

This yellow tree-lichen was widely used as a dye by the Indians of the timbered area of the western United States. The Klamath Indians of Oregon, as well as the Hupas of northern California (Mary H. Manning, letter), use this dye in their baskets, the coloring matter being extracted by boiling. In the case of the Hupas the dye is applied to Xerophyllum leaves, but the Klamaths use it only for the porcupine quills which form the beautiful canary yellow patterns of their twisted tule baskets. The Tlinkit Indians of the south Alaskan coast also use the dye in their spruce-root baskets, the lichen being secured by them not on the coast, but from the interior. (G. T. Emmons, notes.) (See Plate 5.)

Fraxinus nigra.   Black Ash.

The remnants of the Six Nations in New York, Pennsylvania, and adjacent portions of Canada make extensive use of ash, presumably black ash, in their modern splint-basket industry. (T. Donaldson, 1894.)

Helianthus petiolaris.   Sunflower.

A-ka'-u-shi (Moki).

The seeds are used by the Moki Indians of northern Arizona to make a blue dye for use in both coiled and wicker plaques. (W. Hough, notes.) The color produced in the coiled plaques, on sewing material of *Yucca glauca*, is of a dark, almost prussian-blue shade, when the sewing strands are applied with their broken inner surface outward, but of a much lighter shade when the epidermal surface is outward. (Cat. No. 128708, U.S.N.M.)

Hicoria ovata.   Hickory.

The wood of some unidentified species of hickory, probably *Hicoria ovata*, is employed among the remnants of the Six Nations in New York, Pennsylvania, and adjacent portions of Canada in the manufacture of modern splint baskets. (T. Donaldson, 1894.) The inner bark of a hickory is used by the North Carolina Cherokees for yellow patterns in their baskets. (Cat. No. 63077, U.S.N.M.)

Hilaria jamesii.   Galleta.

Ta'-ka-shu (Moki).

The stems of this grass, roughly stripped of leaves and seeds, are used for the filling in of the coiled plaques of the Moki Indians of northern Arizona. (W. Hough, 1898.) In the first few turns of the spiral, which are too short to be made of the grass stems, the packing is of shredded leaves of *Yucca glauca*. (Cat. No. 128467, U.S.N.M.)

Juglans nigra.   Black Walnut.

The Cherokee Indians of North Carolina use the split inner bark to make black patterns in their baskets. (Cat. No. 63077, U.S.N.M.)

Juncus acutus.   Rush.

The Coahuilla Indians of the Colorado Desert, southern California, use the stems to make patterns in their coiled basket bowls. The material, as gathered in a marsh at Palm Springs, is immersed for several days in the muddy water of the spring to render it flexible, and is then dyed a dark olivaceous or almost black color with the juice of a sea blite. (E. Palmer, notes.) (See *Dondia suffrutescens*.)

Juncus balticus.   Rush.

Tsin-a'-u (Klamath).
Kloh-tso'-sĕ (Apache).

The stems of this rush, which is commonly known as wire grass, are often used by Indian children to make small baskets. The practice has been noted among the Klamaths of Oregon and the White Mountain Apaches of the Arizona plateau.

Juncus effusus.   Rush.

Lal'-ûm (Yuki).

The stems of this rush, or wire grass, are used amond the Round Valley Indians of Mendocino County, California, to make temporary baskets, particularly in teaching the Indian girls the art of basketry. (V. K. Chesnut, 1902.)

Juncus textilis.   Basket Rush.

The Luiseño Indians of southern California use the split stems of this rush as the sewing material of their coiled baskets.   (C. Hart Merriam, notes.)   The varying natural colors of the stem at different heights produce a very attractive effect.

Libocedrus decurrens.   Post Cedar.

Wu'-lu-ansh (Klamath).

The split wood of this tree is occasionally woven into rough V-shaped pack baskets by the Klamath Indians of Oregon.

Lonicera interrupta.   Honeysuckle.

Hai-wat' (Yuki).

The long flexible stems are used to a slight extent among the Round Valley Indians of California in the coiled "one-stick" baskets, in which the foundation consists of a single stem.   (V. K. Chesnut, 1902, and notes.)

Martynia louisiana.   Devil Horns.

Ta-g'at'-ĕ (Apache).

This plant, which is often known in books as the unicorn plant, has a large green pod with a slender terminal projection.   At maturity the green outer layer becomes dry and falls off, the remaining interior portion of the projection splitting into two parts or horns which are exceedingly tough and black, and sometimes reach a length of 35 centimeters (13 inches).   Moistened and split they are used extensively to make black patterns in the baskets of various Indian tribes, notably the Apaches, in the desert region of Arizona, southern Nevada, and southeastern California.

Panicularia nervata.   Manna Grass.

Among the Tlinkit Indians of the south Alaskan coast, strips split from the internodes of this grass are sometimes used as an overlay for the patterns in spruce-root baskets, either white or variously dyed. (G. T. Emmons, notes.)

Parosela emoryi.   Parosela.

The Coahuilla Indians, of the Colorado Desert, in southeastern California, give a yellowish-brown color to the rush (*Juncus acutus*) they use in basket making by steeping it in water with the branches of this plant.   (E. Palmer, 1878.)

Philadelphus gordonianus.   Syringa.

Hân'-lĭ (Yuki).

The pithy stems of this shrub, which is locally known as arrowwood, are employed by the Indians of Mendocino County, California, in the manufacture of baskets for carrying babies, a use to which the stems, on account of their lightness, are well adapted.   (V. K. Chesnut, 1902.)

Phragmites phragmites.   Reed.

Tkap (Klamath).

The white patterns in the twisted-tule baskets of the Klamath and Modoc Indians of Oregon are made from this reed.   The part used is the shining surface covering of the stem, taken from less thrifty plants, particularly those which have produced no flower cluster.

Plate 6 is a twined gambling tray of the Klamath Indians living on the head waters of Klamath River, Oregon.   The warp is of twined tule stems, the body of the weft is of the same material, the overlaying in white is with split pieces from the stem of the reed.   The black is twisted tule dyed in mud springs, the yellow borders of the trefoil are in porcupine quills dyed with wolf moss.

Design unknown; the projections on the large ornaments are called arrowheads.   Collection of Frederick V. Coville.

Picea sitchensis.   Sitka Spruce.

Sit (Tlinkit).

The roots of this tree, boiled and split, are the basis material of the baskets manufactured by the Tlinkit Indians of Yakutat Bay, Alaska. (F. Funston, 1896.)   The same use prevails among the Tlinkits of the Alexander Archipelago, notably those of Sitka, Juneau, and Douglas. The Indians of Neah Bay, Washington, and doubtless other tribes also, use the split roots for their coarse burden baskets.   (See Plate 7.)

Pinus edulis.   Arizona Nut Pine.

O-bi' (Apache).

The Apaches of the White Mountain district, Arizona, use the resin of this tree, often called pinyon, as a pitching material for their water baskets.

Pinus lambertiana.   Sugar Pine.

Slender strands split from the root of the sugar pine, woven about uprights of California hazel, are the foundation material of the acorn-soup baskets of the Hupa Indians, northern California.   To make them split more easily the roots are steamed by burying them in sand and building a fire over them.   (Mary H. Manning, letter.)

Pinus monophylla.   Nevada Nut Pine.

The Panamint Indians of southeastern California use the pitch of this tree to make their water baskets impervious to water.

Pinus ponderosa.   Yellow Pine.

The split wood of the root is one of the materials used by the Hupa Indians of northwestern California for the principal part of the weft in closely-woven baskets.   (P. E. Goddard, notes.)

Pinus sabiniana.   Digger Pine.
Pol′-kûm ol (Yuki).

The Little Lake Indians of Mendocino County, California, use the split roots to make their large V-shaped baskets for carrying acorns. The root is warmed in hot damp ashes, and the strands are split off before cooling. (V. K. Chesnut, 1902.)   A similar use extends northward among the Hupa and other California coast Indians as far as Klamath River.   (V. Havard, 1890.)

Populus trichocarpa.   Balm of Gilead.

In northwestern California the Hupa Indians sometimes used the root to fasten the ribs of their baskets at the beginning and to form a round at the base of the sides of the basket. (P. E. Goddard, notes.)

Pseudotsuga mucronata.   Red Fir.

According to the authority of J. W. Hudson, the Pomo Indians of Mendocino County, California, use the roots of this tree in the manufacture of some of their fine baskets.

Pteridium aquilinum.   Bracken.
Bĭs (Calpella).

A form of the common bracken occurring in the western United States is occasionally employed as a basket material among the Indians of Mendocino County, California. (V. K. Chesnut, 1902.)   The part used is the two flat strips of black hard-celled tissue in the rootstock.

Quercus alba.   White Oak.

Splints from the wood of a white oak, presumably this species, are still used by the Cherokee Indians of North Carolina as the material for certain of their baskets.   (Cat. No. 63073, U.S.N.M.)

Quercus lobata.   California White Oak.

The Concow Indians of Mendocino County, California, sometimes blacken their basket strands of redbud (*Cercis occidentalis*) on which the bark is still attached, by soaking them in water containing the bark of this oak and scraps of rusty iron.   (V. K. Chesnut, 1902.)

Rhus diversiloba.   Poison Oak.
Kats′-te (Wailaki).
Mä-tyu′-ya″-ho (Pomo).

The slender stems are occasionally used for horizontal withes in some of the baskets of the Mendocino County Indians of California

(V. K. Chesnut, 1902), while the juice, which turns black rapidly on exposure to air, is the source, according to J. W. Hudson, of a dye sometimes used to stain the purest black strands of the Pomo basketry.

Rhus trilobata.   Threeleaf Sumac.

Si'-i-bi (Moki).
Chĭl-chĭn (Navaho).
Tsĕh' kan'-ĭ (Apache).

Among the desert Indians the slender branches of this bush are used extensively, perhaps more extensively than any other plant except willow, in the manufacture of their baskets. For warp the peeled branches are used. For weft and for the sewing material of coiled baskets the branch is usually split into three strips and the bark and brittle tissue next the pith removed, leaving a flat tough strand. The use of the threeleaf sumac has been noted among the Apache, Panamint, Paiute, Navaho (W. Matthews, 1886), Moki (W. Hough, 1898), and Coahuilla (D. P. Barrows, 1900). (See Plate 8.)

Salix.   Willow.

Brancnes from various undetermined species of willow were widely used among the western Indians, probably more generally than any other plant, particularly in the various forms of coarser baskets. Among the tribes in which travelers have recorded the manufacture of willow baskets, in addition to those given below under the identified species of willow, are the Mission, Mohave, Coahuilla, Cocopa, Yuma, and Coconino Indians of Arizona and southern California; the Zuñi of New Mexico; the Hupa, Yurok, Modoc, Chimariko, Gualala, Nishi-nam, and Yokut of northern and middle California, and the Tinné of the Yukon Valley, Alaska. The split roots of willow are sometimes used for the weft in beginning the hat baskets of the Hupa Indians. (P. E. Goddard, notes.)

Salix argophylla.   Willow.

Bam ka-le' (Pomo).

The Pomo Indians near Ukiah, California, consider this their best willow for the manufacture of coarse baskets. (V. K. Chesnut, 1902.)

Salix lasiandra.   Willow.

A willow, which is referable to *Salix lasiandra* in its broad sense, is used to some extent by the Panamint Indians of Inyo County, California, in their twined baskets, and by the Apaches of the White Mountain Reservation, Arizona.

Sambucus mexicana.   Elder.

The Coahuilla Indians of San Diego County, California, give a deep black color to strands of the threeleaf sumac, used as a sewing material of their coiled baskets, by soaking them for about a week in an infusion of the berry stems of this elder. (D. P. Barrows, 1900.)

Savastana odorata. Holygrass.

The Indians of the northeastern United States and adjacent parts of Canada, such as the Penobscots of Maine (V. Havard, 1890) and the Abenakis of Ontario (Cat. No. 206394, U.S.N.M.), use the long, sweet-scented leaves of this grass in some of their baskets.

Scirpus lacustris. Tule.

Ma'-ĭ (Klamath).

The principal basket material of the Klamath and Modoc Indians of Oregon is the tule, a plant widely used by the tribes of the Pacific coast States in the manufacture of mats. Narrow strips from the surface of the stem are twisted into long threads and these used for their finer twined baskets, giving a great variety of green and brown shades or, when dyed, a black. For coarser baskets whole or split stems are commonly employed, without twisting. The very slender roots of the tule, which occur in great abundance on the stout root-stocks, are used, without any other preparation than drying, to make patterns of a maroon color in the twisted tule baskets. (See Plate 9.)

Scirpus maritimus. Bulrush.

Tsu-ĭsh' (Pomo).

The Pomo Indians of California use for the brown and black patterns of their fine coiled baskets a fiber extracted from the rootstock of this bulrush. Structurally the fiber is the same as that described under *Carex barbarae*. The identification is by Miss Alice Eastwood.

Smilax californica. Greenbriar.

The long and exceedingly strong stems, brought from the watershed of the Sacramento River, are sometimes employed by the Indians of Mendocino County, California, in their basketry. (V. K. Chesnut, 1902.)

Thelesperma gracile. Thelesperma.

O-ha'-u-shi (Moki).

A decoction of the whole plant was formerly used to give a red-brown color to the stems of rabbitbrush (*Chrysothamnus moquianus*) for the patterns in the wicker plaques of the Moki Indians of northern Arizona. (W. Hough, 1898; Cat. No. 128708, U.S.N.M.)

Thuja plicata. Giant Cedar.

The split roots of this tree are the common sewing material for the strong, water tight huckleberry baskets of certain tribes of the North-west Coast from northern Oregon to British America, including the

Klikitat, Cowlitz, Puyallup, Tulalip, Snoqualmie, Skagit, and Fraser River Indians. The Indians of Neah Bay, Washington, and of Vancouver Island, British Columbia, use the split brown inner bark as the warp of their finely woven but artificially dyed flexible baskets. The Nisqualli Indians of Puget Sound, and doubtless many other tribes of the Northwest coast, employ the same material in coarser strands in making rough burden baskets, frequently in conjunction with a warp of split branches from the same tree. (See Plate 10.)

Tsuga mertensiana. Black Hemlock.

The Indians of Neah Bay, Washington, sometimes use split hemlock roots in their coarse openwork quadrangular V-shaped burden baskets. The tree was described by a Neah Bay Indian as having cones 2½ inches long, in which case the species would be the black hemlock instead of the Western hemlock (*Tsuga heterophylla*), which is the commoner of the two at low elevations in that vicinity.

Tumion californicum. California Nutmeg.
K'o'-bi (Pomo).

The split roots of this tree are sometimes used by the Pomo Indians of Mendocino County, California, in the manufacture of their finer baskets. (V. K. Chesnut, 1902.)

Typha latifolia. Cattail.
Po'-pas (Klamath).

Twisted strands made of slender ribbons split from the sheathed portions of the leaves are used by the Klamath Indians of Oregon in their smaller flexible baskets, either to form the body of the basket or to make an ornamental band. The color is a lusterless, slightly ashy white.

Ulmus americana. Elm.
The Sioux Indians of the northern plains region used the inner bark of the elm to make a coarse basket. (V. Havard, 1890.)

Vaccinium membranaceum. Blueberry.
Ka-na-ta' (Tlinkit).

The juice of some species of blueberry, probably *Vaccinium membranaceum*, is used as a purple dye in spruce-root baskets by the Tlinkit Indians of the south Alaskan coast. (G. T. Emmons, notes.)

Vitis californica. Grape.
Shi-ïn' (Pomo).

Among the Hupa Indians of northern California the root is sometimes used to fasten the ribs of a basket at its beginning, and to make a round at the outer edge of the basket's bottom, while in fine hats grape root sometimes makes up the whole weft. (P. E. Goddard, notes.) Portions of the woody stem are used by the Pomos of Mendocino County, California, as a sewing strand for attaching the rims to their pack baskets. The grape strands completely cover the stout withe that forms the basis for the rim, making it more durable and at the same time thickening it so as to give a good means of firmly grasping the basket. (V. K. Chesnut, 1902, and notes.)

Woodwardia spinulosa. Giant Chain Fern.

The Hupa Indians of northern California use a portion of this fern, either white or dyed orange brown with alder bark, in the patterns of their hat baskets. (Mary H. Manning, letter). The parts employed are two slender flat strands, very flexible and leathery when moist, which are extracted from the stalk of the frond.

Xerophyllum tenax. Xerophyllum.

The long, tough, minutely serrated, grass-like, lustrous leaves of this plant, often called squawgrass, are very commonly used by the Indians of the Northwest Coast as an overlaying material to make the white patterns of their baskets. Occasionally it is dyed. The base of the leaf for an inch or more often has a natural faint purple color which is used to good effect. The use of the material extends from the Pit River, Shasta, and Hupa Indians, in northern California, northward through most of the tribes west of the Cascade Range to the Neah Bay and Vancouver Island Indians of the Straits of Fuca. These last two use Xerophyllum leaves, cut to a uniform width by a gauged knife-edge, as the weft of their gaudily dyed flexible baskets.

Yucca arborescens. Tree Yucca.

The slender roots are sometimes used for red figures in baskets of the Panamint Indians of Inyo County, California.

Yucca arkansana. Yucca.

The leaves are used in the basketry of the Kaiowa Indians of Oklahoma. (J. Mooney, notes.)

Yucca baccata. Banana Yucca.

The Mescalero Apaches of southern New Mexico and adjacent parts of Texas, in the region between the Rio Grande and Pecos rivers, use the split leaves of this plant for the main portion of their baskets, and its roots for the red patterns (Cat. Nos. 204646 to 204653, U.S.N.M.). It is probable, I am informed by Mr. Vernon Bailey, that they use also in the same way the leaves and roots of *Yucca macrocarpa*, an arborescent species growing at lower elevations in the same region.

Yucca filamentosa.   Silkgrass.

The leaves of this plant were formerly in use among the Indians of North Carolina as a basket material.   (J. Lawton, 1714.)

Yucca glauca.   Plains Yucca.

Mo'-hu (Moki).

This plant is used in the basketry of the Moki Indians (W. Hough, 1902) of northern Arizona.   In some of the coarser twilled baskets the warp and weft are made up of the narrow unsplit leaves thinned by the removal of a strip from the back.   (Cat. No. 213254, U.S.N.M.) In the coiled plaques the sewing material consists of narrow strips split from the leaves.   The outer surface of the leaves gives various shades of green and greenish yellow or, in the case of the young leaves, white, or they are dyed in several colors.   The dyed strips are often applied with the inner, broken surface outward.   This surface takes the dye more readily and gives a deeper shade.   For the use of the shredded leaves as a packing material in the first few turns of the spiral, see *Hilaria jamesii.*

III. BASKET MAKING

The sallow knows the basket maker's thumb.—EMERSON.

Under the head of basket making are included all the activities involved in and fostered by construction, namely:

1. *Harvesting materials.*—This embraces intimate acquaintance with the places where just the right substances abound, knowledge of the times when each element is ripe, methods of growing, harvesting, and conveying involved, as well as the tools and apparatus used in gathering.   In their rough state much of the materials would be as unfit for the use as quarry clay would be for the potter or crude ore for the metallurgist.

2. *Preparing materials.*—Frequently the raw materials are stored away at the time of harvesting until required for manufacture.   Nature makes the rules for gathering in her own good time.   But this might be the busy season, whereas this art may go on in different seasons. When the time comes for their use special manipulations are necessary, such as peeling, splitting, making splints, yarning or twisting, twining, braiding, soaking, gauging, coloring.   These should each be noted carefully and described for the several basket areas.

3. *Processes of manufacture.*—The materials being ready, the maker seats herself in the midst and begins the technical operations that should be minutely watched, and photographed, if possible.   Collections should also be made of tools, apparatus, and patterns.

Each of these will be examined with minute care, especially the third.   If this art is to be imitated and become a stimulus in technical instruction it is of the utmost importance that the substances be correctly known, that the manipulations of material be familiar, and, above all, that the course of each element in the warp and weft, the foundation, and sewing be understood. Care has been taken to draw correctly the figures used in illustration. They are all in the basketry of the Indians, and, more than that, they are the beginnings of more refined processes and structures.

HARVESTING MATERIALS

Since the materials used in basketry are derived from different parts of a great variety of plants, the gathering of them involves many industries. The harvesting of basket material is no exception to the rule that every human activity begins with a natural process slightly modified. The birds are in a sense the original basket makers, and it is known that some very expert Indian tribes take the grasses and the stems of plants as they find them. They know nothing of drying or

FIG. 1.
MUD SHOES, CALIFORNIA.
Klamath Indians.
Cat. No. 24109, U.S.N.M. Collected by L. S. Dyar.

manipulating. Improvement grows out of study into the nature of substances, until with some tribes the obtaining of raw materials involves quite as much sagacity, toil, and travel as the making of the basket.

For procuring the roots, the apparatus of digging is necessary. To be sure, the hand was the first hoe and the strong arm draws the root from its hiding place, but our Indians had gotten beyond that. The northern Indians, especially those of the Columbia River in western Canada, use quite elaborate forms of this device. It is wonderful to think of the sagacity developed in savage minds by the quest for underground substances and the proper discrimination of the places where the best examples abound.   From the farthest north, in the neighborhood of Point Barrow to the southern portions of South America, roots form substantial materials in basket making, both twined and coiled.   It is not enough to say simply that roots of plants were the materials of the baskets, but it is well known that the savage women knew in each section what plant furnished the toughest and most pliable roots, the localities in which this kind of root reached its best, the plants that yielded brown, red, and black colored splints, which produced unrivaled effects, though the portion above ground gave no sign of the treasures held or the time of year when it was proper to obtain these substances, and the processes by which they could be extracted and saved most economically.   Incidentally to this quest of material, of course, was that of carrying, so that here in the very beginning of our art a host of useful human activities are engendered.   The Klamath invented a peculiar kind of mud shoe to wear when wading about in shallow marshes after roots for their basket work.   (See fig. 1.)

The stems of plants, of grass, rushes, and woody species are to be found in the basketry of almost every portion of the Western Hemisphere.   The young and tough shoots of a single year's growth are choice materials for some purposes, and were eagerly sought.   In those regions where spinous plants yielded the materials, a sort of gathering knife was employed resembling a miniature sickle with a wooden handle. There is a time of year when they are in the best condition for the basket woman's craft.   There are certain parts of the stems which are useful in this direction, while others are valueless.   In woody species the outer layer next to the bark has the toughness of leather, while a little way inward the wood is almost as brittle as glass.   Furthermore, the stems of plants vary greatly in color—different parts of the same stem are in different colors.

Now, the student would be surprised to find in the East, in the West, in the North, and in the South that there is very little more for the savage woman to learn.   Distinguished botanists will say that instead of trying to teach the Indians the use of new plants, the best way to search for new materials to introduce into modern textile arts can be learned from these savage artisans.   The leaves of plants are used in basketry, especially in the South.   In the extreme North, among the Eskimo and Athapascan tribes, no leaves are suitable for basketry. Among the Aleutian Islanders stems and leaves of grass come into play.   Down the Pacific coast of the continent, in southeastern Alaska, British Columbia, and the coast States of the Union leaves, either in their natural color or dyed, are employed with great effect in many types of ornamentation, as will be seen further on.   The range of usefulness, either for texture or ornament, is well known to the basket maker.   In Mexico and tropical America this division of the subject has been developed most. Little mechanism is necessary in this part of the world. A sharpened stick for the root gatherer and a flint knife and mussel shell for the stem harvester complete the outfit. Nimble fingers aided with the teeth were the most useful apparatus.

In her textile gleaning, the savage woman has not been slow to avail herself of the metal appliances introduced by the whites. You will now see her afield with pick and knife of steel gathering the old-time substances.

PREPARING MATERIALS

As is well known, every industry may be divided, either in savagery or in civilization, into four parts: First, that which is associated with taking the gifts of nature, called in this particular instance harvesting; second, the transformation of this material into proper form for special trades; third, the manufacture of useful and ornamental objects; and, finally, the activities of consumption and enjoyment, by which the things may take their places as servants to supply the wants and desires of mankind.

The preparation of materials for basketry consists in splitting and separating the desirable from the undesirable portions; in removing the bark; in taking the soft and spongy matter from the fibrous portion, like soaking and hackling in flax; in making ribbon-like splints of uniform width and thickness; in shredding, as in cedar bark; in twisting, twining, and braiding; in gauging, and coloring.

The apparatus for this intermediate work must have been in aboriginal times very simple, a stone knife and shell for scraping supplementing the work of the fingers and the teeth. The quality of the finished workmanship depends largely upon this secondary process. In those regions of very uniform moisture the plants used were of quick growth and pliable, and it would be easy, even without metal tools, to secure fine splints and other elements in the manufacture; but in those localities where the raw substances were more brittle, fine work would be difficult and indeed was impossible until quite recently. It is a question, therefore, whether anciently some of the modern processes in basketry were known at all. Certainly there was no such delicate basketry made in Canada by the untaught aborigines as can now be procured from their descendants; but in the old graves of California and the adjoining areas wonderful pieces of delicate workmanship are brought from ancient pre-Columbian tombs.

It must not be forgotten that coloring matters were in ancient times among the prepared materials of basketry. Nature furnishes opportunities for diversity of color in the substances themselves. The Indian also knew how to change or modify the natural color of different materials by burying them in mud. The juices of the plants and the mineral substances in the mud combined to produce darker shades of the same color or an entirely different one.   But the savage woman had gone further, for they well knew that certain plants were useful as dyes.   In point of fact, the best dyestuffs of each area had been exhaustively exploited.   A list of these for each area would include a large number of useful plants.   As in gathering materials the simplest processes involve slight artificiality, so in this intermediary art the most primitive basket makers modified little their raw materials.   They did not store them away for the convenient season, and, save that they soaked them before using, practiced none of the refining processes necessary to the highest results.

In each of the culture areas of America the methods of preparing materials were peculiar.

Dr. Walter J. Hoffman [a] described in 1895 the aboriginal process of preparing material for wicker baskets among the Menomini Indians (Algonquin Family) on Lake Michigan.   See figures 110 to 114 of this paper.

A small log of wood, 3 or 4 inches in diameter and as long as it is possible to procure one without knots, furnishes the splints.   (Hoffman's fig. 37.)   These logs are cut when the rings of annual growth are most easily ruptured.   The log is beaten with a wooden mallet. The example shown in Hoffman's illustration (fig. 38) is of modern type, made with steel tools, but the ancient Indian, no doubt, had a much rougher but quite as efficient implement.   The strips thus loosened are torn off one by one as long as the material is sufficiently flexible for basket making.   The next process is the shaping of these splints for the desired work—splitting them, shaving them down thin and smooth, and finishing them for the hand of the weaver.

The basket-maker's awl of bone, the old aboriginal implement, may be seen at work in many camps; but the knife with which the pre-Columbian woman cut her basket material has utterly disappeared from use.   Now, among the Algonkin, the knife of steel vastly improved their art and it raises a question whether in the pristine condition of savagery some forms of basketry were as good as they are at present.   This query applies only to work done in hard wood.

The knife now in use among the Indians for this and other wood-working purposes is an interesting survival from the remote past in Europe.   It is now active in the farrier's shop for paring the frog of the horse's foot, prior to putting on the shoe; but two or three centuries ago, under name of man's knife,[b] it found its way through the entire English and French area of North America.

A curved blade of steel is inserted or laid in a groove on the side of

[a] Fourteenth Annual Report of the Bureau of Ethnology, Part I, figs. 37–41.

[b] The man's Knife among the North American Indians: A study in the Collections of the U. S. National Museum, by Otis Tufton Mason, Report of the U. S. National Museum, 1897, pp. 725–745, 17 figs.

the handle, made fast by wrapping with strong twine. The groove is shouldered so as to take the pressure. The blade is detachable for the purpose of grinding it. It will be seen that if held in the right hand the operator cuts toward himself. This is the ancient method of whittling practiced by the peoples on the western shores of the Pacific Ocean, the Ainos, Japanese, etc. (Hoffman's fig. 39.)

A bundle of splints is shown in fig. 40 of Hoffman's paper of different widths ready for the hand of the basket maker, and in fig. 41 (Hoffman) is a coarse-finished product showing the method of setting up the warp and applying the weft in wicker basketry of the Menomini.

It is not known that the ancient Menomini used any dyes on their baskets whatever. In their modern ware they procure these substances through traders.

The sweet grass (*Savastana odorata*), of which large quantities of baskets are manufactured, was dried in the shade to hold its color. Further, it was rolled into bunches and sewed with sinew, as the Eskimo do in making their coiled baskets. Very old specimens of such ware are preserved in collections. But in the ware now in the market twine and braid of this material are prepared beforehand in large quantities for the future use of the weaver and frequently by different hands.

Farther south in the Eastern basket area the canes for twilled basketry needed no knife for the splitting. A slight blow would crush the stalk, the spongy matter adhering to the inside was scraped away, and the splints were ready for the dyer or the weaver if they were not to be colored.

The following information concerning natural sources of color for basketry and other objects among the Cherokee Indians comes from Miss Harriet C. Wilkie, of Raleigh, North Carolina. The petals of the iris rubbed on a slightly rough surface are said to yield a rich and lasting purple. The blossoms and tender green tops and leaves of the common sneeze weed (*Helenium autumnale*) made into a tea yield a beautiful and fadeless yellow. Long boiling dulls this to a yellowish olive. The common broom sedge (*Andropogon scoparius*), winter dried, yields another yellow, less pure and brilliant, also much affected by continued boiling. The color is known as burnt orange and works beautifully in basketry.

In central Alaska the Athapascan tribes use both spruce and willow for their coiled basket jars and trinket material. Much care is bestowed in splitting the roots and stems, in order to procure uniform sewing material. In the U. S. National Museum the specimens all show care in this regard. The Alaskan Eskimo on Bering Sea also manufacture coiled basketry as well as twined, but it is from dried grass and shows very little care in the preparation. Crossing over to the Aleutian chain, the care bestowed on materials is different.

When Attu weavers wanted the grass to be white it was cut in November, the whole stalk (wild rye), and hung points down out of doors to dry. If grass was to be yellow, the common color, it is cut in the middle of July, and the two youngest blades that are full grown are then cut out and split into three pieces, the middle one being thrown away. The other pieces are then tied into bunches about 2 inches in diameter and hung up to dry out of doors (points down). If the grass is to be cured green it is prepared as when it is wanted to be yellow, but the first two weeks of the curing is carried on in the shade of the dense growth of grass and weeds that is found in the villages. After that it is taken out and dried in the house. Under no circumstances is the sun allowed to shine on any of the grass in the process of curing, which takes about a month or more.

Beautiful coiled basketry is made by the Chilcotin, Harrison Lake, Lower Thompson Indians in British Columbia, Salish on the coast, as well as Klikitat and Tulalip in Washington. Only women and girls occupy themselves with this work. The baskets are made from the small, trailing roots of the cedar (*Thuja plicata*). These are dug up with an ordinary root digger, and pieces of the desired length and of about the thickness of a finger are cut off. These are buried in the ground to keep them fresh. When required they are taken out and peeled or scraped with a sharp stone or knife. They are then hung up until dry enough for use. Next they are split into long strips by inserting and pressing forward the point of the awl used in basket making, made from the long bone of a deer. The pieces which have the desired width and thickness throughout their entire length are used for stitching purposes, while others which split irregularly, or are too short or too thin to be used for that purpose, are put together in bundles to form the foundation of the coils. In the sewing these foundations are kept continuous and of uniform thickness by adding fresh pieces as required. (See Plate 11.)

In other basketry, thin, pliable strips of cedar sap or other wood in pairs, having both smooth sides out, are used for foundation instead of the bunches of split roots. These are stitched in the same manner, but are neither as strong nor as durable nor are they water-tight.[a]

The Upper Fraser and the Lytton bands sometimes use *Elymus triticoides* instead of *Xerophyllum*. The bark used is that of *Prunus demissa*, which is either left its natural light reddish-brown color or is dyed by burying it in damp earth. By thus keeping it under ground for a short time it assumes a dark-brown color; if kept longer it becomes quite black. (Teit.)

The Makah Indians make a red color by mixing vermilion with chewed salmon eggs; black color is a combination of bituminous coal

---

[a] James Teit, The Thompson Indians of British Columbia, Memoirs of the American Museum of Natural History, II, Pt. 4, 1900, pp. 163–392.

and the same carrier; cedar bark is colored black by soaking in mud, and red by means of alder bark chewed. (Swan.)

The Twana Indians, on Skokomish Reservation, Washington, now use a steel-bladed knife and an awl of the same material in basket making. Formerly they employed a pointed stick or bone for their imbricated ware and for pressing home the weft of twined basketry; but in large measure their fingers are their tools. (Myron Eells.) The same remark applies to basket makers in all the culture areas. Fingers and teeth are still in vogue and can not be dispensed with. The metal awl, however, quite displaces that of bone, and it is not surprising to find scissors of the best make added to the steel-bladed knife, especially for clipping off the projecting ends of materials.

Hazel stalks are gathered by Oregon tribes in best form on ground that has been burned over, the young ones springing up straight and strong from the rich soil. The peeled stems are the warp, those split by means of the teeth are the weft, and a dye is made from the bark chewed by the basket maker. (Mrs. Harriet K. McArthur.) The fine white grass, like ivory in smoothness and tint, is obtained at great elevations, their excursions leading them to the summer snow line of Mount Shasta.

PROCESSES OF MANUFACTURE

As you gaze on the Indian basket maker at work, herself frequently unkempt, her garments the coarsest, her house and surroundings suggestive of anything but beauty, you are amazed. You look about you, as in a cabinet shop or atelier, for models, drawings, patterns, pretty bits of color effect. There are none. Her patterns are in her soul, in her memory and imagination, in the mountains, water courses, lakes, and forests, and in those tribal tales and myths which dominate the actions of every hour. She hears suggestions from another world. Her tools are more disappointing still, for of these there are few—a rude knife, a pointed bone, that is all. Her modeling block is herself. Her plastic body is the repository of forms. Over her knee she molds depressions in her ware, and her lap is equal to all emergencies for convex effects. She herself is the Vishnu of her art, the creator of forms.

The Tlinkit in weaving, says Emmons, sits with the knees drawn up to the chin, the feet close to the body, the shoulders bent over, the arms around the knees, the hands in front. Sometimes one knee is dropped a little to the side, and, in the case of old women, they often recline on one hip, with the legs drawn up, the elbows resting on a pillow or blanket doubled up.

In all types of weave the working strands are constantly dampened by dipping the fingers into a basket or cup of water close at hand, or, in the case of embroidery, by drawing the section of grass stem through the lips. The material is kept in a plaque-like work basket called tarlth ("spread out," from its flat bottom and low, flaring sides). Besides the shell or metal knife there is generally a rude awl, consisting of a spike of goat or deer horn, a bear's claw, or a piece of bone rubbed down to a tapering point, and a large incisor of the brown bear or the tooth of the killer whale. These constitute all of the tools and accessories used in basketry. (Emmons.)

Plate 12 represents a Pomo Indian basketmaker. In front of her is an unfinished water-tight basket jar in plain twined weaving. The warp elements are willow rods dressed down to uniform thickness; the weft is of carex root and cercis stems split, the patterns being made in the latter. Photographed by H. W. Henshaw.

Plate 13 represents a Tlinkit woman of Sitka, Alaska, making a twined basket. All the native surroundings are absent—the environment, as men are wont to say—but the artist's mind and skillful fingers remain. She has four elements to handle simultaneously— warp, two wefts, and decorative material. The mouth, therefore, is brought into requisition, as may be seen. The operation consists in twining with finely divided spruce root and wrapping each outside splint with colored straw. The work resembles embroidery when finished and is, in this work, called false embroidery.

There seems to be always an affectionate fellow feeling between the skillful hand of the artisan and the materials which it fashions. The more tractable the latter, the more deft the former. That is not always true in culture. The best endowment does not always yield the best results. But the statement holds good in our art with few exceptions. Where the finest grasses grow, and the toughest roots and stems, they set up a school of mutual refinement between the woman and her work. It needs only a few miles eastward or northward to change the garden into a desert and correspondingly to degenerate the artist. It would be unjust to her ingenious mind to overlook the fact that she has not been utterly cast down by the failure of one kind of material. She is not long in finding out new substances and new technic processes for each environment.

WOVEN BASKETRY

The various processes of manufacture will now be definitely explained. In technic, as already said (p. 190), basketry is either hand-woven or sewed. The hand-woven basketry is further divisible into (A) *Checkerwork*, (B) *Twilledwork*, (C) *Wickerwork*, (D) *Wrappedwork*, and (E) *Twinedwork*, in several varieties. The sewed work goes by the name of coiled basketry, and is classed both by the foundation and the fastening. In addition to these technical methods on the body, special ones are to be found in the border.

A. *Checkerwork.*—This occurs especially in the bottoms of many North Pacific coast examples, and also in the work of eastern Canadian tribes (fig. 2); in matting its use is well nigh universal.

In this ware the warp and the weft have the same thickness and pliability. It is impossible, therefore, in looking at the bottoms of the cedar-bark baskets and the matting of British Columbia (fig. 3) or Eastern Canada to tell which is warp and which is weft. In very many examples the warp and weft of a checker bottom are turned up at right angles to form the warp of the sides, which may be wicker or twined work. A great deal of bark matting is made in this same checkerwork, but the patterns run obliquely to the axis of the fabric, giving the appearance of diagonal weaving. The fine hats of Ecuador are especially noticeable in this deceptive appearance, which is caused by the weaver's beginning the work at the center. Perhaps,

FIG. 2.
COARSE CHECKERWORK.

though there is no positive information on this subject, the North Pacific coast women proceed in the same manner to give a tiled effect to the surface of their matting. When warp and weft are fine yarn or threads the result is the simplest form of cloth in cotton, linen, piña fiber, or wool. The cheap fabrics of commerce are of this species of weaving. In art and industry lattice-work frequently shows the bars intertwined as in checker basketry (fig. 4).

From this results a most stable figure, the elasticity of the material and the friction of the surfaces holding the fabric together. (See figs. 4, 5, 6.)

The pleasing effects that may be produced in

FIG. 3.
FINE CHECKERWORK.

checker are shown in Plate 14. At the bottom is coarse work. At the end of seven rows the warp strips of bark are held firmly in place by a row of twined weaving and then split into four, each sixth one being left whole for artificial effects. At proper intervals broader strips of weft are introduced. In the chapter on ornamentation attention will be called to the variety in this mass of unity by the individual characteristics of each square in the weaving.

FIG. 4.

OPEN CHECKERWORK.

B. *Twilledwork.*—This is seen especially in those parts of the world where cane abounds. In America it is quite common in British Columbia, Washington, Southern United States, Mexico, and Central America, and of excellent workmanship in Peru, Guiana, and Ecuador. The fundamental technic of diagonal basketry is in passing each element of the weft over two or more warp elements, thus producing either diagonal or twilled, or, in the best samples, an endless variety of diaper patterns. (See figs. 5 and 6.)

The example shown in Plate 15 represents a cigar case made by the women of Bolivia, who weave the celebrated Panama hats, the texture being fine twilled work. The ornamentation should be studied carefully, for it consists of twined weaving, in which both warp and weft strands are brought together in pairs and one twined about the other.

| FIG. 5. | FIG. 6. |
| TWILLED WORK. | TWILLED WORK. |

There is no attempt at anything but plain over-two weaving elsewhere in this specimen. To the student of technology it is charming to read in this connection from Ure's Dictionary[a] the labored description of twilled loom work with its hundreds of parts in the climax of a series of inventions initiated with savage women's figures.

Twill, or *tweel.* A diagonal appearance given to a fabric by causing

---

[a] Article Weaving, fourth edition, London, 1853.

the weft threads to pass over one warp thread, and then under two, and so on, instead of taking the warp threads in regular succession, one down, one up. The next weft thread takes a set oblique to the former, throwing up one of the two deposed by the preceding. In some twills it is one in three, or one in four. The Latin *trilix*, a certain pattern in weaving, became *drillich* in German, and hence our word *drill*. *Twill* is derived from *zwillich*, which answers to the Latin *bilix*, and the Greek *dimitos*. The latter survives in *dimity*. See also *samite*, derived from Greek *hexamiton*, six thread.

FIG. 7.
ANCIENT TWILLED WORK.
Pressed on pottery of Alabama. After W. H. Holmes.

The French *touaille* has also been suggested as the etymological source of the word.

The fabrics thus woven are very numerous—satin, blanket, merino, bombazine, kerseymere, etc. When the threads cross each alternately in regular order it is called *plain weaving;* but in *twill* the same

FIG. 8.
ANCIENT TWILLED WORK.
Pressed on pottery of Tennessee. After W. H. Holmes.

thread of weft is *flushed*, or separated from the warp while passing over a number of warp threads, and then passes under a warp thread. (See Plate 16.)

The points where the threads of the warp cross form diagonal lines, parallel to each other, across the face of the cloth. In *blanket twill* every third thread is crossed. In some fabrics 4, 5, 6, 7, or 8 threads are crossed. In *full satin twill* there is an interval of 15 threads, the warp (*organzine silk*) being floated over 15 threads of the woof (*tram*), giving the glossy appearance.

Twills require heddles equal in number to the threads that are included in the intervals between the intersections. This disposition of the warps in the heddles is termed *mounting the loom*, and the

FIG. 9.

TWILLED WEAVING.

Cherokee Indians, North Carolina.

heddles are termed *leaves*. A twill takes its name from the number of leaves employed, as a three-leaf twill, a five-leaf twill, etc.

Twills are used for the display of color, for strength, variety, thickness, or durability.

On a fragment of ancient pottery from Alabama, Holmes also discovered marks of basketry in twilled weaving, as shown in fig. 7.

It will be noticed that material of cat-tail or split cane was used. The effect shown in the figure was produced by passing each weft strand over three warp strands and under one on the side exhibited. On the other side of the texture, no doubt, the process was reversed, the warp strands passing over three and under one. In such work there was opportunity to use double warp and weft, the strips of cane laid together so as to expose two bright surfaces.

In order to vary the texture of twilled work, the ancient inhabitants of the Mississippi Valley knew how to use for warp and weft substances of different widths. On a fragment of ancient pottery from Pope County, Tennessee, Holmes found impressions of ancient basketry. Fig. 8 shows how these ancient weavers utilized wide fiber of bast or split cane for the warp, and string for the weft, passing in their work over two each time. For the uses of woven fabrics on making pottery

FIG. 10.
WICKER BASKET.
Zuñi, New Mexico.
Cat. No. 40291, U.S.N.M.   Collected by J. W. Powell.

and the interesting way in which the history of lost arts have been preserved, see Part VII.

Excellent variety was also produced in this kind of weaving by means of color. Almost any textile plant when split has two colors, that of the outer, or bark surface, and that of the interior woody surface or pith. Also the different plants used in diagonal basketry have great variety of color. By the skillful manipulation of the two sides of a splint, by using plants of different species, or with dyed elements, geometric patterns, frets, labyrinths, and other designs in straight line are possible. (See fig. 9.)

Examples from the saltpeter caves, and modern pieces from the Cherokee, both in matting and basketry, are double. By this means both the inside and the outside of the texture expose the glossy siliceous surface of the cane. By changing the number of warp splints or a stem over which the weft passes, it will be seen in the figure here given that great variety of diaper or damask effect may be produced.

C. *Wickerwork.*—The name is from the Anglo-Saxon *wican*, to bend. Common in eastern Canada, it is little known on the Pacific coast and in the Interior Basin, excepting in one or two pueblos, but is seen abundantly in southern Mexico and Central America. It consists of a wide or a thick and inflexible warp and a slender flexible weft (fig. 10). The weaving is plain and differs from checkerwork only in the fact that one of the elements is rigid. The effect on the surface is a series of ridges. It is possible also to produce diagonal effects in this type of weaving.

Wickerwork must have been a very early and primitive form of textile. Weirs for stopping fish are made of brush, and wattled fences for game drivers are set up in the same manner. A great deal of the coarse basketry in use for packing and transporting is made in this fashion. The Zuni Indians make gathering baskets of little twigs after the same technic, the inflexible warp being made up of a small number of twigs of the same plant, laid side by side. The transition from checker to wicker in some examples is easy. The moment one element, either warp or weft, is a little more rigid than the other, the intersections would naturally assume a wicker form.

FIG. 11.
CLOSE WICKERWORK.
Hopi Indians, Arizona.

The finest specimens in America are the very pretty Hopi plaques made of *Chrysothamnus moquianus* and *C. laricinus.* Short stems are dyed in various colors for weft, the ends worked into the warp and the whole driven tightly home, so as to hide the ends of the warp and even the manner of weaving. (See fig. 11.)

Various patterns are effected on the surface—geometric figures, clouds, mythical animals and persons, and symbols connected with worship. Wickerwork has pleasing effects combined with diagonal and other work. Fig. 12 is a square Hopi plaque, having twilled weaving in the middle and a band of wicker outside of this, the whole finished with rough, coiled sewing on the border.

It has passed into modern industry through the cultivation of osiers, rattan, and such plants for market baskets, covers for glass bottles,

and in ribbed cloth, wherein a flexible weft is worked on a rigid warp.
Also, good examples are now produced by the Algonkin tribes of
New England and eastern Canada.

For commercial purposes, wicker baskets precisely like those of the
Abenaki Indians are thus made.

The white-oak timber is brought to the yard in sticks running from
6 to 40 inches in diameter and from 4 to 18 feet long.   It is first sawed
into convenient lengths, then split with a maul and wedges into fourths
or sixteenths.   The bark is then stripped off with a drawing knife.
The next process is cutting it into bolts at what is called the splitting
horse, to be shaved down with a drawing knife into perfectly smooth,
even bolts of the width and length desired.   These are then placed in

FIG. 12.
TWILLED AND WICKER MAT.
Hopi Indians, Arizona.
After W. H. Holmes.

the steam box and steamed for a half hour or so, which makes the
splints more pliable.   They are taken thence to the splint knife, which
is arranged so that one person, by changing the position of the knife,
can make splints of any desired thickness, from that of paper to that
of a three-fourths-inch hoop.

The oyster baskets and most small baskets have the bottom splints
laid one across another and are plainly woven in checker.

But the round-bottomed baskets, used for grain and truck, are made
by taking from 10 to 18 ribs and laying them across each other at the
middle, in radiating form, and weaving around with a narrow thin
splint until the desired size for the bottom is reached, when the splints
are turned up and set in other baskets, about a dozen in a series, for
twenty-four hours.

They are then woven around with a fine splint and placed on a revolving drum or form and filled up the required hight and set in the sun to dry for six hours.   They are then shaken hard by striking the bottom on the floor, which causes the splints to settle tight together and prepared for the rim.   They next proceed to fasten the handles to the sides and put the rims or hoops on by fitting them into the notches made in the handles and binding them tightly with fine splints.   The different styles are made by using different-shaped drums and variously colored splints, the latter being done by dipping the splints before weaving into dyes.

The most curiously made baskets are those for the charcoal and eelpots.

The charcoal baskets are shaped like a tray and are carried on the head by the coal carriers.

The eelpots are used as traps for catching eels. The wood is prepared for them in the same manner, and they are made on a form about 40 inches long and in the shape of a bottle minus the bottom, and have a funnel arrangement at either end, which is detachable.

FIG. 13.
WRAPPED WEAVING.
Mohave Indians, Arizona.
Cat. No. 24145, U.S.N.M.   Collected by Edward Palmer.

D. *Wrappedwork.* — Wrapped basketry consists of flexible or rigid warp and flexible weft. Examples of this technic are to be seen in America at the present time among the Indians of southern Arizona for their carrying frames.   (See fig. 13.)

The warp extends from the rigid hoop, which forms the top, to the bottom where the elements are made fast. Firmness is given to the structure by means of two bowed rods crossing at right angles at the bottom and securely lashed at the top. The weft, usually of twine, is attached to one of the corner or frame pieces at the bottom and is wrapped once around each warp element. This process continues in a coil until the top of the basket is reached. In some of its features this method resembles coiled work, but as a regular warp is employed and no needle is used in the coiling, it belongs more to the woven series. Hudson mentions the same among the Pomos for holding roof

poles in place.   The wrapping is very close where the rafters come to
a point.   As they widen the weft comes to be farther apart, being
quite open on the outer margin.   This method of weaving was
employed by the mound builders of the Mississippi Valley.   Markings
of wrapped weaving pressed on ancient pottery taken from a mound in
Ohio are to be seen in the Third Report of the Bureau of Ethnology.
(See fig. 14.)

This style of weaving had not a wide distribution in America and is
used at the present day in a restricted region.   When the warp and
the weft are of the same twine or material and the decussations are
drawn tight, the joint resembles the first half of a square knot.   The
Mincopies of the Andaman Islands construct a carrying basket in the
same technic.   Specimens of their work were collected and presented
to the U. S. National Museum by
Dr. W. L. Abbott.[a]   These baskets
resemble most closely the Mohave
specimens, only they are smaller and
more attractive.   The Mincopies and
their neighbors far and near have the
incomparable rattan for warp and
weft, which combines the strength
and flexibility of copper wire.   The
distribution of this wrapped weaving has not been studied.   Plate 17
is a carrying basket in wrapped

FIG. 14.

WRAPPED WEAVING, FROM MOUND IN OHIO.
After W. H. Holmes.

weaving from the Mohave Indians, photographed from the original
now in the Field Columbian Museum, Chicago.

E. *Twinedwork.*—This is found in ancient mounds of the Mississippi Valley, in bagging of the Rocky Mountains, down the Pacific
coast from the island of Attu, the most westerly of the Aleutian
chain, to the borders of Chile, and here and there in the Atlantic
slope of South America.   Indeed, it is found among savages throughout the world.   It is the most elegant and intricate of all in the woven
or plicated series.   Twined work has a set of warp rods or rigid
elements as in wickerwork, but the weft elements are commonly
administered in pairs, though in three-strand twining and in braid
twining three weft elements are employed.   In passing from warp to
warp these elements are twisted in half-turns on each other so as to
form a two-strand or three-strand twine or braid and usually so deftly
as to keep the smooth, glossy side of the weft outward.

The position of the weaver at her task on twined work, in Plate 18,
shows the transition between the humble posture of the primitive
basket maker and her successor later on seated at a loom.   The name

[a] Smithsonian Report, 1901, pp. 475–492, pl. II.

of the weaver in the lower figure is Elizabeth Propokoffono. Her home is on the island of Atka, far out in the Aleutian chain. The Tlinkit weaver sits on the ground in the old-fashioned way, because her warp is rigid and self-supporting; Elizabeth, however, is working in soft grass, both for warp and weft. For this reason the former is suspended, and she is working from below upward. The Haida Indians on Queen Charlotte Archipelago south of her, as will be seen later on, weave in the same manner, the warp resting on a disk fastened to the top of a stake. Enough of modern technical appliances are mingled with this thoroughly aboriginal process to mark a sharp contrast between the woman's fingers and her beautiful basket on the one hand, and her loom-woven clothing, her flat-iron, and the iron hinges on her door on the other hand.

FIG. 15.

PLAIN TWINED WEAVING.

The upper figure is from the Attu Island, also weaving a grass wallet in twined work in front of her underground home or barabara. It is most interesting to observe that her work is supported from a stick in the top of the house, and is mounted precisely as one shown in Plate 1, of Holmes's Prehistoric Textile Art, taken from Hariot,[a] and illustrating industries of the eastern Indians at the period of discovery.

According to the relation of the weft elements to one another and to the warp, different structures in twined weaving result as follows:

1. Plain twined weaving over single warps.
2. Diagonal twined weaving or twill over two or more warps.
3. Wrapped twined weaving, or bird-cage twine, in which one weft element remains rigid and the other is wrapped about the crossings.
4. Lattice-twined weaving, tee or Hudson stitch, twined work around vertical warps crossed by horizontal warp element.
5. Three-strand twined weaving and braiding in several styles.

1. *Plain twined weaving.*—Plain twined weaving is a refined sort of wattling or crating. The ancient engineers, who built obstructions in streams to aid in catching or impounding fish, drove a row of sticks into the bottom of the stream, a few inches apart. Vines and brush were woven upon these upright sticks which served for a warp. In passing each stake the two vines or pieces of brush made a half turn on each other. This is a very primitive mode of weaving. Plain twined basketry is made on exactly the same plan. There is a set of warp elements which may be reeds, or splints, or string, arranged radially on the bottom and parallel on the body. The weft consists

[a] Thirteenth Annual Report of the Bureau of Ethnology, 1896, Plate 1.

of two strips of root or other flexible material, and these are twisted as in forming a two-strand rope passing over a warp stem at each halfturn. (See fig. 15.) Many wastebaskets are woven on this plan.

Plate 19 shows two bowls in plain twined weaving, called Bamtush by the Pomos, which are excellent examples of the possibilities and limitations of this style. They are in the collection of C. P. Wilcomb, of San Francisco. The upper figure, 10 inches in diameter, is from Cloverdale, Russian River, Sonoma County; the lower from Potter Valley, in Mendocino County. The warp is of willow rods, the weft of carex root and splints of cercis. A small space at the bottom is in three-ply braid and the narrow band near the top, with wide twists, is plain twined work over more than one warp stem. (See Plates 34, 44, 71, 72.)

In this connection must not be overlooked a variety of twined weaving in which the warp plays an important part. It is a transition between the plain twine and the next type, the halves of the double warp standing for the independent warp stems of the diagonal weave. If the weft be administered in open work with the rows from a fourth to a half an inch apart and the warp elements be flexible under the strain of weaving, they will assume a zigzag shape.

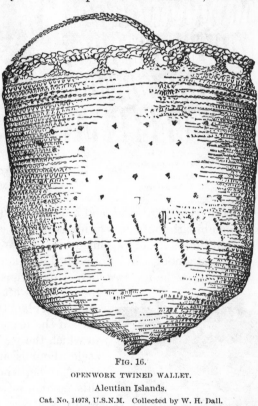

FIG. 16.
OPENWORK TWINED WALLET.
Aleutian Islands.
Cat. No. 14978, U.S.N.M.   Collected by W. H. Dall.

Pleasing varieties of this type of twined weaving will be found in the Aleutian Islands. (See fig. 16.) It resembles hemstitching. The Aleuts frequently use for their warp stems of wild rye or other grasses, in which the straws are split, or a pair used, and the two halves pass upward in zigzag form. Each half of a warp is caught alternately with the other half of the same straw and with a half of the adjoining straw, making a series of triangular instead of rectangular spaces. (See fig. 17.)

A still further variation is given to plain twined ware by crossing the warps. In bamboo basketry of eastern Asia these crossed warps are also interlaced or held together by a horizontal strip of bamboo passing in and out in ordinary weaving. In such examples the interstices are triangular, but in the twined example here described the weaving passes across between the points where the warps intersect

<table>
<tr><td>FIG. 17.</td><td>FIG. 18.</td></tr>
<tr><td>TWINED OPENWORK.</td><td></td></tr>
<tr><td>Aleutian Islands.</td><td>CROSSED WARP, TWINED WEAVE.</td></tr>
<tr><td>Enlarged.</td><td>Makah Indians, Washington.</td></tr>
</table>

each other, leaving hexagonal interstices. (See fig. 18 and Plate 166.) This combination of plain twined weft and crossed warp has not a wide distribution in America, but examples are to be seen in southeastern Alaska and among relics found in Peruvian graves.

2. *Diagonal twined weaving.*—In diagonal twined weaving the twisting of the weft filaments is precisely the same as in plain twined weaving. The difference of the texture is caused by the manner in which the weft crosses the warps. This style abounds among the Ute Indians and the Apache, who dip the bottles made in this fashion into pitch and thus produce a water-tight vessel, the open meshes receiving the pitch more freely. The technic of the diagonal weaving consists in passing over two or more warp elements at each turn, just as in weaving with a single element. But the warp of the diagonal twined weaving never passes over or under more than one weft as it does in twilled weaving. There must be an odd number of warps, for in the next round the same pairs are not included in the half turns. The ridges on the outside, therefore, are not vertical as in plain weaving, but pass diagonally over the surface, hence the name. (See Plate 20, and figs. 19 and 20.)

FIG. 19.
DIAGONAL TWINED WEAVING.
Ute Indians, Utah.

Plate 20 will make clear the difference between plain twined weaving and diagonal twined or twilled work. The figures are of the burden basket, the granary, and the mush bowls of the Pomo Indians, in Lake, Sonoma, and Mendocino counties, California, in the collection of C. P. Wilcomb. Especial attention is here drawn to the infinitely greater possibilities of decoration in the twilled work. The foregoing plate shows that the ornamentation of plain twined basketry is confined chiefly to bands, but here the artist revels in the cycloid, which widens and becomes more intricate as it ascends. It rivals in complexity the best coiled work of the Pomos and should be compared with Plates 29 and 56.

FIG. 20.

DIAGONAL TWINED BASKETRY.
Pomo Indians, California.
Collection of C. P. Wilcomb.

3. *Wrapped twined weaving.*—In wrapped twined weaving one element of the twine passes along horizontally across the warp stems, usually on the inside of the basket, forming a lattice. The binding element of splint, or strip of bark, or string, is wrapped around the crossings of the horizontal element with the vertical warp. (See fig. 21.)

On the outside of the basket the turns of the wrapping are oblique; on the inside they are vertical. It will be seen on examining this figure that one row inclines to the right, the one above it to the left, and so on alternately. This was occasioned by the weaver's passing from side to side of the square carrying basket, and not all the way round as usual. The work is similar to that in an old-fashioned bird cage, where the upright and horizontal wires are held in place by a wrapping of finer soft wire. The typical example of this wrapped or bird-cage twine is to be seen among

FIG. 21.
WRAPPED TWINED WEAVING.

the Makah Indians of the Wakashan family living about Neah Bay, Washington, and in the soft hats of Salish and Shapaptian. (See fig. 22.)

In this type the warp and the horizontal strip behind the warp are both in soft material. The wrapping is done with a tough straw-colored grass. When the weaving is beaten home tight the surface is not unlike that of a fine tiled roof, the stitches overlying each other

with perfect regularity.   Such a simple style of fastening warp and
weft together would seem to have occurred to tribes of savages in
many parts of the world.   Strange to relate, however, excepting in
Washington and the ocean side of Vancouver Island, the process is not
known.   The exception to this statement is to be found in a few spo-
radic cases where, perhaps, Nutka and Makah women had married into
adjoining tribes.   A few of the Salish women make similar ware, and
it will be seen in basket hats of the Nez Percé Indians.   A small collection of this ware came to the
Museum through the Wilkes Exploring Expedition, but the ornamentation is decidedly Skokomish.

FIG. 22.
WRAPPED TWINED WEAVING.
Makah Indians, Washington.

Figs. 23 and 24 show the detail
of mixed twined weaving, diagonal twined weaving, and wrapped
twined weaving, inside and outside
view.   The facility with which
the basket maker combines these
weaves in the same texture gives
her complete control over her material in the matter of ornamentation.
The coloring of the two sides of
the splints of cercis shows, in the
figures, the difference between the
outside and the inside of the basket.   Another element of technic, not
mentioned hitherto, is made apparent here in the requirements of
these three different styles of workmanship controlling the space
somewhat of the warp rods.   Perhaps in no other tribe than the Pomo
is there such free use of any number of textile methods on the same
piece of workmanship to secure different results.

It is possible to combine the several methods of twined weaving
and, calling the aid of color, to produce good effects even in unpromis-
ing materials.   Figs. 25 and 26 show back and front of a square from
a Ute basket jar.   The first two rows are plain twined work, then
come three rows of plain twined work also, though it does not look
like it.   It incloses warp stems in pairs, and the back and front are
alike.   It changes to diagonal merely by alternating warps.   Below
these three rows are diagonal twine, wrapped twine, or Makah weave,
combined with diagonal.   Plate 21 contains five figures, all in diagonal
twined weaving.   They were made by the Ute Indians and collected
long ago by Major J. W. Powell.   They represent first of all the different results of the same technical process in varied materials.   The
specimens are all woven precisely alike.   Fig. 1 has a coarse, inflexible
warp.   Fig. 2 has a finer warp, and hence the twists may be driven
closer home.   Fig. 4 shows the adaptation of modern shape in facili-

tating the carrying. In fig. 5 a fine weft assumes a diagonal shape in being twisted, while fig. 3 is the last word in the story of the water jar.

4. *Lattice-twined weaving.*—The lattice-twined weaving, so far as the collections of the National Museum show, is confined to the Pomo Indians, of the Kulanapan family, residing on Russian River, California. It is so called because it has a vertical and a horizontal warp

FIG. 23.
DETAIL OF MIXED TWINED WEAVING.
(Outside.)

resembling latticework. Dr. J. W. Hudson calls this technic tee. This is a short and convenient word, and may be used for a specific name. The tee-twined weaving consists of four elements, (*a*) the upright warp of rods, (*b*) a horizontal warp crossing these at right angles, and (*c, d*) a regular plain-twined weaving of two elements, holding the warps firmly together. (See fig. 27.)

In all these examples in the National Museum the horizontal or extra warp is on the exterior of the basket. On the outside the tee

FIG. 24.
DETAIL OF MIXED TWINED WEAVING.
(Inside.)

basket does not resemble the ordinary twined work, but on the inside it is indistinguishable. Baskets made in this fashion are very rigid and strong, and frequently the hoppers of mills for grinding acorns, and also water-tight jars, are thus constructed. The ornamentation is confined to narrow bands, the artist being restricted by the technic.

Plate 22 shows two examples of tee weaving. The upper one, 19 inches in diameter, is from Pinole rancheria, Mendocino County, California. The lower one is from Lake County, and both are in the collection of C. P. Wilcomb. The warp is in stems of the willow, the dull colored material of the weft is the root of sedge, the brown and very white colors are in the stem of cercis—the former color being outside bark, the latter of wood next to the bark. (See also Plate 173.)

FIG. 25.

VARIETY IN TWINED WEAVING.
(Outside.)
American Anthropologist, III, 1901, fig. 18.

The technic of these two baskets is as follows: Beginning at the upper edge there is no special border, the ends of the warp stems being cut off; two or three rows of plain twined weaving are at the top; just below will be seen three or four rows of alternating brown and white rectangles; these are also in plain twined weaving, although the twists pass over two or three warp stems instead of one; after that twined tee weaving follows over the entire surface. With an ordinary hand glass the two sets of warp, vertical and horizontal, can be made out, and also the way in which the weft of thin splints is administered. The limitations of ornament to the narrow bands with triangles and parallelograms for the elements are clearly seen. On the plain bands a form of ornament will be noted, in which splints of cercis unite with those of sedge root to form an alternation of wood color and very white. In the colored bands the effects are produced by exposing now the outside or bark of the cercis, now the inside or wood color. No at-

FIG. 26.

VARIETY IN TWINED WEAVING.
(Inside.)
American Anthropologist, III, 1901, fig. 21.

tempt has been made to change the color of these splints artificially.

5. *Three-strand twined weaving.*—Three-strand twined weaving is the

use of three weft splints and other kinds of weft elements instead of two, and there are four ways of administering the weft:

(*a*) Three-strand twine.

(*b*) Three-strand braid.

(*c*) Three-strand, false embroidery, Tlinkit.

(*d*) Frapped twine, Thompson River.

It will be seen in studying these four methods that they are partly structural and partly ornamental, especially the last two. Inasmuch, however, as the Indian woman makes her ornamental work a part of her industrial work, the four methods may be all studied here. Very little was known among the American aborigines concerning additional ornaments given to the textile after the foundation was woven. The part which furnishes strength to the fabric and that which gives decoration were in technic one and the same process.

FIG. 27.

TEE OR LATTICE-TWINED WEAVING.

Pomo Indians, California.

American Anthropologist, III, 1901, fig. 22.

(*a*) *Three-strand twine.*—In this technic the basket-weaver holds in her hand three weft elements of any of the kinds mentioned. In twisting these three, each one of the strands, as it passes inward, is carried behind the warp stem adjoining, so that in a whole revolution the three weft elements have

FIG. 28.

THREE-STRAND BRAID AND TWINED WORK.

(Outside.)

American Anthropologist, III, 1901, fig. 23.

FIG. 29.

THREE-STRAND BRAID AND TWINED WORK.

(Inside.)

American Anthropologist, III, 1901, fig. 24.

in turn passed behind three warp elements. After that the process is repeated. By referring to the lower halves of figs. 28 and 29, the outside and the inside of this technic will be made plain. On the outside there is the appearance of a three-strand string laid along the warp stems, while on the inside the texture looks like a plain twined weaving.

The reason for this is apparent, since in every third revolution one element passes behind the warp and two remain in front. Three-strand twined work is seldom used over the entire surface of a basket. In fig. 30 will be seen the drawing of a very old piece of twined work from the ancient Hopi or Moki Pueblo. The bottom of this old basket jar and a portion of the body, as will be seen, are covered with plain twine weft. The shoulder and neck and two bands of the body are in three-strand twined weaving. A small portion of the inside, seen in the top of the drawing, as will be seen, has the appearance of small two-strand twined work. In fig. 31 is shown a square inch from the sur-

FIG. 30.
BASKET-JAR IN THREE-STRAND TWINE.
Hopi Indians, Arizona.
Collected by J. W. Powell.

face of this jar, enlarged to make plain, the appearance of the two types of technic. The upper portion of the figure has all the appearance of twilled and twined work in two-strand weft. The three-strand work shown in this figure is a Ute motive. The U. S. National Museum collections represent at least seven different styles of basketry technic attributed to the Hopi people of Tusayan, and philologists have come to the conclusion that the Hopi are a very mixed people.

(b) *Three-strand braid.*—In three-strand braid the weft elements are held in the hand in the same fashion, but instead of being twined simply they are plaited or braided, and as each element passes under one and over the other of the remaining two elements, it is carried behind a warp stem. This process is better understood by examining the upper part of fig. 32, *a* and *b*. On the surface, when the work is driven home, it is impossible to discriminate between three-strand twine and three-strand braid. The three-strand braid is found at the starting of all Pomo twined baskets, no matter how the rest is built up.

Fig. 33 is a conical carrying basket of the Klamath Indians of Oregon, collected by L. S. Dyar. It is made of coarse stems of rushes. The warp begins with a few stems brought together to a point at the bottom and as the specimen widens out fresh warp stems are added. These are securely joined together by a continuous coil of weft, which is a three-strand braid. At the beginning these turns of the coil touch one another, but as the work progresses and the basket widens the

FIG. 31.
THREE-STRAND AND PLAIN TWINED WEAVING.

distance from one row to the next increases until they are nearly an inch apart at the top. The braiding is done from the outside, two of the stems showing always there and only one on the inside, resembling common twined weaving. This is the only specimen in the Museum in which the whole surface is braided. In many twined baskets of the

FIG. 32.
THREE-STRAND BRAID.
a, outside; *b*, inside.

Pomo an inch or so at the bottom is thus woven. The top is finished off in the following manner: Three warp ends are braided together for at least 2 inches, turned down and cut off. The hook-shaped ends are held in place by a row of common twined weaving at the top. Just below this and close to the ends is a row of three-strand braid.

Another row of the same kind is made halfway between the upper edge of the solid weaving and the border. A hoop of wood is held in place on the inside by a wrapping of coarse twine. The appearance of three-strand braid in the drawing on the inside of the basket is given by the strands of twined weaving and the ends of the warp bent over. The basket is strengthened on the outside by five vertical rods, and the carrying string is in three-strand braid, precisely as in the body and margin of the basket. Height 22 inches, diameter 23 inches. In the collection of Dr. C. Hart Merriam are two closely woven Klamath baskets in the same technic (see Plate 174). Styles (c) and (d) belong rather to ornamentation and will be described under that heading.

FIG. 33.

CARRYING BASKET, THREE-STRAND BRAID.

Klamath Indians, Oregon.

Cat. No. 24104, U.S.N.M.   After W. H. Holmes.

Something should be said in this connection about the manner of laying the foundation for weaving baskets. In many of the specimens illustrated in this work it will be seen that very little tasteful care has been bestowed upon this part of the work. The Eskimos, for instance, do not know how, seemingly, but use a piece of rawhide, and it is said that the Indians of British Columbia formerly inserted a piece of board or wood at the bottom of their coiled baskets and sewed the coils around an edge of it, but there is method in much of the basket weaving in this point, as will be seen on examining the plates. Miss Mary

White, in her book, More Baskets and How to Make Them, has worked this subject out very carefully.[a]

Figs. 34 to 39, inclusive, show the result of her studies.

Fig. 34 is the simplest form of starting the bottom of a basket. Four warp stems are arranged in pairs and crossed at the center. A

FIG. 34.
WARP STEMS CROSSED IN PAIRS.
After Mary White.

FIG. 35.
WARP STEMS CROSSED IN FOURS.
After Mary White.

strip of wood or a flexible stem is wound twice around the intersection. The figure also shows how additional warp stems may be introduced into this pattern, being thrust between the regular stems. Once they are held firmly in place by two or three rows of common basket weav-

FIG. 36.
SIXTEEN STEMS WOVEN IN FOURS.
After Mary White.

FIG. 37.
WARP STEMS CROSSED IN FOURS
AND TWINED.
After Mary White.

ing, additional warp stems are added, and they are bent out radially as a foundation for the work.

Fig. 35 shows how a start may be made with 16 warp stems crossing in groups of four at the center. Two sets begin at once to divide and

[a] How to make Baskets, New York, 1902; also More Baskets and how to make Them, 1903.

radiate, and after they are held together by three rows of weft the other eight are spread out in the same way. The drawing illustrates exactly the manner in which this is done.

Fig. 36 shows another method of beginning with 16 warp stems, plaiting them into checker pattern at first, then afterwards spreading them out radially.

Fig. 37 brings us into the Hopi Indian type of twined weaving. Here four stems in one direction cross the same number at right angles and are held in place by a row of twined weaving, additional warp stems being inserted at the corners, which spread out radially.

Fig. 38 is a Hopi application of coiled sewing to the beginning of the basket. In Fig. 39 the warp stems are woven together in wicker work in two sets; the first vertical, the second horizontal. As soon as they are in place and held together the work proceeds as in ordinary weaving.

FIG. 38.
SIX WARP STEMS PARALLEL.
After Mary White.

COILED BASKETRY

Coiled basketry is produced by an over-and-over sewing with some kind of flexible material, each stitch interlocking with the one immediately underneath it. The exception to this is to be seen on Salish, Maidu, and other baskets, in which the passing stitch is driven through the wood of the one underneath and splits it.

In the coiled basketry of British Columbia, as well as here and there farther south, this splitting of stitches, so clumsy looking when done without plan, is turned into an element of beauty. The top of each stitch is carefully bifurcated or trifurcated, so that to the uninitiated the sewing appears to have been done vertically instead of horizontally. This type of work may be called furcate coil. (See Plate 23 and figs. 51 and 55.)

FIG. 39.
WARP STEMS CROSSED IN THREES; HELD BY WICKER.
After Mary White.

The specimen (Plate 23) is a remarkable old piece found near Death's Valley, California. Diameter, 6½ inches; depth, 4 inches; colors, dark wood, with line of brown around top. This is one of the finest specimens of furcated stitches. It resembles common Ute basketry of the two-stem variety, and in the sewing the stitches are not driven home tight, but left as wide apart as possible. On the inside of the basket it is plain coiled sewing, showing the foundation rod clearly between the stitches. Passing the awl point between the stitches on the inside, it is carefully pushed through so as to divide the sewing splint of the previous coil exactly in the middle. This gives the appearance of embroidery stitches from the center of the bottom to the outer margin. This specimen of furcated stitching is in the collection of Edward L. McLeod. Those familiar with the coiled basket making taught in the industrial schools will compare this work with their own, in which the colored rafia is hidden in the foundation for a space of wrapping and comes out at the point where the double stitch is to be made.

The transition between lace work and coiled basketry is interesting. In the netted bags of pita fiber, common throughout middle America, in the muskemoots or Indian bags of fine caribou skin thong from the Mackenzie River district, as well as in the lace-like netting of the Mohave carrying frames and Peruvian textiles, the sewing and interlocking constitute the whole texture, the woman doing her work over a short cylinder or spreader of wood or bone, which she moves along as she works. When the plain sewing changes to half hitches, or stitches in which the moving part of the filament or twine is wrapped or served one or more times about itself, there is the rude beginning of point lace work. This is seen in basketry and soft wallets of the Mackenzie River tribes, the Hopewell mound relics in Ohio, here and there in California, and especially among the Fuegians, as well as in many pieces from various parts of the Old World. (See figs. 59, 115).

The sewing materials vary with the region. In the Aleutian Islands it is of delicate straw; in the adjacent region it is spruce root; in British Columbia it is cedar or spruce root; in the more diversified styles of the Pacific States every available material has been used—stripped leaf, grass stems, rushes, split root, broad fillets, and twine, the effect of each being well marked. The gathering and preparation of these materials for use have already been described in the first portion of this paper. It is understood that, as in woven basketry, the grasses, roots, and splints of wood are soaked in water and kept as pliable as possible until the work is done.

In all coiled basketry, properly so called, there is a foundation more

FIG. 40.
BONE AWL FOR COILED
BASKETRY.
Collected by Edward
Palmer.

or less rigid, inclosed within stitches, the only implement being an awl of some kind.   Fig. 40 shows the metatarsal of an antelope sharpened in the middle and harder portion of the column, the joint serving for a grip for the hand.   It was the universal prehistoric sewing implement of savage women and persists to our day.

In every living tribe of basket makers these awls are among the commonest of woman's tools, most serviceable in sewing garments as well. They are dug up in mounds, found in caves, and are rarely absent from the work baskets of mummies in the arid regions.[a]

Frank H. Cushing was of the opinion that the bone awl was far better for fine basket work than any implement of steel; the point, being a little rounded, would find its way between the stitches of the coil underneath and not force itself through them.   The iron awl, being hard and sharp, breaks the texture and gives a very rough and clumsy appearance to the surface, as will be seen in fig. 51.

Coiled basketry in point of size presents the greatest extreme. There are specimens delicately made that will pass through a lady's finger ring, and others as large as a flour barrel; some specimens have stitching material one-half inch wide, as in the Pima granaries, and in others the root material is shredded so fine that nearly 100 stitches are made within an inch of space.   In form the coiled ware may be perfectly flat, as in a table mat, or built up into the most exquisite jar shape.   In design the upright stitches lend themselves to the greatest variety of intricate patterns.

Coiled basketry may be divided into ten varieties, based on structural characteristics.

The foundation of the coil may be (1) a single element, either splint, or stem, or rod; (2) a stem or other single element, with a thin welt laid on top of it; (3) two or more stems one over another; (4) two stems or other elements laid side by side, with or without a welt; (5) three stems in triangular position; (6) a bundle of splints or small stems; (7) a bundle of grass or small shreds.

The stitches pass around the foundation in progress (1) interlocking with and sometimes splitting stitches, but not inclosing the foundation underneath; (2) under one rod of the coil beneath, however many there may be; (3) under a welt of the coil beneath; (4) through splints or other foundation, in some cases systematically splitting the sewing material underneath.   With these explanations it is possible to make the following ten varieties of coiled basketry, matting, or bagging:

A. Coiled work without foundation.

B. Simple interlocking coils.

C. Single-rod foundation.

D. Two-rod foundation.

---

[a] Smithsonian Report, 1882, p. 724, fig. 3.

E. Rod and welt foundation.

F. Two-rod and splint foundation.

G. Three-rod foundation.

H. Splint foundation.

I. Grass-coil foundation.

K. Fuegian coiled basketry (see p. 258).

These will now be taken up systematically and illustrated. (See fig. 41.)

A. *Coiled work without foundation.*—Specimens of this class have been already mentioned. The sewing material is babiche or fine raw-hide thong in the cold north, or string of some sort farther south. In the Mackenzie Basin will be found the former, and in the tropical and

Fig. 41.

CROSS SECTIONS OF VARIETIES IN COILED BASKETRY.

subtropical areas the latter. If a plain, spiral spring be coiled or hooked into one underneath, the simplest form of the open coiled work will result. An improvement of this is effected when the moving thread in passing upward after interlocking is twined one or more times about its standing part. (See figs. 41 A and 100.)

The technical process just mentioned is practiced among the Athapascan tribes of the Mackenzie River drainage. It is doubtful whether anciently the predecessors of these Indian women did such fine work in rawhide. The steel-bladed knife made slender babiche possible, and the thrift brought about by the Hudson Bay Company made it desirable. But it will be seen that the Mound-builders had the weave and could produce in flax texture even more delicate than the muske-moots or hunting bags of the northern tribes.

Fig. 42 represents a carrying frame and net of the Pima and other tribes on our Mexican border. It is supported by a rude framework of sticks. The network is of agave twine and is made of interlocking coils, looking as all-coiled basketry would if the foundation were removed.

FIG. 42.
CARRYING BASKET.
Pima Indians, Arizona.
Cat. No. 126680, U.S.N.M.   Collected by Edward Palmer.

Further on illustrations will be given showing the wide extent of this technical process of coiled basketry without foundation. Examples in the U. S. National Museum come from as far south as Paraguay and even the Straits of Magellan. It is in common use as far north as northern Mexico. Both the possession of different material and the demands of a tropical life have occasioned the employment of this particular technic in articles of common use about the household. Its relation to coiled basketry and bead work is shown by the fact that women in making the fabric use a needle to carry the thread or string around through the row of work preceding. A small rod or mesh gauge is used to secure uniformity in the size of the meshes.

B. *Simple interlocking coils.*—Coiled work in which there may be any sort of foundation, but the stitches merely interlock without catching under the rods or splints or grass beneath. This form easily passes into those in which the stitch takes one or more elements of the foundation, but in a thorough ethnological study small differences can not be overlooked. (See fig. 41 B.)

Fig. 43 represents this style of workmanship on a coiled basket in grass stems from Alaska, collected by Lucien M. Turner. The straws for sewing merely interlock without gathering the grass roll.

FIG. 43.
DETAIL OF INTERLOCKING STITCHES.

In the imbricated basket work of British Columbia and Washington the sewing is done with splints of cedar root and the stitches interlock. Two quite distinct styles of foundation are used, namely, bunches of splints taken from the more brittle and rough interior of the cedar root, and two flat strips of the smooth layer on the outside of the root. The surface of the one will be rugose, of the other, flat and smooth. (See figs. 52, 53, and 54 and Plates 156–161.)

Figs. 44 and 45 represent a type of coiled work in vogue among the Mescalero Apaches. As has been said previously, the Apache Indians, who live in the arid regions of Arizona, made the foundations of their coiled basketry of hard rods. In various tribes these rods are arranged in a foundation after different patterns. It will be seen by examining the drawing here given that three rods form the basis of the coil. They are laid one on another in a vertical row, the

FIG. 44.
FOUNDATION OF THREE RODS LAID VERTICALLY.
Mescalero Apache Indians.

stitches simply interlocking so that the greatest economy of work is effected. It is not known that any other tribe in America practices this peculiar arrangement of the foundation rods. This specimen, Cat. No. 211941, in the U. S. National Museum, was collected by F. M. Covert.

Plate 24 shows a style of coiled weaving called openwork. This specimen, in the collection of C. E. Rumsey, Riverside, California, is termed a grasshopper basket, but it belongs to a type of technic that has a very wide distribution, and probably has nothing to do with holding live insects. The foundation is a bundle of shredded material or grass. The sewing is a splint of hard wood. This is wrapped a certain number of times around the foundation and then caught under the sewing of the coil underneath, the stitches interlocking. Perhaps a few bits of the foundation are caught also in the stitch. After two stitches are made in this way the wrapping continues. It is possible by counting this last as well as the number of stitches to reproduce beautiful patterns on the surface. The ornamentation also may be varied by the use of different colored splints. This specimen is from the Watchumna (Mariposan) Indians of middle California, but examples are in the National Museum collected from Norway, Porto Rico, and Peru. (See Plates 224 and 248.)

FIG. 45.

DETAIL OF FIG. 44.

C. *Single-rod foundation.*—In rattan basketry and Pacific coast ware, called by Dr. J. W. Hudson tsai in the Pomo language, the foundation is a single stem, uniform in diameter. The stitch passes around the stem in progress and is caught under the one of the preceding coil, as in fig. 41 C. In a collection of Siamese basketry in the U. S. National Museum the specimens are all made after this fashion. The foundation is the stem of the plant in its natural state; the sewing is with splints of the same material, having the glistening surface outward. As this is somewhat unyielding it is difficult to crowd the stitches together, and so the foundation is visible between. California is not far behind the East in the quality of material, willow for the basis of the coil, and plants in a variety of colors for the sewing. The Siamese coiled basketry has little of design on its surface, but the American basketmaker may fix whatever her imagination may suggest. The effect of the plain stitching is pleasing to the eye by reason of the regular broken surface. In America single-rod basketry is widely spread. Along the Pacific coast it is found in northern Alaska and as far south as the borders of Mexico. The Pomo Indians use it in some of their finest work.

FIG. 46.

DETAIL OF SINGLE-ROD COIL IN BASKETRY.

The roots of plants and soft stems of willow, rhus, and the like are used for the sewing, and, being soaked thoroughly, can be crowded together so as to entirely conceal the foundation. (See fig. 46.)

Plate 25 represents a collection of Pomo treasure baskets, all in single-rod foundation, called tsai by Dr. Hudson and bam tsha or bam tshai by Carl Purdy. These specimens are in the collection of C. P. Wilcomb; the foundation is of willow rod, the sewing material of sedge root, the design in the cercis splints, the decoration with shells, beads, and partridge plumes. The method of sewing is on all of these baskets the same as shown in fig. 41 C.

Plate 26, Cat. No. 89801 U.S.N.M., is from Point Barrow, Alaska, and was collected by Capt. P. H. Ray, U. S. Army. The material is shoots and roots of willow, and the specimen was secured from Eskimo people living at the extreme northern point of Alaska. It had evidently been procured, however, from Indians near by. On the bottom small rods are used for the foundation and the sewing is in straight lines backward and forward until this portion is finished. Here the foundation rods are somewhat larger and the sewing splints wider. Comparing this specimen, then, with a great many others from the same area, the uniformity in size of the foundation rod is noticeable. It will also be noted that the stitches are not driven home closely, a feature which occurred over and over again in coiled basketry between Point Barrow and the Republic of Mexico.

D. *Two-rod foundation.*—One rod in this style lies on top of the other; the stitches pass over two rods in progress and under the upper one of the pair below, so that each stitch incloses three stems in a vertical series (fig. 47). A little attention given to fig. 41 D will demonstrate that the alternate rod, or the upper rod, in each pair will be in-

FIG. 47.
FOUNDATION OF TWO RODS, VERTICAL.

closed in two series of stitches, while the other or lower rod will pass along freely in the middle of one series of stitches and show on the outer side. Examples of this two-rod foundation are to be seen among the Athapascan tribes of Alaska, among the Pomo Indians of the Pacific coast, and among the Apache of Arizona. An interesting or specialized variety of this type is seen among the Mescaleros of New Mexico, who use the two-rod foundation, but instead of passing the stitch around the upper rod of the coil below simply interlock the stitches so that neither one of the two rods is inclosed twice. This Apache ware is sewed with yucca fiber and the brown root of the same plant, producing a brilliant effect, and the result of the special technic is a flat surface like that of pottery. The U. S. National Museum possesses a single piece of precisely the same technic from the kindred of the Apache on the Lower Yukon. (See figs. 44 and 45.)

E. *Rod and welt foundation.*—In this kind of basketry the single-rod foundation is overlaid by a splint or strip of tough fiber, sometimes the same as that with which the sewing is done; at others, a strip of leaf or bast. The stitches pass over the rod and strip which are on top down under the welt only of the coil below, the stitches inter-

FIG. 48.
ROD AND WELT FOUNDATION.

locking. The strip of tough fiber between the two rods which serves for a welt has a double purpose—strengthening the fabric and chinking the space between the rods (fig. 48). This style of coil work is seen on old Zuñi basket jars and on California examples. This type of foundation passes easily into forms C, D, E, and F. In fact, it is impossible to distinguish between them without marring the specimen. (See fig. 41.)

The specimens shown on Plate 27 are a water bottle and a gathering basket of the Utes; that is, they are of Ute motive. Such pieces, however, are often seen among other tribes and in some of the later pueblos. By looking carefully at the surface of the pictures it will be seen that there may be two rods, the upper much smaller than the other; or on the top of the principal rod will be a splint or two of material. The foundation of such basketry is not uniform in composition, but in motive they are all the same. The strength of the basket is in the principal rod. The joint is made stronger by having between the stitches of two coils an additional rod or smaller piece. There are no wide gaps separating any two styles of weaving, and it will be easily seen that this Ute type passes readily into other forms.

FIG. 49.
WATER JAR IN COILED BASKETRY.
Wolpi, Arizona.
Cat. No. 42129, U.S.N.M.   Collected by J. S. Stevenson.

Cat. Nos. 84596 (upper figure), 42126 (lower figure), U.S.N.M.

F. *Two-rod and splint foundation.*—In this style the foundation is made thicker and stronger by laying two rods side by side and a splint or welt on top to make the joint perfectly tight. The surface will be corrugated. Tribes practicing this style of coiling generally have fine material and some of the best ware is so made up.   It passes easily, as one might guess, into the Lillooet style, in which the two elements of the foundation are thin and flat.   Fig. 49 is a water jar from the Wolpi pueblo, one of the Hopi group, collected long ago by James Stevenson.   It is Cat. No. 42129 U.S.N.M., and was first figured in the Second Annual Report of the Bureau of Ethnology. (See fig. 41 F.)

Plate 28 represents two fine old coiled baskets from the pueblo of Sia, on the Rio Grande River, New Mexico.   In addition to the structure, which consists of two rods and a splint above sewed with willow splints, the stitches interlocking and catching in the welt below, the ornamentation a stepped design, suggestive of pueblo architecture on the upper figure and spirals made up of colored rectangles on the lower figure, needs to be merely pointed out.   The characteristic sought to be illustrated here in this connection is the false braid made on the surface produced by sewing a single splint in a figure of eight weaving, shown in the plate.   The modern Indians of this pueblo do not make basketry of this character, and it is altogether reasonable to think that in the olden times these pieces came into the possession of these people by traffic from Shoshonean tribes near by.   Catalogue No. 134213, U.S.N.M.   Collected by James Stevenson.

FIG. 50.

FOUNDATION OF THREE RODS, STITCHES CATCH-
ING ROD UNDERNEATH.

G. *Three-rod foundation.*—This is the type of foundation called by Carl Purdy bam shi bu, from bam, sticks, and sibbu, three.   Among the Pomo and other tribes in the western part of the United States the most delicate pieces of basketry are in this style.   Dr. Hudson calls them "the jewels of coiled basketry."   The surfaces are beautifully corrugated, and patterns of the most intricate character can be wrought on them.   The technic is as follows: Three or four small willow stems of uniform thickness serve for the foundation, as shown in fig. 50; also in cross section in fig. 41 G.   The sewing, which may be in splints of willow, black or white carex root, or cercis stem, passes around the three stems constituting the coil, under the upper one of the bundle below, the stitches interlocking.   In some examples this upper rod is replaced by a thin strip of material serving for a welt (see fig. 41 F).   In the California area the materials for basketry are of the finest quality.   The willow stems and carex root are susceptible of division into delicate filaments.   Sewing done with these is most compact, and when the stitches are pressed closely together the foundation does not appear. On the surface of the bam shi bu basketry the Pomo weaver adds pretty bits of bird feathers and delicate pieces of shell. The basket represents the wealth of the maker,

and the gift of one of these to a friend is considered to be the highest compliment.

Plate 29 is a beautiful example of Bam shi bu coiled basketry, having a foundation of three Bams, or shoots of Hind's willow (*Salix sessilifolia*). The sewing of the lighter portions is in carefully prepared roots of a sedge, Kahum (*Carex barbarae*), while the designs are in the roots of a bulrush, Tsuwish (*Scirpus maritimus*). Red feathers of the California woodpecker are scattered over the surface. This faultless speci-

FIG. 51.
FOUNDATION OF SPLINTS.

men, now in the collection of C. P. Wilcomb, was made in the year 1896 by Squaw Mary, a noted basket maker, wife of Ned Dunson (Indian), then living at Santa Rosa Creek, Sonoma County, California. She belonged to the Tsar walo division of the Pomos. Diameter of the basket 8⅔ inches, collected by J. P. Stanley.

FIG. 52.
IMBRICATED WORK DETAIL, CALLED KLIKITAT.
Showing method of concealing coil stitches.

H. *Splint foundation.*—In basketry of this type the foundation consists of a number of longer or shorter splints massed together and sewed, the stitches passing under one or more of the splints in the coil beneath (fig. 51). In the Pomo language it is called chilo, but it has no standing in that tribe. In the Great Interior Basin, where the pliant material of the California tribes is wanting, only the outer and younger portion of the stem will do for sewing. The interior parts in such examples are made up into the foundation. All such ware is rude, and the sewing frequently passes through instead of around the stitches below. In the Klikitat basketry the pieces of spruce or cedar root not used for sewing material are also worked into the foundation. (See fig. 41 H.)

In a small area on Fraser River, in southwestern Canada, on the upper waters of the Columbia, and in many Salishan tribes of northwestern Washington, basketry, called imbricated, is made. The foundation, as said, is in cedar or

FIG. 53.
IMBRICATED COIL WORK, CALLED KLIKITAT.

spruce root, while the sewing is done with the outer and tough portion of the root; the stitches pass over the upper bundle of splints and are locked with those underneath. On the outside of these baskets is a form of technic, which also constitutes the ornamentation. It is not something added, or overlaid, or sewed on, but is a part of the texture effected in the progress of the manufacture. (See fig. 52.)

The method of adding this ornamentation in strips of cherry bark, cedar bast, and grass stems, dyed with Oregon grape, is unique, and on this account I have applied the term "imbricated" to the style of weave here shown. (See fig. 53.)

The strip of colored bark or grass is laid down and caught under a passing stitch; before another stitch is taken this one is bent forward to cover the last stitch, doubled on itself so as to be underneath the next stitch, and so with each one it is bent backward and forward so that the sewing is entirely concealed, forming a sort of "knife plaiting."

FIG. 54.
IMBRICATED BASKETRY DETAIL.
Thompson River.
After James Teit.

In some of the finer old baskets in the National Museum, collected over sixty years ago, the entire surface is covered with work of this kind, the strips not being over an eighth of an inch wide. James Teit describes and illustrates this type of weaving among the Thompson River Indians of British Columbia, who are Salishan.   The body of the basket is in the root of *Thuja plicata*, and the ornamentation in strips of *Elymus triticoides* and *Prunus demissa.*   (See fig. 54.)

Imbrication is one of the most restricted of technical processes. Eells says that some women in every tribe on Puget Sound could pro-

FIG. 55.
OVERLAYING IN COILED WORK.

duce the stitch, and he names the Puyallups, Twanas, Snohomish, Clallam, Makah, Skagit, Cowlitz, Chehalis, Nisqualli, and Squaxon. It doubtless originated here.   It is the native art of the Klikitat, Yakima, and Spokanes, all of whom are of the Shahaptian family.   The Thompson and Fraser River Indians have long known the art. (See Plates 68, 74–79, 156–167.)

Fig. 55 is a square inch from the bottom of a Fraser River imbricated coiled basket.   It illustrates several important features in the basket maker's art.   In the first place, the Indians of this area did not know how to make a beginning of the bottom of a rectangular basket with coiled work, so a block was inserted or foundation strips were laid parallel and were whipped together after the manner of coiled work.   This figure also shows how the splitting of stitches before mentioned in sewing may have at first been accidental, the basket maker having in mind only the purpose of placing the stitches in vertical rows.   From this unintentional furcation of the stitches comes the purposeful splitting, the forked stitches being made alike and uniform.   Thus, out of a careless habit has come one of the beautiful ornamentations in coiled basketry.   A third purpose in this figure is to show, perhaps, the initial step in imbricated work.   Indeed, this form of overlaying is seen on many examples of it.   A straw of squaw grass (*Xerophyllum tenax*) is

FIG. 56.
FOUNDATION OF STRAWS IN COILED WORK.

inclosed under a stitch; it is then turned back; a second stitch is made and the strip of grass laid over it.   Thus, over the surface there is an alternation of exposed and concealed stitches by means of this material. This is elsewhere called "beading."

I.   *Grass-coil foundation.*—The foundation is a bunch of grass or rush stems, or small midribs from palm leaves, or shredded yucca. The effect in all such ware is good, for the reason that the maker has perfect control of her material. Excellent examples of this kind are to be seen in the southwestern portions of the United States, among the Pueblos and Missions, and in northern Africa. The sewing may be done with split stems of hard wood, willow, rhus, and the like, or, as in the case of the Mission baskets in southern California, of the stems of rushes (*Juncus acutus*) or stiff grass (*Epicampes rigens*). (See fig. 56, and the cross section given in fig. 41 I.) In the larger granary baskets of the Southwest a bundle of straws furnishes the foundation, while the sewing is done with broad strips of tough bark, as in fig. 57.

FIG. 57.

COIL WITH OPEN SEWING INCLOSING PARTS OF FOUNDATION.

Plate 30 shows specimens of Hopi coiled plaques on shredded foundation made up of the harder parts of the yucca split and rolled into a bundle. The sewing is with tne tough, leafy portion and passes simply under the coil in preparation, the stitches interlocking. Between the refined type of coiled work of this class and the old-fashioned straw beehive or the Mohave granary is a long distance. These thick Hopi plaques have their nearest resemblance in the Moorish basketry of North Africa and leave the question on the mind whether from long contact the Hopi themselves may not have gotten a suggestion therefrom. These specimens are Cat. Nos. 166856 and 166858 in the U. S. National Museum and were collected by James Mooney. (See also fig. 58.)

FIG. 58.

FOUNDATION OF GRASS OR SHREDDED MATERIALS.

K. *Fuegian coiled basketry.*—In this ware the foundation is slight, consisting of one or more rushes; the sewing is in buttonhole stitch or half hitches, with rush stems interlocking. The resemblance of this to Asiatic types on the Pacific is most striking. (See fig. 59.)

Plate 31 is one of the most interesting specimens of basketry found in America, because in its structure it practically imitates the specimens just illustrated from the Straits of Magellan. It is described by

George H. Pepper in Guide Leaflet No. 6 of the American Museum of Natural History. It is called a "sifter," and was found among the relics of the ancient basket makers of southeastern Utah. The outer rows of coiling belong to the single-stick variety. On the rest of the surface the binding material in passing around the foundation rods makes a whole turn on itself between them. The basket is 9½ inches in diameter and 2 inches deep.

WATER-TIGHT BASKETRY

Basketry is rendered water-tight by closeness of texture and by daubing with pitch or asphaltum. Both twined and coiled ware are useful for this latter purpose. It is said of the mother of Moses that she "took for him an ark [a boat-shaped basket] of bulrushes and

FIG. 59.

FUEGIAN COILED BASKET, AND DETAILS.

daubed it with slime and with pitch and put the child therein, and she laid it in the flags by the river's brink." (Exodus ii, 3.) Now, the Egyptians and other Hamites of our day make coiled basketry of type fig. 41 I; that is, with a foundation of shredded material sewed with finely split palm leaf. The foundation is quite thick, so that the ware is strikingly like the Hopi plaques of the Middle Mesa. There is no reason for believing that the ancient ware differed from the modern. In the Interior Basin also baskets are used for pottery by tribes that are not sedentary. (See Plate 32.)

Major J. W. Powell, during his topographical and geological survey of the valley of the Colorado River of the West, in company with Prof. A. H. Thompson, made a collection of water-tight basket work from the Paiute Indians (Shoshonean family) in southern Utah, and additions have been made by Dr. Walter Hough and others. Both coiled and twined work are found in great varieties. Plate 32 represents the varieties of these water-tight carrying jugs or bottles. Fig. 1 of the plate, Cat. No. 11882, is a Tsai a wats, in twined weaving, the pattern being twilled work. Lugs on the side support the broad, soft, buckskin band. The pitch is evenly laid on, just revealing the texture beneath. Height, 7½ inches.

Fig. 2, Cat. No. 10760, is a globose jar in coiled weaving, carelessly done on a splint foundation, as among the Utes. Height, 7½ inches. There are no lugs on the outside, so this piece would be a pitcher rather than a canteen.

Fig. 3, Cat. No. 10758, is a Tsai a wats of squat form in single-rod coiled weaving, with three lugs at equal distances around the shoulder for carrying. Height, 4¾ inches.

Figs. 4 and 5, Cat. Nos. 213101–2, in the U. S. National Museum, are small canteens, collected from the Havasupai Indians, in Cataract Canyon, by Dr. Walter Hough. They are precisely the same in structure as the foregoing, though the Havasupai are of the Yuman family, while the Utes are Shoshonean. Height, 7½ inches and 8½ inches.

Fig. 6, Cat. No. 211020, U.S.N.M., is Paiute water jar for carrying, from the collection of Captain Carr, U. S. Army. The foundation is of splints, and the pitch is carefully restricted to the inside. Horsehair lugs support the headband of old leather. Height, 9 inches.

Fig. 7, Cat. No. 11880, U.S.N.M., is an excellent specimen of twined work in twill, with single rows of three-ply twine and the neck in openwork. In many examples like the one here shown the melted pitch or asphaltum is poured inside and rinsed around until the surface is covered. Height, 9 inches. The rope handle gives the appearance of a pitcher.

Fig. 8, Cat. No. 10759, U.S.N.M., is pear shaped and has wooden lugs upon the sides for the carrying bands. It is twined and twilled weaving and thoroughly overloaded with pitch. The rounded bottom serves to keep the bottle erect. Height, 8½ inches.

Plate 33 is a water jar of the White Mountain Apaches, Cat. No. 213278, U.S.N.M., collected by Dr. Walter Hough. It is made in diagonal twined weaving and covered with pitch. Three lugs of wood attached to the sides are for the purpose of suspension and carrying. The height is 12 inches.

BORDERS ON BASKETRY

Having studied the structural processes on the body of these textiles, it will now be in order to note how the work is finished off. A glance at a lady's workbasket or a waste-paper basket shows how important

such an examination must be. Both in woven and in twined ware
many beautiful specimens will be seen, whose edges differ not in the
slightest degree from other portions of the basket. Indeed, the Tlinkit, the Pomo, and the Mission weavers all frequently affect the plain
border on their ware, and certain kinds of plaques of the Hopi
Indians, said to be the workmanship of unmarried women, leave the
foundation exposed, and the work is suddenly brought to an end.

Another fact will surprise the student, namely, that technically the
border is often in quite another class of weave. This grows, as will
be seen, out of the exigencies of the case. A checker weaving, with
the edges left open all around, would be a flimsy affair. Coiled work
lends a hand in putting a finish on woven work; the latter, or an
imitation of it, on the contrary, becomes an embellishment of the
former. The drawings and the plates will explain more clearly than
words the structure of borders. The motive in this inquiry should be
to learn the steps or evolutionary processes through which the inge-

FIG. 60.

COILED BORDER ON CHECKER WEAVING.

Cat. No. 206390, U.S.N.M.

nious savage woman's mind has
passed in this series of inventions to discover, if possible, a
little truth about the relationship and communication among
tribes in olden times, and to learn
some new manipulations in an
art now becoming popular. It
is like the breaking out of an old
hereditary complaint in the tips
of the fingers. The borders will
be studied in the following order:
The finishing off in checker work,
in wicker work, in twilled work, in twined work, and in coiled work.

The first and simplest method of making borders is illustrated in
examples collected among the Abenaki Indians of Canada belonging
to the Algonquian family. The baskets are made of splints from the
ash, formerly worked out with aboriginal tools (see fig. 60), but
nowadays made by machinery. The foundation of the borders consists of three narrow hoops. Every alternate warp splint is cut off
flush, the others are bent down over the middle hoop and pushed
under the upper row of weaving, having first been pointed. Outside
and inside of this middle hoop and clasping the bends in the warp
splints are the other two hoops, the whole being bound securely
together by a coiled sewing in splint. The specimen here figured is
Cat. No. 206390, U.S.N.M., made by Caroline Masta. Diameter, 5¼
inches; height, 3 inches.

The border of twilled work, when the weaving is finished, resembles
closely the interlacing of a series of crossed warps. In matting made

in this way the ends of the warp and of the weft are bent backward on one another and forced under the texture. In one example a twilled mat is finished out with wicker weaving, both sets of elements being straightened out for warp. (See fig. 12.) The margin is then finished off as if the whole mass had been in wicker weaving. The example here shown was made recently by an Indian woman in the Zuñi pueblo, western New Mexico. (See fig. 61.) The material is stripped leaves of yucca, from which coarse mats, basket bowls, and trays are made. The mat is woven square and a hoop of wood is pro-

FIG. 61.

WEFT AND WARP FASTENED DOWN WITH TWINE.

(*a*, front; *b*, back.)

Cat. No. 215488, U.S.N.M.

vided for the border. The mat is forced down into it, the ends of the warp and weft cut off about an inch above the hoop. They are then bent down on the outside in groups of fours and held in place with one row of twined weaving, as shown in the accompanying drawing, giving both front and back view. The basket is the gift of Mr. G. B. Haggett. Diameter, 11 inches. Cat. No. 215488, U.S.N.M.

In the simplest forms of wicker work the ends of the warp are all cut off in uniform lengths and each bent down by the side of the next warp, or behind one warp and down beside the second warp, or is woven behind and in front of the other warp stems with greater or less intricacy, forming a rope pattern on the outside. So much of wicker basketry as originated with the Indians is very simple in the matter of finishing. Cat. No. 215487 shows how this sort of work is done. The basket is the work of the Zuñi Indians, New Mexico, and is the gift of Mr. G. B. Haggett. Diameter, 9½ inches. (See fig. 62.)

The variation of this type may be seen in the next figure. The

FIG. 62.

THREE-STRAND WARP BORDER IN WICKER WORK.

warp stems are in pairs and are bent in this case to the left at right angles and woven out and in among the next three or four sets, returning to the starting point. It is not altogether certain that this style of finishing the border was invented by the Indians, but they have adopted it. This drawing is made from specimens in the collection of G. Wharton James. (See fig. 63.)

FIG. 63.

BORDER MADE BY WEAVING WARP RODS IN PAIRS.

Collected by G. Wharton James.

In the next example the handle is a stiff splint of hickory, circular in shape. The wide hoop border shown in the drawing and the circular hoop are the framework from which the weave begins. All the smaller warp elements focus at the junction of these two. The widening is effected by the introduction of fresh warp elements as the work proceeds; the weft makes only a short excursion at the beginning around one or two warp stems, the hoop increasing in length as the work widens and additional warp elements are inserted. This specimen is Cat. No. 214558, U.S.N.M., and was collected by Mrs. C. G. Benjamin from the Moravian settlement, North Carolina. Diameter, 5¾ inches. (See fig. 64.)

The term twined basketry is applied to every variety whose warp elements are held together by twined weaving. The warp is either soft filament, or hardwood splints, or roots. The weft likewise may be yarn of flax, wool, or other very pliable material, or it may be rigid splints from roots or tough young wood, such as osier, red bud, sumac, or the like. Such a variety of

Fig. 64.
SINGLE-STRAND COILED BORDER.
Moravian Settlement, North Carolina.
Cat. No. 214558, U.S.N.M. Collected by Carolyn G. Benjamin.

material will demand in the finishing off various kinds of borders. Lieutenant Emmons speaks of the border of the basket as its life and says that while a rent in the side or bottom of a wallet may be sewed with fresh root, the breaking of the edge suggests at once to the woman the gathering of materials for a new basket. The great variety of borders in this type of weaving can be best understood by studying specimens. It will be interesting to begin this by comparing examples from two widely separated areas, namely, the caves of Kentucky and the distant islands of the Aleutian chain, both in soft warp. (See Plate 143.)

Fig. 65.
BRAIDED BORDER FROM WARP.
After W. H. Holmes.

Holmes[a] describes bags of fiber found in a cave 8 miles from Mammoth Cave, Kentucky. The largest is 34 inches across and 15 inches deep. The warp is of 2-strand twine; an ornamental variety is given by introducing two larger cords of a different color at stated intervals. These warps are held in place by regular twined weaving at distances varying from a

---

[a] Thirteenth Annual Report of the Bureau of Ethnology, 1896, p. 34, fig. 8.

quarter of an inch to an inch apart. At the top, where the twined
work finishes, the warp cords are brought together in groups of five

and twisted into a rope for a
short distance. They are then
gathered into a continuous
braid; the ends of those plaited
in are cut off when the ends of
a new set are taken up. This
very elaborate form of border
will also be found later on in
Washington. (See fig. 65.)

The methods of finishing
borders on twined work among
the Salishan tribes are shown
in the accompanying figure.
The Quinaielt wallet (Cat. No.
127843, U.S.N.M., collected
by Charles Willoughby), has
several noteworthy characteristics. The twined weft is vertical, woven over a frail warp.
At the upper margin are outside strengthening rows of
close-twined work. Finally,
the two ends of each vertical
weft element are brought together as one, bent backward

FIG. 66.

TWINED WALLET.

Quinaielt Indians, Washington.

Cat. No. 127843. Collected by Charles Willoughby.

behind the two preceding ones, then forward under a row of twined
weaving, serving to hold them in place, the loose end showing on
the inside. (See fig. 66.)

Turning now to twined weaving on hard foundation, it will
be a matter of surprise that the
Pomo Indians, who make some
of the finest twined basketry in
the world, take no pains in finishing off the upper margin of
many pieces. Cat. No. 165659,
U.S.N.M., is a basket of the
Pomo Indians, collected for the
Bureau of Ethnology by H. W.
Henshaw. Diameter, 11 inches.
(See fig. 67 and Plate 19.)

FIG. 67.

SINGLE-STRAND TWINED BORDER.

Pomo Indians.

Cat. No. 165659, U.S.N.M. Collected by H. W. Henshaw.

The weaving is done when the material is wet and soft, and in drying the weft shrinks and binds itself to the warp, so that the basket

actually wears out before it unravels. Granary baskets, mill hoppers, mush bowls, and other varieties in common use have this sort of margin. In the drawing here shown the weft is supposed to be untwisted, and the whole is enlarged in order to exhibit the texture. When complete the warp is driven close together and the little sticks of alder or willow forming the warp are left protruding.

In the following illustration the same principle obtains of making little or no change in the finishing, but the technic is three-strand instead of two-strand. The figure represents a section of a meal bowl of the Ceyal Pomo, Cat. No. 203287, U.S.N.M., which was collected by J. W. Hudson. (See fig. 68.)

FIG. 68.

THREE-STRAND TWINED BORDER.

Cat. No. 203287, U.S.N.M. Collected by J. W. Hudson.

Plate 34 makes evident the difference between the plain twined border and the three-strand border. In the upper figure the inside of the basket is exhibited and the effect is that of common two-strand twine, but in the lower figure the three-strand twine appears in a single row of weaving on the upper border. The cutting off of the margin is also shown. It is to be understood that the trimming of the ends of the warp stems is not done until all the weaving is entirely finished.

The Hupa Indians in some cases finish the borders of twined work by bending down the ends of the warp and wrapping or seizing them with splints of willow or other tough material. An inch of the border in a basket of the Ray collection in the U. S. National Museum is shown. (See fig. 69 and Plate 170.)

Another example of this woven and coiled work is shown. The basket (Cat. No. 68491, U.S.N.M.) is the work of the Zuñi Indians of New Mexico. It will be seen that the last row of weaving at the top is three-strand. The warp rods or stems extend a little ways upward, then bend sharply to the left. They are then cut so that there will be always three of them included. The coil or seizing of splints holds them all firmly in place. The top of the basket measures 4½ inches in diameter. (See fig. 70.)

FIG. 69.

BORDER OF HUPA TWINED BASKET.

The McCloud River Indians in Shasta County, California, cut off the warp flush and finish the border with what looks like plain twined weaving on the edge, but a regular half knot is tied between each pair of warp stems.

Fig. 71 shows a border of Paiute Indian twined basket, in which the warp rods or stems are bent to the left at right angles and cut off

after passing two or more stems, the object being to have at least three ends in a bunch forming the foundation of the border. The uniting material is a long splint of willow or rhus, passing to the left, up and around the foundation in front of the standing part, and under the upper foundation stem backward, forward to begin another series. It is in fact an application of the half hitch or button-hole stitch.

When these are drawn tight they form an effective border which on the upper margin has all the appearance of a four-ply braid. The basket itself is an example of twined weaving in twilled style, and shaped something like an immense strawberry.

This same process of imitating braid on the border of a basket by the ingenious wrapping of a single splint becomes much more complex in coiled basketry, as will be seen later in many figures.

FIG. 71.

BORDER OF PAIUTE TWINED BASKET.

The figure (Cat. No. 203253, U.S.N.M.) shows a combination of the work just described and the twined-work border formed by bending down the warp. The specimen is from the Pomo Indians. Collected by J. W. Hudson. Diameter, 14 inches; height, 10 inches. (Fig. 72.)

By far the greatest variety in the treatment of borders in twined basketry will be found among the Tlinkit Indians, southeastern

Alaska, and the Haida Indians, on the Queen Charlotte islands. Neither of these great families use coiled work, and they employ little of other types of weaving than the twined. The Tlinkits are more ornamental and use colored grasses in their false embroidery, while the Haidas never employ such decorations, but excel in plain and diagonal twined work and in 3-strand weaving. Lieut. G. T. Emmons, U. S. Navy,[a] has studied these people closely for many years, and the information regarding the borders of these tribes is derived from him.

According to this authority, fully nine-tenths of all the baskets used by the Tlinkits are of the open cylindrical type, in which the border is called upon to sustain more than its proportion of the wear in use. Some tribes have always used certain trimmings, plaitings, or braidings to the exclusion of others, and the work of different periods within tribal limits shows marked preferences. Two principal methods are employed in the finish of the border edge, (1) by trimming off the warp

FIG. 72.
THREE-STRAND WARP BORDER.
Pomo Indians.
Cat. No. 203253. Collected by J. W. Hudson.

ends flush with the last spiral of weave (see Plate 44), and (2) by turning the warp over and fastening it down to the standing part by twined weaving or braiding. The first system is always used with covered baskets and generally with double baskets, where the two borders give protection to each other, with hats and mats, and generally with all types of baskets made for the tourist trade. The second method is employed in all open baskets made for use and in the finer varieties with double warp. When extreme nicety is required, the inner strand or layer of the double warp is cut off two lines of weave below the top, so that when the outer strand is turned down on the standing half the thickness of the border is not increased beyond that of the regular walls. But whether the warp is cut off flush or turned over, the last few spirals of weave are generally strengthened by additional twining, braiding, sennit, or embroidery. There are a few examples in the

---

[a] Basketry of the Tlingit Indians, Memoirs of the American Museum of Natural History, III, Pt. 3, 1903, pp. 229–277.

collection of the National Museum in which the turned reverted ends of warp stems are braided among themselves.

This braided warp is held together by rows of twined weaving.

1. The crudest border, or really want of border, consists in cutting off the ends of the warp even with the last spiral of two-strand weft. This is universally practiced with the covered work basket, and is often the finish of the smaller double basket.   (See fig. 67.)

2. Border with the warp ends cut off flush, the one or more rows of three-strand twined woof around the edge adding strength to this part. (See fig. 68.)

FIG. 73.
TWO-STRAND TWINE, ONLAID FOR BORDER.
Tlinkit Indians.

3. In the third type of border a two-strand twine is laid vertically against the outside of the warp stems and held in place by another two-strand twine passing through the vertical twine and around the back of the warp stems.   The vertical twine appears only on the outside of the basket.   The horizontal twine is seen on the outside and the inside alike.   (See fig. 73.)

4. In the fourth type of border a two-strand twine is ornamented on the outside with false embroidery precisely as on the body.   In some cases a narrow band of this style of weaving occurs at the upper margin and is decorative as well as useful.

5. The Haida and the Tlinkit truncated cone-like hat of root is finished at the border by cutting off the warp ends flush and weaving a

common three-strand or four-strand braid around the warp so that one part goes inside and the other two or three parts remain on the outside.

FIG. 74.
THREE-STRAND BRAID WOVEN IN FOR BORDER.
Tlinkit Indians.

This shows a rope-like ridge on the outside around the edge. (See fig. 74.)

FIG. 75.
BORDER OF BRAID, ONLAID.
Tlinkit Indians.

6. Another style consists in sewing a braid or sennit on the outside of the warp by means of a two-strand twine passing through the first

and around the second. These two styles of finishing hat borders are in use by the Haida in basketry, and may have been borrowed from them. (See fig. 75.)

7. In all open baskets made for use where strength is of primary importance the warp ends are doubled over on the standing part of the next warp splint in the direction of the weave, that is, to the right, and twined down to it with the weft. This finish is found on the oldest pieces of Yakutat work. It is often strengthened by the overlaid embroidery in straw or root around the last few spirals of weave. A number of technical processes employed when the warp is cut off flush

FIG. 76.

BORDER OF TURNED-DOWN WARP WITH TWO-STRAND TWINE.

Tlinkit Indians.

will be found also on the borders of specimens in which the warp is turned down.

8. With the turning down of the warp strands the three-strand woof twining is sometimes used in the place of the two strand.

(9) A later finish, and one generally found on the shallow, basin-like basket used as a work basket in weaving and as a berry screener, consists of a turning down of the warp ends as described, and, in addition, weaving a two-strand twining over the bights, forming a rope-like twist over the outer edge, and thoroughly protecting the more exposed parts of the warp. This character of finish occurs more among the Sitka, Hoonah, and Hootz ah tar tribes. The Chilcat never used it and the Yakutat only in the case of the basket-worker's basket. It is certainly of more recent date, although not of to-day. (See fig. 76.)

(10) The most elaborate finish, peculiar to the Chilcat, used to a degree by the Hooach, seldom found among the Sitka and Hootz ah

FIG. 77.
BORDER OF FOUR-STRAND BRAID, TURNED-DOWN WARP.
Tlinkit Indians.

tar, and practically unknown to the Yakutat, consists in two extra woof strands which, with the original, go to form a regular flat sennit

FIG. 78.
BORDER OF FOUR-STRAND BRAID ONLAID, WARP TURNED DOWN.
Tlinkit Indians.

braided on the turned down warp. This finish is also found on the finest and most elaborate ceremonial hats. (See fig. 77.)

(11) The four-strand braid or sennit is attached to the outside of the border by a two-strand twined weaving. The middle strands of the four-strand braid are crossed each time behind the outer one of the two-strand weft (fig. 78), which also grasp the turned-down warp on the back.

FIG. 79.
BORDER INCLOSING HOOP.
Tlinkit Indians.

(12) The border of the oval covered basket differs radically from that of all others. Here the top of the wall is rolled over on the outside and twined down to the side all around, and sometimes this roll

FIG. 80.
BORDER OF THREE-STRAND BRAID.
Tlinkit Indians.

incloses a thick sized spruce hoop, which adds considerably to the strength and stiffness of the border. (See fig. 79.)

In all instances where the warp ends are turned over, the ends of the woof splints in finishing off the border are twisted and run through the bights of the two or three last warp strands.

Fig. 80 shows a border of a basket hat from the Tlinkit Indians, Alaska, also collected by Lieutenant Emmons. The border represents two rows of regular twined weaving, the finishing in three-strand braid (fig. 74). It will be noticed that in crossing each warp rod one of the three members of the braid passes behind the warp, the other two remaining in front. On the inner side, therefore, the appearance will be that of the ordinary twined work. Cat. No. 168263, U.S.N.M.

Fig. 81 shows a form of border on the twined work of the Haida Indians in Queen Charlotte Islands, British Columbia, in which the warp stems are cut off flush. In this example four splints, or two

FIG. 81.

MIXED TWINED WORK.

Haida Indians, British Columbia.

Cat. No. 89033, U.S.N.M.   Collected by James G. Swan.

rows of twined work, are combined into a braid, as will be seen in fig. 73, the two rows of twining becoming one row of braid. As the braiding proceeds from the end of one warp stem to another the weft splint then on the inside is hooked over the end of the warp stem. In the drawing are shown also the plain twined weaving and diagonal or twilled work, by means of which figures are wrought on the surface of the hat.

In coiled basketry many specimens, often among the finest, as will be seen in the accompanying drawings, have in their borders the same structure as on the rest of the body. For each special type of coiled work there will be a variety of border. Frequently the coiled netting, of which hammocks and other weaves without foundation are examples, is finished off by simply stopping the work. The same would be true in all the varieties of foundation mentioned in the previous section. In the present example the foundation consists of three rods or stems not set in triangular fashion, as in the best Pomo coiled work, but in a vertical series. This makes the rows much wider and economizes the sewing. But the varieties of this type are as numerous as the tribes of Indians practicing coiled weaving. (See fig. 82.)

FIG. 82.

SIMPLE COIL BORDER.

Paiute Indians, Utah.

Cat. No. 14688, U.S.N.M. Collected by J. W. Powell.

Fig. 83 illustrates the same statement already made with reference to the so-called grasshopper basket (Plate 24). The drawing shows how, with a splint foundation, the sewing material interlocks with the stitches underneath, taking up at the same time one or more splints.

In Plate 23, illustrating bifurcated stitches on a basket in the McLeod collection, will be seen the simplest departure from the ordinary coiled sewing on the border. The stitches pass forward one space, through and backward a space, making a herring-bone effect on the upper edge of the basket.

Plate 35, upper figure, illustrates a simple type of border work. The foundation is a bundle of splinters wrapped with splints of spruce root and sewed on here and there in regular order to the coil underneath, being bent between the stitches so as to form a regular sinuous line. On the next round the row is straight, wrapped like the first, and is sewed to the top of the sinuous coil underneath. On the top of all is another row, the bends not being so high, the lower portions being sewed

FIG. 83.

SIMPLE WRAPPED BORDER.

to the joint of the other two. The border forms a series of lenticular openings, with a bar across the long diameter. This method of ornamentation is not confined to one area, an Eskimo specimen from Davis Inlet, northern Labrador, collected by Lucian Turner, being made on substantially the same plan.

Fig. 84 is the border of a coiled basket collected among the Hopi Indians by Victor Mindeleff, Cat. No. 84596, U.S.N.M. It will be seen that the foundation of the coiled work on the body of the basket consists of three rods on the same perpendicular plane. The stitch passes over the three; catches under one of the previous coils, the stitches interlocking. In finishing off this work a single rod is used for the margin or border. It is sewed to the upper rod of the previous foundation in plain coiled work; but while this process is going on a series of three splints are twined around both the foundation and the stitches of the border. When the whole is drawn tight it gives the appearance of a very elaborate double-braided work, looked at from the outside, and a continuous twined or rope work on the upper margin. In order to make the style more compre-

FIG. 84.
THREE-STRAND COILED BORDER.
Hopi, Arizona.

hensible, a drawing from the border of Cat. No. 204833 is introduced, fig. 85, in which the elements of the border twine are in different colors. The two examples just shown illustrate what was previously said about using twined work for the borders of coiled weave, and the opposite among the Tlinkits.

Fig. 86 represents the border of a coiled basket of the Sia Indians of New Mexico, Cat. No. 134213, U.S.N.M., collected by Mrs. Matilda

FIG. 85.
DETAIL OF FIG. 84.

C. Stevenson. A hoop is used for the foundation of the border, and it is first made fast to the regular sewing underneath by means of a simple coiled splint on the outside of this. The ornamental border consists of an ordinary figure-of-eight wrapping, as in doing up a kite string, going from left to right. A splint passes under the foundation rod toward the front, and then forward five stitches over, behind, and under, back three stitches and under. The same process repeated gives the form of a braid on the outside. Finally, by the manipulation of a single pliable splint, effects are produced on the border which resemble three-ply or four-ply braid.

Fig. 87 shows the detail of border on a Havasupai (Yuman) basket, Cat. No. 213259, U.S.N.M., collected by Dr. Walter Hough. It will be seen that two rows are used in the foundation of the border. The strip, or splint, passes under the upper backward, then around in

FIG. 86.

SINGLE-STRAND PLAITED BORDER.

front forward, and under both, then backward to repeat the process by a sort of figure-of-eight movement, passing from left to right. When the work is done and driven home it has the appearance of regular plaiting. Fig. *b* shows both top and side view of the completed work.

The application of border work to other forms of receptacles may be studied here, since the processes are quite akin. In a large area of

FIG. 87.

SINGLE-STRAND PLAITED BORDER.

Havasupai Indians, Arizona.

Cat. No. 213259. Collected by Walter Hough.

North America bark of trees, with some leather, was so easily worked that very little trouble was taken in weaving baskets.

Fig. 88 represents the border of a birch-bark tray formed over a rod of willow, a very simple and effective but quite ornamental method of attachment. Five holes are bored or cut through the bark near the upper border. Two holes are then made, half an inch from the border, and these series are repeated all the way around. The sewing passes around the rod and through the hole in a simple coil, but the effect of the shallow and the deep stitching is quite pleasing. The sewing is done with tough splints from the root of the spruce. The specimen here figured is from the Upper Yukon River, Cat. No. 217750, U.S.N.M., collected by I. C. Russell.

FIG. 88.
PLAIN COILED BORDER ON BARK VESSEL.
Cat. No. 217750, U.S.N.M.   Collected by I. C. Russell.

Fig. 89 is the border of a birch-bark tray from the Tinné Indians, Central Alaska, collected by I. C. Russell, Cat. No. 217744, U.S.N.M. Three slits were cut through the bark near the margin; after an interval of some distance three others, and so on around the entire border. A willow rod serves for the strengthening element, and the spruce root is attached by a series of half hitches or buttonhole stitches. On the inside the effect is a combination of coiled and twined weaving, and on the outside only the vertical stitches of the coil are seen.

FIG. 89.
COIL AND KNOT BORDER ON BARK VESSEL.
Cat. No. 217744, U.S.N.M.   Collected by I. C. Russell.

Fig. 90 represents a border of a Yukon River, Alaska birch tray. It consists of the alternate use of plain coil around a strengthening rod and three stitches, passing down and under a rod on the inside, crossing the standing part to the right through an opening or slit cut in the bark, and up to the beginning. There are three of these half hitches, as they might be called, and then five wraps around the upper rod. From this point the process is renewed.

Fig. 91 is a border of birch-bark tray from the Upper Yukon River, collected by I. C. Russell. On the upper edge a rod is used for strengthening. It is attached to the margin of bark by means of splint of spruce root. The drawing shows the front and back of the method of holding the root and bark together. From the back the splint passes from the hole in the bark obliquely over the rod, down,

FIG. 90.
PLAIN COILED BORDER ON BARK VESSEL.

forward through the bark, backward and behind the standing part, over the rod, down and through the same hole, to start another knot. Practically, then, it is a series of single knots, as is shown in the upper openwork drawing. The Indians who make these birch baskets are called Tinné, or Déné. They live in Central Alaska and belong to the Athapascan family. The specimen is Cat. No. 217247, U.S.N M.

FIG. 91.
COIL AND KNOT BORDER ON BARK VESSEL.
Cat. No. 217247, U.S.N.M. Collected by I. C. Russell.

The ordinary checker and other woven mats are fastened off in the same manner as the baskets.

An interesting and intricate border is made by the Chilkat Indians on their ceremonial blankets. It consists of a number of long strings of mountain goat's wool and cedar bast held together by a few rows of twined weaving at the middle. This is then doubled and sewed to the margin, the ends forming the fringe. (See Plate 148.)

IV. ORNAMENTATION ON BASKETRY

There's magic in the web of it:
A sibyl that had numbered in the world
The sun to make two hundred compasses,
In her prophetic fury sewed the work.
—OTHELLO, III: 4.

Ornamentation in and on basketry is to be studied with three teachers or guides—the technician, the artist, and the folklorist. With the first named are learned the varied materials as to color and texture, the technical elements and their forms, and the methods of assembling them. The artist will show how these elements, on the one hand, open possibilities for æsthetic effects, and how, on the other hand, the stitches and decussations handicap attempts at free-hand drawing. The folklorist examines the pictography, the totemism, the lore and mythology of the ornamentation, with a view of putting the student into intellectual and spiritual relationship with the basket maker. Without her basket-making would be merely a trade or calling, and the art student would be utterly helpless in detecting the alphabet of design. This phase of the subject will be elaborated in the chapter on symbolism.

Great help in this investigation would be derived from a visit to the humble artist to watch the processes through which the fine effects have been elaborated. To this inquiry special attention will here be given. It should be added in passing that in producing her effects the basket maker must be fully equipped for her work before the first stitch or check is attempted. The painter, the potter, and the sculptor may add finishing touches or make corrections after the work is done, but the basket maker is like the musician—every detail in the production must be attended to correctly at the time. There is no chance to go back and remedy defects. Decoration on basketry is studied under the following heads:

A. Form and structure.

B. Ornamentation through color.

Form and color may be studied (1) on the basket as a whole; (2) on the minutest structural elements; and (3) in the designs upon the surface. These will be taken up in order and treated in their relation to the sense of the beautiful, present in the humble Indian woman's mind as well as in those more refined. Growth, progress from pure naturalism to greater and greater artificiality, may be observed here quite as marked as in other activities. To illustrate what is here said by way of introduction, Plate 36 represents a coiled basket of the Mission Indians in the collection of G. Wharton James. The noteworthy characteristics of this basket bowl are the effects produced by variety in designs and color in shades, as well as by symmetry of outline. The sharp contrast seen in the designs are due not to modern dyes, but

to a skillful use of Nature's colors.   Under the descriptions of materials
attention was called to the variety of natural pigmentation in the
stems and roots of the plants used in the construction of the Mission
work.   The center of the specimen is in rectangles the colors of which
alternate between white and dark brown.   The center zone is made up
in straw color, white, and black; the third or outer zone in natural
shades of the stem—white, brown, and black—with here and there spots
of brown introduced into the straw-colored sewing.   The outer edge
is in brown and white.   Anciently the Mission baskets were not nearly
so gaudy looking, but among the frequent transformations in artistic
forms and colors this example illustrates progress in the adoption of
really beautiful motives of a high order.

The elaboration of decoration in form first, and then of color, will
now be taken up more minutely.   The aesthetic side of this part of
the subject is so well explained by Holmes,[a] that it is here only necessary to make plain the technical elements and processes involved in
ornamentation.

As on Pueblo pottery, so on basketry, some patterns are merely
likenesses of things, and that is all.   A step in advance of this is the
portraiture of some particular and sacred natural feature, mountain,
body of water, trait, etc.   Pictography is one grade higher, and,
beginning with attempts at figuring animals and plants entire, runs
the whole gamut of transformation, ending with conventional meto-
nymies, synecdoches, and geometric patterns of the classic type.

FORM AND STRUCTURE

Form in basketry is decided at the outset, not by the desire to create
something artistic, but to produce a useful receptacle.   There is
scarcely a basket so rude, however, that a sense of symmetry and other
artistic qualities did not enter into its composition, both as to its general outline and the management of its details.   These varied forms
are decided in reality by:

(a) Function, which is discussed in the chapter on uses, from the
purely industrial point of view.

(b) Materials, shown in the chapter on manufacture as to their
variety and quality, but here considered as suggesting and restricting
form.

(c) Imitation of natural objects and of forms of utensils in other
materials.

(d) Physiological limitations.   Both in the making of the basket
and in using it the Indian woman had ever in view the convenience of
her own body.   The curves of the basket itself, the length and width,
the proportion of all its parts, as well as convenience of holding,

---

[a] Sixth Annual Report of the Bureau of Ethnology, Washington, 1889, pp. 189–252.

transporting, and utilizing, all had reference to the woman's physical frame.

(*e*) Aesthetic purpose. The desire to produce something beautiful in itself without any regard to other motives.

If there be any beauty in work belonging to the first step it is purely *adventitious*, the weaver did not effect it purposely. In the next higher grade there are no separate elements of beauty, but the utilitarian features are dominated by taste purposely. A third class of aesthetic forms, one step higher, enhance the beauty of the basket, but do not diminish its serviceability. It seems a pity to waste so much prolonged work and lovely design and color on a mere berrypicking basket or a pot for cooking with hot stones, but who will say nay? Finally, usefulness is ignored or sacrificed to pure aestheticism. (See Plates 11, 23, 45, 70, and 71.)

When the very lowly and practical functions of a great deal of this ware are considered one has a striking example of the way in which the sense of beauty may coexist with forlorn poverty and surroundings, as may also be seen by comparing the most skillful basket maker with her workshop. This thought must not be carried too far, however, in understanding the culture status of the woman, since all artists are busy practically with uncleanly materials and do not wear their best attire in the studio. On this same practical side, also, the love of beauty for its own sake may not be the entire motive in the artist's mind; her natural ambition and pride of achievement in technical skill, and perhaps envy, have much to do with preeminent success—quite as much with her as with artists at the other end of civilization. The same discrimination is made by art critics in the highest walks of culture. The singer or musician who renders a technically difficult piece may be stimulated quite as much by pride of performance as by the overpowering influence of aesthetic feeling. It is difficult to sound the depths of the Indian woman's motives, but in the matter of shape, as will be seen, her masterpieces are fine models of symmetry and grace. Quite every plate in this paper will illustrate in some way or another what will be said respecting the ornamentation of Indian basketry in the six geographic areas. In each one of the phases under which shape as a decorative element is studied there will be found a response in the different parts of the hemisphere.

The study of form and structure in the ornamentation of basketry will be now considered under the heads named: First, the shape of the basket as a whole; second, the minute structural elements out of which all designs on basketry are formed, and third, the designs on the surface of the basket and their combination into symbols or composite ornamentations. (See Plate 37.)

SHAPES OF BASKETS AS A WHOLE

The shapes of basketry have relation to the forms of solid geometry. The cube, the cone, the cylinder, the sphere, are the bases of all simple and complicated varieties. In softer material basketry approaches matting. The products are then flat or pliable, although the process of manufacture is the same. Among the eastern tribes of the United States the Algonkin and Iroquois baskets are all cylindrical or rectangular in outline. The same is true of the tribes in the Southern United States, although the greater flexibility of the reed cane invites the basket weaver to a wider diversity. In the Interior Basin and everywhere else the wild flax and other fibrous plants abounded, the sack, rectangular in outline, prevailed, but in the western portions of Canada east of the Rocky Mountains the prevalence of birch bark occasioned a variety of solid forms. The Indians of the Interior Basin also employ the cylinder largely. The same is true of the Eskimo, of Alaska, while the Aleutian Islanders, especially in the outer islands, having the flexible wild grass to work with, return to the form of the bag or satchel. The cylinder and the rectangle prevail among the Haida and Tlinkit, while the soft wallet, rectangular in outline, were more common farther south. The Salish and other tribes of Indians, of Columbia and Washington, diversified in their tribal and linguistic elements, produced many forms of baskets. Those in touch with the Hudson's Bay Company were very quick to imitate the shapes of packages used by them. In this region, also, since the boiling with hot stones was a prevalent method of cooking, the basket pot, somewhat cylindrical in motive yet more in the form of a truncated cone, was seen in every house. What is said about the diversity of form among the Salish tribes is true all along the Pacific coast of the United States. Here also is to be found the conical baskets in great abundance, since the people were partly vegetarians or diggers. The carrying basket is a prominent feature in collections from this area. From these simple geometric forms were developed dishes, jars, bottles, packing cases, and so on, in unlimited numbers, combining the cylinder, the cone, and the rectangle. In many of these the jar-shaped necks of pottery are imitated, in which the elements of the sphere and the spheroid are used.

In giving the forms just indicated to basketry the Indian woman has always in mind the elements of the beautiful as well as of the useful. It is considered a reproach to violate the rules of bilateral symmetry or proportion in form. A superficial view of a large collection of baskets from any portion of America would strike the most careless observer as the fruits of thoughtful and painstaking labor on æsthetic lines. These forms are often said to be mere imitations of something the savage woman has seen in nature or in other arts. Imitation is indeed one of the elements in this problem, but it is an entire misconception of the underlying plan to suppose that the skillful weaver is a slave to natural patterns. Indeed, it might also be averred that she is less subservient to such things than artisans of much higher grade. On entering the workshops of civilization one sees the walls loaded with designs and models after which to work, but rarely would the observer see an Indian woman looking to any other source than her own imagination for the model of her basket; strictly speaking, she never makes two alike. A close observation of the weaver at her work demonstrates the fact that the eye, the hand, the curves of the body, the angles of the lower limbs, all contribute their share to giving beautiful forms to basketry. The following illustrations will show the gradations of general outline through which basketry passes, the maker keeping always in mind the sense of pleasure to be awakened or gratified.

They are as follows: *a*, flat forms; *b*, dish forms; *c*, bowl forms; *d*, jar forms; and *e*, miscellaneous forms.

(*a*) The simplest of these is the flat tray, mat, wallet, sail, gambling plaque, and more. They assume endless varieties of outline, and through the stimulus of trade all sorts of shapes result, table mats of standard patterns in Sitka and Vancouver Island, rectangular wallets in Washington, Idaho, and Montana, but especially the gambling plaques of California.

Plate 38 shows two flat plaques of this form, the upper one from the Tule River country, Tulare County, California, the lower one from Madera County, both in the collection of E. L. McLeod, of Bakersfield, California. The coiling, if well done, would produce the circular outline. The Indian woman who constructed the plaque made the stitches under the spell of this art motive. A number of additional examples of artistic forms in flat basketry will be found in Plates 6 and 61.[a]

(*b*) Use cooperates with beauty in deepening the basket into a shallow plate as among the Hopi (Moki) for the sacred meal in their prayer ceremonials, but more attractive still are the so-called Navaho ceremonial baskets. (See Plate 39). These beautiful objects have attracted much attention also through their association with Navaho ceremonies. They are called ghost drums, wedding baskets, and various other names, all associated with the Navaho religion. The dish baskets shown in the plate are in the collection of Fred Harvey. The same form exists along the Pacific States wherever meal or other vegetal diet is eaten. They are the common dish in which the mush is served throughout the acorn-bearing parts of California. It is an excellent example of adaptation to use, consistent at the same time with correct æsthetic expression. Doing her best in producing the proper form

---

[a] W. H. Holmes, Report of the U. S. National Museum, 1900, pl. XLI.

she was not hampered by the fear of lessening utility. Figures of similar shapes will be seen in Plates 93, 216.

(c) Deepening the plate or dish gives the bowl an unlimited number of forms and emancipates the basket maker. All through the southwestern United States the olla is the prevailing form. It is a segment cut from a sphere, marvelous in symmetry when the production of a master hand. Departing from this simple outline, varieties are produced by flattening the bottom and straightening the body until the truncated cone and regular cylinder are reached. The quality of the material used may have a little to do with the general outline, but it is charming to see how easily the savage woman overcomes the obstinacy of nature and persuades reluctant wood to do the work of grass and soft fibers. Cylindrical forms are in favor with the Aleuts, with the Haidas of Queen Charlotte Islands, with the Tlinkits of southeastern Alaska, and some tribes in Washington and Oregon. In the eastern parts of Canada and the United States cylindrical forms are mixed with rectangular. The baskets shown in Plate 40 are in the collection of E. L. McLeod, of Bakersfield, California. These are all from Kern County, and include hats as well as domestic forms. It will be noticed that some of the examples have straight conical bodies and others are curved outward, but none are incurved. As models for modern basketry these shapes can not be improved upon, since they are grounded in the structure of the human body itself. Reference will be again made to the baskets in this plate when the elementary forms are studied that go to make up the designs. The photograph does but half justice to the basketry from this region, which adds to the beauty of outline and variety of design the charms of tints and colors in varied materials.

(d) Baskets with constricted borders go by the general name of bottlenecks. If a motif be sought outside the desire of the Indian artist to have it thus, there is a style of old Pueblo pottery at hand which stands preeminent in southwestern United States.[a] After the body of the vessel or basket is built up to the required height the work is drawn into the form of a jar or bottle. Attention has already been called to the fact that no pottery existed formerly on the west coast of North America. The few exceptions to this rule only intensify this absence. The place of pottery is taken by basketry, even for cooking. There is no limit to the pine trees yielding gum which will render basketry water-tight. The bottle-shaped basket soon appears and is installed as Aquarius of the Utes, the Apache, and other tribes and as a seed vessel. No sooner was its office fixed than it began to dress up in artistic form, and the inimitable bottleneck of the Panamint and other tribes in the Inyo-Kern and Tulare area appeared. The Apaches

---

[a] J. W. Fewkes, Seventeenth Annual Report of the Bureau of Ethnology, 1898, Plates 130, 131, 143.

are having the last word at this point in the adoption of correct æsthetic forms purely European. Plate 41 shows a group of Kern County bottlenecks in the collection of E. L. McLeod. Plate 42 illustrates a lot of Apache ollas in the collection of J. W. Benham, of New York City.

That these pretty jar shapes have little significance so far as tribes are concerned is shown by the fact that they occur all the way from Point Barrow in Alaska to southern California.

(e) This class includes all odd forms whatever. They are frequently made in imitation of objects that struck the Indian woman's fancy. The very best examples of this are the imbricated baskets of the Fraser-Columbia drainage. A good collection of them tells the whole story accurately, starting from the conical forms, with foundation of splints and bottoms in shape of a watch spring to be found on the Klikitat and the Thompson River and ending below and above the Fraser mouth with flat and uniform foundation and straight lines in the bottom, the last shapes in the series being nothing more than imitations of Hudson Bay Company's packages, trunks, cradles, and so on. These bizarre shapes are not confined to the mere imitation of white men's devices. The demands of ceremony and religion required special forms of basketry. (See Plates 43, 157–172.)

Finally, ornamentation in the form of the basket as a whole has kept pace with the multiplication of uses. The first contact of the Indians with the whites created new desires in their minds. Furthermore, it was not long before they discovered their best interests to lie in the direction of service to their conquerors. The supply of new wants and responses to the demands just mentioned would necessarily break in upon the ancient régime. Not at first, however, did the new object respond to the best workmanship. Plate 44 represents a part of the outfit of a Tlinkit Indian in the service of the Russians. Among his other accouterments there must be a receptacle for ammunition. This must conform to those already in use. The result is the three forms shown in the plate. First, a small jar-shaped holder with a basketry cap-like cover; second, a bullet holder, in which the one basket fits exactly over another; third, a combination in which the cover is attached to the basket by means of a running string. All of these forms are shown in the plate. While drawing attention to these designs it will be well to examine their characteristics. The cover of No. 2 is plain twined weaving of the old-fashioned sort. The attractiveness of the work is in its regularity, both of vertical lines and horizontal weaving. The under portion of this double basket is covered over with false embroidery designs. No. 1 is an evident departure from ancient shapes, and the surface is covered with poor work in embroidery. No. 3 is more worthy of scrutiny. On the outer basket, or cover, plain weaving and embroidery alternate in single lines and narrow bands. The lower, or inside, basket has its surface enveloped in embroidered weaving of excellent character and is wrought in three colors. The specimen is in the collection of L. H. Brittin, of Edgewater, New Jersey.

MOSAIC ELEMENTS IN DECORATION

The composition of the basket, its molecular elements, so to speak, is guided largely by the materials. In cross section they are in their coarsest forms round, then half round, resulting from splitting whole stems. The finer sorts arise from further subdivision of stems, being roundish on the outside and flat within; or flat on both surfaces, as in the Canadian ash splints and the flat foundations of Fraser River baskets; or ribbon-like, as in basketry made of palm leaves; or thread-like, as in the coiled basketry of the Pomo, sewed with split sedge root as fine as pack thread. These various kinds and grades of materials in their tractability are dependent on climate, latitude, and phytogeography in the first place, and finally upon the maker's grade of culture, on the form and function she had in mind, as well as on the higher forms of fine art, social rivalry, and mythology. (See Plate 45.)

In ultimate structure, basketry is free-hand mosaic or, in finest materials, like pen drawings or beadwork, the surface being composed of any number of small parts—technically decussations, stitches, or meshes, practically separate from one another so far as the effect on the eye is concerned. These mosaic parts are with some materials quite flat on the outer surface, as in the best matting and bags, while in others they stand out on account of the coarseness and rigidity of the wood. The object of mosaic ordinarily is to produce a flat surface for pavements or floors. The term "mosaic," here used as a simile, applies to such as is seen in mural decoration, where projections and depressions are wrought into artistic designs. In much basketry the separation of the stitches and exposure of a warp beneath having another color have precisely the same effect. In many examples the stems and roots are thoroughly soaked and rendered plastic and then pressed home, the parts being forced together, in which case the little elements become spindle-formed or hexagonal. Mosaic effects in basketry may be—(a) Tessellate, as in checker or twilled weaving; (b) concentric, as in wicker and twined weaving, and (c) radiate in all coiled weaving. These must be kept in mind.

Unity in variety, the underlying principle of all æsthetic composition, finds its first step illustrated in the making up of a basket. The perfection of an Indian basket in its artistic technic is monotony, or monotechny, if such a word existed. In looking at a clumsy bit of work done by a child, or a beginner, one is aware of painstaking effort to make all the checks or stitches alike, ending in failure. In the most elegant pieces the victory is won, unity is achieved. With her mouth for a vise and other purposes, with a flint knife, and the educated fingers, the patient and skillful artist formerly brought all her filaments to uniform thickness. At present scissors, awls, knives, and gauges (all of metal) aid her immensely in her task. The eyes and hands cooperating, in some instances through a hundred thousand efforts, produce elements of astonishing uniformity. This unity is of a very high order; for in many examples, coupled with a monotony of elements absolutely under control of the artist there is at the same time a charming variation in width and length of parts in harmony with, and made necessary by, the widening and narrowing of the basket. This unity in a myriad of details is the more noteworthy in a basket-maker's art, in common with that of all other textile workers, because the individual elements are not lost or destroyed in the operation. The exceptions to this are rare, as in a few California specimens, where the coiled sewing is entirely obscured by overlaying of feathers. Usually the perfection of the stitch is the aim of the worker.

Plate 46 is a rare coiled basket made by a Washoe woman named Datsolalee. It is in the collection of A. Cohn, Carson City, Nevada. The piece measures 8½ inches high, is 12 inches wide, and 6 inches wide at the opening. The stitches number over 50,000, being thirty to the inch. The body color is a rich light gold, and the figures are in red and black. It weighs 16 ounces, and is valued at many hundreds of dollars. The figures on the basket represent birds migrating or flying away, the motto being, "When the birds leave their nests and fly away, we shall move." The shape of this piece and the quality of the sentiment in the markings are excelled only by the inimitable quality of the work on the surface. It is difficult to conceive of a more perfectly uniform piece of handiwork than this.

In pottery all vestiges of coiling and molds are commonly obliterated. In a very few examples of ancient ware there seems to have been an aim to perfect the coiling and render its detail monotonous and artistic, but in the many thousands of other examples the potter has erased the marks of the fingers, the paddle, and the mold. On the other hand, the whole development of the art of basketry has been an effort to perfect the individual stitch, or mesh, or check, if necessary to make any number of thousands of them exactly alike over the entire surface of a large receptacle, or to study the greatest possible number of variations that may be given in form to these primary elements consistent with the unity of the whole effect. The Eskimo near the mouth of the Yukon must have only lately acquired the art of basket making. With coarse hay for the foundation and sinew for thread they produce the clumsiest excuses for basketry, ugly in form, slovenly in stitching, and utterly devoid of designs on the surface, while the Aleuts, close by, have unique elementary forms and work with surprising uniformity. With the monotony or uniformity of the mosaic elements in any basket one must not fall into the error of thinking that there is not the greatest variety of fundamental shapes in the things to be monotonized. They vary in outline and relief in position with reference to the horizon; that is, the rim of the basket, in relative proportion to the whole and its parts.

FIG. 92.

CHECKER ORNAMENT IN TWO COLORS.

After W. H. Holmes.

In checkerwork the basketry tiles, one might call them, keeping in mind the use of the word mosaic, are squares or rectangles in close or open work. The mosaic of checkerwork pleases by its uniformity, and yet many baskets made by hand with tools not over refined have in them enough of variety to relieve them from the dull monotony in machine products. Flexibility in materials, as between hard-wood splints and those of cedar bark and palm leaf, offers all the chance the weaver needs to play tricks in reliefs. The eye is never wearied in rambling up and down among these crooked paths. There is possibility of variety even in checkerwork, through changing the width of warp and weft elements. Oblong rectangles there mingle with tiny or larger squares in tessellated surfaces. (See Plate 14 and figs. 96 and 97.)

FIG. 93.

AMAZONIAN BASKET DECORATIONS IN CHECKER.

After F. H. Cushing.

What is here said concerning the æsthetic effects produced in the plainest kind of checkerwork by simple alternation of the colors is illustrated by fig. 92, after Holmes in the Sixth Annual Report of the Bureau of Ethnology already quoted.

Fig. 93 is a more interesting illustration from the Amazon region, from a drawing after Frank H. Cushing. The surface of the basket is mosaic in two colors, made up of little square blocks, and by their alternation not only sloping and vertical patterns are produced, but the most intricate labyrinth of fretwork. There is no limit to the pos-

sibilities any more than there is to the Italian workman making a tessellated pavement with marble blocks in white and black.

As soon as the weaver steps outside of her monotonous checkerwork into the province of wicker, or especially twilled weaving, the possibilities of ornamentation are infinitely multiplied. In plain weave, wicker elements are sigmoid or spindle-shaped; on twilled weaving, they are oblong rectangles. Passing into the most intricate damask effects in modern linen weaving, in which materials of one color only have to be used, it will be seen how greatly varied this sort of ornamentation may be made. The elements of wickerwork mosaic

FIG. 94.
TWILLED WORK IN TWO
COLORS.
After W. H. Holmes.

are horizontal, but twilled weaving, in single elements may be both vertical and horizontal in the same piece. The three accompanying figures are from Holmes and show better than words the possibilities of the little squares and rectangles for decoration. In fig. 94 in two colors the white work is under two and over one; the weft over one, two, or

FIG. 95.
DIAPER TWILLED WORK IN TWO
COLORS.
After W. H Holmes.

three and under one; the result being a series of sloping designs of great beauty. Fig. 95 in precisely the same materials shows how by varying the count the pattern is changed. Fig. 96 is interesting because it exhibits a widespread type of mat weaving farthest away from loom work. The woman begins at the corner to weave. All the little blocks are rectangles; all stop at the same angle, and the result is a perfect Greek fret in two colors. (See Plate 47.)

In twined weaving the effect of the single rows is funicular one way and corrugated the other. If the reader will notice any number of twined baskets in plain twined weave, it will at once become apparent that it has its limitations. The Pomo make only bands in it to represent the skin of a snake or some such motive. The Haida and Tlinkit vary the ribbed effect with decorative overlaying or three-strand weft. With the diagonal twined work the case is entirely different. The boldest of spiral designs covering an immense surface are wrought in weaving in twilled fashion. Nothing can excel the Pomo, Pit River, and other northern California carrying baskets in attractiveness of decoration. In openwork twining, where the warp has a chance to show its versatility, as in mound-builders' ware, but especially in Aleutian wallets, the pleasing effects in a single color are without end. For examples of the great variety in twined-work decoration see Plates 19, 21, and 48.

Plate 48, illustrating twined decoration in its elements is a representation of food bowls of the Klamath Indians of southern Oregon. These old specimens were among the first received at the U. S. National Museum and were collected by George Gibbs, Cat. No. 7568, U.S.N.M. The resources of ornamentation used by the Klamath Indians are fine stems and rods for the fiber, different colors in the wood, and superadded elements for decoration. Much of their work

FIG. 96.
DIAGONAL TWILLED ORNAMENT.
British Guiana.
After W. H. Holmes.

is done in soft material and in the type of overlaying used by them the ends are fastened off carelessly on the inside of the structure so as to give a rough appearance.

Further illustrations of Klamath ornamentation, as well as that of their kindred, the Modocs, will be found in Plates 167, 174.

One of the prettiest and boldest attempts at securing effects in twined weave in the U. S. National Museum is from the vast cemetery of Ancon in Peru. The illustration (fig. 97) shows the decorative belt on a small workbasket made from rushes. One might be deceived into thinking that the motive came from the Yokut Indians of California (figs. 98 and 99), but a glance at the texture reveals a different method of achieving the same result. The warp is double, consisting of two straws side by side as in the Aleut wallets. At the bottom are three rows of plain twined weaving, each twist inclosing two warps.

Follow these pairs up to the top of the basket and note that the two rows of twined weaving—one dark, the other light—also inclose pairs, but not the same pairs, between the single twinings. Here seven human figures are woven in black on a brown ground. The pairs are holding in their hands between them a rhomboid object, reminding one of an Iroquois wampum belt in which two warriors are shown as bearing the sacred pipe. The weaving on this space is twilled mixed with twined, the latter being subservient to the former. The warp elements no longer are worked in pairs, but singly. The twined weaving on them is twilled on the brown body surface and vertical across the black rectangles, making the double warp conform to the twined weaving below everywhere save on the feet. All this is finger work and deserves a prize for its maker both for the plan and the size of the molecules.

FIG. 97.
HUMAN FIGURES IN TWINED WEAVING.
Ancient Peru.
After W. H. Holmes.

Coiled basketry, on the contrary, is made up of radial elements only, which are the stitches, some being long and thin, others short and wide. The æsthetic effects depend on the quality of the material. The very coarsest ware of the Utes and the Klondike nations has little beauty of texture, while that of the Alaskan Tinné or the California Washoe, Panamint, or Pomo is faultless. In finer coiled work, when the stitches barely interlock, they appear to stand one over another from row to row; but when the stitches pass underneath one of the rods at least of the foundation below there is an alternation of stitches with open spaces on the surface resembling twilled weaving, each one being wedged between two, over and under. It is impossible to trace any ornamentation in coiled work among the eastern Indians of North

America through lack of material. The Arctic Alaskan coiled basketry also is lacking in color features. It is not until the Salish tribes of British Columbia are reached that attempts are made to produce beautiful effects in the primitive coiled elements of ornamentation. The resources of the artist are fourfold.

(1) Her regular stitches are in tough root splints coiled in such manner that the smooth outer surface of the last year's growth is exposed to view. Seldom will the rough inner splints which constitute the

FIG. 98.
DESIGN ON COILED BOWL.
Tulare Indians.
Cat. No. 19691, U.S.N.M. Collected by Stephen Powers.

foundation come into sight through or between the stitches, Indeed, there is a type of weaving in this area in which smooth, thin strips of wood are laid together in pairs so that when the warp is exposed it is the bright outer surface that is seen. The Salish woman is not backward in making most of her opportunities with the dull brown color of the cedar in that she has learned to practice uniformity in the stitches themselves.

(2) Mention has already been made of splitting stitches in the sew-

ing of these savage women. It is done in such a careful manner that it becomes an element of beauty, otherwise it would become a contribution to ugliness. Examples of this work will be seen in Plate 24.

(3) Another resource of ornamentation in the elementary American work of coiled basketry has been well used by the Salish Indians— that is the so-called beading, which consists in running a strip of bright grass in and out among the coiled stitches at regular intervals. Many examples of brown cedar sewing with bright golden-colored straws for the beading are in the U. S. National Museum. This arrests the radial effect of the coil stitches and substitutes the concentric or parallel motif.

FIG. 99.
DETAIL OF FIG. 98.
After W. H. Holmes.

(4) The last elementary resource referred to among the Salish tribe is imbrication, which will be more minutely described in the section devoted to color in ornamentation. The sewing on such specimens is entirely obliterated and the surface reconstructed in yellow, red, brown, and wood color, the effect being tesselate mosaic.

Among the California tribes these coiled elements, being much smaller in size than those in the baskets of the Salish tribes, afforded opportunity for different artistic effects. An inspection of the work done by Pomo, Maidu, and other tribes of northern California shown in many plates and figures will prove this.

Fig. 98 is from the surface of a beautiful coiled basket of the Tulare Indians, Tulare County, California. It gives an opportunity of studying the elementary stitches on the best of coiled work. These Indians have at their command four colors, that of the root or wood with which the body of the basket is sewed; black filaments taken from the root of a peculiar sedge; where the redbud or cercis is available, the outer bark is a rich brown and the inner side quite white; in addition there is a bright reddish root, *Yucca arborescens.*

The stitches are, of course, hexagonal in form, but the pressing of the wood together gives them quite an oval outline, and they naturally, in the course of sewing, incline toward the right. With these colors and oval elements to which the artist is bound to restrict herself, the attempt is here made to produce a step-formed cycloid. In the spaces between each two designs is the figure of a man. It is interesting to note how, under such narrow restrictions, so good effects can be produced.

FIG. 100.
PIMA CARRYING FRAME.
Southern Arizona.
Cat. No. 76033, U.S.N.M. Collected by Edward Palmer.

In southern California among the Tulare and other neighboring tribes, as well as among the Apache and Navaho, most pretentious figures are attempted in coiled elements. Fig. 99, after Holmes, in the Sixth Annual Report of the Bureau of Ethnology (fig. 339) furnishes a good example of what is here mentioned, but the farthest departure from old-fashioned types is exhibited in the work of the Apaches, who attempt all sorts of animal forms in coiled work, and the Pima tribes, who lose themselves in labyrinths and frets.

The basket from which this elementary rectangle is taken will be found illustrated on Plate 30, in Report of the U. S. National Museum for 1884.[a]

Plate 49 shows two covered jars in exquisite coiled work, brought from Santa Barbara, California, by William Alden Gale, of Boston, between 1810 and 1835, and owned by the Misses Eaton. The upper basket is 11 inches high and 5 inches wide; the lower 15½ inches wide and 10 inches high. They are introduced here for the purpose of calling attention to their combination of æsthetic qualities. One does

---

[a] See also Stephen Powers in Contributions to North American Ethnology, 1877, p. 256.

not know which to admire most, their forms, the fineness of the stitches, the simple but effective designs, or the charming effect of color both in the patterns and in the mosaic work.　Covers on baskets from this area are rare and may not be ancient.　It is just suggested that their motive came from the old preserve jars common in ships' outfits a hundred years ago.

In fig. 100 the ornamentation has all the features of lacework; indeed, it might be called the beginning of lace.　The detailed drawing above the figure shows, however, that the example is simply a piece of coiled basketry from which the foundation rows have been carefully withdrawn and only the sewing remains.　In the long stitches between the thread has been simply wrapped twice around the standing part instead of once.　It is within the weaver's power to make this change at any moment from single wrap to double wrap, the result being a figured surface, as in the lower drawing.　This sort of ornamentation has rare existence north of the present boundaries of Mexico, but may be found all through tropical America.　The example here shown was procured from the Pima Indians of the Piman family in Arizona and Mexico, but beautiful examples were also collected by W J McGee among the Papagoes, their kindred.

DESIGNS IN DECORATION

The fundamental checks, decussations, stitches, and meshes of which the mosaic of basketry is made up are used, associated or not with color, in forming designs or patterns on the surface.　Compare the severely plain Haida cylinder wallet with the exquisitely decorated hat from the same tribe.　Both are in the color of the spruce root, but the latter resembles fine lacework on account of the delicate pattern covering its surface.　All Indian tribes know how to give variety to unity by simply making up various technical compositions that add no new processes.　These compositions are aggregations of simple forms which are the alphabet of the Indian woman's most intricate patterns. It matters not how complicated the whole design may be, it is composed of the following simple parts:

(*a*) *Lines in ornament.*

(*b*) *Squares or rectangles.*

(*c*) *Rhomboidal figures.*

(*d*) *Triangles.*

(*e*) *Polygonal elements.*

(*f*) *Complex patterns.*

It may be well to devote a little more space to the consideration of these.　Many seemingly incomprehensible patterns become clear when resolved.　At the same time the secret of their pleasure-giving quality is revealed.　Just as a subtle pleasure creeps into the mind in scrutinizing the uniform stitches on the surface of the Washoe basket (Plate

46) so, in a higher sense, the orderly recurring of the same geometric shape over and over in an intricate design adds to the enjoyment of the whole. These elements are not exact, however, being hand-made and bounded by lines produced by the curved forms in most basketry. The artistic effect is thus heightened.

(a) *Lines in ornament.*—It may not have occurred to the reader to observe how scrupulous almost every Indian basket maker is to relieve the monotony of her work by a simple line of some other kind of weaving. It would be safe to say that no basket is without them. In the entire Hudson collection in the National Museum there is not a twined basket whose texture is not improved in more than one place by a line in a different style of technic. These lines may run in almost any direction, and, as in the Haida hat, be worked into geometric figures.

Plate 50 is a collection of Pima basket bowls from southern Arizona belonging to F. M. Covert, of New York city. It shows how many different effects are produced in the same tribe by the mere administration of lines wandering about. In some of the figures shown it will be seen how easy it is for a row of stitches to become double and then to add or to make additional rows at the ends or on the sides, to separate lines or to give to a line any sort of curved effect. This is especially noticeable in fig. 3. The line may pass by further additions into rectangles, triangles, or geometric figures. The Indians of the southwestern portion of the United States have exhausted the situation in this matter of meandering lines.

(b) *Squares or rectangles.*—The next simplest form upon which the basket artist may venture is the square or rectangle, which may be a band of two or more rows interrupted by vertical spaces, perhaps in another color. It is a matter of counting the same number over and over as the work progresses, and is one of the first steps in arithmetic. In a Pomo gift basket the square patterns on the bottom are the mats on the floor, and so the simplest of weaving motives lends itself to symbolism. In the plainest forms of work the checkers or squares are oriented at right angles to the horizon or border of the specimen. Variety is effected by the position of the squares and their relation one to another and to other decorative elements. A delightful effect is produced on matting especially where the squares or checkers are oblique to the borders. Such work is to be seen in America, but was much more common in the islands of the Pacific.

The rectangle gives a wider scope still to variety in artistic effects. Bands of rectangles are to be seen around basketry, and more complicated forms are made up of them or have them in their composition. A departure from the rectangle, but in the same line of workmanship, is the parallelogram. Such work is easily produced in the diagonal or twilled weaving. An excellent example of an intricate design made up of rectangles in various positions and relations one to another is shown in the old Skokomish wallet from Washington in the collection of F. Harvey. (See Plate 51.) The decorations on this wallet consist of vertical collections of geometric figures, one hanging from another, in suits of four. Each one of the designs which go to make up the whole decoration in its simplest elements is a rectangle. The projections from the sides of these are the same, and the wolves around the upper border are simply a collection of the same elementary design, the head, the neck, the body, the legs, the tail, each one is the same. On the larger rectangles are nests of geometric figures of the same class, one inclosed in the other by widening lines. The entire effect on the surface is produced by the clever use of a single element.

In many examples, when the rectangular figure is set obliquely the pattern on the basket appears to have a rhomboidal form. The types of weaving have much to do with the administration of the rectangle, whether it be radial or concentric. In diagonal weaving the long axis is horizontal, but in coiled work the long, slender rectangles are perpendicular. In loose coiling the figures become rhomboidal on account of the longer slope of the stitch. Twined work produces an infinite number of rhombs in rows having ragged edges. In the style of weaving produced by the Makah the separate elements are rectangular on the inside, but they form a charming patchwork of rhombs on the outside. The rectangle aside from color, which will be studied later, lends itself to ornament by its relief, its proportions, and its position. The relief depends on the material, which may be soft inner bark or bast, or pliant leaves. On the other hand, it may be soft fillets of ash and stems of willow or coarse brushes as in the fish weir. When the projecting elements are intractable the possibilities of plain geometric ornamentation are limited in the extreme, but with fibers highly flexible and well-soaked materials the field of the decorator becomes greatly enlarged.

Plate 52, a large bottle-shaped granary of the San Carlos Apache Indians belonging to the fine collection of F. S. Plimpton, of San Diego, California, shows what is meant by proportion. Upon the surface of this coiled basket will be found stepped patterns rising in a cycloids from the bottom to the neck and even to the rim of the specimen. Each one of these spaces is covered with black and white rectangles, or as near as rectangular forms can be made on a globular surface governed in length and width by the widening or narrowing of the specimen. In the spaces between these patterns so made up are men and horses, but even these have square heads, bodies, legs, and feet. The fingers on the men are in proper shape. An amusing departure is manifest in the effort to give a little shape to the tails and ears of the horses.

(c) *Rhomboidal figures.*—With the parallelogram or rhomb, the surface of the basket has a tessellated or mosaic appearance. These figures also may be oriented with reference to the borders, but the patterns become oblique, and more pleasing diaper effects are caused when the figures are not oriented with reference to the horizon or border. Plate 53 shows a number of beautiful bowls in the collection of C. P. Wilcomb from Kern, Inyo, and Tulare counties, California. They are introduced here for the purpose of showing how, on many of them, diamond-shaped patterns have been worked into basketry with excellent effect. Associated with these geometric form polygons are also the elements of cycloids, covering almost the entire surface. Radiating from the bottom, triangular spokes proceed to the outer margin and these are decorated with diamond patterns and irregular polygons. The human form and other typical patterns are united with those now under consideration. The majority of the decoration, however, is in the simple elementary geometric shape here considered.

(d) *Triangles.*—On the surface of basketry the triangle, as an element of design in mosaic, does not occur in the single stitch or check, but it is found in open-work basketry, as among the Aleuts, where the warp is bent backward and forward or crossed. By the combination of elementary parts triangular effects in great variety are obtained. In this technic a triangle is not a three-sided figure with straight outline, but a pyramid made by piling up rectangles, vertical or radial in coiled basketry, horizontal or concentric in woven basketry. The base of the triangle may be straight but the sides are notched and stepped as in the bead work.

A great many symbolical designs of arrowheads, mountains, and other artificial and natural objects which suggest the three-sided form are produced on both coiled and woven basketry, the base of the triangle being at the top, at the bottom, or on either side of the figure. The conical or the globular basket lends itself most cheerfully to this element in design. On cylindrical, and especially on vertical vasiformed basketry, for ornamental effects the triangle easily passes into curved figures of infinite variety. After the foundation of the figure is laid on a certain round of weaving or coiling it is possible on the next round to widen or narrow above either end of this line. In some examples a sweeping cycloid beginning at the base, narrows and curves to the right or left, terminating with the outer border. The Filipino hat makers are exceedingly fond of creating a series of these triangle cycloids in different colors, some of them turning to the right, others to the left. The California basket maker also produces flame-like effects with elongated triangles. There seems to be no end to the versatility of this figure on globular basketry.

Plate 54 represents two of the Tulare bowls in the collection of F. S. Plimpton. The upper figure, especially, shows in its bands of decoration in brown and black how the rhomb and triangle cooperate to produce regular and pleasing decoration. The lower figure is a better illustration of the use of narrow parallelograms, combined in lines concentric and radial, to give expression to phenomena such as lightning.

Plate 55 is an imbricated box from the Fraser River country, in British Columbia. Excepting the parallel bands, the front and body of the basket are covered with white and dark-brown triangles, no other elementary geometric figure being introduced. Each triangle is an example of the limitations before mentioned, which practically cut the basket maker off from free-hand drawing. The geometricians say that a circle is a polygon with an infinite number of sides. With them all curved lines resolve themselves into the rectilinear. The basket maker does not stop there, but resolves rectilinear forms into still minuter rectilinear forms of another class. The mosaic elements on the basket are most regular squares of imbrication. There is for her no other way to make a triangle. This specimen is in the collection of F. Harvey.

(e) *Polygonal elements.*—What has been said of the triangle is also true of polygonal figures--that is, of those having more than four sides. These figures may be produced in the texture of baskets in openwork. They are also brought about by uniting different forms of checks or stitches in the same piece of work. On the hats of the Haida Indians and on twined work of the Pacific coast excellent diaper patterns are woven. In closely packed basketry the individual stitches assume the form of the hexagon, after the manner of the bee's cell. On matting, wallets, bags—that is, on flat surfaces—all of the geometric figures before mentioned having straight borders occur. In many rhombs the ends are cut off by boundary lines of bands and turned into hexagons.

However, as soon as basketry begins to assume curved outlines, borders that would be straight on a flat surface are bent in one or more directions. The effect of this, both in the single mosaic element and in the larger designs, is to change the figure from a hard outline to one that is far more graceful. In a coiled basket the foundation coil is curved horizontally, but the stitches cross these at right angles. In a coiled bowl with globose bottom there are three sets of curves with different radii—the horizontal curve of the foundation, the curve of the pattern, and the vertical curves of the stitches. The shapes of polygons that may be worked on the surface of basketry are legion. The designs which may be made out of these are even more numerous. It will be possible to illustrate only a limited number of them, but the reader may be pleased to turn from plate to plate in the decorations on the surface of basketry in the various chapters to see how versatile the Indian woman's mind was in making the best of her limitations. Being confined to angular elements, having no opportunity to introduce the curve, except so far as the body of the basket itself made straight lines curved, it became necessary to rack her ingenious brain to satisfy her cravings for expression of the beautiful with straight lines only. (See Plates 56–59.)

(*f*) *Complex patterns.*—The most striking artistic effects in basketry are realized when the simple lines, bands, and geometric figures are united and modified to suit the weaver's fancy, to fit the general shape of the object, and oftentimes to correct a miscalculation on the part of the maker. The effect of lines is changed by breaking, curving, setting at different angles, widening, and coloring. Geometric figures become subsidiary to and are lost in mythological compositions, but they are the organic parts of the whole design.

Plate 60 will illustrate what is here said about the production of intricate designs by combining two or more of the separate elements in the foregoing paragraphs. In every one of the bowls shown in this plate a circular form in basket work is attained by using material of the same color in the coiling at the bottom. From these central beginnings designs in triangles, squares, rectangles, and polygons are built up into labyrinthian decorations for the whole surface. In the middle figure of the bottom row five patterns radiate from the central circle, each one of which is made up of three groups of rectangular figures in black and white. Specimens are in the collection of J. W. Benham.

Plate 61 will interest the student as an example of bold design, being the American eagle, with expanded wings. It will surprise him to note how, with the use of straight-line figures before mentioned, some little life is given to the neck and to the talons of the bird by the fine marking of stitches, which lend themselves somewhat to curved effects. It can not be said, however, that this treatment is a success.

ORNAMENTATION THROUGH COLOR

Quite as much as form, the colors in basketry are an element of beauty. As in basket forms the sense of pleasure is awakened by the mass, by the minute elements, and by the shape of patterns or designs, so it is with colors. One does not know which to admire the most—the subdued shades of the natural materials, the pretty effects of the infinite variety of hues in the stitches, or the combinations of patterns in ornamentation through colors furnished by Nature's laboratory, which the importunate Indian women of America have secured in their tireless quest. The gamut of shades runs from pure white through the yellows and browns to sooty black, and age only ripens the effects. The peculiar golden shade of an old piece from California will set the connoisseur's face aglow. No doubt a part of this admiration springs from association of ideas such as age, rareness, the seeming disparity between the maker and her art, and, maybe, the pride of ownership.

When it is remembered that for utilitarian purposes merely not one speck of this artistic coloring is needed, and further noted that great fatigue and search and critical judgment are necessary in order to assemble materials for a single basket, surely no one will withhold admiration from the creator of colored ornamentation in basketry. One can scarcely begin to appreciate her struggles and triumphs until the effort is made to reproduce her results.

Ornamentation by means of color is effected in basketry through the following processes, already hinted at in the chapter on basket making:

(*a*) By employing materials which are of different colors by nature. This has been partly described in the foregoing sections.

(*b*) By the use of dyed materials.

(*c*) By overlaying the weft and warp with thin strips of pretty materials before weaving or by wrapping strips about them in various ways.

(*d*) By embroidering on the texture during the process of manufacture, called false embroidery.

(*e*) By covering the texture with plaiting, called imbrication.

(*f*) By adding feathers, shells, beads, and other ornamental objects.

In the making of designs on basketry, dyeing, overlaying, false embroidery, and imbrication are merely artificial methods of repeating and heightening the decorative effects already shown to be possible through use of materials in their native colors. No new designs are added, symbolical or otherwise. The effect of new forms in elementary technic has already been mentioned. But the artist obtains an immense advantage in the number of colors as well as the richness of shades and harmonies. After all, excepting in California, there are only a few colors in tough fibers to select from in any area. If it were not for pretty grasses which have brilliancy of color, but little tenacity, and the bright dyes in mineral and vegetal substances which have no value as textiles, the æsthetic power of basketry would be greatly curtailed. There are two or three small linguistic families of Indians in California that seem to have gathered unto themselves every kind of basket decoration. As in the island of Crete the culture of the ancient peoples about the eastern Mediterranean seem to have assembled, so in the Pomo and Mariposan tribes of Indians the composite art reached its climax of decoration. Is it not marvelous that here hundreds of years ago, perhaps, broke out the first basketry epidemic; not as now resulting in a fever to own them merely, but manifesting itself in a passion for making them. In the chapter on uses it will be seen that this passion was intimately related to the most sacred feelings that dwelt in the soul of the maker, namely, those associated with the spirit world. It is also true that the natural materials for other forms of art expression were lacking or not courted.

(*a*) *In natural materials.*—Color in basketry is effected, first, by the materials from which the structure is made up. In the Aleutian Islands the ware is in the color of the wild grass stalks, unripe and ripe; farther south the spruce root decides the shade, and in British Columbia cedar root and bast and bark give a brown or white appearance to the ware. In eastern Canada ash splints are white and brown; so are the baskets made therefrom, but the cane of the Southern States has a glossy yellow-green surface, and that predominates in Cherokee and Choctaw ware.

Among the bewildering varieties of baskets between British Columbia and Mexico the foundation colors will be decided by that of the Indian hemp, spruce and cedar root, bulrushes, cattail stems, shoots of willow and rhus, roots of sedges and agave, roots of yucca, and so on.

In this connection it must not be overlooked that these same materials are not lacking in responsiveness to the severest æsthetic demands of the artist. The Abenaki woman knows that last year's growth of black ash is almost as white as snow, while the rings of growth farther in are brown. She therefore makes warp of one and weft of the other, or bands of them alternately, much to the embellishment of the surface. The commonest fishwoman on the coast of British Columbia will show you that cedar root has three colors—that of the woody portion, the brown of the outer bark, and the newest wood nearest to the bark. She also knows how to overlay with grasses. The California cercis, or red bud, has a pretty reddish-brown bark, but the wood inside is pure white. Remarkable suggestiveness to a wide-awake mind exists in the yucca leaf of the Southwest, which may be used in basketry, whole or split. The outside is mottled green in a number of shades, while the inside is white. The leaf of the yucca (*Yucca arborescens*) is green, the root a reddish brown.

Holmes calls attention to the possibilities of æsthetic effects in a single color shown in a workbasket from the ancient cemetery of Ancon, Peru, produced through variety in the management of diagonal weaving. There will be found on all these workbaskets (1) ordinary diagonal weaving, over and under two or three or more; (2) bands of greater or less width formed by laying a piece of wood or cane between warp and weft and then continuing the weaving on the other side; (3) the forming of hinges and ridges by twining in each weft element about two or three warps before continuing the weaving. The herringbone effects are produced by leaving in front alternately warp and weft in the padded bands. If the number of rows of common diagonal weaving is even, a herringbone effect is seen; if odd, the checks in the two rows will be parallel. In Mexico and Central America the valuable yuccas give color to all textiles, as do the palm leaves in South America. (See figs. 207–209.)

It is said that the Japanese in sawing up logs will keep the planks bound together until the workman is ready to use them, and when the carpenter places them in a ceiling or a piece of furniture he is careful to have the ends abut on each other as they were together in nature. The grain, in such case, fits and produces odd but pleasing forms. In the same way the basket maker, by showing discretion and taste with roots or stems of different shades, succeeds in producing cloud effects upon the basket or mat. So nature comes in to the assistance of the Indian woman in her elementary steps. She does not start out with the design in her mind which she will produce in color, but by using the colored elements she is able to get her effect with less forethought. Indeed, it can be seen that in such a way the earliest thoughts of beauty might have been awakened.

Plate 62 shows two coiled Mission baskets in the collection of G. Wharton James; the upper one is 10 inches and the lower one 11¾ inches in diameter. They are made of rush, but the interesting feature for which they are introduced here is the design—the upper figure might be called the keystone pattern, the body of the bowl having two zones of patterns in brown and black material, each one made up of wedge-shaped figures, narrow on the inside and widening outward. These patterns are in four parts, each one surmounted by a middle piece extending two rows beyond the next pair and each pair of the series ending two rows nearer to the center. They are of equal width. A narrow wedge separates the four groups. Between the zones is a band of white preserving the outline of the border. The lower figure is a five-pointed star, the border of the segments being curved as in the orange-peel pattern. The central figure might be called a sun design, which, though it be modern, shows the adaptability of the Indian mind to invasion by suggestion.

A second step in color resources, without going away from the natural and necessary structural elements, is in the use of different materials. Very few areas in the Western Hemisphere are so poor in resources as to have only one good basketry plant. On the Great Lakes ash, hemp, and sweet grass are white, brown, and green; in the Southwest rhus is white and martynia is black; in California willow is woody white; cercis is red outside and snow-white inside, and at least one sedge has black root, and the yucca a red one. Most dainty effects are secured in coiled basketry by sewing with strips from quills of flickers and other highly colored birds. Not to pursue the statement too far, it is only in Alaska and the Straits of Magellan that the body of our textile does not contain varied material.

The moment a savage woman has in hand these variegated substances her fancy is emancipated. Warp may be of one plant and weft of another, either in plain checker or in twilled weaving. Wickerwork is not entirely irresponsive to the opportunity. In twined weaving the two strands of the weft may differ in color, so that the result will be the mottled line. If the warp stems be odd in number, then on the next round the colors on vertical lines will not match. With these simple resources the basket-maker may play an unlimited number of melodies. An excellent example of lines in simple and two-color effects from southeastern Alaska is shown in colored plate 67.

But the ambitious artist is not satisfied with flecked lines and mottled surfaces, and broad bands in one color. Her bands are divided into rectangles, triangles, and rhomboidal elements. The zones of element are widened and the geometric patterns composing them are multiplied and variegated. Those who have large collections may have noticed how the several styles of technic behave in this regard. Checkerwork is little restrained, so also are wicker and twilled ornamentation; but in twined and coiled ware the case is entirely different. Plain twine and the Pomo tee work venture little beyond the banded ornament. The same is true of most coil types; but the twilled or diagonal-twined work and the three-rod coil leap over the parallels and spread themselves out in bewildering cycloids of colored patterns, or, keeping to the angular elements, the weaver covers a large surface with fretwork in endless variety. All of this is wrought into the structure of the basket in the substantial everyday material, which possess tenacity and color as well. Quite a number of tribes in the southwestern United States use no superadded material or dyes whatever, and yet the tribes of the Piman family excel all others in the endless variety of fretwork on their basketry produced with splints in wood color and the undyed splints from the pod of the cat's claw, or *Martynia louisiana*. (See Plate 63.)

(*b*) *By dyeing.*—The colors of natural textile materials were still further diversified with dyes and paints, the latter either stamped, stenciled, or applied freehand. At the present time the cheap and obtrusive dyes and paints of the trades supplant the aboriginal and more attractive substances. The latter have also become more difficult to procure as civilization has preempted the ground.

The artificial coloration of basketry material was known to the American savages in pre-Columbian times. For mineral dyes they use earth colors, burying the splints in different soils, where they acquired permanent shades. Vegetable dyes were known from Alaska southward everywhere. The substances used were such as have the power of directly fixing themselves within the texture of the basket material. It is true and also interesting to note that certain of the processes of the Indians in dyeing their basketry materials were, all unconsciously to them, foreshadowings of the later and more complicated processes in which a mordant is employed to fix the dyestuff in the materials. The Indian had no knowledge of the effects produced. They discovered the fact, but their theories would lead into dreamy myths in which the personeity of the dyestuff would be the prominent characteristic.

Plate 64 shows twilled basket No. 76778, U.S.N.M., from the New Orleans Centennial Commission. It is a basket of the Chetimacha Indians of Louisiana made in split cane in the natural color and dyed. The union of textile effects and the three colors—orange, black, and straw color—are most pleasing, the motive being ellipsis and rhombs made by the use of small squares and rectangles. The upper portion of the figure also shows how a diaper effect may be produced on the surface by the lights and shades of the uncolored material.

It is useless to tarry about the eastern basket makers in search of native dyes. There is no doubt of their having possessed them. The porcupine-quill workers about the Great Lakes and all the way to the Arctic circle are still adepts in the art. In the National Museum are little wallets of bladder from Anderson River, Canada, each one filled with porcupine quills dyed in a separate color.

The basket weavers of Yakutat Bay, in southeastern Alaska, color their splints of spruce root from which they weave their twined basketry with dye from the willow. They scrape the roots of willow and make a decoction in a wooden tub in which they soak the spruce-root splints. Their neighbors of the same linguistic family had a more extensive laboratory in color. For more than a hundred years they were in contact with the Russians and from them obtained good dye-stuffs and knowledge of processes. Many an old piece of their basket ware, although it has stood hard use in all the years and in spite of all, has grown more beautiful with age.

Plate 65 shows two covered baskets of the Tlinkit Indians in twined work which are inserted here for the purpose of exhibiting the influence of modern traffic. Cæsar in his Commentaries speaks of the Belgians as being the most manly of all the Gallic tribes, because merchants less frequently went among them and sold them the things that tended toward effeminating their minds. The Mercatores have also been among the tribes of the Northwest. On the right-hand basket even the bands that would show some little survival of the ancient wood color have been dyed, while the red, yellow, black, and white shades are in aniline. The form of these baskets is also borrowed from civilization, and the handles in braided ware are not aboriginal. Cat. Nos. 168267, 168268.

The wood of the alder, when freshly cut, says Swan,[a] is soft and white and easily worked, but a short exposure to the air hardens and turns it to a red color. The bark chewed and spit into a dish forms a bright-red dye pigment of a permanent color, which is used for dyeing

---

[a] The Indians of Cape Flattery, Washington, 1870, p. 43.

cedar bark or grass.   Governor Dagget, writing of the Indian women
on the Hupa reservation in northwestern California, uses almost precisely the same language with reference to making a dye pot of their
mouths.   The processes of weaving there are in twined work and suggest connection with the Washington state tribes.

The Navaho Indians, according to Washington Matthews, employ
native dyes of yellow, reddish, and black.   In their blankets they have
also wool of three different natural colors, white, rusty black, and gray.
The black dye is made from the twigs and leaves of aromatic sumac
(*Rhus trilobata*).   They put into a pot of water leaves and branches of
the sumac.   The water is allowed to boil five or six hours.   Ocher is
reduced to a fine powder and slowly roasted over a fire until it assumes a
light-brown color.   It is then combined with an equal quantity of Piñon
gum (*Pinus edulis*), and again the mixture is placed upon the fire and
stirred.   The gum melts and the mass assumes a mushy consistency.   As
the roasting progresses the mass is reduced to a fine black powder.
When it has cooled it is thrown into the decoction of sumac, with which
it forms a rich, blue-black fluid.   This is essentially an ink, the tannic
acid of the sumac combining with the iron of the ferric oxide in the
roasted ocher.   The whole is enriched by the carbon of the calcined
gum.

Reddish dye is made from the bark of the *Alnus tenuifolia* and
the bark and root of *Cercocarpus parvifolius*, the mordant being fine
juniper ashes.   These dyes are now applied by the Navaho.   The
so-called Navaho blankets are in three colors.

For yellow the flowering tops of *Chrysothamnus graveolens* are boiled
about six hours, until a decoction of deep yellow is produced.   The
dyer then heats over the fire some native alunogen (native alum)
until it is reduced to a pasty consistency.   This she adds to the
decoction and puts the whole in the dye to boil.   From time to time
a portion is inspected until it is seen to have assumed the proper
color.   The tint produced is nearly lemon yellow.

Julian Scott makes the statement that the Coconinos or Havasupais
in northwestern Arizona use only black in the ornamentation of their
basketry, while the Apaches and Wallapais use black and red also.

(c) *By overlaying.*—This process of ornamentation consists in laying a strip of pretty grass, dyed or in the natural color, on the outside of one or both the strands in woven or coiled weaving.   It is
virtually furnishing a dull-brown strip of root with a bright-colored
bark.   By this ingenious combination beauty and strength cooperate
in the result.   The weaver has it always in her power to twist the
strand so as to hide this bark side or bring it into view.   The Hupa
Indians especially, but many other tribes in northern California and
northward, do the weft of their beautiful twined weaving in somber
materials.   The men are most adept in lining the backs of their bows

with sinew shredded and mixed in glue. In a similar way, as though
one had suggested the other, they line the back of the weft strands
with bright straw. It is not glued, since the weaving would hold it
in place. When the Hupa reveals the straw side of the strand at every
half turn, she covers the surface of her basket with straw color which
turns to gold with age. The overlaying of only one of the two weft
strands gives a freckled effect on the surface. In some of the tribes
the pattern does not show on the inside.

This will be a good place in which to mention a kind of overlaying
common in countries where the cane abounds. The outside of the
stem is glossy and may be dyed. The inside is spongy and unat-
tractive. By laying two strips together, so that the smooth surface
may be outward, there would be really a double fabric with two
glossy surfaces. The southern Indians also frequently passed only
one of the pair of splints over or under weaving.

Fig. 101 shows a style of wrapping done in Mexico City.[a] The illustration is from a hand wallet.
The body of the checker
weaving is in hard, flattened
straws of varying shades.
Each warp straw is wrapped
with two fillets of thin material in darker color so as to
leave small squares on the surface set diagonally. When
the plain weft is run among
the warp elements, the surface of the fabric is covered
with larger and smaller
squares in white set in tri-

FIG. 101.
WRAPPING WEFT FILLETS WITH DARKER ONES.
After W. H. Holmes.

angles of darker material. The white squares run diagonally across
the surface. There are endless variations produced by this wrapping
added to the body of the fabric.

This overlaying must not be confounded with the many tricks which
cunning women play with the strands of the regular twined weaving,
which are frequently of brilliant straws of squaw grass and other
pretty materials. (See Plates 146, 164, 170, 177 and 178.)

Plate 66 represents twined basketry of the Klamath River Indians
of various types, and is here introduced for the purpose of showing
how the tough weaving material may be overlaid with basketry and
other colored filaments so as to conceal the foundation both outside
and inside. It has been shown in the chapter on processes, however,
that the exposure of the overlaying material need not occur on the

[a] W. H. Holmes, Sixth Annual Report of the Bureau of Ethnology, 1888, p. 227, fig. 330.

inside. These specimens are Cat. Nos. 204258, collected by Mrs. Carolyn G. Benjamin; and Nos. 19286 and 19282, collected by Livingston Stone.

Akin to the "beading," so common in the Fraser River coiled basketry to be mentioned, is an ornamental effect produced in twined work by the onlaying of colored straws in regular geometrical designs and catching the angle under the strand of the weft. Holmes [a] figures an example of this from the Klamath Indians in northwestern California, a rare process in North American Indian basketry. (See fig. 102.) It reminds one of the stamps for printing tapa cloth used in the Polynesian area.

Beading is the insertion of narrow strips of pretty grass or other material into the sewing of coiled baskets, passing it under one, over the next, and so on. Plain beading produces a broken line of dark and light color alternating, and shifts the direction of the elemental

FIG. 102.
BEADING ON TWINED WORK.
Klamath Indians.
After W. H. Holmes.

figure from vertical to horizontal. If several rows are made, figures are produced by the process of twilled weaving. The basket maker may pass her filament over and under as many stitches as she chooses; she may make the elements of any row immediately over those of the preceding row, or they may alternate. The Fraser River Salish are adept in this on many of their imbricated baskets. Especially on the ware whose coils have flat foundations is beading effective. (See fig. 103.)

(d) *False embroidery.*—This is a method of ornamentation in which the outer surface of a twined basket is covered wholly or in part with designs, but they do not show on the inside. The Tlinkits excel in this, calling it uh tah yark tu twage (outside lifted up and put around). It has the appearance of being sewed on after the weaving is done. The process is described on the next page, and many figures in this paper show examples of it. Plates 71 and 74, in color, demonstrate more plainly how effective false embroidery may be made. The body of all Tlinkit and Haida ware is in dull-brown shade of spruce root. The saving feature which lends itself cheerfully to ornamentation is the pliability and even fiber of the young roots. Nothing can be more pleasing to the eye than a fine old Haida hat, its surface covered with intricate patterns. The Tlinkit false embroidery in subdued colors, yellow, red, and black, contrasts harmoniously with the cinnamon-

---

[a] Sixth Annual Report Bureau of Ethnology, p. 227, fig. 331.

brown spruce root. Also the restful manner in which this work changes the slope of the elements in the weaving should not be overlooked. The twined weaving is made up of a series of little mosaic elements lying down one upon another like a row of bricks that have

FIG. 103.
BEADING ON COILED WORK.
Clallam Indians, Washington.
Cat. No. 23512, U.S.N.M. Collected by J. G. Swan.

fallen. The incline of the stitches in false embroidery is in the opposite direction. In Plate 67 charming effects are produced by alternating the plain weaving and the embroidery. (Emmons.)

The twined false embroidery might be classed technically with three strand twined weaving. (See figs. 29, 31, and 104.) The warp is in normal position. The weaver selects three strands for weft, two of spruce root and one of brightly colored grass. They all have their places in the weaving, but the third, or decorative element, instead of taking its turn to pass behind the warp, remains on the outside and makes a wrap about the strand that happens to be there. The

FIG. 104.
OVERLAID TWINED WEAVING.

wrapping may pass, also, over two by skipping every alternate twist of the warp. The Thompson Indians vary the mode of wrapping by passing a strip of corn husk or other soft material entirely around the twining each time, showing the figure on the inside.

(e) *Imbrication.*—This term, derived from the Latin imbrex, a tile, is applied to a style of decoration used in Washington and British Columbia by the Klikitat and many of the Salish tribes, and most closely allied in technic with the feather work on basketry farther south. Leaves of *Xerophyllum tenax*, strips of wild cherry bark or of the inner bark of the cedar, in natural color or dyed black, are laid over the sewing of the coiled work. The juice of the Oregon grape is used to produce a bright yellow dye. The separate elements of the imbrication are squares or rectangles, varying in size with the fineness of the workmanship. But the mosaic effect is most striking, and designs of intricate character are successfully expressed in it. The Salish tribes about the Fraser mouth have learned to widen the coils by using thin strips of wood, often half an inch wide, as foundation of the coil. This increases the size of the imbrications and of the patterns. (See page 254 and Plate 68, also Plates 11, 43, 45, and 55.)

Ornamentation in Thompson River basketry is produced by imbrication and by beading (for detail drawing see figs. 52 and 53 and Plate 102). Imbrication is done by bringing the piece of grass over the outside of the last stitch and forward, then doubling it back and catching the double end with the next stitch. The outsides of Klikitat, Cowlitz, and Thompson baskets are completely covered in this manner, so that the whipped cedar splints can only be seen from the inside. Lillooet baskets have the lower part of the body plain, while the Chilcotin baskets have a separate band in the middle of the body. The grass used is that called Nho'itlexin. It is long, very smooth, and of a glossy yellow-white color (*Xerophyllum tenax*). To make it whiter diatomaceous earth is sometimes spread over it and it is then beaten with a flat stick on a mat or skin. The grass is seldom dyed, as the colors are said to fade soon. (Teit.)

(f) *Feather-work, beads, etc.*—The California baskets adorned with feathers are called jewels. They no longer serve vulgar uses. The beautiful productions covered with styles of ornamentation before described have often the marks of fire, the stain of berries, the smell of fish about them, proclaiming that they were not above combining the beautiful with the useful. The feather baskets sacrifice use to beauty.

The tribes of eastern America have not employed feathers in basket work in recent times. The nearest approach to it is the porcupine-quill work of the Indians in Canada and the United States. The quills are dyed and set on the surface of birch baskets by thrusting the sharp ends into the bark. The old historians tell of gorgeous feather robes made doubtless in the Indian fashion of twined weaving, which is akin to basketry. The Eskimo, Aleut, Haida, and Tlinkit do not ornament baskets with feathers, but they do apply in dainty fashion to some of them worsted, hair, and furs. Neither do the tribes of the Fraser-

Columbia area. It is the California tribes chiefly that have developed the art, of which they practice two styles. In the one tiny bits of colored feather are sewed by their shafts to coiled basketry just to give a hazy effect to the surface. Plate 70 is an excellent example of this. It will be observed that the elaborate pattern in black is not obscured in the least by the feather. In the other process the feathers are laid one upon another so thickly that the surface of the basket is hidden. The addition of so much extraneous matter thickens the foundation and coarsens the work. As previously remarked the best examples of coiled sewing are not to be found in the feathered baskets.

Plate 69 is a colored illustration of a feathered basket of the Pomo Indians from Sonoma County, California, in the collection of C. P. Wilcomb. It is examples such as these that technically are called jewels. The foundation is a three-rod coil, the sewing is with split sedge root (*Carex barbaræ*), and the stems of the feathers are caught under the stitches. The feathers on this rare specimen are as follows:

Red—Woodpecker (*Melanerpes formicivorus*).
Green—Mallard duck (*Anas boschas*).
Orange—Oriole (*Icterus bullockii*).
Yellow—Meadow lark (*Sturnella neglecta*).
Black—Quail (*Lophortyx californicus*).
White wampum (Kaya)—Disks of *Saxidomus nuttallii*.
Red wampum (po)—Disks of *magnetite*.
Pendants of abalone, *Haliotis* sp.
Long diameter—9 inches.
Colored plate kindly furnished by C. P. Wilcomb.

Plate 70 is a feathered jewel basket of the Upper Lakes, who are Pomo Indians, in Lake County, California. The stitches are of the coiled work over three rods and interlocked beneath. The yellow feathers are from the breast of Jushil, the meadow lark (*Sturnella neglecta*); the red ones are the throat and scalp feathers of Katatch, the woodpecker (*Melanerpes formicivorus*); and the black feathers at the top are from the crest of Chikaka, the quail (*Lophortyx californicus*). In recent forms pretty feathers of the peacock and other showy birds gotten in trade are used. The perforated disks are money from the clam shell, Kaya (*Saxidomus nuttallii*); and the iridescent pendants are cut from Tem, or the haliotis shell, which is quite abundant on the Pacific coast.

The following list of plants used in coloring have been identified by Frederick V. Coville, Botanist of the Department of Agriculture:

Alnus rhombifolia—White alder.
Amaranthus palmeri—Amaranth.
Berberis nervosa—Oregon grape.
Carthamus tinctorius—False saffron.

Covillea tridentata—Creosote bush.
Delphinium scaposum—Larkspur.
Dondia suffrutescens—Sea blite.
Evernia vulpina—Wolf moss.
Helianthus petiolaris—Sunflower.
Parosela emoryi—Parosela.
Quercus lobata—California white oak.
Rhus diversiloba—Poison oak.
Sambucus mexicana—Elder.
Thelesperma gracile—Thelesperma.
Vaccinium membranaceum—Blueberry.

V. SYMBOLISM

All the high and low
Of my wild life in these wild stems I snare;
The jagged lightning and the star I show;
The spider and the trailing snake are there.
—ANNA BALL.

All industry leads to fine art and all savage arts begin at the foot of the ladder and end " beyond the bourne of sunset." In this apotheosis, basketry is the rival of stone working, wood carving, skin dressing, and pottery. The merely useful basket has some beauty, but the exalted specimen of handiwork is the acme of intelligent discrimination in the materials as well as of hand skill and taste, and leads up to the choicest textile productions. Its maker must be botanist, colorist, weaver, designer, and poet, all in one. But could the windows of her mind be thrown open wide there would be seen, in addition to all these, the mystic love of her tribe alive and active. In the old days of unsophisticated savagery, no doubt, there was everywhere in America the overseeing and guiding presence of the mythic in the practical. Its relics are still to be found on fragments of pottery especially, and there is no reason to doubt that it reigned in other departments of activity. The old-time basket makers were under its spell everywhere. It would be an interesting study, but it can not be pursued here, to find out how far the various peoples of Europe in settling down upon the lands of the savages had by their ethnic traits and beliefs gradually eliminated or modified those of the aborigines in the matter of symbolism.

Besides the unmodified artistic motives in the designs on basketry, there still survives in the Pacific coast area a symbolism more or less connected with Indian cosmogony. The maker is a sorcerer. In such tribes as the Hopi this idealism in design is still alive and active. Among the Algonkin Indians of the Atlantic States the thought seems to have escaped entirely from the design, and the Indian woman making her baskets at the seaside resort, at the springs, or at Niagara

Falls has no more idea of putting a thought into the colors and patterns which she weaves than though such a thing never existed. The designs are changed to suit the whims of the buyers. Idealism is buried in commercialism. Tracing the motive around the Arctic region there still is found no pattern in basketry until southern Alaska is reached. In the birch-bark ware of middle Alaska and Canada, and in the rawhide-parfleche receptacles of the Sioux and other Plains tribes, the mythical conception is reawakened. The Ojibwa about the Great Lakes preserve all sorts of ancient patterns in porcupine-quill work on birch bark, while the Sioux, the Arapahos, and Kiowas paint upon their parfleche cases the totemic symbolism of their tribes.[a] It is well to keep in mind these other symbolic representations in speaking of basketry, since they raise questions of origins and relationships. Boas is inclined to refer the designs on Salishan basketry to the tribes inland across the Cascade Mountains.

The Haida Indians of Queen Charlotte Archipelago make wailets and hats of spruce root, now and then weaving in a band of black, but the ware is extremely plain. Its decoration depends upon the various types of weaving employed and painted symbols. But the Tlinkits on the mainland and islands of southeastern Alaska, on the other hand, cover the surface of their baskets, made precisely similar to those of the Haidas, with symbolism connected with their daily life. It has been thought that anciently the Tlinkits made baskets like the Haida, without colored ornaments, and that the designs on the baskets have no mythological significance. The Chilcats, however, who are akin to the Tlinkits and live on the mainland, cover the surface of their fringed robes with their totemic symbolism in most subtle fashion. The technical process on these blankets is precisely the same as that on the baskets, only the blankets are made in soft wool while the baskets are in hard material. Coming farther southward the land of the imbricated basket is reached. The sybolism on this ware has been worked out by Livingston Farrand.[b] Further on these designs will be taken up with greater detail. As the inscriptions on Assyrian slabs have preserved the thoughts and lore of Mesopotamia and the hieroglyphics of Egypt held secure for millenniums the story of the oldest of empires, so in a much humbler fashion the myths and stories of these Indians have been in the olden times symbolized on their basketry. There is no Rosetta stone nor alphabet of design for their decipherment, all the more diligent must the present seeker be to save the evanescent records. The basket is frequently made for no other end than to record the legend.

---

[a] A. L. Kroeber, The Arapaho, Bulletin of the American Museum of Natural History, XVII, 1902, pp. 1–150.

[b] Basketry Designs of the Salish Indians, Memoirs of the American Museum of Natural History, II, 1900, Pt. 5, pp. 393–399.

The Salish tribes of Washington and Oregon, and those of California, Arizona, and New Mexico, all place some kind of designs on their basketry.   Whether it has a symbolical significance or not has to be determined in each case by inquiry.   Looking at the whole field as revealed in collections and publications, the following classes of objects and phenomena sought to be represented seem to be complete:

1. Natural phenomena, such as lightning, sunrise, clouds, and sky.
2. Natural features of objects, such as mountains, lakes, shores, and rivers.
3. Plant phenomena, including splints of the plant used to make the design.
4. Animals and parts of animals.   There is no end to this species of design, from the attempt to represent the entire animal alive and in motion, to the few stitches which stand for a part of the creature, perhaps a wing, a fin, an eye, or a tooth, to show what the animal might be.
5. Human beings, either full or in part.
6. Devices used by the Indians in their occupations, arrowheads especially.
7. Ideas connected with the Indian thought and life; for example, such as the opening in a Navaho basket.
8. Mythical personages connected with sorcery and witchcraft.
9. Their gods and heavenly beings.

In thinking of symbolism the sign or form on the basket and the thing signified must be kept separate in the mind.   The sign may be at the beginning pictorial and pass down through changes and abbreviations to a mere outline that has no suggestion in it, or a simple geometric figure common in the technic may become a mythic being, by making here and there a significant addition through suggestion.

When it is remembered that the Indian represents in a general way the childhood of the race, one has but to revert to that period of life to recall how a spot of ink or a meaningless form was transformed into a picture of something real or ideal.   A fundamental geometric figure on basketry may in similar fashion by the addition of a line or two become almost any design, the visible home of any symbol.

In this paper, devoted more particularly to the technical side of basketry, the manner of realizing the symbol is still important.   However, it is not so much sought to teach that a certain design represents a butterfly as to see how the woman put the form into the texture of her basket.

The sculptor, the painter, the carver, and the potter are more realistic than the basket maker, since the making of portraiture and pictures are easily within their reach.   Yet nothing is more common among them all than abbreviation and synecdoche.   Not only are they under the spell of symbolism, but the symbol is curtailed to the lowest terms.   A fin stands for a whale, incisor teeth for a beaver, the beak for a bird, and often the image is completely obliterated in the symbol.   Now the basket maker is still more handicapped by her technical limitations and driven to symbolism if she did not largely invent it.   For pictorial effects on the surface, the maker is hampered by the limitations of weaving and sewing. It will be found, therefore, that her temptations are to pass more quickly to the symbolic stage of representation. It is well to remember also that just as on the baskets themselves the symbolism, starting with pictures, has in some tribes been reduced to its lowest terms, so in the basket maker's mouth the legends have become faded into concrete words and then into meaningless terms, yet the thought is there. Of a certain form on a basket plaque the Hopi woman would say it is the bird that carries messages to the rain god; another tribe would call it a bird; a third name it wings, and finally it becomes an empty geometric design. Again, the student himself passes through a process of initiations as the subject is exploited.

It is said that Pompey declared, when he had drawn aside the veil of the Holy of Holies, at Jerusalem, "The Jews worship nothing." With some such feeling the collector of baskets begins his quest. The first impression is that no set patterns were in the maker's mind. She has a sense of the beautiful and loves to give her fancy free rein. Indeed, the reticent and suspicious basket maker helps the delusion. A little later the discovery is made that the patterns stand for things, but still for general notions. It is only after long familiarity and systematic converse with old basket makers that the veteran collector learns that the belief that these patterns stand for mountains, lakes, rivers, men and women, deer or other mammals, flying birds or bird tracks, fishes, insects, flowers, plants, heavenly bodies, or articles of use and worship merely is but a fraction of the truth. They are concrete, standing not for all or any, but for one, and underneath them is charming folklore. Mrs. Shackleford tells of a certain intricate pattern on a Washington basket that it represents ripples, but on patient inquiry it was found to mean the subtle movements in the under waters of a certain lake upon a special occasion. To appreciate symbolism fully one must know the sign, hear the story, and then study the skies, the landscape, and the social environment.

To attempt to discover an alphabet in this primitive art would be useless, for each tribe adapts old and new standard forms to its own concept myths. The artists alone, in every case, can interpret them. This existence of concrete stories in art form is not confined to basketry. Dr. Boas is authority for saying that the intricate totem post and composite painting of the North Pacific coast can be interpreted only by the carver. The attempt to find a clue to the mystery of their composition is hopeless, for none exists. As soon as the perfection of monotony or uniformity has been reached in the technic to form the basis of real art, there ensues a variety no less thorough and diversified in the ornamentation for symbolizing the same idea. The rule in the Indian woman's mind seems to be reduced to a formula like this: "The minimum of variety in the technic, the maximum of variety in the symbolic." Or, in other phrase, variety of symbolic expression in the unity of the real art. One looks carefully at a set of drawings like those of Emmons, Farrand, Fewkes, or Dixon, and turns to a familiar collection to find the same symbols. They are not there; or, rather, they are hiding there. It is a question whether there be two baskets alike in design among any tribe. This is the real charm of savage hand work as compared with the rather dull uniformity of machine products. All the tribes of the West that have preserved their symbolisms have at the same time made the most of their liberty to modify the original.

The subject of symbolism may be studied from several points of view, the technic, the elaborative or historic, and the ethnic. Beginning with the technic as the easiest, symbolism is wrought in checker, twill, wicker, twine, and coil. Looking at a coarse piece of matting made up of monotonous squares, it is not easy to see how the story of creation or tribal preservation could be wrought into them. But with finer elements and the introduction of color, a part of the difficulty vanishes. In point of fact, however, there is little evidence that sentiment was wrought into checker, or even into twilled weaving. There is no essential difficulty in the way. Mosaic in stone or other hard material is made up of little blocks, chiefly squares, and both the twined and the coiled basketry surfaces contain innumerable designs made up in small squares in black or other color.

Symbolism may be studied in its elaboration or historic development. The history of a symbol on basketry is the same as that of a design on pottery or a painting on hide. Perhaps, since the technical demands are more exacting, the progressive appearance of the ideal is more rapid and the hiding of the original more complete. A moment's thought makes it clear that one is dealing simply with a universal law of mental development. The basketry of any one tribe will show what is meant. On a single Hopi plaque it is not rare to see side by side the complete figure of a bird or butterfly with outspread wings and near by an abbreviated cross which means the same thing. (See Plate 47.)

Another specimen constructed by the same hands will have the cross but not the birds. By and by enough examples are brought into comparison to show the process of fading out through which the realistic becomes only a skeleton. There is a celebrated Japanese painting showing seven stages in the life of a beautiful girl. As she passes into womanhood, through all its years, behind the real face the pretty child is seen, and even the skull that lies among the flowers shows to the beholder, after a moment's gaze, the lovely girlish face. In the last relic of symbol on basketry to the trained eye of mythology the same transition takes place. The comparison of an ordinary lot of California basketry, their zigzag lines, arrowheads, mountains, and crossing paths, with such treasures as are in the Merriam collection, each gathered from the hand of the maker, together with the song of the soul whose melody is written there also, makes plain what is here set forth.

Professor Farrand calls attention wisely to the fact that in the reduction of symbols to their lowest terms very dissimilar forms have converged until the same figure does duty for many objects, the technical exigency or strain predominating. This has led to differences of opinion among native connoisseurs and frequently confusion to the ethnologist. The same observation would be true in working the other way. It is only in most recent times that psychologists have appreciated the power of suggestion in helping one to determined action.

Recently a package of beautifully marked shells were sent to the National Museum as the probable origin of designs in savage art. Nothing could be farther from the truth. Form does not come to the savage artist's mind in that way. Whether the symbol arise by contraction or expansion, the artist is the creator of new forms, working always within the school of her materials and tools.

Wicker basketry in its worst state is positively ugly. In the eastern part of North America no attempt is made to put a legend upon it, but in New Mexico and Arizona it is found in two forms side by side, one as plain as undressed stems can be made and the other at the topmost point of pictorial representation. In Oraibi, the most western of the Hopi (Moki) towns, are made the pretty little wicker plaques called Katchinas. The finding of fragments of these in ancient ruins by Dr. Fewkes is good proof that they have long been made by the Hopi. Farther on, the designs themselves will be examined. They are mentioned here rather to show that where there is a will with the human species, of whatever color, there is a way. Examples of Katchinas are shown in Plates 85 and 93. The Hopi wicker plaques are made up of short stems of *Chrysothamnus* that have been previously smoothed and dyed in as many colors as are needed. The work resembles closely that in porcupine quills. Figures do not show effectively on the back, for the reason that a single stem often passes over only one warp element. Symbols of complex pattern are also frequently finished out with the brush. In many of the intricate symbols on the Katchinas the narrow limitations of the material and the curve of texture that can go in one direction only put the artist to her wits' end for conventionalisms. She does not mind, but goes ahead. True, a rainbow must be upside down, the sky goddess must have rectangular eyes and mouth. There is no perspective, the round must be flat, and even those features that are out of sight must be brought to view. Never mind, the ideal wins and the plaque is finished.

With twined work the case is different. All its varieties are capable in themselves of expressing ideas even in one color, but as soon as overlaying, embroidery, and the use of different hues are added there is practically no end to the possibilities. In this connection the reader may be reminded again that designs must not be confounded with symbols.   The former are apparent and constant and extremely limited, the latter ideal and as varied as an Indian woman's fancy.   But in the chapter on ornamentation it was seen how varied in different hands and materials twined patterns might be made.   Twined ware is, if anything, at the start the coarsest of all, for what could be ruder than the wattling of a fish weir or the wall of a granary?   Taking the geographic areas in turn, it is not until southeastern Alaska is reached that an attempt to tell a story in twined decoration occurs.   Even there the symbol exists more in the false embroidery on the surface than in the twined work.   In point of fact, however, whether studied with Emmons for southeastern Alaska; with Farrand on Salish ware; or with Dixon in northern California tribes, it is not in twined work that the most exalted and idealized symbolism has been wrought.

Coiled ware also has such a variety of technical treatment, with the whole color scheme of nature to select from, that in practice there is no limit to the form and combination of designs or of symbolism.   In these the weaver secretes her thoughts.   You must ask her what they mean.   Rarely is one of her symbols widespread.   In the next tribe the sign will stand for quite something else.   It is well to observe here that a vast deal of coiled basketry has no symbol or design on it whatever.

Ethnic symbolism.—Recurring to the six ethnic areas which for convenience have been adopted in this publication, basketry has lost all trace of symbolism among the Indians of eastern North America.   It can not be for a moment supposed that they have none, for with Algonquian, Siouan, Kiowan, the substitutes for basketry, rawhide receptacles, as well as moccasins, cradles, and objects in three dimensions, are covered with idealism in painting and embroidery.

To understand the richness of this survival of aboriginal symbolism the student will receive his principal aid at hand in the researches of A. L. Kroeber among the Arapaho.[a]   Four hundred and fifty-eight distinct symbols are given in figures covering Indian ideas from common objects to spiritual beings.   All the closing pages of the above-named paper (pp. 138–150) must be examined carefully in order to comprehend both the sign and the thing signified, the thought and the overthought, the text and the symbolic context in Arapaho embroideries, paintings, and three dimension designs.   The closing paragraph will give the gist of Dr. Kroeber's study:

The closeness of connection between this Arapaho decorative symbolism and the religious life of the Indians can not well be overestimated by a white man.   Apart from the existence of a great amount of decorative symbolism on ceremonial objects not described in this chapter, it should be borne in mind that the making of what have been called tribal ornaments is regularly accompanied by religious ceremonies;

---

[a] Symbolism of the Arapaho Indians (Bulletin of the American Museum of Natural History, XIII, 1900, pp. 69–86); Decorative Symbolism of the Arapaho (American Anthropologist N. S., III, 1901, pp. 308–336); The Arapaho (Bulletin of the American Museum of Natural History, XVIII, 1902, pp. 1–150).

that some styles of patterns found on tent ornaments and parfleches are very old and sacred, because originating from mythic beings; that a considerable number of objects are decorated according to dreams and visions; and, finally, that all symbolism, even when decorative and unconnected with any ceremony, tends to be to the Indian a matter of a serious and religious nature.

The Eskimo also and the Aleuts perpetuate no thought or myth in basketry symbols. The etchings of the former on ivory are also modern and were learned from outside teachers. It is not in these that the idea is to be sought. Not for a moment is it to be thought, however, that there is no symbolism existing. All the life is wrapped up in hunting. The long, dark winter, the return of the sun with the innumerable retinue of life in the air and in the waters gives the keynote. It is in the drama of hunting and the masks worn in dances that symbolism is embodied.

On the Pacific coast from Alaska to the peninsula of California and in the Interior Basin the tribes have been left to their own devices through the centuries, and it is here that survivals of symbolism are to be sought. They will be found in one place full of life and ancient spirituality; in another stung by civilization, they are as torpid as the spiders that are placed in their nests by the mud wasps.

The name Tlinkit applies to a number of basket-making tribes in southeastern Alaska. In their charming archipelago they have developed a unique scheme of symbolism growing out of their mode of life. This has been thoroughly studied by Lieut. G. T. Emmons, U. S. Navy, in his collections in the American Museum of Natural History, New York, and the identifications here made are on his authority.[a] They cover a wide range of meanings. Supplementary to this basket symbolism, or rather preeminent over it, are the Chilkat blankets and the endless variety of carvings in stone, horn, and wood, and the symbolic paintings on all sorts of surfaces. The following identifications are from specimens in the U. S. National Museum:

> Ars suck har ha yar ku, "Spirit voice, or shadow of a tree."
> Kah thluckt yar, "Water drops."
> Kisht, "The crossing."
> Klake da kheet see tee, "Single tying around."
> Klaok shar yar kee kee, "Head of the salmon berry cut in half."
> Ku Klate ar ku wu, "The Arctic tern's tail."
> Kuk thla ku, "Flaking of the flesh of fish."
> Shon tche kulth kah katch ul tee, "Tattooing on the back of the hand of an old person."
> Shuh tuck ou hu, "Shark's tooth."
> Shar dar yar ar kee, "Work on Shaman's hat."
> Thlul k yar nee, "The leaves of the fireweed."
> Ut tu wark ee, "An eye."
> Ut kheet see tee, "Tying around."
> Yehlh ku wu, "Raven's tail."

---

[a] Basketry of the Tlingit Indians, Memoirs of the American Museum Natural History, III, 1903, pp. 229–277.

Plate 71 shows specimens of twined wallets made of spruce roots, for carrying berries and other articles of food on the back.   The left-hand figure in this plate is Catalogue No. 20704 in the National Museum and was collected by James G. Swan, at Sitka, Alaska.   It is an excellent specimen of twined weaving, with what is here called false embroidery.   The figures on the surface, determined by Lieutenant Emmons, are as follows: The two wide bands contain the following ornaments: The large five-sided figures in the middle are the "Shark's tooth;" the chevron pattern covering the shark's tooth means the "Flaking of flesh of fish into narrow strips;" the small triangular figures are the "Salmon berry cut in halves," but in this arrangement also called "Water drops;" the narrow middle band is rendered "Single tying around;" below the ornamental band the cross-shaped figure represents the "Raven's tail."

The right-hand figure in this plate is also a berry basket.   The two wider bands have the same design, having a bar in the middle with its ends bifurcated, known by the Tlinkit as "The crossing."   The triangles in these bands stand for "The salmon berry cut in halves."   The middle band is "Tying around."   The vertical designs at the bottom represent "An eye" on one side, and on the other side "Shark's tooth."   The five-sided figure with a reentrant angle stands for "The Arctic tern's tail."   Catalogue No. 21560, U.S.N.M., collected by J. B. White.

The right-hand figure in Plate 72, Catalogue No. 20704A in the National Museum, collected by J. G. Swan, is a cylindrical basket in twined weaving.   The upper part of the body of this basket is divided into three bands worked in straw, natural color, and dyed red and brown.   The symbols in the upper and lower band are (1) the "Spirit voice, or the shadow of a tree," in zigzag lines; (2) vertical rows of rhombs, which indicate the eye; the middle band, made up of sinuous lines on rectangular figures is called "Tying around."   The allusion may be either to the fact that this figure constitutes an encircling band, or to the sinuous pattern itself.   On the lower part of the body the fretted pattern, with three rectangles inclosed in the bents like the bars on an epaulette, stands for "The tattooing on the back of the hand of an old person."

Plate 37 represents two small, beautiful baskets with rattles in the tops, made by the Tlinkit Indians of southeastern Alaska.   Both of them are covered over the entire surface with false embroidery in three colors.   The small patterns on the baskets portray the salmon berry and the triangular figures stand for shark's teeth.   These are fine old specimens collected in 1875 by Dr. J. B. White, U. S. Army.   Catalogue No. 21562.

Plate 73. The bottom figure is a covered basket on the Tlinkit Indians, Catalogue No. 168282, collected by Lieutenant Emmons.   The warp is crossed, and the weaving is in twined work ornamented with false embroidery. The upper band and the one across the middle of the body represent "The salmon berry cut in half," while the band of the shoulder and the one at the bottom stand for "The leaves of the fireweed."

The upper covered jar on the same plate illustrates the combination of false embroidery and the use of two colors in the material out of which the specimen is woven. This specimen is Catalogue No. 9112 U.S.N.M., and was collected in Alaska by Lieut. F. M. Ring, U. S. Army.

The Haida Indians on Queen Charlotte Islands are near to the Tlinkit in arts, but weave no symbols into their basketry. They paint various designs on their ceremonial hats and have no end of richest symbolism on their canoes and carved in wood and slate. They also now engrave on silver and keep alive the poetry of their ancient art.

The following story, collected for Lieutenant Emmons by a friend, proves that the basket is not altogether out of touch with their world of myth:

Once upon a time there were two Haida Indian orphan girls living on Queen Charlotte Islands, British Columbia. After being punished by their stepmother for eating up a store of deer tallow they resolved to run away. They wandered about in the forest a long time and were eventually rescued by the "seek quan ni" (Black Bear tribe), one of whom married the girls. Years afterwards these girls determined to visit the scenes of their sad childhood. For their journey back from the forest to places of human habitations their good totem spirit directed them to weave two baskets apiece large enough to fit over the end of the thumb. These they were directed to fill with crumbs of various kinds of cured meats and deer tallow. As in the miracle of the five loaves and two fishes which sufficed for a multitude, the contents of these tiny baskets furnished food for the two women on their journey of many moons. Arrived at the entrance of their father's house their baskets suddenly became very large, so large, in fact, that it required the strength of many slaves to take them into the house. The women found their stepmother still alive. They offered her the various meats and tallow which they had brought from their forest home. More, and yet more food they pressed upon her until the unhappy woman died of overeating.

Professor Farrand selected happily the most versatile of all the North American families of Indians for his studies, the Salishan. Among these the Lillooet and Thompson baskets, of British Columbia, supply the flat and round types of imbricated coiled work, and the Quinaielt, on Puget Sound, the overlaid twined weaving. The Klikitat ware is not included, but a comparison of its symbols with the Salish would be profitable. The line of development in symbolism among the Salish tribes has been from the pictorial to the geometric.   Professor Farrand finds that the use of animal designs is by no means predominant.   This was seen to be true on the Tlinkits also, while the Chilcat (Tlinkit) blanket shows the dissected and distorted motives described by Boas.[a]

The list of symbols on the baskets of the lower Thompson Indians is given by Mr. James Teit.   It is made up of:

1. Arrowhead pattern (tataza, arrowhead).
2. Root pattern (múla, a variety of root).
3. Butterfly pattern (nkíkaẋeni, butterfly).
4. Star pattern (nkokucên, star).
5. Packing strap pattern (tsupîn, packing strap).
6. Zigzag pattern (skolotz, crooked).
7. Box pattern (luka, grave box).
8. Eagle pattern (haláu, eagle).

Each of these words is compounded with the suffix "aist," pattern; but the lower Thompson also have symbols for snake or snakeskin, snake or snake tracks, rattlesnake tail, grouse or bird tracks, bear foot or bear tracks, bird or geese flying, fly, beaver, deer, horse, man, hand, tooth, leaf, shells (dentalia), stone hammer, comb, necklace, net, root-digger handle, leggings, canoe, trail, stream, lake, mount, air, lightning, and the same is true of other Salishan tribes.

Plates 74 to 79, reproduce Professor Farrand's figures and the descriptions are from his monograph.[b]   These illustrations, being most of them in a difficult technical process called imbrication furnish excellent studies in mosaic pictographs.   The elements are all little squares in different colors, varying from one-eighth to one-quarter inch in dimensions.   Much charity is needed in detecting the thing in the symbol.   The shark's mouth with its horrid teeth, is rather intensified by the angularity of the design, but most of the things represented are hidden in the symbol.

Plate 74, fig. 1, shows a coiled and imbricated berry basket of the Lillooet Indians, British Columbia.   It has a pyramidal form, flat foundation in the coils, and the decoration is in two segments or bands. The designs are flies, arrowheads, and half circles (?).   The lower stripes are clusters of flies.   Height, 10½ inches; 1 inch = 7½ stitches, 4½ coils.   Compare Cat. No. 213535 U.S.N.M.

Plate 74, fig. 2, shows a twined and overlaid basket of the Quinaielt Indians, Washington.   Its design represents flounders.   Height, 5½ inches; 1 inch = 8 twists, 12 rows of weaving.

Plate 74, fig. 3, shows a coiled and imbricated basket of the Lillooet Indians, British Columbia, with structural elements the same as in

[a] The Decorative Art of the Indians of the North Pacific coast, Bulletin of the American Museum of Natural History, IX, 1897, pp. 123–176.

[b] Basketry Designs of the Salish Indians, Memoirs of the American Museum of Natural History, II, 1900, pp. 393–399.

figure 1.   Its design is a head, with mouth, teeth, and hair along the back of the head.   The stripes below are arrowheads.   Height, 11 inches; 1 inch=7½ stiches, 4 coils.

Plate 74, fig. 4, represents the end of Plate 75, fig. 6, Lillooet.   The design is said to typify flies.   Compare example 216422 U.S.N.M.

Plate 74, fig. 5, shows a coiled and imbricated basket of the Lillooet Indians, British Columbia.   The two segments are preserved in the design as in figures 1 and 3.   The structural features are also the same.   The design is a head, with open mouth, below are arrow heads. Compare fig. 3.

Plate 74, fig. 6, represents a coiled and imbricated basket of the Lower Thompson Indians, British Columbia.   Special attention is called to the ridged surface caused by a bundle of splints.   On this plate are shown the two radically different methods of laying the foundation for the coil.   The two narrow black and white stripes on the upper portion are made by beading, and represent earth lines. The lower figures are grouse tracks.   Height, 6 inches; 1 inch=6½ stiches, 5 coils.

Plate 75, fig. 1, represents a coiled and imbricated cooking basket of the Lower Thompson Indians, British Columbia, with a design of flying geese.   The foundation of the coil is of splints; the distinctive characteristic is that the ornamentation covers the whole surface and is not divided into bands.   Height, 9 inches; 1 inch=6½ stitches, 4½ coils.

Plate 75, fig. 2, shows a coiled and imbricated covered basket or trunk of the Lower Thompson Indians, British Columbia, while the design is of a rattlesnake's rattle.   Height, 5 inches; 1 inch=6 stitches, 3½ coils.

Plate 75, fig. 3, represents a wrapped twined bag of the Yakima (Shahaptian family) Indians, Washington.   The National Museum has many bags from Shahaptian tribes showing Farrand's symbols.   The design is of flying birds.   Height, 22 inches; 1 inch=7 stitches, 9 rows.

Plate 75, fig. 4, shows a coiled and imbricated basket of the Lower Thompson Indians, British Columbia.   Its design is a snake trail or track.   Height, 9½ inches; 1 inch=6½ stitches, 3½ coils.

Plate 75, fig. 5, shows a coiled and imbricated basket of the Lower Thompson Indians, British Columbia.   The design indicates a snake trail.   In technical elements this example is Thompson, but the crenelated form of design is widespread and has many interpretations. Compare Plate 74, fig. 1; also Merriam's butterfly design, page 332. Height, 13 inches; 1 inch=6½ stitches, 3½ coils.

Plate 75, fig. 6, represents a coiled and imbricated basket of the Lillooet Indians, British Columbia.   The shape and flat foundation are Lillooet, but the solid design over the whole surface is not so. The design shows flies, snake tracks, and arrowheads (side view). Height, 10¼ inches; 1 inch=5½ stitches, 2 coils.

Plate 75, fig. 7, is a coiled and imbricated globular basket of the Lower Thompson Indians, British Columbia. The design represents a snake coiled around the basket and exists on baskets in other Salishan tribes. The vertical line interrupting the coils shows the limitation of this style of weaving, made up of a continuous spiral and not of a series of rings. Height, $7\frac{1}{2}$ inches; 1 inch=8 stitches, $4\frac{1}{2}$ coils.

Plate 75, fig. 8, is a coiled and imbricated basket of the Lower Thompson Indians, British Columbia. This beautiful example is true to type in all except the angular design. The designs represent butterflies' wings. Height, 14 inches; 1 inch=6 stitches, $3\frac{1}{2}$ coils.

Plate 76, fig. 1, is a coiled and imbricated basket of the Lillooet Indians, British Columbia, the upper design representing intestines; the vertical stripes in the lower segment are flies. Height, 11 inches; 1 inch=7 stitches, 4 coils.

Plate 76, fig. 2, is a coiled and imbricated basket of the Lillooet Indians, British Columbia, with a design representing a net; the interspaces show deer shot by arrow, deer, man, dogs, flies. The flat coil in the bottom, the absence of angles, the design over the surface are noteworthy in the Lillooet. Height, $13\frac{1}{2}$ inches; 1 inch=6 stitches, $3\frac{1}{2}$ coils.

Plate 76, fig. 3, is a coiled and imbricated basket of the Lillooet Indians, British Columbia, with a design representing a man with feather in his hair, bow and two arrows, and at either end a notched ladder (?). The lower segment is beaded. Height, $8\frac{3}{4}$ inches; 1 inch=8 stitches, $5\frac{1}{2}$ coils.

Plate 76, fig. 4, shows a typical coiled and imbricated basket of the Lower Thompson Indians, British Columbia. The design is a plant with fernlike leaf, end view. Height, $8\frac{1}{2}$ inches; 1 inch=$7\frac{1}{2}$ stitches, $3\frac{1}{2}$ coils.

Plate 76, fig. 5, shows a coiled and imbricated basket of the Lillooet Indians, British Columbia, having a design representing arrowheads and flies. In technic this example represents the older forms. Height, 11 inches; 1 inch=7 stitches, 4 coils.

Plate 77, fig. 1, shows a coiled and imbricated basket trunk of the Lillooet Indians, British Columbia. The structure and form are decidedly Hudson Bay Company in motive. The design represents arrowheads of different shapes. Height, 9 inches; 1 inch=$5\frac{1}{4}$ stitches, $3\frac{1}{2}$ coils.

Plate 77, fig. 2, shows a bag in twined weaving with wrapped ornament of the Wasco Indians (Chinookan family), Washington, with designs representing flying birds, men, and sturgeon. Height, $8\frac{1}{2}$ inches; 1 inch=8 twists, 12 rows.

Plate 77, fig. 3, is a coiled and imbricated basket trunk of the Lower Thompson Indians, British Columbia; design, arrowheads. This specimen shows the intrusion of Hudson Bay Company forms into the upper country. Height, $6\frac{1}{2}$ inches; 1 inch=7 stitches, 4 coils.

Plate 77, fig. 4, represents a coiled and imbricated basket of the Lower Thompson Indians, British Columbia, with a design showing a packing strap or tump line, possibly a net. This is a good type in technic, form, and decorations. See also figs. 6, 7, and 8. Height, 11½ inches; 1 inch=6½ stitches, 4 coils.

Plate 77, fig. 5, is a coiled and imbricated packing basket of the Lower Thompson Indians, British Columbia, with a design representing grave or burial boxes. This is an interesting hybrid, with Thompson stitch and decoration on a Coast box, having even the added foot. Height, 6¾ inches; 1 inch=7 stitches, 4½ coils.

Plate 77, fig. 6, is a coiled and imbricated basket of the Lower Thompson Indians, British Columbia. The design indicates crossing trails, possibly stars. Height, 14 inches; 1 inch=6½ stitches, 4 coils.

Plate 77, fig. 7, is a coiled and imbricated basket of the Lower Thompson Indians, British Columbia. Legend, stone hammer, side view. Compare example 217438 U.S.N.M.

Plate 77, fig. 8, is a coiled and imbricated basket of the Lower Thompson Indians, British Columbia. Height, 9 inches; 1 inch=7½ stitches, 3½ coils.

Plate 77, fig. 9, shows a twined and overlaid basket of the Quinaielt Indians, Washington, with a design representing a fish net. Height, 7½ inches; 1 inch=5 twists, 8 rows of weaving.

Plate 78, fig. 1, shows a twined and wrapped wallet of the Upper Thompson Indians, British Columbia, with a design representing lakes, lakes connected by streams, ducks flying toward the lakes, and animal footprints. Figures 1–4 are akin to the Shahaptian work in Washington, with the exception that the decorative filaments are wrapped about both elements of the twine. Height, 21 inches; 1 inch=9 twists, 13 rows of weaving.

Plate 78, fig. 2, is a reverse of preceding, having a design of arrowheads and crossing trails.

Plate 78, fig. 3, is a twined and wrapped wallet of the Upper Thompson Indians with a design showing three rows of lodges. Height, 23 inches; 1 inch=5½ twists, 8 rows of weaving.

Plate 78, fig. 4, is the reverse of No. 3, and has a design showing household utensils.

Plate 78, fig. 5, is a twined and overlaid wallet of the Quinaielt Indians, Washington, having a design representing a mountain chain. Height, 8 inches; 1 inch=6 twists, 8 rows of weaving.

Plate 78, fig. 6, shows a twined and overlaid basket of the Quinaielt Indians, Washington. Its design is called a mountain chain. Height, 10 inches; 1 inch=5 twists, 7½ rows of weaving.

Plate 79, fig. 1, is a coiled and imbricated basket of the Lower Thompson Indians, British Columbia. The design is said to represent mountains with lakes in the valleys. Height, 14½ inches; 1 inch=6½ stitches, 3½ coils.

Plate 79, fig. 2, is a twined and overlaid basket of the Quinaielt Indians, Washington, with a design representing waves or ripples on the water. Height, 10 inches; 1 inch=5½ twists, 9 rows.

Plate 79, fig. 3, shows a twined and overlaid basket of the Quinaielt Indians, Washington, with an unknown design. It is widespread, however, and resembles a cluster of marsh plants. Resembles motives in northern California. Height, 6¼ inches; 1 inch=7 twists, 10 rows.

Plate 79, fig. 4, is a coiled and imbricated basket of the Lillooet Indians, Washington, with a design representing lightning. Compare Plate 75, figs. 1 and 2, where it stands for flying geese. Height, 5 inches; 1 inch=8 stitches, 3½ coils.

Plate 79, fig. 5, is a coiled and imbricated ware of the Lillooet Indians, British Columbia. The design is said to be of meaning unknown revealed in a dream. Height, 10 inches: 1 inch=5 stitches, 3½ coils.

Plate 79, fig. 6, is a coiled and imbricated basket of the Chilcotin Indians, British Columbia, with an unexplained design. This rare piece is noteworthy for having three or four bands or segments of independent designs. It shows in its technic little influence of foreign culture. Height, 8½ inches; 1 inch=6½ stitches, 7 coils.

For the northern California and southern Oregon tribes the guide to the study of symbolism is Roland B. Dixon.[a] who divides basketry into three types (see fig. 163.):

I. *Northwestern type* includes the area occupied by the Hupa (Athapascan), Karok (Quoratean), Yurok (Weitspekan). The technic is twined work overlaid.

II. *Northeastern type* comprises Modoc and Klamath (Lutuamian), Shasta (Sastean), Pit River (Palaihaihan), Yana (Yanan), Wintun (Copehan), and Maidu (Pujunan). The technic is twined and coiled.

III. *Pomo type.*—This versatile people of the Kulanapan family in its technic is cosmopolitan, using both twined and coiled ware in every variety. The Yuki and the Costanoan are left unclassed.

Three groups of symbols are distinguished by Dixon—animal designs, plant designs, and representations of natural or artificial objects. For the Pomo symbols he relies upon Carl Purdy, collector of material from that people in the American Museum, New York. For the northeastern group, Dr. Dixon has made exhaustive personal observations and illustrated the symbols in Plates I–XVI of his monograph.

The following story applies to a beautiful piece of basket work from the Yuki Indians, now in Round Valley Agency, Covelo, California. They are associated with the Wailakis, who are Athapascan, but the Yuki themselves form a separate family. Catalogue No. 131108 in the U.S.N.M., Plate 80, is called a sun basket, of Yuki manufacture,

---

[a] Basketry Designs of the Indians of Northern California, Bulletin of the American Museum of Natural History, XVII, 1902, pp. 1–32.

collected by N. J. Purcell, and in order to complete its history it is necessary to know what the Yukis believe to be the origin of the world. "In the beginning there was no land; all was water. Darkness prevailed everywhere. Over this chaos of dark waters hovered 'On-coye-to,' who appeared in the form of a beautiful white feather, hence the love of the Yukis for feathers. In time the spirit became weary of his incessant flight through the murky space and lighted down upon the face of the water. Where he came in contact with the water there was a whirlpool that spun his body round and round. So rapid became the motion that a heavy foam gathered about him. This became more dense and expanded in width and length. It gathered up the passing bubbles until it was a huge floating island. On the bosom of this rested the snowy form of On-coye-to. As he lay upon this island after an almost endless flight through the dark space, the idea of a permanent resting place came into his mind. So he made the land and divided it from the water. From the form of a feather he assumes that of a man and rested upon the land. Still there was no light, and the spirit was troubled. On-coye-to saw far off in the firmament a star, po-ko-lil-ey, and resolved to visit it and learn how it emitted its sparkling light. After a long journey he arrived and found a large and beautifully lighted world, inhabited by a numerous, hospitable people. Still, he saw not whence came the light. He was allowed free access to all the habitations save one, ' the sweat house.' This was guarded night and day, and was accessible only to sick persons. Finally a great hunt was planned, and as the time drew near all was prepared for the occasion. But On-coye-to feigned sickness, that he might investigate the sweat house. When the morning arrived for the hunt he was too ill to accompany the hunters. A council was held to determine whether this stranger should be admitted to the sweat house, which is even now a sacred place with the Yuki tribe, and it was decided to give him the benefit of this house of medicine, religion, gambling, and many other practices. A few old men were left to administer to his wants and to see that all went well. As he entered the sweat house he was almost blinded by the light that flashed upon him. As he became accustomed to it he looked around him and discovered its origin. Hanging high over his head in several baskets were as many beautiful suns. Having found the fountain of light he waited patiently until the old men were all asleep, then climbed cautiously to what seemed the brightest of the suns, took down the basket which held it, slipped from the sweat house and made his way rapidly back toward his own world. He was hotly pursued by the indignant warriors, but he arrived safely after many adventures. He hung the sun in its basket far in the east, then surveyed it. It did not light up to suit him and he moved it a little higher. Still it did not suit him, so he continued to move it on and on, and is moving it to the present day." Thus the Indian accounts for the moving of the sun, and thinks not that the earth moves.

The basket here shown is believed to be a copy of the same in which the sun was stolen from the other world and brought to this. On the bottom is a piece of polished abalone shell cut round to represent the sun. Below this is suspended a new moon, then a fish, and all around the sides hang pieces of the same shell, which the Yuki say represents the stars. (N. J. Purcell.)

As before mentioned, Dr. Dixon relies on Mr. Purdy for the symbolism on the Pomo basketry. The collection was made in 1900, and the names of designs given. Since that time more information has come to Mr. Purdy, and some of the terms are changed. The U. S. National Museum has the collection of Dr. J. W. Hudson for comparison, made some years earlier. The interpretations of the symbols by the two men are quite as interesting a study in the psychology of the collectors as of the Indian basket women. From Dr. Hudson's manuscript accompanying his collection the following notes on symbolism are taken. The underlying thought in his mind is that each separate social group of the Pomo has peculiar types of basketry known by the keynote in the ornamentation, which is the totem of that group.

Both in painting and in feather decoration the following colors have a significance with the Pomo:

> Red: bravery; pride. (Personified by the woodpecker.)
> Yellow: amatory; success; gaiety; fidelity. (Lark.)
> Blue: demoniac cunning; perfidy. (Jay.)
> Green: astuteness; discretion; watchfulness. (Duck.)
> Black: conjugal love; beauty. (Quail.)
> White: riches; generosity. (Wampum.)

The following interpretations of signs were given by Dr. Hudson in connection with his collection of basketry secured by the U. S. National Museum:

Baiyakan (Baiyak, net mesh). Same as Mr. Purdy's. The design is an alternation of dark and light squares between two boundary lines.

Bishekamak, deer's hoofs or trail made by those animals in the mud. Very rare pattern, once common to the Taco (Yukian) of Potter Valley. Consists of two right-angled triangles joining so as to represent the track of a deer's hoof.

Bishemao, deer's loins, the mottles on the buck's rump when struggling out of the slime of Clear Lake at the creation. Parallel lines with the inclosed space filled with dark and light parallelograms.

Bisheo, deer's teeth, seen by the primal Indians when that animal called to them for help as he struggled in the mud. A row of little squares with open spaces between.

Danokakea, Mountain Waters tribe, totem of a tribe once living 6 miles north of Upper Lake, in the mountains at the headwaters of McClure Creek, and a close affinity and neighbor of the Pomo of Potter Valley. A band of equilateral triangles in two colors alternating.

Ka wi na ote, or *Ka wi na mi yak,* turtle neck. A charm of halved turtle backs strung one above the other, indicated by three equilateral triangles, one resting on another.

Katsha, arrowheads often represented on the basket as strung together and worn as necklaces.

Katshak, arrowhead. A row of equilateral triangles bounded by two lines and touching by their bases, or having the apex of each one touching the middle of the base of the other.

Kawinateedi, turtle backs which were seen floating on the waves of Clear Lake. A series of rhombs adjoining one another.

Kea, quail plume. Totem of the confederated tribes of Lake County, California, especially those living in the valleys around Clear Lake. This excludes the Napo, Kabe napo, rock village; and Kura napo, water-lily village, who had no recognized totems. The Yokaia also claimed the Kea totem, being close kin to Lake tribes, though living across the range. L-shape and Z-shape designs in color. Most common of Pomo symbols.

Misakalak, blacksnake, a totem recognized as belonging to the Shokowa of Schokowa valley, around Hopeland. Represents a snake trail. Two parallel lines near together with a sinuous pattern between.

Na wa kai, a totem consisting of a series of ponds connected by a slough, and this tribe is totally extinct, yet the pattern is often seen in the Yokaia village and called Baketch, or man's spit. This is a row of squares made up of dots.

Poma, red earth. Named from the mound of siliceous earth in Potter Valley, whence all Pomos sprung, and from which, to this day, their ceremonial yeast or sacrament is dug to be mixed with their bread and eaten. The totem of a Potter Valley tribe. Pomo = red (stone) mine or quarry, where argillite or magnetite is mined for wampum. A row of triangles in red splints.

Shakobiya, grasshopper elbows, or the spines on the tarsi. Trail noted in mud. It consists of a line of right-angled triangles joined at their bases.

Shakokamak, grasshopper tracks made in the mud at creation. Parallel rows of dots in fours.

Tsi yo tsi yo, up and down, the word Ka being understood. "Waves" rolling back from the shores of Clear Lake, releasing the new-born creatures. Three zigzag lines parallel and oblique. Certain Lake County Pomo tribes use the term tsi yo tsi yo, signifying waves, or the marriage of the east wind to the waters of Clear Lake, representing it by a series of dotted parallelograms in stepped pattern.

Carl Purdy's vocabulary of Pomo symbols on basketry is as follows:

Baiyakan (Baiyak, net), band of rectangles, called meshes; also, snake.

Bishe mao, or *mia,* backbone or ribs of a deer. Rectangles or rhombs en échelon.

Butterfly pattern, Long Valley Indian (Copehan).

Chi kakh, quail.

Dalan, halved. (Yokaia, dilan.)

Dan, opening. (Compare the path in Navaho baskets.)

Itchi cu we; len we is naked, or bare and naked; itci tcu we, bare of design—i. e. not ornamented.

Ka pok poko, short design, rhomb or rectangle in the middle.

Ka tio tio, waves (Ka, water, and tio tio, rippling); or Kahio, or Kalio (?).

Kailakama, crow foot (kai, crow, and akama, foot).

Kalcha misit, arrow points. (Yokaia.)

Kalen le lan, white mark in the middle.

Katcha, arrowhead.

Katcha, arrow; Katcha da lan, arrow halved; Katchi mi set (or misit), arrow points.

Kawina ritcha, turtle neck.

Kèyá, quail tip.

Kèya, tip or top.

Lelan (lilan) in the middle.

Mato, large; Kalcha mato, arrowhead large.

Mi sit, point; or miset (?).   Upper Lake Pomo.

M sa kalle, spiral, or snake; name of a certain spotted snake.

Pau shna, acorn top (Pau, corn, and shna, head).

Sakalle (Yokaia for snake).

Siot sio, zigzag, waves.

Tchikaka ke-ya, quail tip (Tchikaka, quail; ke-ya, top knot).

Una leu, crossing.

Utcha, neck.

Mr. Purdy's interpretations of Pomo symbols will be found in Dr. Dixon's paper before quoted.   If the reader have a collection of Pomo baskets, an examination of the symbols on them in comparison with the Dixon plates will demonstrate what liberties the basket weaver took with her designs.   May be, it were better to say, what struggles she made to realize a design or symbol under general and special limitations.

POMO (KULANAPAN) DESIGNS, DIXON'S PLATES

Arrow point.   (Plates 29, 30, 33, 36.)

Buckeye tree.   (Plates 27, 34.)

Crossing tracks.   (Plates 28, 29, 34, 36.)

Crow's track.   (Plates 34, 35.)

Grasshopper leg.   (Plate 27.)

Leaf.   (Plate 27.)

Meshes in fish net.   (Plates 30, 31, 33, 34, 35.)

Quail tip.   (Plates 27, 28, 29, 36.)

Red mountains.   (Plates 27, 30, 31, 33, 34, 35.)

Spotted fawn skin.   (Plate 27.)

Unknown designs.   (Plate 32.)

Zigzag.   (Plates 28, 29, 30, 32, 33, 35, 36.)

To illustrate the technic of symbolism, Plate 81, Catalogue No. 203398, collected by Dr. J. W. Hudson, is presented.   It shows a gift basket of the Pomo Indians, made by a Yokian woman whose name is Keshbim, who worked upon it seven months.   The pattern is a pictograph of a feast, the bottom of the basket being tule mats (bitsan) interspersed on the assembly hall floor, not shown in the figure.   The band of rhomboid figures around the bottom is the roof of the dance lodge with its rafters crossed and interlaced, and the dancers, male and female, are celebrating the Ma a ca ka (food-falling) harvest (acorns).   The Pomos have four seasons in their year, beginning on the first full moon (tha na bu sa da, thumb moon) in July, and Sa ha nim, smoke-floating time, has four moons; Ma a ca ka has three moons, beginning with Ba too da, index moon.   Kat sa na, green earth, has three moons, and Kat sa mi, green-things time, has three moons.   This basket, under the old régime, would have been presented to some friend during the feast, demanding a very handsome return, for no one appreciated a fine piece of work like a Pomo woman.   The foundation is of willow rods.   The sewing is not done with linen thread as one would suppose, but with roots split so fine that in some places the sewing shows 60 stitches to the inch.

Dr. Dixon has made careful personal investigations concerning the symbolism on the basketry of California tribes east of the Sacramento River. [a] The following designs with their tribal assignments may be found in Dr. Dixon's plates:

WINTUM (COPEHAN) DESIGNS

Arrow points. (Plate 23.)
Bear's foot. (Plate 23.)
Bent elbow. (Plate 23.)
Cross waves. (Plate 24.)
Deer excrement. (Plate 24.)
Empty spool. (Plate 24.)
Fish tail. (Plate 23.)

Flying geese. (Plate 23.)
Leaves strung. (Plate 24.)
Pulled around. (Plate 24.)
Rattlesnake. (Plate 23.)
Striped. (Plate 24.)
Water snake. (Plate 23.)
Wolf's eye. (Plate 23.)

MOQUELUMNAN DESIGNS

Eye. (Plate 26.)

Quail tip. (Plate 26.)

PIT RIVER (PALAIHNIHAN) DESIGNS

Arrow point. (Plate 22.)
Lizzard. (Plate 23.)

Skunk's nose. (Plate 22.)

MAIDU (PUJUNAN) DESIGNS

Deer excrement. (Plate 25.)
Earthworm. (Plate 25.)

Rattlesnake. (Plate 25.)
Water snake. (Plate 25.)

NOZI (YANAN) DESIGNS

Wolf's eve. (Plate 25.)

House. (Plate 25.)

Dr. Dixon's conclusions are of interest. Designs are subject to much variation, chiefly through different arrangements of elementary and constant forms in the pattern. If there are two or more types for the same element they are never found together. Designs are essentially the same on coiled and twined basketry, but most of the Maidu baskets are coiled, and there is suggestion of acculturation from the Pit Rivers. Function and form of the basket have something to do with symbols, certain designs being restricted to plaques, others to soup bowls, and so on. The spiral line is a favorite in massing symbols. Some of the patterns are found everywhere in the Maidu area, others are quite restricted. In most cases, and this is the universal testimony, the intent of the design is not clear from mere inspection, but must be explained before it can be understood. The author's summary of Maidu symbols is the very large variety and number, the frequency of animal designs, the unusual predominance of plant designs, the number in which the realism is obscured, the

---

[a] Basketry Designs of the Indians of Northern California, Bulletin of the American Museum of Natural History, XVII, pp. 1–32, 37 plates.

tendency to spiral and zigzag patterns, and the well-nigh universal practice of putting but a single design on a basket.

Plate 82, fig. 1, is a Washoe basket 8½ inches high, 12 inches wide, and 6 inches across the opening. There are 30 stitches to the inch. Colors, red, black, and brown. Weight, 16 ounces. The legend is named "Migrating," or "When the birds leave their nests and fly away we shall move." The lower left-hand basket, fig. 2, is 7 inches high, 11½ inches across, and 6 inches over the opening, with 30 stitches to the inch. The body is light-gold color, and the ornamentations are in red and black. Weight, 15 ounces. The legend is, "Rays of the sun ascending." An attempt to imitate the radial appearance of the light at sunrise. The lower right-hand basket, fig. 3, is 7 inches high, 6 inches across the opening, and 11½ inches in diameter, with 30 stitches to the inch. The body is light-gold color and the decorations are in red and black. Attention is invited to the intricate combination of squares and triangles, stepped patterns, and rhombs to form the total design on the surface. These symbols relate to the different ranks or degrees in the chieftancy of the tribe which they are entitled to receive by inheritance. This information is based on the studies of A. Cohn, of Carson City, Nevada.

Plate 83 is a Tulare bottle-neck, collected on Tule River, Tulare County, California, and is in the collection of C. P. Wilcomb. The material and sewing are similar to those in other Tulare baskets. The ornamentation deserves especial attention. The bands of rhombs on the body and the part on the upper border which resembles the shaftment and feather of an arrow are common to the region. On the middle of the body, however, is a band of ornamentation which resembles the Egyptian ankh. It is useless to speculate on the origin of this symbol, since the Indians in this part of California have been in touch with the Latin-American race for centuries. In this Inyo-Kern-Tulare subarea Dr. C. Hart Merriam finds the crenellated design to be associated in symbolism with the spasmodic flight of the butterfly as it flits among the flowers (see Plates 41, 188, 192, 194) and calls attention to the dispersion of the symbol as far north as southeastern Alaska.

Designs were found by Dr. George H. Pepper[a] on the ancient basketry from the caves of southeastern Utah. He refers them to symbols as they are now understood among living tribes, but recognizes that such forms do not stand for the same object always, even in the same tribe. The designs given are the butterfly of the Maidu, water-fowls, mountain, and sun. A glance at the beautiful workmanship and the designs on Dr. Pepper's specimens at once places them not

_____

[a] The Ancient Basketmakers of Southeastern Utah, Guide Leaflet No. 6 of the American Museum of Natural History.

in the Ute or Shoshonean family, but with the exquisite basket-making tribes westward in California.   They have the three-rod foundation. The upper one is 17½ inches in diameter and 5 inches deep.

The basket having the butterfly design was found over the body of an infant, and this led the finder to the conviction that the forms had some mythic significance.   These specimens, and many more, belonging to the Wetherill, the McLeod, and Graham collections are now in the American Museum of Natural History, New York.   (See Plate 84.)

The Pueblos called Hopi in northeastern Arizona were visited by the Spaniards in the early part of the 16th century.   Having no gold to tempt the avarice of the conquerors, they were let alone.   On their coiled and wicker baskets, used in their religious ceremonies, are shown the personages and phenomena most intimately associated with their cult.   I am indebted to Dr. J. Walter Fewkes for the interpretation of their symbolism.

The basket shown in Plate 85 is peculiar to the Hopi village of Oraibi; has a picture of the Corn Maiden (Shalakomana or Palahiko-mana).   The head bears the representation of a tablet which is symbolic of the rain clouds.   The colors represent the rain clouds of the four cardinal points: Yellow, the north; blue, the west; red, the south; white, the east.   Usually in representations of this maiden the Hopi hair puffs are represented.   A design on the forehead stands for an ear of corn, which is one of the symbolic marks of this maiden.   There ought to be represented in the middle of the forehead, dependent from this ear of corn, a fragment of Haliotis shell.   This is for the rainbow.   The two eyes appear as bands, and should be of different colors, the left green or blue, the right red.   The two bands below the eyes are meant for facial markings which are generally triangular in shape.   Green and red stripes on the chin represent the rainbow. On paintings the bow is curved the other way, but the restrictions of basket making require the curve to be downward.   The blanket on the body is a garment made of feathers, the individual feathers being represented by blue and red bands.   This is the earth goddess or corn goddess.   Interesting descriptions of the ceremony in which this Corn Maiden or sky goddess is engaged will be found in Dr. Fewkes's interesting paper[a] on the Minor Hopi Festivals.   On Plate 24, opposite page 494 of his article, is illustrated the Palahiko-mana dance.   She is shown as the central figure.   The headdress, body garment, and embroidered blanket are represented in full.   The headdress is decked with feather plumes, and altogether the appearance is more striking.   The basket weaver has done her best where her pictorial ability gave out, at least, to indicate the presence of even the clan markings on the face, which in the drawings picture the human hand.

---

[a] American Anthropologist, N. S., IV, 1902, pp. 482–511.

The top figure, Plate 93, shows the birds of the four cardinal points, two very much enlarged and two smaller. The stripes on the border are the tail feathers of the larger birds. The limitations of the basket maker are well shown in the specimen, in that all perspective is neglected and every part of the body brought to the same plane; the feet are turned around so as to show the toes.

The lower figure in the same plate represents one bird. The head on the upper margin having rain-cloud appendages, the beak being represented by an extension on the right hand side. The wider symbolic colors are abbreviated in every part. The bend in the knee is shown by the rectangular spaces representing the leg. (See Plate 93.)

The basket shown in Plate 47 was made at the Hopi village of Oraibi. The symbols on this basket represent the sky birds of the four cardinal points, two of which are larger, two smaller, apparently made so for want of room. The central figure represents the heart of the sky with geometrical rain-cloud figures. The sky god has a number of names.

In the upper figure (see Plate 216), the designs have got past the pictorial stage, and the meaning could only be known by consulting the maker of the basket. It is doubtful whether she did any more than what she saw her mother do. It might be possible, if a large series were had, to follow this symbol outward to the known pictorial form.

The lower figure in this plate represents the four birds of the cardinal points. The standard colors of the cardinal points are not all in the design because the basket itself is yellow, which deprived the workwoman of the privilege of representing the north. The symbol is very highly conventionalized.

The figures on both examples, Plate 30, denote rain clouds.

The same types of symbolism, occasioned by the climate, the physical features and productions of the arid region will be found at Zuñi and among the Rio Grande Pueblos.[a] Symbolism on the basketry of Middle and South America has not been worked out.

[a] F. H. Cushing, A Study of Pueblo Pottery, Fourth Annual Report of the Bureau of Ethnology, Washington, 1887, pp. 467–521.

For a fuller explanation of the rich symbolism surviving in the Pueblo region the reader must consult the papers of J. W. Fewkes, to be found illustrated in the American Anthropologist, N. S., V, 1899–1903, and in the reports of the Bureau of American Ethnology.

A Study of Textile Art in Its Relation to the Development of Form and Ornament, Sixth Annual Report of the Bureau of Ethnology, Washington, 1889, pp. 189–252; also, Prehistoric Textile Art of Eastern United States, Thirteenth Annual Report of the Bureau of Ethnology, Washington, 1896, pp. 3–45

VI. USES OF BASKETRY

Blessed shall be thy basket and thy store.—DEUTERONOMY, XXVIII: 5.

Nature has provided members of the animal kingdom with receptacles which are a part of their anatomy. The camel has its water sack, the ruminant animals have their extra stomach for the storage of grasses, the squirrel carries nuts in. the pouch in the side of his cheek, and certain insects are provided with various means of transporting food to a distance. It remained for the human race to invent appliances to accomplish similar results, and basketry forms one of the principal means adapted to such needs. There is practically no limit to the uses to which basket-work weaving has been put. The enumeration of these uses in detail will show what a prominent place the receptacle has had for holding water, food, and other precious objects, for gathering the materials connected with industry and for transporting them. Basketry also enters into the house, the furniture, the clothing, the armor, the domestic economy, the family life, and religion of the American tribes.

There are a multitude of secondary uses of baskets which will be mentioned in the proper place. Certainly they have done as much as any other industry to develop the intellectual life of savage women, both a knowledge of the resources of nature and a taste for aesthetic products. It will also be found that there is no gulf between basketry, beadwork, lacework, and loom work. There are times when the basket weaver suspends her work and, with the use of her fingers alone, imitates the products of most complicated weaving frames. The highest steps in basket making will be the first steps in the great mechanical art which now costs so many millions of dollars and employs so many human beings.

Before the coming of the European, basketry supplied nearly every domestic necessity of the Indians, from an infant's cradle to the richly-decorated funerary jars burned with the dead. The wealth of a family was counted in the number and beauty of its baskets and the highest virtue of woman was her ability to produce them. Some domestic vessels were named for the particular service they performed; as bi-ti-bo-um' (dishes), or Ká-dem (water giver) among the Pomos; but the majority were known by their weave or shape. Vessels of the Tee weave, says Hudson, bore the brunt of culinary usage, as pots, pails, roasters, etc. There were two varieties of sifters; the coarse pshu-kǎń separating the crumbs for nut cake, etc., and the ma-a-pó-i, or finer sifter (a conoid utensil), which, slightly tilted and struck sharply within by the finger tips, spills the chaff over the outer margin.

The great value of her work reflected upon the maker herself. It was the most expert woman in basketry, says Miss Jennie C. Carr, who brought the highest price, namely, two strings of shell money.

Of old basketry some examples are clean while others are soiled and dilapidated. The former had the good fortune to fall into careful hands half a century ago, when they were new, and have with the years merely faded down to their indescribable shades. The other precious old pieces have been

> Dipped in baths of hissing tears
> And battered by the shocks of doom.

The study of structure in basketry, as in other activities, leads to investigations concerning functions and use. Among the least favored tribes in this regard there is a similarity to the lower forms of animal life where the same structure performs a number of processes. It is also common to see among plain sort of people and the uneducated one utensil used for many purposes. So with the little advanced tribes of Indians there will be one technical process in basket making and very small variety of forms for many uses, but when the more advanced and skillful tribes are reached there is a differentiation of function and along with it corresponding differences in structure and technical processes even in the same piece.

In the study of function there are two inquiries of equal value, namely, (1) the geographic distribution of functions together with the particular types of basketry that are used to perform these offices from place to place, and (2) tribal origins and purposes in order to connect function with ethnological and geographical studies. In each one of the six areas into which the Western Hemisphere has been divided the uses to which baskets are put will be decided by the animals, plants, and minerals that are indispensable to the happiness of the people, and the forms and characteristics of the baskets will depend upon the plants that are to be had for making them. On the seashore there must be clam baskets and fish baskets. In the interior there will be berry baskets; and in those regions where no pottery is to be found cooking baskets, in which food is boiled by means of hot stones, are among the commonest objects in sight. From the other point of view a more subtle question arises, whether ethnology has anything to do with basket materials or things to be carried in them. In tracing the history of invention during its primitive stages it will at once be recognized that the art of basket making was greatly stimulated by the multiplication of ends to be served; that the inventive faculty having such a versatile and accommodating material found scope for its own enlargement and improvement. In the end it becomes apparent that the art and the artist have set themselves one to the other "like perfect music unto perfect words." The basket adapts itself to the woman's life. It is not easy to pin any special structure upon a definite tribe, however, since women were captured or ran away mayhap into other tribes. A quiet system of pedagogy was going on all the time in basketry, as well as in other activities. The uses of basketry will be given in further detail, the topics arranged in alphabetic order.

An interesting phase of the struggle between use and beauty is to be seen in the compromises which they make for space on the same basket. The jewel, the cremation chef d'œuvre, the precious gift to a friend, may be covered with designs, have the most beautiful on the bottom, or where the maker's fancy led her. On the other hand, the piece for common uses is a despair of the artist; it is bereft of ornament. Among the Tlinkit of southeastern Alaska, while the covered trinket baskets are decorated to the ground, the cylindrical food baskets are plain near the bottom, and in many examples half the way up the body. This compromise in decoration is more apparent in the heavy coiled work of the British Columbia tribes. Boxes for show, cradles, and such examples are surrendered to the decorator, while the berry baskets and cooking pots have their decorations chiefly on the upper portion of the body. This fact limits the motives in the design. On old pieces it is melancholy to see how the hard wear of years has invaded the sacred precincts of art and destroyed even the symbols of religion. On the California basketry art was predominant. The spirals descend nearly to the bottoms of the mush bowls and the carrying baskets, but a glance reveals at the point of strain a patch of ordinary strong weaving or a protective covering.

As previously mentioned, baskets are receptacles of some kind or other. They do not of themselves usually perform work, but are used for holding the materials and apparatus of work. The art of basketry, however—that is, the plication or working of somewhat rigid materials—easily passed out of the mere making of receptacles into the construction of all sorts of objects needed in daily life.

The uses of basketry are either industrial or ideal. Industrially, they are connected first with the whole range of obtaining food or nourishment and the other natural materials upon which all history depends.

With the secondary industries, called manufactures, with transportation, and with consumption or enjoyment, one has but to take a stroll along the crowded dock, as in a great seaport, or the busy warehouse of any modern city, to become familiar with the infinite number of ways in which the basket lends its services to the comfort of the human race.

All of these functions, so intricate and diversified in civilization, are represented in savagery by much more simple occupations, from which, however, the basket is never absent.

Beyond the drudgeries of life lie its beatitudes, and here the basket is also present. In fine art, in social functions, in birth, in lore, in custom, and even in burial it is not absent.

A detailed description of the way in which these functions are performed by basketry, with abundant illustrations, will show just what is meant in these declarations.

IN THE CARRYING INDUSTRY

Carrying in baskets was done by the Americans on the head, on the back with head band or breast strap, and in the hands; about the home the basket was scarcely ever absent. It was the strongest of all Indian fabrics, easily made into any shape convenient to the load or the carrier, and it was lightness itself. In a hemisphere almost devoid of pack animals, where woman was the ubiquitous beast of burden, is it any wonder that she invented the most economical of devices for holding and transporting? Since nothing grows where it is wanted, an attempt to enumerate the things transported in baskets would be to list every natural material that contributed to the Indian's happiness. Mineral, vegetal, and animal substances are all in there. Clay from the quarry, water from the spring, stones for working, firewood, edible roots, fruits, and seeds, textile materials, fish, flesh, and fowl are a part of the freight ever on the move throughout the culture areas.

The carrying basket did not lose its multitudinous functions for women with the departure of savagery. One has only to look into market houses and stores, walk along the streets, or visit farms in the country to be convinced of this.

They are borne on the head, shoulder, hips, or knees; they are hung to the body in every possible fashion, and carried by two or more persons with the hands—all for loading ships, cars, or wagons. They are used also as panniers on the backs of animals, and smaller and better specimens are used by the interminable procession of children and buyers and travelers.

The transportation basket did not cease as a stimulus to invention with its holding things and spurring the maker to do her best in its composition. It waked up her mind in other directions. Her feet had to be fitly shod to gather materials; thus sandals were often in basket work. Her clothing required adjustments to new occupations and exposures in the new activities made possible by the art. Even the baskets of other functions were perfected and new functions were created by the carrying art.

In the report of the U. S. National Museum for 1894[a] a large num-

---

[a] O. T. Mason, Report of the U. S. National Museum, 1894, pp. 237–593, pls. 1–25, figs. 1–257.

ber of illustrations are devoted to showing the variety of ways in which baskets may become vehicles among the aborigines of our hemisphere.

Edwin Bryant describes the moving of a Sioux camp near Fort Laramie in 1846.[a] The tent poles were fastened to the sides of the ponies for travaux. Crosspieces were lashed to these and small children were confined in cages made from willows in the form of crates for crockery, having doors on the sides.

The Moki, or Hopi, Indians of to-day, in addition to the woven head ring and the ordinary head straps for carrying loads, have in use a breast band of yucca fiber for dragging loads over the ground. (See figs. 105 and 106.) The Papago women fit a lacework frame to the back in carrying loads for long journeys. (See fig. 106.)

The Apaches make a special pannier in twined work, one of which

FIG. 105.
BREAST BAND FOR HAULING.
Zuñi, New Mexico.
Cat. No. 70962, U.S.N.M.
Collected by James Stevenson.

FIG. 106.
CARRYING FRAME.
Papago Indians, Mexico.
After W J McGee.

will fit the human back, and two may be used on a donkey.

Plate 86, from a photograph by A. W. Ericson, represents a Hupa Indian woman using the carrying basket for firewood. On her head she wears one of the beautiful little conical basket caps of this tribe, common in collections. A band of leather passes across her forehead, and the load of wood is supported on her back. There is no other function of basketry so universally widespread as this.

According to Muhlenpfordt the Pimas and Maricopas make a basket

---

[a] Rocky Mountain Adventures, p. 110.

boat which they call "cora," woven so tight as to be waterproof without the aid of pitch or other application. And upon the same parallel of latitude, along the Gulf of Mexico, the Indians used to cross the rivers on floats of cane woven together and called "cajen." Bundles of cane were laid together sidewise, and over them others, the whole being woven together.[a]

Formerly mats were used by the Makah as canoe sails, but at present they are employed for wrapping up blankets, for protecting the cargoes in canoes, and for sale to the whites, who use them as lining of rooms, or as floor coverings (James G. Swan).

Besides the endless carrying of things among the Indians, called transportation, there is, it must not be forgotten, a large amount of passenger movement. The cradle, or, more correctly, the papoose basket, was the beginning of devices for carrying persons. Except a little riding by people of note on the backs of men in the Andes, only infants were passengers in aboriginal days throughout America.

FIG. 107.
TWINED CRADLE.
Hupa Indians.
Cat. No. 126519, U.S.N.M.   Collected by P. H. Ray, U. S. A.

For the infant there were three zones of going about in the Western Hemisphere, the Arctic, the Temperate, and the Tropical; speaking technically, the zone of the fur hood, the zone of the carrying frame, and the zone of free motion. The Atlantic province tribes made use of flat boards or racks, the Eskimo mother carried her babe safely ensconced in her ample hood of fur. The cradle of southeastern Alaska and the mainland near by were troughs, but most of the Pacific tribes made their papoose frames of basketry, and it is to these that attention is invited. In nearly all of them the feet and head are left free.[b] The Hupa Indians, on the Hupa Reservation, in northwestern California, belong to the Athapascan family in Alaska and northwestern Canada, and that may account for the resemblance of their cradles in form to those of birch bark made by the tribes of that northern region.

---

[a] Du Pratz, History of Louisiana, London, 1763, II, pp. 228–229. Dumont also mentions rafts of poles and canes.

[b] O. T. Mason, Primitive Travel and Transportation. Report of the U. S. National Museum, 1894, p. 521.

Structurally, they are in plain twined weaving, with here and there a row of wrapped twine and false braid. In passing, it may be noted that these Hupa babies are not strapped on a board as among the eastern tribes, nor are their heads bandaged as are those of the tribes along the coast of British Columbia.[a] (See fig. 107.)

IN DEFENSE AND WAR

Basket armor of the tribes on the Pacific Coast is made of narrow slats of wood, recalling those in the bottoms of some of the Lillooet Indian baskets in British Columbia. The slats are associated with straight rods of hard wood. These are woven with cords in regular twined weaving. The twine is finely spun and laid on so as to produce an ornamental effect upon the surface. This basket ornament has been

FIG. 108.
STICK ARMOR TWINED TOGETHER.
California.
After W. Hough.

found in caves of the Aleutian Islands, also among the Tlinkit Indians of the Pacific Coast as far south as the Hupa Indians of the coast of California. In some specimens wicker weaving takes the place of twined weaving.[b]

An examination of Hough's Plates 7, 8, 9, 10, 11, 13, 14, and 15 will show how the weft of twine in basketry is transferred to slat armor worn anciently by the Tlinkit, Aleut, Takoo, Shasta, Hupa, and Klamath Indians was held together.

Fig. 108, reproduced here, illustrates one in which the twined basketry was applied to this sort of armor.

---

[a] See Report of the U. S. National Museum, 1887, p. 178, fig. 11.

[b] Walter Hough, Primitive American Armor. Report of the U. S. National Museum, 1893, pp. 625–651.

The Massawomekes, on the Chesapeake Bay, had similar basket shields or armor. Smith[a] speaks of them as made of little small sticks woven " betwixt strings of thin hempe and silke grass," but so firmly that no arrow could possibly pierce them. Comparing this description with the figure above leaves no doubt of the similarity of the defense on both sides of the continent.

IN DRESS AND ADORNMENT

Basketry, laying aside its chief function of holding something, is even now used extensively among many tribes in dress and adornment of the person. It was mentioned in the section on carrying that the exigencies of going about stimulated the inventive faculty not only in the basket industry but in other crafts accessory to travel. The foremost of these companion arts is that of sandal or shoe maker. It is true that boots of hide and moccasins of tawed skin are the commonest supply of this want, but there is a vast portion of America where the sandal holds sway. They are made of tough fiber and woven in wicker, checker, twill, twined in a number of fashions. Some of the cliff-dwellers' sandals are studies in weaving three and even four ply. Many of them are figured in a paper on Primitive Travel and Transportation.[b] (See Plate 87.)

But, far more than the feet, the head claims the basket weaver's art the world over. ·In America the basket hat clings to the Pacific slope. As soon as the Indian area is reached in southeastern Alaska the hat bursts into bloom. It is made not only for comfort, to save the eyes of the hunter from the glare, and to act as an umbrella, but the handy weaver, having first scoured the earth for the most delicate spruce root, exhausts her artistic skill in its composition. The Tlinkit woman and the Haida woman solve the problem differently. Given the task to make the most elegant hat that can be done in spruce root, the Haida artist relies upon her delicate fingers to get the result. Twined weaving is her technic, but plain and twill and three-ply are so happily blended that she discards color. The Tlinket, just a whit less refined in touch, or maybe not having such perfect material, resorts to color. The designs are not always wrought, but are frequently painted, while beard of seal, abalone shell, and beads exhaust the possibilities of decoration. These hats are made for men as well as women. Indeed, the finest are doubtless made for men to wear on the chase, with the conviction that a hunter must not only do his best but wear his best.

The use of the basket in clothing reaches its climax in the California hats. In a description of the costume worn by Hupa Indians in

---

[a] John Smith, History of Virginia; Richmond, 1819, p. 185.

[b] Otis T. Mason, Primitive Travel and Transportation, Report of the U. S. National Museum, 1894, pp. 237–593.

northern California a large collection of designs on their basket hats are shown in Plates 3, 4, and 5 in the Ray collection from the Hupa Reservation,[a] and on Plate 6 of the same paper will be shown the relation of basketry to foot gear. (See Plate 88.)

Excepting the head gear and the foot gear, the American Indian in places needed protection from rain and cold. The robes made from the tender skins of rabbits and other small animals by cutting them into strips and making them into blankets by twined weaving were widely diffused in North America from Virginia to the Pacific. Wherever the tough cedar bark abounded soft capes and robes were made therefrom by the same women who made the baskets. The rain cloaks of middle America, if they are not of oriental origin, are knotted and do not belong to basketry. Other basketry dress was chiefly ornamental. Leggings reaching to the knees made up by well-known processes are to be found. A great deal of ceremonial regalia, even that from buckskin, is put together by basketmaker's processes.

IN FINE ART AND CULTURE

Basketry has been most useful as the patron of fine art and culture. Like all other human activities, it passes from the homely useful to the useless beautiful, and in so doing combines the two qualities whose union was long ago said to be the acme of excellence. The best art critics will say that in many of their productions the American Indian woman had, by obeying the voices within, attained a high degree of excellence. The practice of this superb work, and the admiration of it, elevated her; her abject state is not her fault.

There is no doubt that in the centuries of sorrow men have suffered more than women, since all their old occupations in which they excelled have been destroyed and hope with them; but the pride of excellence remained with the woman, who easily surpassed the whites in the work she was allowed to continue. That thousands of children are now being taught her art is witness of this.

Plate 89 shows two coiled baskets from Tulare County, California, specimens of the combined art of three or four well-known basketmaking stocks who have united at this point—the Shoshonean from the east, the Mission Indians from the south, and the makers of coiled basketry from the north. In the upper figure the basket bowl is in open sewing over a grass foundation, with ornamentation in plain vertical stripes. Every item of form, color, and design in this specimen has in it the true element of art.

The lower basket is jar-shaped, in closer weaving and more uniform in texture, but its design is especially attractive. The base is a rectangular outline, but the pattern is made up of hourglass form

---

[a] Smithsonian Report, 1886, pp. 205–238.

flanked by two triangles. The body color is that of the material, the hourglass is black, and the triangles in reddish brown. Especial attention is called to this figure. It occurs many times in the basketry in the Merriam collection. It is also seen in McLeod's specimens from the Kern County tribes. The symbolism is not known, nor is there any attempt at imitation of natural objects in these figures, which are natural size in the plate.

Plate 90 shows the resources of the western California tribes of Mendocino County for heightening the beauty of ordinary coiled basketry. The abalone shell, having been ground away from the back, the nacreous surface becomes one of the most beautiful natural objects. The beadlike ornamentation around the edges is the money of the tribes, the feathers are the crests of the partridge, and forming the body of the basket the plumage of various species of birds is sewed on in bands. These objects, of course, have no other value than to show the taste and skill of the maker, and they are chiefly employed in making presents to friends, who are expected to give something quite as good in return.

Emulation in aesthetic ideals and technical skill, a potent factor in education and refinement, found unrestrained opportunity in basketry. It is doubtful whether pottery excelled this art in the demand for scrupulous care in every movement. Many of the best pieces in California ware are marked with the monogram of the maker; and these special marks are often at the bottom of a piece, as though the artist with consciousness of excellence had felt the Horatian thrill when the poet wrote: *Sublimi feriam sidera vertice.*

A sense of beauty in detail was the motive which led the basket maker to search the fields and dig into the earth for fiber. It educated her mind and sharpened her judgment. In order to secure the plume of the quail, the crest of the woodpecker, the shoulder tips of the blackbird, the mottled feathers of the duck, and more, the woman must catch her birds. So she becomes an inventor, more dangerous than the owl, more skillful than the hawk, more subtle than ·the serpent. At first the inventions were crude enough but effective in damming the waters and barricading the air. Ministering to these called forth a new grade of artificialities; culture grew by what it fed upon until it is not possible to comprehend in one grasp the multitude of materials, the variety of technical methods, the shapes, the designs and their meanings, involved in what one forlorn woman had to master in order to graduate in her art.

Dr. Washington Matthews[a] figures the so-called Navaho basket plaque as a drum, and says that the art of basket making is little cultivated among them to-day, because it was neglected through the development of blanket weaving. The material is the twigs of the

---

[a] American Anthropologist, VII, 1894, pp. 202–208.

aromatic sumac. The work is done in coiled weaving. The foundation is in roots of the same material, and in starting the basket the butt of the rod is placed in the center, the tip toward the periphery all the way to the end of the work Around the middle is a band in red, and branching from this band outward and inward triangles in black. The band is not continuous, but at one point is intersected by a narrow line of a colored wood. At first this seemed to be an imitation of the Pueblo "line of life" on pottery, but the Navaho line is put there to assist in the orientation of the basket in the medicine lodge when the light is dim. In playing their game the butts and tips of the Navaho give preference to the butt end of the gambling stick, associating the idea with that of the position of the warp in the coiled basket. When the basket is finished the butt of the first twig and the tip of the last twig in the outer edge must be on a line with this radial opening. When the basket is used in ceremony this line must lie east and west. The stick for this drum is made from the leaves of the yucca bent together, wrapped and sewed. The dull ghostly sound accords well with the other portions of their ceremonies.

IN PREPARING AND SERVING FOOD

The basket is closely connected with the Indian kitchen and dining room, if these terms be allowed. After the purveyor has gleaned from the waters, the air, the range, or the field, with appropriate devices, and the patient carrier has emptied her baskets at the tent side, and forsooth the miller has put through their exercises quite another series, the cook and caterer take up the burden. She is generally the selfsame woman who made the baskets and performed the forenamed drudgeries. But she is prepared for this task as well. There is first of all the mixing bowl or basket, about the shape of the bread trays in millions of kitchens. The coiled method suits the purpose, especially in their manufacture, since to be solid and water-tight are desirable, and weight is not an objection; yet there are tribes that make excellent mixing bowls in twined work. (See Plates 50, 53, 92, 93.)

It must not be supposed that basketry cooking pots are placed over a fire, as one of metal. Great preparation and skill are necessary to success. The basket must be substantial and water-tight; the proper kinds of stones must be selected and cleaned. After heating to a high degree they must be dipped into water to reduce the heat. A red-hot stone would spoil the broth, sure enough. Tongs of wood of a certain species and bent just so must be made ready, and paddles for incessant stirring.[a]

---

[a] For illustrations of cooking with hot stones see W. H. Holmes, Report of the U. S. National Museum, 1900, pp. 170–173, pls. 9–15.

Plate 91 shows two of the best examples of Klikitat imbricated basketry. The foundation is seen in the basket exposed, consisting of a bundle of rude splints of cedar root; the sewing is with prepared splints of the same material, and in both figures it will be seen that no ornamentation ever occurs on the inside of this type. The method of laying on the outer ornamentation has already been explained in the earlier part of this paper.

The designs are made up of rectangular figures in the grass color for the body, with yellow material dyed with Oregon grape, cherry bark, and cedar bark. The designs represent in the upper figure geese migrating; the lower, some species of swamp plant.

The border of the lower figure is in false braid, laid on the upper row of sewing. The stains on the lower basket show that it has been used in gathering berries for a long time; the upper one has not yet seen use. Both of them, however, are vessels for gathering and cooking food.

This cooking with hot stones is mentioned by many older writers, which proves that it was not an innovation with the discovery of America. After the cooking of the food, the next thing was the serving of it, for which purpose there were a number of forms in basketry for holding the fish or mush and for the individual eater.

Plate 92 represents a collection of baskets used for preparing and serving food. The lower figure is a cooking basket in which either mush or fish can be prepared to eat by means of hot stones. Spoons are made from the horns of the Rocky Mountain sheep or goats, and may be used for the individual eater. The upper basket is for draining food or for holding fish or some hot substance and allowing the water to drain off. The other figure shows the method of twined weaving and introducing a new splint into the texture.

Plate 93 shows two of the meal trays of the Hopi Indians in northern Arizona. When the coils are left open, as in these examples, they are said to have been made by an unmarried woman. The base or foundation of the coil is the shreds of yucca stems and the sewing is done with the rib-like strips of the leaves. The colors used in dyeing are those employed also by the weavers in the same region, but of recent years common cheap dyes of traders have taken the place of the native colors. The mythology of the figures in the plaques is explained on page 333.

Plate 94, from a photograph by G. Wharton James, shows a young unmarried woman of the Oraibi pueblo preparing the corn meal for bread making. The chimney is interesting as a first chapter in the history of draft. Fire is built in the corner of the room and a few adobe bricks supported on a log of wood form the flue. A few pieces of brick on the upper part of the roof continue the chimney. Other utensils common in the pueblo life are seen. The young woman wears her hair in the fashion of the tribe.

IN GLEANING AND MILLING

Gleaning or harvesting, storing away, and milling, what a vast number of men are nowadays employed in them. Women are not absent from them altogether in the United States and nothing is more common in the Eastern Hemisphere than to see harvest fields and all activities associated with root and seed gathering thronged with them. The industry was almost solely hers in America. Baskets are named for their part in these crafts. There are picking baskets, root baskets, berry baskets, and on to the list of acorns, fruits, seeds, and roots without end. Carrying baskets are universal, but there are a great many of them used by this set of workwomen, and it will be found that special varieties have been devised for these pursuits.

Also, as every other important invention calls for a host of subsidiary devices, there must be wands for beating off seeds, sieves for separating grain from chaff, fans for the same purpose, roasting trays in which the raw material is parched before grinding. Brooms are made from basket fiber, hoppers for the top of the millstone also, and the open, generous bowls to hold meal. All this is before the cooking processes are reached. If the meal is not to be used up at once, all thrifty tribes had learned to store up vegetable supplies against the day of need. The granary basket was the rival of the pit and the wooden crib. There must have been something refining about this entire round of activities. In many of the baskets associated with them the ornamentation is exquisite. The hunter and the fisherman had scant encouragement to cultivate the æsthetic sense in their employments; but nuts, seeds, grain, most fruits, and roots are clean. Even berries when they stain do not soil the outer part of the receptacle, so the Fraser River tribes adorn the upper portion of the baskets with beautiful patterns. The lower part is left plain. The use of baskets in the plant quest was well-nigh universal. The eastern Indians employed the cane or split ash for their wicker or twilled baskets. As far as the cane extended, even to Guiana and Brazil, this is true. The ingenious cassava strainer belongs to this class.

Plate 95 shows the domestic utensils of the upper Amazon tribes for various household purposes. Palm leaf, out of which fiber is made; the fiber itself, used in various forms of domestic utensils; baskets in two types, twined and crossed warp weaving. The cassava strainer on the left is in twined weaving, so that when the weights are taxed the bag is increased in size and the water forced out of the cassava. The specimen shown was collected for the U. S. National Museum by J. B. Steere.

Lewis H. Morgan writes [a] that in the art of basket work, in all its varieties, the Iroquois Indian women also excel. Their baskets are

---

[a] League of the Iroquois, 1851, p. 382, showing twined baskets.

made with a neatness, ingenuity, and simplicity which deserve the highest praise. Splint is the chief material, but they likewise use a species of sweet grass, and also corn husks. Among these various patterns, which are as diversified as convenience or ingenuity could suggest, the most perfectly finished is the sieve basket. It is designed for sifting corn meal, to remove the chit and coarse particles after the corn has been pounded into flour. The bottom of the basket is woven in such fine checks that it answers very perfectly all the ends of the wire sieve. Another variety of baskets was made of corn husks and flags very closely and ingeniously braided. In their domestic economy the basket answered many purposes. Cat. Nos. 221161–3, U.S.N.M.

From the historians of the discovery it is learned that basketry was used in connection with the gathering and preparing of food. Bartram mentions the use of a sieve which the Indians of Georgia have for straining a "cooling sort of jelly called conti, made by pounding certain roots in a mortar and adding water." Dumont describes the sieves and winnowing fans of the Indians of Louisiana. The Indian women, he says, make fine sieves with the skin which they take off of the canes; they also make some with larger holes, which serve as bolters, and others without holes, to be used as winnowing fans. They also make baskets very neatly fashioned, cradles for holding maize. By comparing this statement with what is said about the California gleaners it will be seen that the Louisiana tribes knew how to sift meal, leaving the coarse particles inside the sieve, and also to separate seeds from chaff, and finally from coarse material, by beating over the edge of a tightly woven basket.

Du Pratz also says that for

sifting the flour of their maiz, and for other uses, the natives make sieves of various finenesses of the splits of cane.

John Smith, speaking of the Indians of Virginia, says they

use a small basket for their Temmes, then pound againe the great, and so separating by dashing their hand in the basket, receiue the flowr in a platter of wood scraped to that forme with burning and shels.

Strachey makes the following statement:

Their old wheat they firste steepe a night in hot water, and in the morning pounding yt in a morter, they use a small baskett for the boulter or seaver, and when they have syfted fourth the finest, they pound againe the great, and so separating yt by dashing their hand in the baskett, receave the flower in a platter of wood, which, blending with water, etc.

There are no gleaning baskets in the Arctic and few in northern Canada. Birch, elm, and pine bark usurp the place of textile materials. But all along the southern border there were gleaners and a variety of basket forms in their hands. Maize, wild rice, roots, nuts, and berries were food staples. Checker matting, wicker basketry, and twined bagging supplied the receptacles.

For the basket maker there are four Alaskas:—Athapascan, and

Eskimo, where there is no gleaning or milling; Aleutian, in which the harvests come from the sea, and the daintiest of twined weaving is made in grass stems; and southeastern Alaska, which shall receive further notice. Storage baskets are attributed to them by early voyagers. Nowadays the ware is small, no piece exceeding half a bushel in capacity. Since seafaring is mixed with hunting and gleaning the fields, the gathering basket leads a busy life. Plates 136–149 represent the types, which, large and small, are chiefly cylindrical in shape. The methods of manufacture and decoration have been described.

In Gerstaecker's Journal is the following account of seed gatherers in California:

While I was standing there a couple of pretty, young girls came from the woods with flat baskets full of flower seed emitting a peculiar fragrance, which they also prepared for eating. They put some live coals among the seed, and, swinging it and throwing it together to shake the coals and the seed well and bring them to continual and close contact without burning the latter, they roasted it completely, and the mixture smelled so beautiful and refreshing that I tasted a good handful of it, and found it most excellent (p. 375).

Edwin Bryant, in his Rocky Mountain Adventures, gives this description of the acorn harvest:

We soon learned from them that they were a party engaged in gathering acorns, which to these poor Indians are what wheat and maize are to us. They showed us large quantities in their baskets under the trees. When dried and pulverized, the flour of the acorn is made into bread or mush, and is their "staff of life." It is their chief article of subsistence in this section of California. Their luxuries, such as bull beef and horse meat, they obtain by theft, or pay for in labor at exorbitant rates. The acorn of California, from the evergreen oak (*Quercus ilex*), is much larger, more oily, and less bitter than on the Atlantic side of the continent. In fruitful seasons the ground beneath the trees is covered with nuts, and the Indians have the providence, when the produce of the oak is thus plentiful, to provide against a short crop and the famine which must necessarily result to them from it by laying up a supply greater than they will consume in one year (p. 240).

The Hupa Indians for collecting seeds, according to Prof. P. E. Goddard, use the basket in the shape of a common burden basket in closely woven style.[a] They also made large storage baskets of close-twined work called djelo, the base being of greater diameter than the top.[a]

Plate 96 represents the harvesting outfit of the Hupa Indians on Hupa Reservation in northwestern California. There is the open-work-twined basket for picking the seeds, the carrying basket in openwork with a decorated band at the top for bearing the crop home, the granary basket, which bears significantly on the outside the image of destructive worms that eat the crop after it is harvested. The woman's head has a pad of soft-twined work on the forehead, across which the buckskin band of the carrying basket rests. The outfit of

---

[a] Life and Culture of the Hupas. Publications of the University of California, I, 1902, pl. xxii, fig. 2.

the mill consists of a large basket at the bottom for catching the acorn meal and millstone set in this for grinding, a hopper basket, most elaborately made, resting on the rock to hold the acorns that are being ground. A similar hopper is shown below, both in its form and structure. The pestle for grinding the acorns and the broom for sweeping up the meal complete the paraphernalia. Throughout the entire acorn area implements resembling these will be found.

The outfit for the Pomo acorn mush maker in Mendocino County, California, is illustrated by V. K. Chesnut[a] in his paper on Plants Used by the Indians of Mendocino County, California (fig. 71 and Plates 13, 18), issued in 1902, by the Department of Agriculture, Washington.

It consists of eleven pieces: The picking basket for the individual gatherer; the holding basket for receiving the contents of number one; the cone-shaped carrying basket, with headband; the granary basket at the home, holding two or more bushels, many of them have beautiful covers; the basket hopper, open at the bottom to fit on the mortar stone, the work of strengthening these tax the ingenuity of the weaver; the mat for the meal to be placed under the millstone; the sifting plaques, in openwork for coarse separating and tightly woven, for shaking the waste over the edge; the cooking pot of the closest weaving; the dipper; the eating bowls, and the daintily woven basket hat.

William H. Holmes illustrates at length the acorn harvesting and milling industry in northern California, carrying and hulling the nuts, pounding them in stone mortars, grinding the meal, separating the coarse particles, cleaning the meal by shaking and blowing, leaching in sand and using hot stones for cooking in basket pots.[b]

Plate 97 is a group of baskets in plain-twined weaving (Bamtush) in the collection of C. P. Wilcomb, of San Francisco. It consists of a conical carrying basket, mill hopper, granary basket, and mush bowl. The carrying basket is in plain-twined work throughout. Even the narrow bands near the top are no exception, for though each twist in the twine passes over two warp stems, on the next round the same two are included in the twist above. Casting the eye upward will show that in the upper band next to the border the same motive occurs, but the same pairs of stems are not inclosed in the twist. The effect of this ornament is quite pleasing, as the two bands with intervening space form an endless zigzag pattern. The border of this basket is formed by bending the warp stems down as the foundation of a coiled work which is strengthened by a hoop of wood. The bands of ornamentation on this and the other baskets in this group is explained under "Symbolism."

---

[a] Contributions to the National Herbarium, VII, pp. 295–408.
[b] Report of the U. S. National Museum, 1900, pls. 10–15 and 22.

The mill hopper is also in plain-twined weaving, strengthened with three narrow bands of tee weaving. The granary basket and the mush bowl are noteworthy especially on account of the peculiar method of finishing the work by merely cutting off the warp stems.

Plate 98 represents two specimens in the collection of C. P. Wilcomb, both of them from Tulare County, California. The upper figure is a bowl connected with body in twined weaving. The diameter is 14⅝ inches. The ornamentation is in four bands, the lower broken, the second in chevron pattern, the third human figures, the fourth the standard hour-glass pattern. On the margin are spots in black material in groups of fours. The lower figure represents a typical mortar stone with pestle and hopper, in this case glued to the upper surface of the millstone. The ornamentation on the upper is also the standard band of hexagonal figures.

Plate 99 represents a Yokut woman on the Tule River Reservation shaking acorn meal and sifting it for making mush.

In Plate 100, the same collection, is represented a Havasupai (Yuman) Indian woman screening corn in a roasting basket with hot stones and blowing out the chaff, using the specimen both for parching and cleaning the seeds.

Plate 101 shows a Coahuilla (Shoshonean) woman grinding acorn flour on a mortar stone, on the top of which has been cemented a hopper basket with open bottom. This method of grinding is extremely old, inasmuch as some of the pieces of ancient baskets in prehistoric graves, found by Mr. Pepper and others, are in this type and stitch of basketry.

Speaking of the Apache Indians and others farther south, Capt. John G. Bourke mentions their fanning trays for grinding the seeds of grasses. Hot stones are placed in them, with the coarse material and the chaff is burned out. The Captain also mentions that the trays are wet to keep them from burning. This can not be a universal practice, because in some of the specimens in the Museum the texture is very much charred.

Plate 102 shows the most primitive form of storage, holding several bushels, used by the Mohave Indians in the desert between Mexico and southern Arizona. It resembles more a bird's nest than a textile preparation. The specimen is in the Field Columbian Museum, Chicago, and to the courtesy of C. L. Owen and G. C. Simms I am indebted for the photograph.

The Mohave and other tribes have curious granaries for storing mesquite beans, corn, etc., near their houses. A platform is constructed on high poles; upon this is placed a round, bottomless basket from 3 to 5 feet in diameter and 2 to 3 feet deep. These are made of arrow-weed stalks tightly interwoven. When filled the top is sealed with mud to keep out rain. In specimens examined by Owen and Simms, of the Field Columbian Museum, several of these nest-like baskets were clustered on the same platform and a rude fence served for inclosure.[a]

IN HOUSE BUILDING AND FURNITURE

House and furniture were here and there constructed of basket work, so the basket maker became architect and cabinetmaker. Of the former, the wall may have been constructed like a huge, coarse basket, with upright stakes for warp and brush, canes, rushes, or leaves of palm for weft. The roof, also, especially in its framework, was in some tribes an immense shallow basket bottom inverted. The rafters were the parallel or radiating warp and the interlacing vines the openwork woof into which many kinds of thatch were fitted.

Accessory to the house, whether a woven structure or not, were fences, awnings, screens, and shelters. They were woven after the fashion of the walls. In middle America and the tropical portions of South America, but far more skillfully in the Philippine Islands and all about the Indo-Pacific, the mat and light basketry serve for seclusion and decoration among the houses. Open checkerwork, twilled weaving, wattling, or twined textile are as effective as they are light and easily put together. When they were moving about, or in situations where a compact dwelling would have been burdensome, it was an affair of only a few moments to imitate the nest-building birds and throw together a wickiup or leaf shelter of some kind.

The winter houses of the Pomo Indians were a rude kind of feathered basketry. They are described by Carl Purdy[b] as domes of wickerwork, thatched heavily with grass or tules (p. 443, with illustration). The summer houses were of wickerwork covered with boughs, and the tribe moved several times a year as acorns, fish, game, or dry quarters were desirable. They solved the problems of transportation by moving themselves about.

Furniture had not the pretentious meaning that it possesses in civilization. The bed for the Indians was the most desirable luxury. Their chairs were mats of many styles of weaving and many colors. All of them were plicated by hand and were the production of the basket maker.

But the bed was not always a basket. In the North it was the warmest fur and robes; in many tribes the mat took the place of the robe, and over a wide area the hammock was chair by day and bed at night. In some of these the twine is knotted or netted and the hammock is in no sense a basket. Throughout the Southwest a resting device is formed by the very ancient basket-makers' process of stringing a number of stiff rods together by three or more rows of weaving. (For a Hopi bridal costume case see Plate 103.)

---

[a] For illustration see Newton H. Chittenden, Land of Sunshine, 1901, p. 202.
[b] Land of Sunshine, XV, May, 1901.

IN MORTUARY CUSTOMS

The basket is intimately associated with Indian life in the "last act." Not only fabrics woven in basketry technic were wrapped about the dead and used to protect the body, but on the sentimental side examples of the finest workmanship were either deposited or burned with their makers.   Plate 104 is taken from Pepper's account of the basket-making Indians of Utah, and is interesting as exhibiting the method of burial among the ancient tribe of southeastern Utah in the canyon country.   These old people must have lived long in these curious retreats, for on top of their graves are found deposits made by later tribes.   The corpse was placed in the hollow of a rock, covered with a rabbit-skin robe made in twined weaving.   On top of all was turned upside down a coiled basket.   The plate shows the method of administering the blanket and the basket, and the lower figure of the plate declares the type and style of weaving used by these ancient basket makers.   The foundation is of three-rod type.   The four figures on the surface near the margin are like the butterfly design seen on some modern ware, but the symbol is not known.   Horatio N. Rust tells of a young Indian girl who was dying of consumption.   She wore on her person a small basket of beautiful workmanship and gave it to a young American, begging him to have her buried in a coffin and the little basket placed within.

Another Indian, Roherio by name, living in the southern California country, tells of his wife, who, when dying, called him to her and said: Take my basket cap, which I have always worn since I have been your wife, and burn it, with everything that is mine.   He obeyed her and burned two trunks full of personal property.

Clarence King describes vividly, in his Mountaineering in the Sierra Nevadas, a cremation scene:

In the opening between the line of huts a low pile of dry logs had been carefully laid, upon which, outstretched and wrapped in her blanket, lay the dead form of "Sally," the old basket maker, her face covered in careful folds.   Upon her heart were the grass-woven water bowl and her latest papoose basket.   The flames slowly lapped over, consuming the blanket, and caught the willow papoose basket.   When the husband saw this the tears streamed from his eyes; he lifted his hands eloquently, looking up at the sky and uttering heartbroken sobs.   All of the Indians intoned in pathetic measure, "Himalaya, Himalaya," looking first at the mound of fire and then out upon the fading sunset.

The desert region of Peru was favorable to the preservation of delicate textiles, and it is in the cemeteries of this region that large quantities of basketry in every style of weaving here described have been found.[a]   (For lace work see Plate 105.)

---

[a] For basketry (coiled and twined) from graves in Peru, see Eleventh Annual Report of the Peabody Museum, pp. 280–292.

IN RELATION TO THE POTTER'S ART

Pottery and basketry were in America, especially among the savage tribes, both the work of women. Before answering the question how far one art was useful to the other, attention must be called to the fact that in eastern United States both prevailed almost universally. In the Arctic, excepting the rude pottery of Alaska on Bering Sea, and on the Pacific from Mount St. Elias to Santa Barbara Islands, the tribes made only basketry. Those of the interior basin and all southward were expert in both.

It was formerly believed that in the eastern division of the United States, especially, pottery was made to a large extent in basketry. Eminent students held this opinion and there seemed to be abundant evidence of its truth. Cushing figures a basket with clay inside to protect the former in the cooking of seeds and grains.[a]

Holmes now believes that the extent to which good baskets were used for modeling pottery in this province has been greatly overestimated. There are innumerable examples of basketry and other textile markings on earthenware, and he divides them into five classes.

1. Impressions from the surface of rigid textile forms.

2. Impressions from cloth and nets.

3. From woven textures used over the hand or modeling implement.

4. From cords wrapped about modeling paddles or rocking tools.

5. Impressions of bits of cords or other textile units, singly or in groups, applied for ornament only and so arranged as to produce textile-like patterns.

In modeling a clay vessel a basket might be used as a support and pivot. It might assist in shaping the bodies of vessels, assuming to a limited extent the limits of a mold. Also, the mat upon which a plastic form rests will leave impressions that firing will render indelible. The tribes of the Pima linguistic family produce jars and baskets of the same shape; but if a row of Zuñi or the Hopi pottery be compared with a row of their basketry they would not suggest that either one was the predecessor and occasion of the other. Laying aside the inquiry whether the basket was the progenitor of the pot, inasmuch as the same hands often produced both, the former unwittingly rendered itself immortal by its many little helpful attentions to the latter in its formative stage. The pot was afterwards fired and worn out and broken into fragments that were buried out of sight. In these last years the archeologist exhumes the shards, washes them carefully, and makes casts of their surfaces in plaster or artist's clay. A glance shows that, though the surfaces of the shards are much worn away by time, the lines in the little cavities are as sharp as when the clay and

---

[a] William H. Holmes: American Anthropologist (N. S.), III, pp. 397–403; also F. H. Cushing, Fourth Annual Report of the Bureau of Ethnology, 1886, pp. 483–493.

the basket made each other's acquaintance centuries ago.   (See Plates 106, 107.)

In the shards examined by Eggers and Holmes one fact is preserved that no historian recounts, namely, that twined basketry as varied and beautiful as that of the Aleutian Islanders was made by the tribes in the Mississippi Valley before the fifteenth century.

AS A RECEPTACLE

Very few of the Indian tribes of America were so unsettled in life as to be without a home.   About such a place accumulated personal property and provisions for the future, large and small.   On the Great Plains of the West, receptacles were made of rawhide gaudily painted. On the MacKenzie drainage, bark of the white birch was the material, decorated with quills of the porcupine dyed in many colors.   But for holding the bone awl and the sinew thread, the trinkets belonging to dress, the outfits of fisherman and hunter, the basket and the wallet were well-nigh universal.   In the industries and other activities of life in which materials, utensils, apparatus, in a word, things were involved, there were receptacles for holding them.   The basket maker herself has a kit of appliances for making her wares.

One of the primary functions of basketry, if not the very first, was to contain or restrain something.   The weir, fence, wing of the game drive, wall of the house, besides many smaller objects of the coarsest weave were invented long before basketry became cooking utensils or works of ceremony.   The myriads of Indian baskets sold at railroad stations and summer resorts have gone back to first principles and are made for the sole purpose of holding.

In the north the small tools of the fur worker and trinkets are easily lost in the snow.   The workbasket or something in its stead is universal.   About Point Barrow the Tinné (Athapascan) Indians make coiled baskets in several styles of weaving.   These are traded to the Eskimo.   On the Bering seacoast of Alaska rougher trinket cases appear.   The Attu makers of dainty wallets in grass, living away out on the Aleutian chain, are quite as skillful in the manufacture of cigar cases, which, by the way, are nothing more than two of their old-fashioned cylinders fitted one into the other and flattened.   Receptacles of basket wood, with no other function than just to hold things, are to be found in all the areas of the Western Hemisphere, in all sizes from the granary down to the sheath for an awl, in every one of the technical processes and in every degree of fineness.   It is the one function of universal application.

Plate 108 is an ammunition holder in twined basketry from the Tlinkit Indians of Sitka, Alaska.   It is ornamented by false embroidery.   The interesting fact concerning this specimen is that as soon as these Indians came in contact with the Russians they began to imitate modern forms of apparatus in textile material. This telescope basket was used by the owner for holding caps, bullets, or other delicate objects for hunting. It also shows that the acculturation of form did not begin recently, but took place as soon as the Indian woman's eye rested upon some novel and attractive form. This specimen is Catalogue No. 1156 in the U. S. National Museum and was collected by James G. Swan.

Plate 109 represents a woman's workbasket of the Tlinkit Indians, of southeastern Indians, in twined weaving, ornamented in false embroidery. Doubtless the form is derived from Russian motives, but it is extremely common among the Indians in this locality and is useful in a thousand ways for holding material. This specimen was collected in Sitka, Alaska, by J. J. McLean.

The Fraser River tribes in British Columbia illustrate also what is said about the power of suggestion in modifying form, and even structure, in an art. The bulk of their stalwart baskets are made for cooking and harvesting apparatus. But where the Hudson Bay Company's and Malayo-Pacific packages came into view, another class of baskets appeared, fashioned in their shapes and ornamented over their entire surfaces. (See Plates 43 and 44.)

IN RELIGION

The one who carried the sacred basket in the Greek religious processions was called the Kanephoros, and it will be remembered that in the consecration of Aaron and his family to the priesthood, among the multitude of paraphernalia was the basket of shew bread.[a]

In one tribe, at least, of American aborigines—the Hopi of northeastern Arizona—bread consecrated to the service of religion is set before the altar in beautiful plaques of coiled and wicker basketry, on which the emblems of religion are wrought in colors.

By religion is meant beliefs about a spirit world, with all its inhabitants and their relations with mankind; this is creed, and cult, or worship. "The best for the gods" is the talisman in the rudest faiths as in the highest. So it will be found that basketry devoted to religion is worthy of its object.

In the autumn, during the months of September and October, the Hopi Indians of northeastern Arizona celebrate their basket dances. They have been studied by Dr. J. Walter Fewkes and J. G. Owen. The basket dance is a public exhibition, closing a series of secret rites, the whole festival being called *Lalakonti*. It is rather a posturing of the body in rhythm, together with songs, during which baskets are carried by women or thrown as gifts among the assembled spectators. Those taking part in these dances are in two groups—the basket

---

bearers, or chorus, and the basket throwers, or *Lakone manas*. The only man participating is a priest called the *Lakone taka*.

The costumes of the participants, the method of holding and throwing the baskets, and the struggles of the men for the specimens are all carefully described by Dr. Fewkes.[a]

In archæological studies at the Chevlon ruins, about 15 miles east of Winslow, Arizona, a large amount of basketry was found in the graves. Much of it had the form of plaques like those still used in Oraibi and the Middle Mesa. The inhabitants of the old pueblos at Chaves Pass were also clever basket makers, and had the same beliefs as their descendants concerning the kinship and close relationships of life between spirit beings and men.

With reference to these basket dances, Dr. Hough says the baskets used are shallow, circular trays, either coiled or wicker, invariably of Hopi manufacture and all decorated in colors. The designs on the *Lalakonti* baskets are various, and there seems to be a greater use of symbolic figures than in those specimens commonly offered for sale. In some examples the designs are conventionalized merely to the extent of adapting them to the field of the basket and the exigencies of the weaving. In most cases, however, the design is in the last stages of convention and the original motive is lost.

Plate 110 shows the portion of the Hopi *Lalakonti* ceremony in which the baskets are introduced by the young women.

The uses of baskets of the plaque type by the Moki may throw light on the reason for their occurrence in the "basket dances." In the household these plaques are devoted to various purposes; ground meal is heaped upon them in high cones by the grinders, or dry food, such as piki bread or dried peaches, is served in them. A basket being difficult and laborious in construction and high priced, besides being easily soiled and unsuitable for the uses to which pottery is put, is employed in cases of nicety, or, one might say, of luxury. Whenever presents are exchanged it is proper to carry them on basket trays.

Baskets form an important part of the paraphernalia of the religious fraternities, being used to at least as great an extent as pottery for containing sacred meal, the prayer-stick offerings, etc. Usually new plaques are prepared for sacred use upon the altars and in the service of the fraternities, notably the *Lalakonti*. It may be found that plaques are almost entirely of ceremonial import.

Sometimes baskets are placed on the walls of rooms as a decoration. This was observed at Sichomovi, where a frieze of Cohonino baskets decorated a room in the house of Wa lu tha ma.

The use of baskets in religious ceremonies by the Navaho Indians is described in Dr. Matthews's paper, The Mountain Chant, a Navaho

---

[a] J. Walter Fewkes, Journal of American Folk-Lore, XII, 1899, pp. 81 and 96.

Ceremony. (See page 515.) Among the Yaquis of northern Mexico baskets are used for holding palms, which they use in their sacred ceremonies. The Hupa Indians, on the Hupa Reservation, in one of their dances hold baskets in their hands, examples of which were

FIG. 109.
CEREMONIAL BASKET.
Hupa Indians, California.
Collected by P. H. Ray.

collected by Captain Ray, of the U. S. Army, and illustrated in the Smithsonian Report for 1886, Plate XI, fig. 45. (See fig. 109.)

Prof. P. E. Goddard[a] describes the use of this basket in the ceremony. (See Plate 111).

IN SOCIAL LIFE

Baskets played a role in the etiquette of the Indians. The Choctaws, in sending a gift of fruit, use a heart-shaped basket to convey a sentiment of sincerity. (See Plate 134.) The wedding basket of the Pomos is an exquisite production in twined weaving. During a marriage festivity the bride's mother presents her son-in-law with a large, handsome basket, which he must immediately fill with cakes and pine sugar for the guests. It is thereafter known as chi-mó pi-ká, or dowry. On such occasions the artist is incited by a combination of powerful motives to do her best. Among the same Indians the gift basket, presented by the maker as a token of friendship, is a masterpiece not only in fineness, but in the exquisite sentiments of its design. In the National Museum are good examples both of the wedding and of the gift baskets. (See Plates 112–114.)

The Gualala style of gambling, says Powers, prevails all over the state, but the Tulare have another sort, which pertains exclusively to the women. It is a kind of dice throwing, and is called *U-chu-us*. For a dice they take half of a large acorn or walnut shell, fill it level with pitch and pounded charcoal, and inlay it with bits of bright-colored abalone shells. For a dice table they weave a very large, fine basket tray, almost flat, and ornamented with devices woven in black or brown,

[a] See Life and Culture of the Hupa, University of California, 1903.

mostly rude imitations of trees and geometrical figures. Four squaws sit around it to play, and a fifth keeps tally with fifteen sticks. There are eight dice and they scoop them up with their hands and dash them into the basket, counting one when two or five flat surfaces turn up. (See Plates 115, 116.)

The rapidity with which the game goes forward is wonderful, and the players seem totally oblivious to all things in the world beside. After each throw that a player makes she exclaims *yet-ni* (equivalent to "one-y"), or *wi-a-tak*, or *ko-mai-eh*, which are simply a kind of sing-song or chanting. One old squaw, with scarcely a tooth in her head, one eye gone, her face all withered, but with a lower jaw as of iron, and features denoting extraordinary strength of will—a reckless old gambler, and evidently a teacher of the others—after each throw would grab into the basket and jerk her hand across it, as if by the motion of the air to turn the dice over before they settled, and ejaculate *wiatak*. It was amusing to see the savage energy with which this fierce old hag carried on the game. The others were modest and spoke in low tones, but she seemed to be unaware of the existence of anybody around her. [a]

The plates show two varieties of the Yokut gambling trays, the flat and the dished. The former is in the National Museum, collected by W. H. Holmes; the latter is in the C. P. Wilcomb collection, collected on the Tule River.

IN TRAPPING

One of the earliest and most primitive uses of basketry textile was in connection with the capture of animals. In a paper on traps published by the Smithsonian Institution, [b] the word *trap* is defined as "an invention for inducing animals to commit self-incarceration, self-arrest or suicide." The basketry traps are used principally for penning or impounding animals and not for killing them. In every one of the areas mentioned, coarse wickerwork or twined weaving are used in this function and there is little doubt that many of the very finest processses of weaving by hand were derived originally from coarse work of this character.

The Pomo Indians make a trap for catching fish from *Juncus effusus*. The interesting feature about these objects is that they are a gross production in brush of the rare Mohave carrying basket, in which the weft is wrapped once about each warp element in passing.

---

[a] Contributions to North American Ethnology, III, 1877, pp. 377, 378.

[b] Report of the Smithsonian Institution, 1901, pp. 461–473.

IN CARRYING WATER

Nearly everywhere throughout the Western Hemisphere the Indian was encamped near springs of water, and in his journeys about for hunting and other purposes knew always where to obtain it. An exception to this is the arid region of the western portion of the United States.

Among the Shoshonean tribes and in the pueblos, seeking out, carrying, and storing water was the chief industry and most of the religious ceremonies and prayers were with reference to rain.

The canteen and the larger carrying jar among the sedentary tribes was of pottery, but with the Utes, Apaches, and other unsettled tribes these vessels were of water-tight basketry made with round or conical bottom, so that in settling on a level the center of gravity would bring the vessel into an upright position and thereby keep the water from spilling. (Plates 32, 33.)

The transportation and storage of drinking water is one of the functions of pottery. Aquarius, the water bearer of the sky, is represented with a jar in his hands, and the spirits that haunt the springs in classic mythology are all of them friends of the potter. The Indians of the Atlantic area were well supplied with water and had vessels of clay. The Eskimo made bottles of sealskin; so did the tribes of the Pacific coast as far south as the Columbia. But in the interior Basin of the United States, Indians of the Shoshoean, Athapascan, and Yuman families substitute basketry for pottery in their canteens, jugs, pitchers, and small tanks. These are made in coiled or twined ware, and sealed with pine tar in the north and asphaltum in the south. It is probably owing to the unsettled life of these tribes that they out and out invented this ingenious substitute for fictile ware. There is no lack of clay, for pueblos in the midst of the region are the last strongholds of Keramos in America. And there was in pre-historic times no lack of pottery there, as the supply of charming whole pieces and precious fragments bear witness.

The most interesting connection of hydrotechny with basketry was discovered in a cliff-dwelling 3 miles north of White River Agency, on the White Mountain Apache Reservation, Arizona, by Charles L. Owen, of the Field Columbian Museum, Chicago. On the floor of the cavern baskets were built without bottoms. The warp was of willow shoots with the leaves on. The weft was in juniper and willow twigs in twined weaving or wattling. The interstices were filled with puddled clay, to make them useful for receptacles of water, which had to be transported from the canyon 300 feet below. An example brought away, No. 68876 in the Field Museum, measures 4 feet 10 inches in diameter and is 15 to 20 inches in height. (See Plate 102.)

The occurrence of basketry water receptacles is a good problem in the study of the parallelogram of subjective and objective forces which originated and developed special arts in primitive times everywhere. In this particular example, the originators of cement-tightened baskets had good textile material, knew the arts of weaving them, were on the move in desert countries where water sources were far apart, and could easily secure the pine sap or the asphaltum for tightening purposes.

Plate 117 illustrates the water jug or pitcher of larger size, called O-oats by the Paiutes. Most of these are in coiled weaving, but even there a variety of technic is shown both in the foundation and in the sewing.

The upper figure is a pitcher-shaped water carrier with globular body, used also for holding seed. The coiled foundation is of two or more rods, the stitches are wide apart and overlap in what is called in Pomo, *tsai* work. The border is in oblique coiled sewing, and the handle is an afterthought set on the neck. Its height is 10 inches. This specimen, Cat. No. 11249 in the National Museum, was collected in southern Utah by Major J. W. Powell.

The lower figure is a much neater specimen in which the foundation is a single rod and in sewing the stitches simply interlock with those underneath, giving a very much more regular form to the surface. The border is in oblique coiled sewing. There are lugs on the side for the purpose of carrying, and the headband is of soft deerskin. This specimen is Cat. No. 11876 in the U.S.N.M., and also was collected in southern Utah by Major J. W. Powell.

The Powell collection contains a large number of these carrying jars in coiled work. They differ in the form of the body somewhat and in the length and shape of the neck, but in other respects, in structure and function, they are the same.

Plate 118 shows two Navaho Indian girls carrying water in their *tusjehs*, or basket jars, after G. Wharton James.[a] The photograph is interesting also in illustrating the two methods of suspending burdens employed by the Indians. The girl on the right has a band across the top of her head, while the one in the rear supports the load from her shoulders. The latter method is also common in the south, especially in Mexico. The baskets are made in coiled weaving and dipped in pitch to make them water-tight.

ALPHABETICAL LIST OF USES

Armor made of slats and rods woven together.

Awning mats in front of cabins.

Bags for everything; for gathering, carrying, and storing, made in every quality.

Bait holding.

Bases for pottery-making (primitive wheel); also forms for portion of vessels.

Beds of matting in basketry.

Boiling baskets, for cooking flesh or mush.

[a] Indian Baskets, Pasadena, California, 1902, p. 31.

Bread, mixing or serving.

Burden baskets in endless varieties.

Burial caskets and deposits.

Cage for insects, birds etc.; also for children on Sioux travois.

Canoe covers, for cargoes (Swan).

Canteen, for personal water supply.

Cape, poncho, or other garment to cover the shoulders, both in animal and vegetable fiber.

Carrying basket, an immense class, with infinite variety of form and universal distribution.

Carrying chair, Guatemala and Peru.

Ceremonial objects; trays in rites and before altar, carried in dances, struggled for, etc.

Chef d'œuvres, to show the best one could do.

Chests for treasures, regalia, and fine costume.

Children's toys; imitations of more serious objects.

Clothing; robes of twine, with or without feathers; hats, jewelry, capes, fringes, petticoats, leggings, moccasins, and receptacles for these.

Coffins of canes and reeds wattled together.

Cooking baskets, used with hot stones.

Cradles or pappoose frames, quite widely distributed.

Creels, all varieties of fishermen's baskets.

Cremation baskets, burned at the woman's grave.

Cult baskets, Hupa basket wand (Ray), Hopi plaque (Fewkes).

Curtain mats for partitions.

Cushions in boats and kaiaks.

Dance baskets, used in ceremonies.

Ditty baskets for small articles of hunters.

Dress. (*See* Clothing.)

Drinking baskets or cups.

Drum, in Navaho ceremony.

Drying tray for fruit.

Eagle traps and cages.

Etiquette baskets, for giving away on the proper occasion.

Fences of coarse basket technic; hunting fences.

Fine art in basketry.

Fish, holding, transporting, creels, bait baskets.

Fish trap, fish weirs, fykes, etc.

Food-serving baskets.

Foundations for pottery.

Fringes on garments, in refined basket technic.

Furniture in basketry.

Gambling baskets.

Gathering or harvesting.

Gift baskets.

Granary or storage.

Grasshopper baskets, so called.

Hammocks in basket work.

Harvesting, fan or wand for beating seeds.

Hats for men or for women.

Head rings, olla rings for carrying.

Hedges, employed chiefly in game drives.

Hoppers, for acorn and other mortars.

Houses, walls, roofs, floors, doors, and other parts.

Inclosures for the beginning of domestication.

Insect cage, for lighting and other purposes.

Jewel baskets, chef d'oeuvres of woman's art.

Jewelry, woven in finest material for adornment.

Leggings in twined weave.

Lined with clay for cooking.

Love baskets.

Marks on pottery.

Meal trays, useful and sacred.

Medicine, associated with sorcery.

Milling outfit, grinding, hoppers, brushes, sieves, etc.

Moccasins or sandals.

Molds for pottery.

Money, mechanism of exchange.

Mortuary baskets of many kinds and functions.

Mud sandals, Klamath, for going in marshes.

Mush bowls for mixing or serving.

Musical instruments, rattles and drums.

Offerings of food to dead, and mortuary objects.

Paho, or prayer-stick wrappings (ancient graves).

Panniers, with saddles.

Papoose baskets.

Partitions for dwellings.

Patterns for pottery.

Picking baskets, for gathering nuts and fruits.

Pitcher basket, with wide mouth.

Plaques, for meal.

Plates or platters.

Ponchos. (See Capes.)

Pottery. (See "Marks on Pottery;" also used to line roasting trays (Cushing).)

Prayer basket, Pahos.

Preparing food, mixing mush, bread, etc.

Quivers.

Receptacles of all sorts, for cooked food, dried fish, and all kinds of preserved meats and fruits. The basket maker herself keeps her splints and stems in a basket.

Religion, used in services of.

Roasting trays, for poaching seeds.

Robes of shredded bark.

Roof of basketry.

Sacred meal trays.

Saddlebags, of late application.

Sails, in both continents.

Seats, at home, in boats, etc.

Seed baskets, harvesting, carrying, and storage.

Seed beater, for harvesting.

Serving food, for single persons or a company.

Sieves, for screening or for shaking.

Skirts, both of common and ceremonial dress.

Sleeping mats.

Storage, fish, berries, pemmican, acorns. All tribes stored some kind of food.

Trade, medium of.

Treasure baskets, those considered treasures.

Trinket and feather storage, also herbs, gum, paint, etc.

Vizors of Katchina masks, made from segments of coiled basketry (Ute type), Hopi.

Washbowl, in ceremonies.

Water bottles, drinking cups, etc., of basketry dipped in pitch.

Water transportation, rafts of cane, mats for sails.

Wedding blanket or cover.

Winnowing baskets for seeds.

Zootechny, or the arts associated with animal life.

VII. ETHNIC VARIETIES OF BASKETRY

For all arts belonging to humanity have a common bond and are included, as it were, in the same kinship.—CICERO.

The technical processes, the decorations, and the symbolism that may exist in the single basket having been scrutinized, it is in order to examine the geographic distribution of these forms in relation to ethnology and environment. Geography has much to do with human enterprises. It does not furnish the ingenious mind nor the skillful hand, but it does supply their materials for their exercise and set bounds in which the mind and hand soon discover how to reach their best.

America was, in aboriginal times, unequally occupied by native peoples. On the Atlantic slope in both continents vast areas were in possession of single linguistic groups called families. On the Pacific slope there were also a few influential families, but the rule was otherwise. Wedged in among the mountains wherever there was an inclosure abounding in food supply there were crowded what seemed to be shriveled remnants of once larger peoples, or fragments of disrupted families.

At once arises the query, Did they bring with them and preserve uncontaminated the stitches and patterns of their priscan basketry and keep the ancient models unchanged? It is to be feared that they did not, and that is why the ethnologist becomes embarrassed in trying to harmonize ethnology and technology. There are, notwithstanding, certain general effects which may be associated with definite peoples.

1. In the Eastern province the prevailing families were Algonquian, Iroquoian, Muskhogean, Caddoan, and a few remnants of smaller ones, in some instances numbering at present less than a hundred persons. The Siouan and other buffalo-hunting tribes on the plains will be omitted because the hide of the slain animals furnished them with receptacles as well as other conveniences of life. The basket makers in their territory belong elsewhere.

2. In the Alaskan province an interesting state of affairs existed with reference to the matter here investigated. In the interior of the peninsula are the Athapascan (or Tinné) tribes. Around the coast line dwell members of the Eskimauan family, having entirely different materials, workmanship, and technical processes. It will be seen later that the Eskimo as a whole are not skillful basket makers. There has been contact, however, between the two linguistic families. The Aleutian peoples are very different in this art from the Eskimo, their ware being among the most highly admired on the continent. In southeastern Alaska the Koloschan family are found, who are different from the Athapascans in the interior of the peninsula in that they do not make coiled basketry at all. The same is true of the Haida or Skittagetan family, in the Queen Charlotte Archipelago.

3. In the Frazer-Columbia province, including the drainage of these great rivers, the Salishan family, the Wakashan, the Shahaptian, and the Chinookan are the present basket-making families. As in the Siouan areas, so here a few small fragments or survivals fill in the gaps and waste places, but contribute little to the technical processes involved. In the discussion of basketry in this province a special characteristic will be brought out.

4. The California province, including also southern Oregon, is the most mixed of all in its ethnology. Many stocks of people whose languages are not known elsewhere, and many fragments of stocks that have a larger existence in other parts of America, are wedged into the mountain valleys and drainages of the streams. Nature has been most lavish here in her materials, and the finest textile plants for making baskets are to be found in California. The diversity of technic is almost as great as that of language. Few styles of weaving or coiling exist that do not have their representatives among this interminable labyrinth of valleys.

5. The Desert, or Interior province, is occupied in its northern portion by the great Shoshonean family, which extends from the forty-ninth parallel to Costa Rica, pushes its way over the Rocky Mountains into the Mississippi drainage and across southern California to the Santa Barbara islands on the Pacific coast, giving and receiving technical suggestions in its way. In the southern portion of this

interior province, Athapascan tribes, the Navaho and the Apache, the Yuman, and the Piman family are basket makers.

6. The sixth province includes Middle and South America, not because all the basketry in these regions is on the same plane, but owing to the small collections received from these quarters. A great portion of it is in the Torrid zone, where palm leaf and tough cane and reeds await the basket maker. There will be missing the characteristics of the North American tribes, and also local weaves will appear worthy of study.[a]

Unlike pottery, this fabric is not destroyed by frost, so that wherever textile material could be obtained there was no meteorological reason why the basket should not be forthcoming. The Athapascans of Alaska and northwestern Canada, possessed of both willow and spruce root, at once developed the coiled ware which their descendants, the Apache, are still making in Arizona.

East of the Rocky Mountains, in the Atlantic drainage of Canada and the United States, at the present time checker and willow work are practiced almost universally; but in the mounds of the Ohio Valley quite well diffused twined ware is found. The Gulf province afforded excellent cane (*Arundinaria macrosperma, Arundinaria gigantea, Arundinaria tecta*), and here, both in ancient times and in modern, diagonal plaiting of basketry and matting was prevalent in all tribes. The Plains province in its central portion relied chiefly on the hide of animals for its receptacles. But around its borders will be found intrusive processes of manufacture in twined, diagonal and coiled workmanship.

On its Pacific slopes North America is the home of basketry. From Attu, the westernmost island of the Aleutian chain, to the borders of northern Mexico is to be found practically every type of this art.

In Middle America, including southern Mexico and the Central American States, pottery was exalted among receptacles, and excellent fibers usurped the function of the coarser pliable materials of basketry.

Owing to differences of climate, rainfall, and other characteristics of environment, the materials for basketry vary greatly from region to region throughout America, and this in spite of all ethnic considerations. Again, the motives for the use of basketry differ from place to place, so much so that peoples of one blood make one ware in this place and another in that. Finally, however, it must never be for-

---

[a]The author acknowledges that many statements made in this ethnic portion of the work are at second hand and has been fortunate in being able to consult men of expert information. The Hudson and the Merriam collection, in Washington City, the Benham, Tozier, Emmons, Teit, Long, Whitcomb, McLeod, and others of the west coast have been placed cheerfully at his disposal. To Mr. C. C. Willoughby, Dr. Boas, Mr. Pepper, Dr. Dixon, Dr. Kroeber, and others mentioned in these pages, he is indebted for constant favors. He hopes that errors will be condoned.

gotten that the ideas, utilitarian and artistic, in the minds of the manufacturers themselves, serve to bestow special marks upon the work
of different tribes so as to give to them ethnic or national significance
under any circumstances.   In the following chapters the typical forms
of the various families of Indians will be illustrated.

Were there no mixture of tribes it might be possible to state in
every case the maker of each specimen from the technic and the ornamentation, though this opinion must be held with reserve.   Throughout the entire continent the practice of capturing women was common;
in each case the stolen ones carried to their homes the processes they
had been familiar with in their native tribe.   The Twana Indians on
Puget Sound practice ten different methods of basket making; the
Pomo Indians have eight processes; the Hopi Indians of Arizona have
at least five.   It is well known that each one of these tribes belong to
synthetic families.   In order to comprehend the extent of this relationship between the tribe and the art, the various basket-making
groups will be defined and the types of their work illustrated.   (See
Plates 154, 155.)

The mixing of basket work through the traveling about of women
is well illustrated in the story of Maria Narcissa, told by E. L. McLeod,
of Bakersfield, California.   Maria was born at San Gabriel mission
and brought up in Tejon Canyon.   There she retained the knowledge
of her native speech and learned the dialects of the surrounding tribes.
She married an American, reared and educated a large family of children, and is still living.   On her testimony tribes from the north as
far up as Tule River would come down to Tejon for social and religious
purposes, hold great feasts and dances, and gamble on the gaming
plaques.   Parties came longer journeys from San Fernando, San
Gabriel, Ventura, Santa Barbara, and Santa Inez, and Mr. McLeod
finds undoubted evidences of these meetings in the technic and the decorations on basketry.   (See Plates 115–116.)

From the Tule River country there came the beautiful flexible work,
an improvement on the Fresno ware.   But the Tejon basketry
excelled, the pieces were better finished, there was more emulation, a
greater variety of patterns, showing the influence of both north and
south.

There was trading of materials likewise, for you will see fine old
pieces from the caves on the Tejon with mission bottoms and Tejon
tops, also old specimens from caves in Santa Barbara County which
were made in Tejon.

LIST OF BASKET-MAKING TRIBES

The following list includes the names of those tribes known to collectors as makers of any kind of basketry, especially in North America, together with the linguistic families to which they belong, and their locations.

Abenaki, Algonquian family, Maine and Canada.

Aleut, Eskimauan family, Aleutian Islands.

Algonquian family, northern frontier and Canada, many tribes.

Apache, Athapascan family.   See Chiricahua, Jicarilla, Mescalero, San Carlos, White Mountain, Arizona, New Mexico, and Oklahoma.

Apache-Yuma, Yuman family, Palomas, Yuma County, Arizona.

Arapaho, Algonquian family, Shoshoni Agency, Wyoming; and Oklahoma.

Arikara, Caddoan family, Fort Berthold, North Dakota.

Ashochimi, Yukian family, near Healdsburg, California.

Atsuge.   See Hat Creek, branch of Pit River.

Attakapa, Attakapan family, southern Louisiana.

Attu Island.   See Aleut.

Auk, Koluschan family, Gastineaux Channel, southeastern Alaska.

Basket-Makers, Ancient Shoshonean family, Grand Gulch, southeastern Utah.

Bella Coola.   See Bilhula.

Bilhula, Salishan family, northwestern British Columbia.

Cahuilla.   See Coahuilla.

Calapooia, or Kalapuya.

Calpella, Kulanapan family, Ukiah, California.

Carriers.   See Thompson Indians.

Cayuse, Waiilatpuan family, Umatilla Agency, Oregon.

Chaves Pass Ruin, Hopi pueblo, Arizona.

Chehalis, Salishan family, Chehalis River, Washington.

Chemehuevi, Shoshonean family, Arizona and California boundary.

Cherokee, Iroquoian family, North Carolina and Indian Territory.

Chetimachas, Chetimachan family, Louisiana.   Also written Shetimachas.

Chevlon Ruins, Hopi pueblo, northeastern Arizona.

Chickasaw, Muskhogean family, Indian Territory.

Chilcotin, Athapascan family, Tsilkotinneh or Chilkyotins, distinct from Carriers, British Columbia.

Chilkat, Koluschan family, southeastern Alaska.

Chinook, Chinookan family, southeastern lower Columbia River, Washington.

Chippewa, Algonquian family, northern United States.

Chiricahua Apache, Athapascan family, Arizona and Oklahoma.

Choctaw, Muskhogean family, Louisiana.

Chukchansi, Yokut tribe, Mariposan family, Sierra region, California, north of Fresno.

Clallam, Salishan family, Washington.

Clatsop, Chinookan family, Clatsop County, Oregon.

Coahuilla, Shoshonean family, Coahuilla, Kawia, Kauvuya, Agua Caliente, Santa Rosa, Cabezon, Torres, Twenty-nine Palms and Cahuilla reservations, California; also Saboba, southern California.

Cocahebas.   See Merriam's list, page 468.

Coconinos.   See Havasupai, Yuman family.

Cocopa, Yuman family, near Mexican boundary, Arizona, and Lower California.

Concow, Pujunan family, Round Valley, California.

Coos, Kusan family, Coos County, Oregon.

Coquille.

Couteau. See Thompson Indians.

Cowlitz, Salishan family, Cowlitz River, Washington.

Coyotero Apache, Athapascan family, southern Arizona.

Coyuwee. See Paiutes.

Creeks, Muskhogean family, Southern States and Indian Territory.

Diegueños, Yuman family, San Diego County, California. Capitan Grande, Sequan, Santa Ysabel, Campo, Cuyamaka, and Morongo reservations.

Diggers, Pujunan family, (a popular name applied to vegetarian tribes), California, east of the Sacramento.

Eel Rivers, Athapascan family. See Flonho.

Eskimo, Eskimauan family, Arctic America.

Flathead, Salishan family, misnomer for Salish.

Flonho or Lolonkuh, Athapascan family, Eel River, California.

Fraser River, Salishan family, British Columbia.

Galice Creek, Kulanapan family. See Pomo.

Gallinomero, Kulanapan family, Cloverdale, California.

Garotero, Athapascan family. (Same as Coyotero.)

Gualala, Kulanapan family, Mendocino County, California.

Haida, Skittagetan family, Southern Alaska, Dall, Prince of Wales islands, Queen Charlotte Islands, and British Columbia.

Hat Creek, Palaihnihan family, northeastern California, branch of Pit Rivers.

Havasupai, Yuman family, Cataract Canyon, Arizona.

Hoh, Chimakuan family, Neah Bay, Washington.

Homolobi, ancient ruin near Winslow, in Arizona.

Hoochnom, Yukian family, Round Valley, California, Eel River.

Hoonah, Koluschan family, Cross Sound, Alaska.

Hopi, Shoshonean or Hopean family, Pueblos, northeastern Arizona. Wrongly Moki.

Hualapai. See Walapai.

Huicholes, Piman family, Zacatecas, etc., Mexico.

Hupa, Athapascan family, Trinity River, California.

Iroquois, Iroquoian family, northern frontier and Canada.

Jicarilla Apache, Athapascan family, northern New Mexico, Jicarilla Agency.

Kabinapo Pomo, Kulanapan family, Clear Lake, California, western part.

Karok or Cahroc, Quoratean family, Klamath River, California, Lower Salmon River and down Klamath to a few miles above Waitspeh.

Kaweah, Mariposan family, middle California, not Coahuilla.

Klamath, Lutuamian family, Klamath County, Oregon.

Klikitat, Shahaptian family, Yakama Reservation, Washington, Klikitat County, Oregon.

Kohonino, same as Havasupai.

Lillooet, Salishan family, western British Columbia.

Little Lakes, Kulanapan family, Round Valley Reservation, California.

Lolonkuh, Athapascan family, Eel River, California.

Luiseño or San Luis Rey Mission, Shoshonean family, Mesa Grande, Potrero, Temecula, Rincon, Los Coyotes, Pauma, and Pala reservations, villages at San Luis Rey, and San Felipe, California.

Lummi, Salishan family, north Puget Sound, Washington.

McCloud or Winnemem, Copehan family, northern California.

Maidu, Pujunan family, east of Sacramento River, California, Sacramento to Honey Lake, from Big Chico Creek to Bear River, California.

Makah, Wakashan family, Cape Flattery, Washington.

Makhelchel, Copehan family, Clear Lake, California.

Maricopa, Yuman family, southern Arizona.

Mattoal, Athapascan family, northwestern California.

Mayas, Mayan family, Yucatan and lands adjacent.

Melicite, Algonquian family, Quebec and New Brunswick.

Menomini, Algonquian family, northeast Wisconsin.

Mescalero Apache, Athapascan family, Mescalero Agency, eastern New Mexico.

Mewas. See Miwok.

Micmac, Algonquian family, Nova Scotia, New Brunswick, and Quebec.

Missions, a great many villages, Shoshonean and Yuman families, southern California.

    Agua Caliente (Shoshonean), a rancheria in western San Diego County.

    Augustine (Shoshonean).

    Coahuilla, Kawia (Shoshonean).

    Comoyei, Yuman family, all Yuma dialects between Lower Colorado River and Pacific Ocean and 32° to 34° north, Comoya, Quemaya, called Diegueños on the coast.

    Cuchan, Yuman family, Yumas so called.

    Cupania, in Agua Caliente.

    Diegueño, Yuman family, in Capitan Grande, Campo, Cuyamaka, Inaja, Sequan, Santa Ysabel, Mesa Grande, San Felipe, Manzanita villages.

    Kawia, Shoshonean family. See Coahuilla.

    Matayhoa, possibly the Diegueno village of Mataguay, in western part of San Diego County.

    Piute, Shoshonean family, at Twenty-nine Palms.

    Playanos, Shoshonean family, coast tribes of Coahuilla.

    Saboba (School), Shoshonean family, Tahktam village, San Jacinto Valley.

    San Felipe, Yuman family, a Diegueño rancheria of this name was 70 miles northeast of San Diego in 1883.

    San Fernando, Shoshonean family, related to San Gabriel.

    San Gabriel, Shoshonean family, also Kizh dialect, Tobikhar of Loew.

    San Juan Capistrano, Shoshonean family, formerly Netela dialect, Gaitchim of Loew, called Juaneños.

    San Lucania, Shoshonean family, also Cabezon, Potrero, Pala, Pauma, Rincon, Temecula, Puerto de la Cruz, Puerta Ygnacia, Torris, and Matajaui.

    San Luis Rey (de Francis), Shoshonean family, formerly Kizh dialect.

    Santa Inez. Same character of baskets as Santa Barbara.

    Santa Rosa.

    Serraño, Shoshonean family, Morongo, San Manuel, the Serranos or "mountaineers," formerly Tahktam, a division of Tabikhar.

    Takhtam (men), Shoshonean family, called Serranos, dialect, Coahuilla.

    Tule River, remnant of Tejon.

    Yuma, Yuman family, evidently the Cuchan or present Yumas.

Miwok, Moquelumnan family, California, from the Sierra to the San Joaquin River, from Cosumnes to the Fresno.

Modoc, Lutuamian family, Klamath Agency, Oregon, east of Shasta, north to Goose Lake Valley.

Mohave, Yuman family, between Fort Mohave and Ehrenberg, Lower Colorado River.

Moki or Hopi pueblos, Shoshonean family, northeastern Arizona.

Monos, Shoshonean family, sierras east of Yosemite, California.

Muckleshoot, Salishan family, Puget Sound, Tulalip Agency, Washington.

Nakum, Pujunan family. See Maidu.

Napa or Suisun or Solano, Copehan family, Sacramento River, California.

Natano, band of Hupa.

Navaho, Athapascan family, southern Utah, New Mexico, and Arizona.

Navarros, Kalanapan, Punta Arenas, California.

Nehalem, Salishan, Oregon.

Newooah. See Merriam's list, page 469.

Nez Percé, Shahaptin family, Nez Percé Agency, northern Idaho.

Nims. See Merriam's list, page 468.

Nishinam, Pujunan family, Sacramento Valley, California.

Niskwalli, Salishan family, or Nisqualli, Columbia River, Washington.

Nomelaki or Numlaki, Copehan family, Round Valley, California.

Nozis, Yanan family, south of Pit Rivers, California.

Nutka, Wakashan family, West Vancouver Island. See Makah.

Ojibwa, Algonquian family, Michigan.

Opata, Sierra Madre, Sonora and Chihuahua.

Oraibi, Shoshonean family. (See Hopi) Hopi pueblo.

Paiutes, Shoshonean family, Nevada agencies, Reno, Carson and Wadsworth on central route of the Southern Pacific Company; Tule River Reservation, Kern River, White River, Poso Creek, Sierras near Walker Pass, eastern Nevada, Pyramid Lake, Schurz, Hawthorne, Virginia City.

Panamint, Shoshonean family, Death Valley, Inyo County, California.

Papago, Piman family, south of Tucson, Arizona, and Sonora, Mexico.

Patawat, Wishoskan family, Humboldt Bay to Arcata, California.

Patwin, Copehan family, Sacramento River, California.

Pawnee, Caddoan family. See Arikara.

Penobscot, Algonquian family, Old Town, Maine.

Peruvian, Kechuan family, Highlands of Peru.

Pima, Piman family, Gila River, Arizona.

Pit Rivers, Palaihnihan family, Pit River, California.

Pomo, many subdivisions, Kulanapan family, Mendocino and Lake counties, California.

Potter Valley, Kulanapan family, Round Valley, California.

Pueblos: of the Rio Grande, Tanoan and Keresan families; those of the Zuñian family are in New Mexico; Shoshonean pueblos are in northeastern Arizona.

Puyallup, Salishan family, Puget Sound, Washington.

Queets, Chimakuan family, northwest Washington.

Quilleute, Chimakuan family, northwest Washington.

Quinaielt, same as Quinaults, Salishan family, west Washington.

Redwoods, Yukian family, Round Valley Reservation, California.

Rogue Rivers, Athapascan family, Grande Ronde Reservation, Oregon.

Round Valley tribes. See Concow, Little Lakes, Nomelakki, Pit Rivers, Redwoods, Wailaki, and Yuki.

Saboba Mission, Shoshonean, southern California.

Salishan family, great variety of technic and many tribes, Washington and British Columbia.

San Carlos, Apache, Athapascan family, southeastern Arizona.

San Felipe pueblo, Keresan family, Rio Grande River, New Mexico.

Santa Barbara Mission, Moquelumnan family, southwestern California.

Santa Rosa Mission, Yuman family, San Diego County, California.

Santa Ysabel, Yuman family, San Diego County, California.

Seminole, Muskhogean family, Florida.

Shasta, Sastean family, in Shasta and Scott Valley, California.

Shoshoni, Shoshonean family, Great Interior Basin, Montana.

Shushwap, Salishan family, British Columbia.

Sia, Keresan family, New Mexico, a Rio Grande pueblo.

Sikyatki, ruin, ancient Hopi pueblo, northern Arizona.

Siletz, Athapascan, Siletz Reservation, Oregon.

Sitka, Koluschan family, Alaska.

Siwash, Chinook jargon for "Savage," general name for Northwest Coast Indians.

Skagit, Salishan family, North Puget Sound.

Skokomish, Salishan family, or Twana, upper Puget Sound, Puyallup Agency, Skokomish Reservation, Skokomish River.

Snohomish, Salishan family, upper Puget Sound, Tulalip Agency and reservation, northeast of the Skokomish.

Solano. See Napa.

Spokan, Salishan family, Montana and Washington.

Squaxin, Salishan family, Puget Sound.

Suisun. See Napa.

Tarku, Koluschan family, Tarku Inlet, Alaska.

Tatu, Yukian family, Round Valley, United States Indian Agency, California.

Tejon, Tulares of Tejon Pass, Moquelumnan family.

Thompson Indians, Salishan family, also Couteau or Knife Indians, British Columbia, southern interior of British Columbia, mostly east of Coast Range, in valleys of Fraser, Thompson, and Nicola rivers.

Tillamuk, Tillamook County, Oregon.

Tinné, Athapascan family, name for tribes in Alaska and Canada.

Tlinkit, Koluschan family, southern Alaska.

Tolowa, Athapascan family, Crescent City, California.

Tonto Apache, Athapascan family, southern Arizona.

Towanhoo. See Twana.

Tsinuk or Chinook, Chinookan family, Columbia River, Washington.

Tulalip, Salishan family, Tulalip Reservation, Washington.

Tulares, Moquelumnan family, Tule River, California.

Tule Rivers, Mariposan family, southern California.

Twana, Salishan family, Puget Sound, Washington.

Umatilla, Shahaptian family, Umatilla and Morrow counties, Oregon.

Umpqua, Athapascan, Grande Ronde, Oregon.

Ute, Shoshonean, in Utah under many names.

Viard or Weeyot, Wishoskan family, Eel River, California.

Waiam, Shahaptian family, village rather than tribe, Des Chutes Rivers, Oregon.

Wailaki, Copehan family, Sacramento Valley, California.

Walapai or Hualapai, Yuman family, northwestern Arizona.

Wallawalla, Umatilla Agency, Oregon.

Wappo, Yukian family, Alexander Valley, California.

Warm Spring Apaches, Athapascan, Chiricahua, Mexico.

Wasco, Chinookan family, The Dalles, Oregon.

Washo, Washoan family, Reno, Carson, and Wadsworth, on central route of the Southern Pacific Company, western Nevada, Genoa, Gardenville, Washoe, Franktown.

White Mountain Apache, Fort Apache Agency, eastern Arizona.

Wikchumni, Yokut tribe, Mariposan family, Sierra region, California.

Wintun, Pit River Indians, Copehan family, Sacramento River, California.

Wuksatches. See Merriam's list, p. 469.

Wushqum, Chinookan, Columbia River, Oregon.

Yakima, Shahaptian family, Washington.

Yakutat, Koluschan family, Yakutat Bay, southeast Alaska.

Yamhill, Kalapooian family, Willamette Valley, Oregon.

Yana or Nozi, Yanan family, near Redding, California.

Yaqui, Piman, Sonora, Mexico.

Yoalmani, Yokut tribe, Mariposan family, Tule River Reservation, California.

Yoerkali, Yokut tribe, Mariposan family, Tule River Reservation, California.

Yokaia, Kulanapan family, Ukiah Valley, California.
Yokuts, Mariposan family, mid-California.
Yuki or Ukie, Yukian family, Round Valley, California.
Yurok, Weitspekan family, Klamath River, California.
Zuñi, Zuñian family, western New Mexico.

EASTERN NORTH AMERICA

For thus the tale was told
By a Penobscot woman
As she sat weaving a basket,
A basket or *abaznoda*
Of that sweet-scented grass
Which Indians dearly love.
—CHARLES GODFREY LELAND.

Eastern North America will include the tribes east of the Rocky Mountains. Many of them are now basket makers, but archeology is doing excellent service in helping to complete a map of this area in order to determine the distribution of the various technical processes that obtained in aboriginal times. The few types of the art that now survive must not be taken as covering the ground of ancient weaves. The recovery of the latter by the Bureau of American Ethnology, the Peabody Museum, and other explorations is one of the most wonderful contributions of the spade to the ethnologist. Though basketry was anciently made of grass, hemp fiber, bark, young stalks, and sapwood, and for that reason is the most perishable of human manufactures, under favorable conditions salt mines, nitrous caves, the desert's aridity, metallic earths, and even fire have kindly preserved enough of the delicate textures to reveal the processes of weaving in vogue many centuries ago.

Indian women in the Mississippi Valley used to decorate the outsides of clay vessels by pressing string and basketry products on the soft material before burning. Thus they preserved the record of the art for all time. By applying modeler's clay to these ancient fragments the texture is at once revealed. In Popular Science Monthly[a] will be seen account of experiments with these sybilline shards, by George E. Sellers. William H. Holmes simultaneously made larger investigations and published accounts of experiments by him on Mound Builders and other ancient pottery of this area.[b] He carefully washed the fragments of their ware and made casts of the outer surface. The result was astonishing. Natural forces had eaten away and greatly obscured the marks of textiles on the outside surface of the shards, but in the bottom of the cavities, filled for centuries with earth, the impressions have been carefully preserved, and "the manner in which the fabric in all its details of plaiting, netting, and weaving were constructed can be brought out quite as graphically as

[a] Vol. XI, 1877, p. 573.
[b] Third Annual Report of the Bureau of Ethnology, 1884, pp. 393–425.

though one were examining the surface of the original vessels." On the surfaces of rocks the paleo-botanist discovers the delicate impressions of leaves. In these indelible lines he reads the names of species of trees that grew millenniums ago. So, through these impressions on potsherds the archeologist is able to discover lost arts of whose existence all other evidence has perished. (See Plate 107.)

All along our northern frontier and in many parts of Canada the Iroquois and Chippewa now fabricate baskets from the ash, birch, linden, and other white woods and the vernal or sweet grass (*Savastana odorata*). The method of manufacture is universally the same; it is the plainest in-and-out checker and wicker weaving. (See Plates 117 and 121). The basketry is far from monotonous, however, for the greatest variety is secured by difference of form, of color, of the relative size of the parts, and of ornamentation. In form the baskets run the whole gamut as among the Haida and Makah, guided by the maker's fancy and the demands of trade. These Indians all live on the border of civilization and derive a large revenue from the sale of their wares. The colors are of native manufacture—red, yellow, blue, green, alternating with the natural color of the wood. To begin with the rudest, let us take a dozen or sixteen strips of paper half an inch wide and cross them so as to have one-half perpendicular to the other half, woven in checker at the center and extending to form the equal arms of a cross. Bend up these arms perpendicular with the woven checker and pass a continuous splint similar to the framework round and round in a continuous coil from the bottom to the top. Fit a hoop of wood to the top, bend down the upright splints over this, and sew the whole together with a whipping of splint, and you will have the type basket. (See figs. 9 and 10 on Plate 119.) Now, by varying the width of the splint used to cover the sides a great difference of appearance is secured. The complete operation among the Menominees was studied out by W. J. Hoffman,[a] and will be seen in figs. 110 to 114. In the National Museum are baskets made of uniformly cut splints not over one-sixteenth of an inch in width.

Finally, the Algonkin, as well as the Southern Indians, have learned to decorate baskets with a great variety of rolls, looking much like the napkins on the table of a hotel. The weaver draws a splint under the warp stick, gives it a turn up and down, or two turns in different directions, and draws the loose end tightly under the next warp stick but one. This operation is repeated, forming around the basket one or more rows of projecting ornaments. Morgan bears testimony to the skill of the Iroquois women in the art.[b]

The basket woman at her work sits upon the ground in front of her lodge, or frequently of a little booth or shelter—the first step in the

---

[a] Fourteenth Annual Report of the Bureau of Ethnology, 1896, p. 260.
[b] The League of the Iroquois, 1851, pp. vi–55.

evolution of the artist's studio. The materials which she gathered long ago with much pains, and has been hoarding up, are within easy reach. Her hands and her teeth are both available in her work, aided by only a small supply of tools. A number of Indian women at work will be seen in different connections throughout this paper.

Plate 120 shows Caroline Masta, an Abenaki Indian woman from Pierreville, Canada, seated in her humble laboratory at Belmar, New Jersey. Her materials are of black ash (*Fraxinus nigra*) and sweet grass (*Savastana odorata*). The former has been worked out by machinery in Canada, and is piled up around her; the latter is gathered and braided by her relatives, and sent to her all ready for the last step in manufacture. This Indian woman conducts a thriving business, not being able to make up ware as fast as there is demand for it. Specimens of her work are shown in Plate 119, photographed by Herbert B. Rowland.

To illustrate more fully the survival of the old art in the new era, Plate 121 represents three Chippewa women near Saginaw, Michigan, making splint baskets. They are seated no longer in the midst of wretchedness, but in an apple orchard. The clothesline and the receptacles filled with fruit mark the changed life. It will be noticed, also, that the woman on the left is using for her splints a gauge set with metal blades. Indeed, the broad strips lying on the ground were worked out by machinery. Checkerwork and wickerwork are the only forms of technic practiced by these Chippewas. It will not be assumed by anyone that the improvement in environment has redounded to the benefit of the savage art. The baskets are the common frame ware, and often the best of them bear no comparison in refinement with the work of their most savage sisters on the west coast. Photographed by Harlan I. Smith.

The acme of the northern Algonkin weaving is in twilled matting. The operation, technically, is just on the border between free-hand plaiting and loom work. Plate 122 is a mat plaited by a Chippewa squaw, about 50 years old, at Grand Marais, Minnesota. It is of cedar bast made in strips a quarter of an inch wide, and is in three colors— one the natural tinge of the material and the other two dyed. The interesting features are, first, that the weaving is done from below upward, as in the Haida basketry and in the work carried on by Virginia Indians in the days of John Smith.

A small rod or stiff cord of bark is suspended by means of eight loops from a pole resting on two forked sticks. This is to give free motion to the woman's hands. Over this the warp strings are suspended freely. The Chilkat blanket weaver, also, as will be seen, has no other machinery. For a few rows the weaving is simple checkerwork of the plainest kind, and then begins a series of twilled patterns over two and under two. But even this simplest technic so lends itself to charming effects of light and shade that there is not a monotonous square inch on the surface. Another band of plain weaving is followed by zigzag and angular work, inclosing lines and squares, giving birth to a very pleasing effect. Some of the oldest pictures preserved in the early chronicles of the Algonkin Indians, to whom the Chippewa belong, show them weaving in exactly the same fashion.

The mat described above was made for Capt. R. D. Gaillard, U. S. A., in a single day, the work beginning at 9 o'clock in the morning and the finished product being delivered 2 miles away at 4 o'clock in the afternoon. It is 6 feet 5 inches long and 4 feet 5 inches wide.

The Menomini Indians of the Algonquian family, living in northern Wisconsin, are quite expert in various forms of basket work and hand weaving. Mats are woven from the leaves of rushes, flags or cattails, and cedar bark. They are for roofing temporary structures, such as medicine lodges, for partitions, floor mats and wrappings, and for various purposes in the canoes. The leaves and stems are strung

Fig. 110.

ASH LOG FOR MAKING SPLINTS.

Menomini Indians.

After W. J. Hoffman.

together by means of threads made of basswood fiber. In this they imitate a kind of textile well distributed throughout North America formerly.

The mats shown on Plates 21, 22, and 23 of Dr. Walter J. Hoffmann's paper[a] on this tribe are made from the inner bark of the cedar, cut in strips averaging one-half inch in width, in mixed, twilled, and checker weaving, which, combined with the native color of the material and dyed strips, produce the greatest variety of diaper patterns. They do not differ essentially from Captain Gaillard's mat just described.

The baskets of the Menominees resemble those of the eastern Canadian Indians. A log of elm wood is beaten until the space between the annual layers of growth is destroyed; the thin strips are then pulled off, cut to a uniform width, and scraped as smooth as possible. At present gauges of steel are used for the purpose. The weaving is done in checker, twilled, and wicker work. A section of the beaten log, showing the annual layers loosened, the mallet of wood, and the modern knife, resembling the "man's knife" throughout all the northern tribes, are shown in figs. 110 to 114. For the finer kinds of bag-

---

a Fourteenth Annual Report of the Bureau of Ethnology, 1896, p. 260.

ging the inner bark of the young sprouts of basswood is employed. It is removed in sheets and boiled in water with a quantity of lye. This softens the fiber and prepares for the next process, which consists in pulling bunches of the boiled bark forward and backward through a hole in the shoulder blade of the deer. The fiber is twisted into yarn and made into cord or twine by winding on the thigh with the palm of the hand. This advance in the preparation of the textile elements paves the way for twined weaving.

FIG. 111.
WOODEN MALLET
FOR LOOSENING
SPLINTS.

Fig. 1, Plate 123, is an example of hexagonal weaving in a Mackenzie River snowshoe in which the vertical elements answering to warps are crossed and not interlaced, and the fabric is bound together by the weaving in and out of a single rawhide thong. Fig. 2, on the same plate, illustrates the next step in this weaving, and is suggestive of a feature in the twilled basketry taken from graves in a cemetery at Ancon, Peru, namely, the method by which a bar of the snowshoe frame enters into the weaving and widens the meshes. Most beautiful effects are produced on the surface of these snowshoes by the different methods of administering the warp. This has been carefully worked out by John Murdoch in his paper upon the Eskimo of Point Barrow, Alaska,[a] and is referred to here simply to show how the methods of weaving in basketry are to be seen in other materials for other purposes.

In fig. 3, same plate, the warps at certain points in the manipulation are twisted in pairs about each other, a technical process in vogue throughout middle America, beginning as far north as the Mohave country in southern Arizona. It might be called the first step in lace making. Fig. 4, same plate, introduces another element of complexity wherein the warp elements instead of being twisted around each other are wrapped once or twice about the weft, so that the primitive lace work is effected both vertically and horizontally.

FIG. 112.
BASKET-MAKER'S
KNIFE OF NA-
TIVE WORK-
MANSHIP.

Charles C. Willoughby, of the Peabody Museum, Cambridge, Massachusetts, is of the opinion that coiled basketry was used among the Ojibwa Indians (Chippewa) on the Great Lakes before contact with the

---

[a] Ninth Annual Report of the Bureau of Ethnology, 1892, pp. 342–352.

whites, and mentions very old specimens now in the possession of that museum, and others have been seen in private collections. The foundation coils are of sweet grass and about one-quarter of an inch in diameter. In some very old specimens the sewing is done with looped stitches, being continuous from the edge toward the center of the basket and not following the coils, as is usual. He also finds the following references to old basket work of the New England Indians. (See Plate 124.) Gookin is quoted, writing in 1674, with the following words:

Several sorts of baskets, great and small, some of them hold 4 bushels or more, and so on downward to a pint. * * * Some of these baskets are made of rushes and some of bents (coarse grass), others of maize husks, others of a kind of silk grass, others of a kind of wild hemp, and some of bark of trees. Many of these are very neat and artificial, with the portraitures of birds, beasts, fishes, and flowers upon them in colors.

The soldiers under Captain Underhill, after destroying the Pequot fort in Connecticut in 1637, brought back with them "several delightful baskets." Brereton (1602) found baskets of twigs "not unlike our osier." Champlain saw corn stored in "great grass sacks." Josselyn

FIG. 113.

COIL OF BASKET STRIPS.

writes, "Baskets, bags, and mats, woven with bark of the lime tree and rushes of several kinds, dyed as before, some black, blue, red, yellow." In 1620 the Pilgrims found on a cache at Cape Cod "a great new basket, round and narrow at the top and containing 3 or 4 bushels of shelled corn, with 36 goodly ears unshelled." The New England Indians were probably not less expert basket makers than other tribes to the west and south. Does not the fact that the three distinct forms of weaving—twined, checker, and coiled—still found among the Ojibwas seem to indicate a survival of these types from prehistoric times all over the great Algonkin area? A few years back this type of coiled work was more in vogue than at present. The next specimen described will take the reader a long way from the Great Lakes. (C. C. Willoughby.)

Plate 125 shows the detail of a flat coiled basket of the Eskimo about Cumberland Inlet, eastern Canada. The foundation likewise contains a bundle of straws, but badly put together and sewed with sinew thread, the stitches being wide apart and caught beneath a few straws of the preceding coil. The bottom is flat and the walls drawn in so as to give a compressed shape. This interesting specimen has been many years in the National Museum and is credited to Capt. C. F. Hall, the Arctic explorer. It may be compared with others of the same type from the southern Canadian border. Catalogue No. 10203; height, 1¾ inches. A much later specimen also from the Eskimo is shown in the next plate.

Plate 126 is openwork coiled basketry of the Eskimo of Davis Inlet, eastern Canada. The foundation is of straw and the sewing is done in the same material, the stitches merely interlocking. The noteworthy characteristic of the basket is the slight amount of sewing in certain portions. The bottom is not unlike the work of the western Eskimo, and, indeed, is a typical illustration. There is a little splitting of stitches, but probably not designed. On the sides the openwork is produced by wrapping the foundation with the straw for one-half an inch and then sewing, as in ordinary coiled work, the angles to the coil below. This may be compared in the wrapping with the openwork coiled basketry of the Kern County Indians in California. (See fig. 196.) Sewing of exactly the same style is to be found in northern Europe, and the suggestion is made that this particular method among the eastern Eskimo is an acculturation. To come nearer home, coiled basketry in rafia that is taught in the schools is largely in this wrapped and sewed method. The Eskimo of this area were for centuries in contact with Norse settlers. This specimen is 8¼ inches in length, and was collected by L. M. Turner.

FIG. 114.

FINISHED WICKER BASKET.

Plate 127 gives the profile and inside view of a shallow coiled basket tray of the Comanche Indians, living on the plains east of the Rocky Mountains, used principally in gambling. The foundation is of rods and splints, the sewing with leaf of yucca (*Yucca arkansana*). Especial attention is invited to the furcate stitches, designedly and symmetrically split. This technic relegates the basket to the Ute or Shoshonean area, west of the Rockies. The Comanches belong to the Shoshonean family. Its diameter is 9 inches.

In the National Museum are four small, dish-shaped, coiled gambling baskets, Catalogue Nos. 6342, 8427, and 153932, gathered from the Rees or Caddoan Indians, the other one from the Mandans, who are Siouan. These baskets are made from willow, on a two-rod foundation, but roughly assembled and sewed with splints of the same material. The borders are all well done in false braid. No more interesting specimens are to be found in this collection.

There are four other gambling baskets of the same type, but of different material, and are fairly made. The foundation is a single stem of, perhaps, willow, the sewing in the leaves of yucca (*Yucca arkansana*). Catalogue Nos. 152802, 152803, 165246, and 165765, and gathered from the Cheyenne, Arapaho, and Kiowan Indians in Indian Territory.

Finally, modern pedagogy has found in the long leaves of the Georgia pine a material by means of which poor people may weave a little of the sense of beauty into their lives.

Plate 128 is a covered basket, made near Augusta, Georgia, from the leaves of the pine by a native Georgia woman, under the instruction and patronage of Mrs. Percy H. Babcock, of Hudson, Ohio. The sewing material is tough, brown linen thread. The interesting characteristic in this specimen is the undesigned resemblance between the stitching and that on the Hudson Bay Eskimo specimen, as well as the old Chippewa specimen in the Peabody Museum, in Cambridge, Massachusetts.

Coiled work, as was shown in the chapter on weaving, changes to lace work by omitting the hard foundation. In this Eastern Area two witnesses, far apart in time, are here to testify to the widespread ancientness of a coiled work now universal in tropical America.

Figs. *a* and *b*, Plate 129, represent the method of weaving in the game bags, or muskemoots, of the Dog Rib and other Athapascan Indians in northwestern Canada for domestic purposes. These tribes and their relatives in central Alaska use the birch-bark vessels for all sorts of domestic purposes. For transportation they do not make regular baskets, but buckskin wallets, in which a process of coiled weaving now to be described is employed. The sides and borders of the game bags are of dressed skin of moose and reindeer. For the body of the bag the same material is cut into fine string and rolled. This material is called "babiche." It is quite evident that before the introduction of the steel knife this material was much coarser, as may be known not only from the game bags, but also from the snowshoes. By examining fig. *b* a small section from one of the muskemoots will show how the work is done. The border of the bag on its lower edge is pierced at equal distances for the reception of the first row of weaving. Through these holes the babiche is strung by half hitches, or what is called "buttonhole stitch." The work proceeds in the same manner round and round until it is desirable to make a variation in the technical process. In the middle of the drawing it will be seen how this is done. The end of the babiche is carried through a stitch in the row above and twisted one and a half times about itself. As many turns as is desirable can be made, and thus the ornamentation may be varied. This method of coiled work, the first described in the table of methods (page 248), does not occur again among the Indians until the borders of Mexico are reached, where the tribes in their carrying nets, and farther south in their wallets and hammocks, employ precisely the same method of workmanship. This specimen, Catalogue No. 2023, with several others in the U. S. National Museum from the Dog Rib Indians of northwestern Canada, was collected by Bernard R. Ross.

Warren K. Moorehead found examples of the muskemoot weaving in the Hopewell mounds, Ohio. There was nothing but an easy portage here and there to hinder passage by water from the mouth of the Mackenzie to the neighborhood of the Hopewell mounds. Examples in Peabody Museum, Massachusetts, and in the Field Columbian, Chicago, prove the identity of technic. (See figs. 115 and 116.)

FIG. 115.
COILED BASKETRY.
Hopewell Mound, Ohio.
After C. C. Willoughby, Peabody Museum.

FIG. 116.
COILED BASKETRY.
Hopewell Mound, Ohio.
After C. C. Willoughby, Peabody Museum.

There is a general impression that the baskets of the ordinary soft character described were used by these eastern peoples in the manufacture of pottery and were ruthlessly destroyed in the burning, but Holmes's investigations tend to show that pliable materials had been almost exclusively employed. In the Pueblo region the case was quite different, though there is no evidence of the burning of the basket.

The twined wallets or other fabrics used were removed before the vessel was burned or even dried. In many cases handles and ornaments were added after these impressions were made, also incised designs were executed in the soft clay after the removal of the textile.

It is quite evident that textile impressions were used to enhance the beauty of the vessel, not to support the clay in process of construction.

In many examples, notably the salt vessels of Saline River, Illinois, the fabric was applied after the vessel was finished, inasmuch as the loose threads sag or festoon toward the rim. Simple cord markings arranged to form patterns have been employed on many examples. And in those cases where basketry textile was pressed on the surface it was not the common, careless weaving, but the elegant designs, as will be seen in the plates.

The textile markings on pottery, ancient and modern, are of five classes:

1. Impressions on the surface, made by rigid basketry, used in molding and modeling.

2. Impressions of pliable fabrics on the soft clay.

3. Impressions of woven textures used over the hand or on a modeling or malleating implement.

4. Impressions of cords wrapped about modeling or malleating paddles or rocking tools.

5. Impressions of bits of cords or other textile units, singly or in groups, applied for ornament only, and so arranged as to give textile-like patterns.[a]

Fig. 117.
WICKERWORK FROM CAVE IN KENTUCKY.
After W. H. Holmes.

If the reader will turn to the classification of basket-making methods (p. 190), it will be noticed that many of these are to be found in the ancient basket ware impressed on pottery by the eastern Indians. Referring to Professor Holmes's paper, openwork checker weaving is very rare among impressions on clay. Foster illustrates one example on pottery from a mound on Great Miami River, Butler County, Ohio. Checkerwork of the close type, on the other hand, was practiced in nearly all the Atlantic States, upon the testimony of pottery fragments.

From potsherds found in the State of New York, closely packed checkerwork patterns have been copied. Charred fabrics from mounds in Ohio reveal the coarsest kinds of oblique checker weaving. Holmes illustrates an example in which the oblique work imitates mat plaiting without a frame, worked from a corner. The selvage and the weft cross the texture obliquely.[b]

---

[a] W. H. Holmes, American Anthropologist (N. S.), III, 1901, pp. 397–403.

[b] See Thirteenth Annual Report of the Bureau of Ethnology, 1896, pl. VII, fig. c.

Not only checkerwork, but twilled work in cane and in twine and wickerwork in soft material have been brought to light by cave explorations in the Western and Southern States. In the Third Annual Report of the Bureau of Ethnology Holmes figures an example of wickerwork in soft materials from a cave in Kentucky. (See figs. 117, 118, and 119.) [a]

To show the distribution of this ancient style of weaving, reference is here made to—

1. Coarse oblique checker twilled work from Ohio, made of twine.

2. In the same volume (fig. 12) is shown a fragment of twilled cane matting from Petite Anse Island, Louisiana. It has been preserved all these years by salt. (See fig. 126.)

FIG. 118.

CHARRED FABRIC FROM MOUND.

After W. H. Holmes.

FIG. 119.

CHARRED FABRIC FROM MOUND.

After W. H. Holmes.

3. Plate 2 in Holmes's report shows a mat of split cane from a rock shelter on Cliff Creek, Morgan County, Tennessee. It is 6 feet 6 inches by 3 feet 4 inches. The variety of twilled effects and the patterned border leave nothing to be desired.

4. In a mound near Augusta, Georgia, a fragment of twilled matting was found attached to the surface of a bit of copper, Holmes's fig. 11. The interesting feature of this example is that on the side shown the warp passes over one and under four, the weft, over four and under one. His fig. 15, from Alabama, is similar, only the formula is three and one.

5. Fig. 14 is from an impression of twilled weaving on a fragment of pottery found in Polk County, Tennessee. Three characteristics of this fragment claim attention. The warp is of fine twine, the weft of

[a] Thirteenth Annual Report of the Bureau of Ethnology, 1896, pl. VII, figs. c and d.

coarse yarn; the work is over two, both in warp and weft; the weaving is oblique. The effect of this technic is pleasing and unique, the components being bands of close work alternating with bands of open-work, made up of sloping elements giving great variety to unity.

It will be seen that the checker and the twilled work in ancient eastern North America had about the same distribution as now.

Twined weaving was common throughout the Middle and Eastern States of the Union in prehistoric times. Fabrics of this class were employed by the ancient potters in nearly all of the States. Every variety of twined weaving known to the modern Indian was practiced

Fig. 120.
TWINED FISHTRAP.
Virginia Indians.
After Thomas Hariot.

by the old-time people—the mound-builders especially. Holmes figures examples from pottery in Tennessee, Georgia, Arkansas, Illinois, Missouri, and Iowa. Even the intricate and delicate forms of twined weaving described on page 234 as zig-zag or divided warp and crossed warp were well known.

The ancient pottery of the Mississippi Valley furnishes many examples of this, as will be seen in Holmes's papers.[a]

Traces of wattled work are found in the mounds of the Lower Mis-

---

[a] Prehistoric Textile Fabrics of the United States, Third Annual Report of the Bureau of Ethnology, 1884; Prehistoric Textile Art of Eastern United States, the same, Thirteenth Annual Report, 1896; and, A Study of the Textile Art, etc., Sixth Annual Report, 1888.

sissippi Valley, where imprints of the interlaced canes occur in the baked clay plaster with which the dwellings were finished. In the same connection John Smith, Butel-Dumont, Du Pratz, Lafitau, and John Lawson are quoted on the use of wattling for houses, inclosure, biers, and burial platforms. A fish trap with long wings done in twined wattling is figured in Hariot and here reproduced from Holmes. (See fig. 120.)

The illustration shows a warp of stakes driven into the bottom of the stream close enough together to let the small fry pass through and to offer no impediment to the flow of water. Brush or poles constitute the warp. The rivers of the Atlantic coast teemed with shad, herring, rockfish, sturgeon, and more, in the spring, and it is permitted to infer that twined fish traps were universal there.

Plate 130, thanks to the preserving care of potsherds, introduces the reader to the old basket makers of no one knows how many centuries ago. From three fragments, selected out of myriads and shown in the plate on the right hand, the casts on the left being in plaster, one might think himself studying specimens from the Aleutian Islands or the Great Interior Basin. The figure at the bottom is in plain openwork of twined weaving, the material being a soft bast, perhaps of native hemp. Hundreds of wallets indistinguishable in texture from this are now brought from around Bristol Bay, Alaska. The figure in the middle is openwork twined weaving in diagonal pattern. The warp strands are in pairs and flexible, making the interstices triangular and giving to the weaving the appearance of "fagoting." If the weft were forced close together, the texture would be the common twilled work of the Pacific slope. The upper figures are also twined, but of rarer style, the warp being set diagonally. This figure is worthy of note in two respects. The workmanship in twisting of the threads is superb. One would have to look a long time through a collection of twined weaving of the present day to see threads near so fine. Not until the outermost island of the Aleutian chain was reached would the specimen appear. The other characteristic is the sloping warp, a thing of rare occurrence in twined weaving.

A further glance at basketry technic preserved in impressions on pottery and in caves shows plain twined weave, open or closed, with vertical or oblique warp; twilled weaving in twined weft and twined weaving with zigzag warp; three-ply twined weaving, and a style of twined work, which for exhausting possibilities of variety in warp treatment will vie with any modern example. The material is good twine, the warp is administered in groups of sixes, oblique toward the right. The weft is a two-ply twine which in crossing the warp takes in a strand at each half turn and is twisted tightly in the open spaces. The pattern is varied by bands of close weft in three rows, above and below which the groups of six warp strands are split into threes.

Attention is called to Plate 8 in the Thirteenth Bureau Report, where is shown ancient twined work preserved by being wrapped about copper celts.[a] (See figs. 121–122; also Plate 107.)

Plate 131 represents an open twined wallet of the Ojibwa Indians (Algonquian stock), at Angwassag Village, near St. Charles, Saginaw County, Michigan. The native name is Na Moot and it is made from the inner bark of the slippery elm (*Ulmus americana*). Other bags of the same technique in the U. S. National Museum are from the elm bark associated with red and black yarn. The technic of these wallets is so interesting in the sur-

FIG. 121.
TWINED WEAVE FROM ANCIENT POTTERY.
Tennessee.
After W. H. Holmes.

vival of ancient weaves that they justify a special description. The weft is plain twined weaving; all the ornamentation, therefore, is effected by means of the warp, which is partly vertical, but more of the zigzag type seen in many Aleutian Island wallets. In all of the specimens examined the warp is made up of twine, partly in the material of the weft and partly in colored yarns. The diameter of the warp twine, especially the yarns, seems to be greater than the length of the twists in the weft, so that there is a crowding which brings one color to the front and leaves another color inside—that is, the figures that are brown on the outside will appear in yarn on the inside and the reverse. To be more explicit, beginning at the lower edge of any one of these wallets the warp may be in pairs, the elements of which separate and come together alternately in the rows of weaving. On the outside of the bag two elm-bark warp strands will be included and appear; in the next half twine two yarns will be included and show on the inside of the wallet. After this zigzag process goes on

FIG. 122.
TWINED WEAVE FROM ANCIENT POTTERY.
Tennessee.
After W. H. Holmes.

---

[a] Thirteenth Annual Report of the Bureau of Ethnology, 1896, figs. 21–26, and plates VII and VIII.

for a short distance the weaver changes her plan, omits the bark or the yarn warp altogether, but continues the twining process, catching the warp in every other half turn of the twine. Again, there will be a row or two of ordinary twined weaving with straight warp, when she returns to her zigzag method, covering the entire surface therewith. At the top of the bag an inch or less of plain twined weaving in which the warps are vertical and included in pairs brings her to the outer border, where all the warps are twisted together and turned back to be fastened off in the texture. In an old example in the National Museum long, cut fringes are sewed to the upper margin and to the sides of the bag.

The photographs of the twined bag shown in Plate 131 were taken by William Orchard, of the American Museum of Natural History, and presented to the National Museum by Harlan I. Smith. On one side a mountain lion and the other an eagle with geometric figures are shown in black. The technic of this particular example from left to right would be five vertical rows of plain twined weaving; nine rows of mixed warp, but plain weaving; a course of braided warp in which the four elements of two rows of warp are braided together and included in the twine. On the other side is a similar administration. The middle portion shows zigzag twined weaving, figured. Above this is a row of three-ply twined weaving, as among many of the Western tribes; above this three rows of plain twined weaving in openwork including all the warps. At the top the warps are twisted and fastened into the texture. It must be clearly understood that the figures which show black on the outside—that is, the eagle and the lion—will be white on the inside, necessarily. The colors used in the small specimen of the National Museum are the natural color of the bark mixed with brown, black, and blue yarns. The National Museum is indebted to Andrew John, a Seneca Indian of New York, for a number of specimens of modern Iroquoian twined ware from corn husks.

There was a decided lack of coiled basketry in all this vast region. Every kind of hand-woven ware was known. Algonquian, Iroquoian, Siouan, and Muskhogean tribes of the present, and all the cave-dwelling, mound-building, ancients, seem, so far as the evidence points, to have known little of coiling.

From this hasty survey of ancient hand weaving in basketry and the other receptacles, as well as in matting, webbing, sandals, and such products of the textile art as resemble basketry, it is now allowed to examine their modern representatives in the southern portions of the same area.

In the States of North Carolina, South Carolina, Georgia, Florida, Alabama, Mississippi, and Louisiana are many Indians still living, remnants of the Cherokees (Iroquoian); Choctaws, Creeks, Chickasaws, and Seminoles (Muskhogean), and the almost vanished Attakapas and

Chetimachas. Some of them were removed fifty years ago into the Indian Territory. Through the lowlands of these States grow the interminable cane brakes, and from the split cane all these tribes make their basketry. They follow the twilled pattern of weaving. Even now there may be purchased in Mobile, New Orleans, and other Southern cities little baskets of yellow, red, black, and green cane woven in twill, crossing with the woof two or more warp splints, and managing the checks so as to produce diamonds and various zigzag patterns on the outside. The Choctaws make a basket oval at the top and pointed below for presents,

FIG. 123.
DETAIL OF TWILLED BASKETRY BORDER.
Choctaw Indians, Louisiana.
Cat. No. 24143, U.S.N.M. Collected by Father Roquet.

averring that this shape imitated the heart, which always accompanies every gift. The handles of their basketry are very clumsily put on, marring greatly the appearance of the otherwise attractive object.

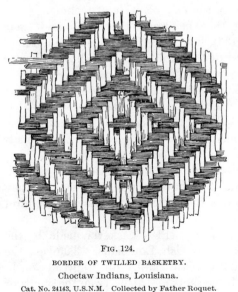

FIG. 124.
BORDER OF TWILLED BASKETRY.
Choctaw Indians, Louisiana.
Cat. No. 24143, U.S.N.M. Collected by Father Roquet.

Often in weaving two thin strips are laid together, the soft sides inward. The evident motive in doubling the thin strips is to have both sides of the basket or mat glossy and smooth. Further on it will be noted that in twined weaving, where the strands of the weft are from split roots, both sides are rendered smooth by revolving each strand half a turn as it passes through between the warp stems. (See p. 406.)

Figs. 123 and 124 show the detail of twilled basketry among the Southern tribes, both in the coarser and finer varieties. In fig. 123, *a* and *b*, will be seen the border. Each weft strand crosses four warp strands. In this example the warp, however, does not cover each time the same number of weft strands; the consequence is a nearly horizontal diagonal effect in the pattern. To form the border a few of the warp filaments are bent down and inclosed in a wrapping of the same material.   Underneath this is a row of twined weaving, which holds in place those warp elements that do not enter into the texture.   A much neater example of work of this kind is shown in the next figure, where the filaments are more carefully prepared and manipulated and the border more neatly finished, but the technical process is the same.   The artistic effect of plain twilled work is shown in this example.

Fig. 124 exhibits the process of crossing in what might be called diaper or figured work.   The effect is heightened by dyeing black one set of the filaments, either warp or weft.   In that case the figures stand out most prominently.   The entire effect of this sort of weaving, however, is in the endless combination of rectangles, black and white, all having the same width and different lengths.

The basket shown in this dissected weaving is Choctaw, Catalogue No. 24143, in the U. S. National Museum, collected by Father Roquet, of New Orleans.

Plates 132–133 represent the twilled basketry of the Chetimacha Indians, Chetimachan family, who have their home on Grande River and the larger part in Charenton, St. Marys Parish.   The name is derived from the Choctaw words *tchuti*, "cooking vessels," *masha*, "they possess."   Mr. Gatschet in 1881 found about fifty individuals still living.   The material of their work is the cane (*Arundinaria tecta*) and all of their weaving is in the twilled style of technic.

Compared with the work of the Choctaws (Plate 134) and their neighbors, the Attakapa (Plate 135), it is more picturesque and attractive, the colors being the original of the cane, red and yellow.   Similar work is to be seen in the northern part of South America, especially in Guiana.   The interesting feature of the Attakapa weaving is that frequently the specimens have the appearance of being double—that is, both the outside and the inside of the receptacle presenting the small surface of the cane.   At once the work connects itself with matting found in the caves of Kentucky and Tennessee.

Plate 133 represents a fine collection of old Chetimachas in the collection of Mrs. Sidney Bradford, of Avery Parish, Louisiana.   They should be examined carefully, since they were posed so as to exhibit the technic of the various parts.

Plate 135 shows a small number of twilled basketry made by the Attakapa Indians living in Calcasieu Parish, Louisiana.   They are the last remnant of an independent linguistic family once spread southward along the Texan coast.   The baskets are made from the stems of the cane.   The outer tough layer is split off and dyed if necessary.   It is then worked into twilled ware, which by the texture and variety of colors shows elegant designs.

These specimens, Catalogue Nos. 165735 to 165739 in the U. S. National Museum, were collected in Louisiana by Mrs. William Preston Johnston.

The Cherokee make the handsomest clothes baskets, considering their materials. They divide large swamp canes into long, thin, narrow splinters, which they dye for several colors, and manage the workmanship so well that both the inside and outside are covered with a beautiful variety of pleasing figures; and though for the space of 2 inches below the upper edge of each basket it is worked into one, through the other parts they are worked asunder, as if they were two joined atop by some strong cement. A large nest consists of eight or ten baskets contained one within another. Their dimensions are different, but they usually make the outside basket about a foot deep, a foot and a half broad, and almost a yard long.[a]

A type collection of this ware was made for the National Museum by James Mooney.[b]

Fig. 125 shows one of the oldest and most beautiful baskets in the National Museum, presented by Drs. Gray and Matthews, of the Army. Four bent poles constitute the framework. Those at the sides are 10 inches apart at the top, 4 at the bottom, and are quite concealed in the structure. The end pair cross these at right angles and descend 6 inches to afford a rest for the load. The carrying strap is of rawhide. The weaving is in twilled work, with diaper patterns made in narrow strips of bark, some having their outer, some their inner surface exposed.

FIG. 125.
TWILLED BASKET.
Arikara Indians.
Cat. No. 84340, U.S.N.M.   Collected by Gray and Matthews.

The weaving was done by an Arikara woman in Dakota. Now, these Indians are not Sioux, but belong to the Caddoan family spread over Louisiana and Texas. It should not be surprising, therefore, to find baskets similar to those of the Cherokees and the Gulf tribes in their hands.

In close connection with wickerwork and checkerwork is twilled or diagonal technic from many localities, especially in the South. An interesting example is illustrated by Holmes,[c] the two elements, the warp

[a]James Adair, History of the American Indians, London, 1775, p. 424.
[b]Nineteenth Annual Report of the Bureau of Ethnology, 1900, p. 176.
[c]Third Annual Report of the Bureau of Ethnology, 1884, p. 416, fig. 98.

and the weft, are entirely different material, one a finely spun thread, the other a loose, coarse filament several times wider than the former, and are woven together in the ordinary plan of under two and over two, and yet the difference in the width and tension of the two elements produces a most charming effect which is not lost, after many thousands of years, in the cast taken from the surface of the fragment. (See p. 225.) An example of matting, also illustrated by Holmes, was taken from a piece of pottery found in Alabama. It is worked in the diagonal style, but on one side the warp passes over one and under three, and, consequently, though the matting was destroyed hundreds of years ago it is certain that on the other side of the fabric the weft made a similar figure, but vertical. (See p. 225.)

Fig. 126.
ANCIENT TWILLED MATTING.
Petit Anse Island, Louisiana.

The caves of Kentucky furnish specimens of ancient textiles preserved in nitrous earth, and fig. 117 is an illustration of one of these, revealing a wicker type of weaving in soft materials, not found on pottery, however.[a]

One of the most interesting examples of this ancient work is illustrated by Foster, also taken from a mound on Great Miami River, Ohio. It has a warp of twine on which the weft is wrapped round

[a] Third Annual Report of the Bureau of Ethnology, 1884, p. 403, fig. 67.

and round. (See p. 241.) Only one family of Indians on the whole Western Hemisphere at present employ this technic, the Yuman, of Arizona. (Fig. 13; compare fig. 14 in the chapter on processes.)

It is an interesting fact that the Andamanese, living halfway round the world, employ the same method of workmanship on their open fish baskets.

Fig. 126 is from the photograph of a specimen of ancient twilled matting from Petit Anse Island, near Vermilion Bay, coast of Louisiana, presented to the Smithsonian Institution by J. F. Cleu, in May, 1866. Petit Anse Island is the locality of the remarkable mine of rock salt, exploited during the civil war, and from which, for a considerable time, the Southern States derived a great part of their supply of this article. The salt is almost chemically pure and apparently inexhaustible in quantity, occurring in every part of the island, which is about 5,000 acres in extent, at a depth below the surface of the soil of 15 or 20 feet. The fragment of matting here photographed was found near the surface of the salt. No vast antiquity can be argued on this account, but the specimen is without doubt very old and a relic of the weavers who lived a long time before the discovery of America. The material consists of the outer bark of the common Southern cane (*Arundinaria tecta*) and has been preserved for so long a period both by its siliceous character and the strongly saline condition of the soil.

ALASKA AND THE NORTH PACIFIC

There is a charm in the name of such Indian materials as spruce root, wild rye, and cedar bark, but they would be useless to us without the Indian touch.
—Mary White.

For convenience of study a line may be drawn across the map of North America from Dixon Entrance northeastward so as to have Queen Charlotte Islands and the makers of coiled basketry that are inland to the north of it. The tribes included will be Athapascan, Eskimauan, Koluschan, and Skittagetan. Among the two first named twined and coiled work in many styles of weaving will be found, while the two last named and their northern neighbors, the Aleuts, have avoided coiled basketry altogether. In Plate 136 are gathered types of the peninsula of Alaska, Athapascan, Eskimo, and Aleutian, embracing hard coil, soft coil, closed twined work, open twined work, straight warp, crossed warp, and hemstitch, gathered by E. W. Nelson.

In studying the basketry of this area the following division, according to tribes and families, will be found convenient:

1. Athapascan (interior of Alaska).
2. Eskimo (around shore).
3. Aleuts (Aleutian Archipelago).
4. Tlinkits (southeastern Alaska).
5. Haidas (Queen Charlotte Archipelago).

ATHAPASCAN COILED BASKETRY

Perhaps no other family of American tribes has such a variety of contacts with neighbors of different linguistic families and of limitations in environments having little likeness to one another. This northern branch of them, as will be seen in Father Morice's list,[a] is in touch along their southern border with Algonquian descendants of Mound Builders on the Ohio, with birch-bark workers in northern middle Canada, and with Pacific coast tribes here and there. Some of these were noted in speaking of Region 1, page 379, with illustrations. Further on other contacts will be shown. The distribution of the family is given by Powell on his linguistic map of North America.[b]

Here the Athapascans are in touch with Eskimo; indeed, most of

⅓

FIG. 127.
COILED WORKBASKET.
Tinné Indians, Alaska.
Cat. No. 89801, U.S.N.M.   Collected by P. H. Ray.

the specimens of their ware shown were procured from the latter in trade. Their technical methods will be best understood through illustrations.

The northern Tinné practice several varieties of technic in their coiled work. The tribes of the interior of Alaska make a very coarse coiled basket now becoming common. Some of the very old pieces have the buttonhole stitch in the sewing.

In a collection of pieces no two will agree either in shape or composition.

The best of the ware is from near the Mackenzie mouth, where dyed feathers are used for decoration. Some of the oldest specimens in the National Museum entered in the first catalogue are coiled basket trays of the Athapascan Indian tribes living in Fort Simpson at the mouth of the Mackenzie River. Splints of willow and spruce root are employed in the work and the ornamentation is meager, consisting of stripes on the side, and borders in quilled work dyed in different colors. These specimens vary from 6 to 8 inches in diameter, and were gathered by R. MacFarlane, B. R. Ross and W. L. Hardesty.

Fig. 127 is a coiled basket jar of the Tinné Indians near Point Barrow, Alaska. The specimen belongs to the single-rod type, in which one rod or stem constitutes the foundation. The sewing is done with split stems of willow, passing over the rod in progress and under the one forming the coil underneath. The illustration here given of this specimen is from Murdoch's paper on the Point Barrow Eskimo.[c]

---

[a] Transactions of the Canadian Institute, Toronto, IV, 1894, Pt. 1, No. 7.

[b] Seventh Annual Report of the Bureau of Ethnology, Washington, 1891, p. 55.

[c] Ninth Annual Report of the Bureau of American Ethnology, 1892, pp. 326–327.

It is said to have come from Sidaru. The owner declared that it came from the Great River in the South, which Mr. Murdoch interprets to mean the Kowak, flowing into Hotham Inlet. The Eskimo are in the habit of going to this place in order to trade with the Indians, and thus this coiled basket found its way into the possession of the Eskimo at Point Barrow. This figure is 336 on page 326 in Murdoch's paper. Catalogue No. 89801. Height, about $3\frac{5}{16}$ inches. Collected by P. H. Ray, U. S. Army.

Catalogue No. 89802 in the U. S. National Museum is a conical workbasket, with a sealskin top for a drawing string to keep the contents from falling out. It is in coiled weaving over a single rod, from Sidaru, northern Alaska, near Point Barrow, collected by Lieut. P. H. Ray, U. S. Army. It is similar in technic with No. 89801. Its height is $4\frac{1}{2}$ inches, and it has been described by Murdoch. (See fig. 128.)

FIG. 128.
COILED WORKBASKET.
Tinné Indians.
Collected by P. H. Ray.

Catalogue No. 56564 in the U. S. National Museum is an Eskimo woman's workbox (Aguma, ama, ipiaru) in coiled basketry, from Point Barrow, Alaska, also collected by Lieutenant Ray. The material is willow and the technic is coiled work of

FIG. 129.
COILED WORKBASKET.
Tinné Indians.
Collected by P. H. Ray.

the single-rod type. The neck of the basket is of black tanned sealskin and is tied with a string of the same material. Height, $1\frac{3}{4}$ inches. It has been described by Murdoch. (See fig. 129.)

Take an example from another part of Alaska. Fig. 130 is a coiled basket of the Tinné Indians who are settled on the Lower Yukon River. The foundation is a single rod of spruce root and the sewing is done with splints of the same material. It belongs to the type of coiled work called a single rod (see p. 250); the stitches interlock with those underneath and inclose also the rod of that coil. Each stitch, therefore, really incloses two foundations. In the explorations of Dall, Nelson, and Turner, in this long stretch of river bottom were collected many specimens showing transition between Indian and Eskimo activities.

On the bottom the basket maker has taken the greatest pains to split the stitches of each coil with those of the coil beyond, giving to each one, looked at from the center, a bifurcated appearance which is quite ornamental.   The same technic will be observed further on in examining the workmanship of the Thompson River Indians in British Columbia, and ·by their neighbors; the Chilcotin, belonging to the

FIG. 130.

COILED WORKBASKET.

Tinné Indians.

Cat. No. 24342, U.S.N.M.   Collected by Lucien Turner.

same linguistic stock.   The Eskimo woman also in making her coiled basket work splits the stitches of her coil and sews through them. This process is kept up on the body of this specimen half the way up.

FIG. 131.

DETAIL OF COILED BASKET.

Tinné Indians.

Collected by Lucien Turner.

Above that it ceases, as shown in the square inch enlarged fig. 131.   The coils vary considerably in width; the stitches also are not of the same size, so that there is by no means the uniform regularity, either horizontally or vertically, that one observes in the California area.   It will be noticed, too, that the top of each stitch is narrowed by reason of the crowding.   Over the entire surface of this specimen it is quite impossible to see the foundation rod because of this crowding of stitches.

This specimen, like many others from the Athapascan area, is jar shaped, and under good conditions would hold water.   Catalogue No. 24342 in the U. S. National Museum.   Collected, with many others, on the Lower Yukon River by Lucien M. Turner. Diameter, 8½ inches; height, 6¾ inches.

It is a long way from middle Alaska to the Hupa Valley, northern California. The basket here shown is No. 126520 in the U. S. National Museum, collected by Captain Ray.[a] It is introduced to show a single wonderful coincidence between the work of Tinné and Hupa, who speak languages of the same family in regions wide apart. It is coiled work. (See fig. 132.)

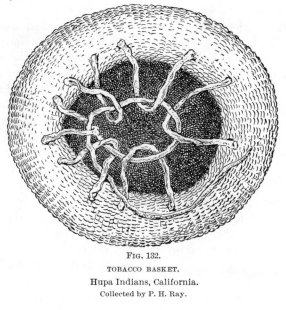

Fig. 132.
TOBACCO BASKET.
Hupa Indians, California.
Collected by P. H. Ray.

ESKIMO BASKETRY

Baskets not only have an infinite variety of uses from village to village, but among each people they have a multitude of uses. From the shore of Norton Sound to the Kuskokwim the women are expert in weaving grass mats, baskets, and bags. Grass mats are used on the sleeping benches and for wrapping around bedding. They are used also as sails for umiaks. They now frequently serve as curtains to partition off the corners of a room or sleeping platform. Small mats are placed also in the manholes of kaiaks as cushions. The bags are used for storing fish, berries, and other food supplies, or for clothing. Smaller bags and baskets are made for containing small articles used in the house.[b]

Two types of basket work are found in close proximity among the Eskimo in the neighborhood of Norton Sound and Bristol Bay, north and south, the twined and the coiled. In the former (fig. 133) the

[a] Smithsonian Report, 1886, Pt. 1, pl. xv, fig. 67.
[b] E. W. Nelson, Eighteenth Annual Report of the Bureau of Ethnology, 1900, pl. 74.

treatment is precisely the same as in those of Aleutian Islands to be described, but the Eskimo wallet is of coarser material and the weaving is far more rudely done. Quite as interesting as the wallets is the matting. (See Plate 136.)

At Chuwuk, on the Lower Yukon, Nelson saw a woman making one of these mats and watched the process she employed. A set of three or four straws was twisted and the ends turned in, forming a strand, a number of which were arranged side by side with their ends fastened along a stick, the primeval loom, forming one end of the mat and hanging down for the warp. Other strands were then used as woof. By a deft twist of the fingers it was carried from one side to the other, passing above and below the strands of the warp; then the woof strand was passed around the outer strand of the warp and twined to repeat the operation. The strands were made continuous by adding straws as necessary, and with each motion the strands were twisted a little so as to keep them firmly together. By this simple method a variety of patterns are produced.

Grass bags are started from the bottom where the strands of the warp, consisting of two or more grass stems, are fastened together and extend vertically downward. The woof is formed by a double strand of grass, each of which is twisted about itself and both twined with the strands of the warp inclosed in the turns; both are continually twisted as the weaving progresses. In coarsely made bags the strands of the woof are spaced from an inch to two inches apart, and those of the warp at intervals of from a quarter to half an inch. These bags have a conical bottom, which slopes from the center to the sides. At the mouth the ends of the warp are braided to form a continuous edge.[a]

The lower figures in Nelson's group of Alaskan basketry (Plate 136) show plainly the matting, the closely woven twined wallet, and the openwork. Plates 137 to 145 in this paper are all excellent illustrations of the ware here described. The specimens are in the U. S. National Museum.

Plate 137 will show better the detail, body and bottom, of one of the twined wallets of the Norton Sound Eskimo. The warp and the twining of the bottom are of a very coarse, rush-like grass. The bottom is in openwork and oval. In this example the warp is radiating from a median line; in others the strands are laid parallel, so that they form a rectangle. At the boundary line between the bottom and the body of the wallet there is a row of three-strand weaving, the rows running in opposite directions, as will be seen in the drawing. The body is of rush color; the spotted lines on the cylindrical portion are in black, produced by the insertion of rags and bits of hide. This

---

[a] Eighteenth Report of the Bureau of American Ethnology, 1900, pl. LXXIV.

effect may be varied by mixing two strands of different color in the twine. The fastening off at the top is done by working the warp strands into a three-strand braid, turning down on the inside of the vessel, and cutting off an end whenever a new warp thread is taken up by the braid. Frequently the last three or four warp straws are not cut off, but braided out to their extremities in order to form a handle for the basket.

In order to show how the warp and weft are administered in this far north region, a square inch of a wallet is represented much enlarged, fig. 133. The openwork producing parallel figures is effected by leaving spaces between the different lines of twining. The four rows at the top of the drawing are plain, solid, twined weaving; the fifth row from the top is twined in an opposite direction, giving the effect of a three-strand braid between the two rows; the third row from the top represents imperfectly the effect produced by the three-strand work. It is interesting to find this method of basket weaving so far north.

FIG. 133.

DETAIL OF ESKIMO TWINED WALLET.

Collected by E. W. Nelson.

The student will notice farther on that very much of the elegant use of the warp in ornamentation, so common with the Aleuts, who speak a kindred language and live near by, is lost. It will be seen, however, that with their rude materials and tools the Eskimo have still acquired the art of making a great variety of basketry, showing that they have had a multitude of teachers. This specimen, Catalogue No. 38872 in the U. S. National Museum, was collected, with many others, at Norton Sound, by E. W. Nelson.

To furnish a means of comparison between the two sides of Bering Sea, Plate 138 is a twined wallet of the Chukchi people of Kamchatka. The foundation is of straw laid parallel, and the weft is of plain twined weaving, the rows one-half an inch apart. The border is finished off by gathering the ends of the warp into a braid. The decoration on this basket is effected first by coloring warp strands black and grouping them systematically, and also by three narrow bands of black twined weaving near the top. Its height is 12 inches. This specimen, now in the American Museum of Natural History, New York, was collected by the Jessup Expedition.

To pursue the comparison farther into Asiatic territory, Plate 139 is a wallet in twined weaving from Kamchatka, introduced here for

comparison with the Chukchi type just shown.   The warp is of coarse
hemp cord; weft or filling is of grass stems in natural color dyed
black.   The bottom is ornamented with bands in two colors; in each
band there are alternate rows of black and white stitches arranged
perpendicularly; in the next band they are oblique, and in the next
perpendicular, forming a interminable mass of changing patterns,
having a very pleasing effect.   The body is covered with alternations
of plain and variegated bands in which the white and black are administered in triangles, rectangles, chevrons, and zigzag patterns.   The
work on this wallet is finely done.   The effect of the ornamentation is

FIG. 134.
COILED BASKET.
Eskimo Indians, Alaska.
Cat. No. 38469, U.S.N.M.   Collected by E. W. Nelson.

very attractive—on the top the ends of the warp are bent down and
held in place by loops of sinew thread.   The work nearest like this
will be found quite common on the eastern side of Bering Sea and on
the Pacific coast of America.   The writer is indebted to Dr. Franz
Boas for drawing attention to these similarities.

    Its height is 13 inches.   This specimen, now in the American
Museum of Natural History, New York, was collected by the Jessup
Expedition.

    The coiled variety of Eskimo basketry, previously mentioned, con-
sists of a bunch of grass sewed in a continuous coil by a whip stitch

over the bunch and under a few stems in the coil just beneath, the stitch looping under a stitch of the lower coil. When this kind of work is carefully done, as among the Indians of New Mexico, Arizona, and California, and in some exquisite examples in bamboo from Siam and in palm leaf from Nubia, beautiful results are reached; but the Eskimo basket maker does not prepare her foundations evenly, sews carelessly, passing the thread sometimes through the stitches just below and sometimes between them, and does not work her stitches home (fig. 51). It can not be said that she has no skill with the needle, for her embroideries in fur, intestines, and quill are excellent.

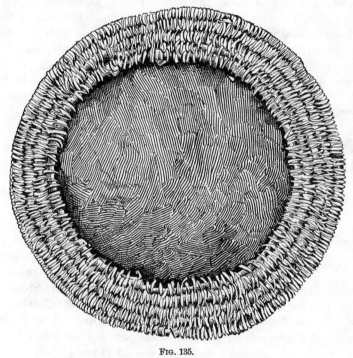

FIG. 135.
BOTTOM OF FIG. 134.

Most of the baskets in the Eskimo collection in the National Museum were gathered by E. W. Nelson and have a round bit of leather in the bottom to start upon (fig. 135). The shape is either that of the uncovered bandbox or of the ginger jar.[a] Especial attention should be paid to this form of stitching, as it occurs again in widely distant regions in a great variety of material and with modifications producing striking effects. (See figs. 134, 135.)

The Eskimo women employ in basket making a needle made of a bird bone ground to a point on a stone (fig. 40). Fine tufts of rein-

---

[a] Eighteenth Annual Report of the Bureau of Ethnology, 1900, pl. 74.

deer hair taken from between the hoofs are modernly used in ornamentation, just as the California women catch the stems of feathers
under their stitches as they sew.

Figs. 135 and 136 will illustrate this rude type of coiled basket of
the Eskimo about Norton Sound. It is quite certain that the art of
basket making is not an old one with these people. They have not
learned how to begin the work from the center of the foundation, and
always leave a circular space, either vacant or to be filled with some
other substance. In the example here shown a piece of hide 4 inches
in diameter and irregular in outline constitutes the starting point.
Holes are punched around the edge of this, as shown in the detail
drawing (fig. 135), and the foundation of grass stems and leaves is
sewed immediately to this with strips of the same material, not with
any regularity or neatness. The basket has a cover, which is also
interesting in its leather hinges, fastening, and handle. It must be
admitted, however, under the stimulus and demands of trade, that the
art is improving. Specimens are at this
date brought home that are vastly better
made than any of the old pieces in the
National Museum; charming cloud effects
are produced in sewing by using straws of
different tints.

FIG. 136.
DETAIL OF ESKIMO COILED BASKET.

This specimen, Catalogue No. 38469, in
the U. S. National Museum, was collected
by E. W. Nelson.

Catalogue No. 127891, in the U. S. National Museum, is a small jar-shaped coiled
basket from the Kowak River region, north
of Bering Strait, Alaska, collected by Lieut. George M. Stoney, U. S.
Navy. The foundation of the coil is a small number of slender grass
stems. The sewing is in material of the same kind. The special characteristic of this specimen is that, in the sewing, the grass filament is
wrapped once around the foundation and on the next turn is locked in
the stitch underneath. This is an economical method of working, but
it weakens the basket. The work on this specimen is slovenly done.
It has a small piece of leather in the center of the foundation. Height,
1¾ inches. This example is a waif. It comes from the Arctic Ocean
area, and most of the pieces in the Museum from near by are Tinné
and gotten by the Eskimo in trade. More curious still is the extra
wrap about the foundation every time a stitch is taken. The rafia
coiled baskets made in some of the schools are similar.

Catalogue No. 35962, U. S. National Museum, is a basket jar of the
Eskimo at Kushunuk, Alaska. The flat bottom is in open-twined
weaving of grass stems. The sides are in coiled work of the same
material, the outline being rectangular, with rounded corners. The

notable feature of this piece is the union of two fundamentally different methods of manufacture, the twined and the coiled.

Its height is $4\frac{11}{16}$ inches, and it was collected by E. W. Nelson.

Catalogue No. 36190, U. S. National Museum, is a coiled basket jar of the Eskimo on the Lower Yukon. The bottom is a piece of sealskin 3 inches in diameter. The coiled work on this specimen is unique. A grass foundation is held together by half hitches or buttonhole stitches in the same close together. There are 16 rows. The stitches pass over the foundation, lock with the stitches underneath, and in returning make a turn about the standing part. The technic is not half hitch, but, if the foundation were pulled out, would resemble the twisted coils in the Mackenzie River game bags, muskemoots (Plate 129), or the work on the textile from Hopewell mound, Ohio. (See fig. 116).

Catalogue No. 153686 in the National Museum is a coiled basket jar of the tribes on the Lower Yukon, Alaska. The foundation is a flat piece of hard wood, varying in width, overlaid by a small splint, which gives an uneven line on the outside. The sewing is done with strips of willow rods without bark. The stitches pass over both strips of the foundation and are caught between the two strips of the foundation coil underneath. This is the only specimen of its kind in the Museum from Alaska. The use of a broad foundation gives a flat appearance to the surface, something like that of the Mescalero basketry in Arizona. A handle is attached, the technic being the same as that of the basket. It is probably of Indian manufacture. Its height is about $4\frac{3}{8}$ inches, and it was collected by J. Henry Turner.

Catalogue No. 127482 in the National Museum is a coiled basket jar of the Eskimo, Togiak River, emptying into Bristol Bay, Alaska. The foundation is a piece of sealskin. The rows of the basket are built up by coiled work, with straw for foundation and sewing. The peculiar characteristic[a] is the neat and regular manner in which the stitches, in passing outward, split the underlying stitch of the previous coil. On the surface these stitches pass from top to bottom in regular vertical lines, resembling feather stitch. The upper margin is ornamented with a row of birds' feet. Its height is $2\frac{1}{5}$ inches, and the specimen was collected by I. Applegate.

Catalogue No. 127483, U. S. National Museum, is a coiled basket jar of the Eskimo on Togiak River. A rude ornamentation is attempted on the surface near the top by overlaying the foundation with a band of brown material underneath the stitches. Much will be said about this device of overlaying among Indian tribes farther south.

---

[a] See Report U. S. National Museum, 1884, pl. IV, showing furcated stitches.

Its height is 2 inches, and it was collected by Mr. Applegate.

The upper figure in Plate 140 is a covered basket in coiled work of the Chukchi people of Kamchatka.   Foundation, a piece of sealskin; bottom, coarse coiled work in straw held together by sewing in sinew thread, the stitches being one-half inch apart.   The body is built up of coiled sewing, similar to that of the Eskimo of Alaska.   Decoration, bands of chevron pattern in black.   Hinge and fastening of sealskin.   Top decorated with six-pointed star.   Diameter, 7 inches.

This specimen, now in the American Museum of Natural History, New York, was collected by the Jessup expedition.   The students of culture will be interested in the results of this exploration, which settle the question of unity of industries in the two continents.

Fig. 2 in Plate 140 is an oblong coiled basket of the Chukchi people of Kamchatka.   In the foundation, as in the Eskimo baskets, an oblong piece of sealskin is inserted.   The people of this north region do not seem to know how to make the coil beginning which prevails among the Indian tribes.

Around this sealskin the bottom consists of a continuous coil of grass stems held together by a wide, open coiled sewing in sinew thread.   The body is built up on a grass foundation with sewing in the same material, resembling precisely the work done by the Eskimo of Port Clarence.   Three rows of coiled work at the top are like that at the bottom, and over all is a band of sealskin rawhide with holes here and there for carrying.   Its height is 9 inches.   This specimen, now in the American Museum of Natural History, New York, was collected by the Jessup expedition.

The bottom figure on Plate 140 is a braided and coiled wallet of the Koryak people of Kamchatka.   The foundation is a strip of sealskin. The body is built up in a continuous coil of six-strand braid, as in making hats.   The decoration consists of alternating plain with colored rows of braid.   Loops of sealskin on the top serve for fastening and carrying.   This is a rare type of basketry in America.   Its height is 13 inches.

There is a small specimen in the U. S. National Museum, obtained by Captain John Rodgers, U. S. Navy, in 1852–5, made in the same way.   As his expedition was on the Arctic coast of Asia, this piece also may have come home from that quarter.

Plate 141 is a covered coiled basket in the collection of F. Harvey. It is from the Lower Yukon River country and represents one of the best types of Eskimo work.   Especial attention is called to the evenness of the stitches, which interlock and at intervals gather in a few of the straws of the foundation.   The mottled surface of the basket should also be noted in connection with the delightful effects produced by simply managing the natural colors of the straw with which the sewing is done.   Attention has been directed to the glorification of this technical method by the Mission Indians in California. This specimen represents the very best coiled work that the Eskimo can make.

In 1874, William H. Dall contributed to the U. S. National Museum a number of specimens of twined basketry, from Attu and other islands far out in the Aleutian chain. (Catalogue Nos. 19476–19480). There for the first time this exquisite weaving was brought to light. Warp and weft are straws of beach grass[a] and the workmanship will compare favorably with that of any other basket makers in the world. In the conical wallets, which resemble in outline those of the Eskimo and southeastern Alaskan tribes, the warp straws radiate from the center of the bottom. On the body the twined weft, always the same plain two-strand work, is applied to the warp so as to give rise to several technical varieties, which may be classified as follows:

1. Plain twined weaving, the weft driven home (Plate 142).

2. Open twined work, there being open spaces between the rows of weaving, but the warp strands are parallel.

3. Crossed warp, in which there are two sets of warp elements, one half inclining to the right, the other half toward the left. The twined weaving binds the decussations, making hexagonal meshes. This type has an interesting distribution on both sides of the Pacific.

4. Divided warp. A pretty effect is produced by these Aleut basket makers, who split the warp, or divide it, if it consists of straws in pairs, and twining the weft straws around two halves of the same straw and next around two half straws not of the same but of adjoining stalks. If the warp be of straws by twos, the left side member of one pair is entwined with the right-hand member of the adjoining pair. On the next round there is an alternation, the straws that belong together being entwined. The result of this is a series of lozenge-shaped openings or meshes (figs. 16, 17). The general appearance of the surface resembles a form of needlework called hemstitching. The Aleuts in doubling the warp do not place one element behind another as do the Tlinkits, but alongside. This enables the weaver to convert her technic into some other type in the successive rounds. She may have plain twining, crossed warp, zigzag warp, or hemstitch at any moment.

5. Diverted warp. By this is meant a form of weaving in which certain warp straws are deflected from the perpendicular for a few courses and then brought back or changed to the upright position again. The result of this is a most pleasing effect (Plate 143) and of the greatest variety on the surface. Attention has been previously

---

a *Elymus mollis*, Sitka, Norton Sound, Kotzebue Sound; *Elymus arenarius*, Norton Sound to Point Barrow; *Elymus sibiricus*, Sitka. Rothrock, Smithsonian Report, 1867. For a description of the Eskimo and Aleuts, see W. H. Dall, in the Contributions to North American Ethnology, I, 1877, pp. 7–106.

invited to the similarity of mound builder's work in the Mississippi Valley to the playing with the warp of which the Aleuts were so fond. Away down among the mummies of Peru are found relics of weaving of precisely the same sort.

Ornamentation is produced by what looks like darning or whipping one or more rows of colored grass after the body is formed. It is in effect the false embroidery of the Tlinkits farther south. The worsted patterns are woven into the texture and do not show at all on the inside. (See fig. 16.) Another plan of attaching the ornamentation is very ingenious, but not uncommon. Two strands of colored straw are twined, and at every half turn one of the strands is hooked under a twist on the body of the basket by a kind of "aresene" work or false embroidery with twine. This ornament has a bold relief effect on the outside and is not seen at all on the inside.

The making of the beautiful twined ware is not new in these small islands. Lisiansky[a] affirms that the Aleuts made baskets called "ishcats," in which they keep all their valuables.

To begin with the eastern tribes, Catalogue No. 2192, in the U. S. National Museum, is a twined wallet of the Aleuts (Eskimaun family) on Kadiak Island, Alaska. Native name, Enakhtak. It is made entirely of Topkhnaluk or wild rye (*Elymus*). The lower stalks are chosen because they become yellow through want of light. The wallets are woven from the standing grass, generally in July and August, by the women, while engaged in curing salmon. In order to secure uniformity in texture the broader leaves are split. An ordinary knife is used to cut the grass, but no other apparatus than nimble fingers has to do with the manufacture. The twining is called agankhak. The Kadiak baskets are used chiefly in gathering berries and also in straining a kind of wine made from them. This specimen was collected by Lieut. G. T. Emmons, U. S. Navy.

These wallet baskets are woven without ornamentation, or may be a line or so near the mouth, often effected by introducing one or more rows of black rags, the warp strands forming a heavy plaited rope-like border, which permits carriage by means of cords through the openings. In the Kadiak wallets the Tlinkit border is also imitated where the warp ends are bent down and held by twined weaving.

Catalogue No. 14978 in the U. S. National Museum is a typical old Aleut wallet. The cylindrical part is covered with meshes in diamond pattern, shown in fig. 9, Plate 136. The ornamentation on the surface is produced by false embroidery with strands of red, blue, and black worsted. The continuous line between the open stripes is formed by false whipping with a single thread of worsted on the outer stitches of one of the twines of straw. The border is a complicated braid.

_____

[a] Voyage Round the World, 1803–1806, London, 1814, p. 181.

A square inch of this weave, enlarged (see fig. 17), taken from the part of the texture where the rectangular meshes or plain work pass into the lozenge-shaped meshes, will show the peculiar method of separating the warp threads and working the halves alternately to the right and to the left.[a] In the bottom row the pairs of warp straws are perpendicular and gathered into the twined weaving so as to produce rectangular spaces. All the rows above this are in the pattern here described. From the Attu Island, collected by William H. Dall.

Plate 142 shows the fine close-twined work done on the extreme western islands of the Aleutian chain. The specimen here described is Catalogue No. 204588, U. S. National Museum, the gift of Mrs. Mary L. D. Putnam, of Davenport, Iowa. Its noteworthy features are the crossed warp and the patterns worked in colored worsted on the surface. The material is beach grass, some species of Elymus. The false embroidery on the surface, there can be no doubt, is borrowed in its method from the Tlinkit Indians of southeastern Alaska. Among the old Aleut wallets, of which there are many in the National Museum, the weaving does not begin to be so fine as on this later ware. It is the same story of progress. With the possession of better knowledge, of superior tools, of gauges for sizing the straws, and, above all, of such demands for their products as to stimulate emulation to its highest pitch, the Atka and Attu weavers have reached their climax.

Plate 143 is introduced to show the technic of variety No. 5, diverted warp combined with variety No. 2, or open work. Fig. 1 illustrates the general effect of this combination. Attention has been called before to the enigmas awakened by the great variety and exquisite taste of these people, our first possession in the Eastern Hemisphere. In figs. b and c the detail will be better understood. In fig. b the first row has parallel warp. In the next row each pair of continuous warp straws are crossed. In the third row they proceed vertically, and so do most of them in the fourth row, but here and there they are crossed again back to the position they occupied in the second row. These, too, continue in the oblique direction in the fifth, sixth, seventh, and eighth rows, crossed in each with a straw of that particular row. In the upper course they return to the vertical position. The twined weaving is precisely the same in every case. It does not vary whether in the closed weaving or open weaving. No artistic effect is expected therefrom. In this plate, where the decorative form is started in the bottom row and begins to widen out all of the intersections within the parallelograms are crossed. At the tenth row, above the upper border of the drawing, the straws return to their vertical position immediately over the starting point.

---

[a] See Report of the U. S. National Museum, 1884, pl. I, fig. b.

These two are only specimens of the innumerable ways of producing effects in Aleutian baskets by changes in the warp.

It will add to the interest in the Attu weaver to see her at her work. Plate 144, taken by Engineer C. Gadsden Porcher, of the United States Revenue Marine, shows her at the front door of her barabra or underground hut. She is essentially a cave dweller. The framework of the house may be driftwood, wreckage, or timber deposited by ships. Over this moss from the tundra is piled, and nature plants her garden.

The first thing that demands notice is that she is weaving upward—upside down, a careless first thought would say. The bottom of her fine wallet is suspended from a pole, most primitive of warping beams, stuck into the roof of the barabra. John Smith's Indians used a limb of a tree (fig. 148). The Bristol Bay Eskimo now employ a stick supported on forked stakes; so do the Chilkats for their highly-prized blankets, and the tribes farther south to make cedar-bark garments. Indeed, the loom is about to be born. With a lens it will be seen that the basket maker is doing the best work, in which every variety of Aleutian technic is engaged. Her costume shows her to be in the current of world-embracing commerce and thought. The plants about her and the precious work of her fingers, together with the ideas in her attentive mind, are survivals from the past.

TLINKIT BASKETRY

The basket work of the Tlinkit Indians is superb. Everyone who sees it is struck with its delicacy of workmanship, shape, and ornamentation. Most of the specimens in the National Museum collection are of the bandbox shape, but they can be doubled up flat like a grocer's bag. (Plates 65 and 67.) The material of foundation and sewing is the young and tough root of the spruce, split, and used either in the native color or dyed brown or black. The structure belongs to the twined type before mentioned and there is such uniformity and fineness in the warp and woof that a water-tight vessel is produced with very thin walls. In size the wallets vary from a diminutive trinket basket to a capacity of nearly a bushel. All sorts of designs in bands, crosses, rhombs, chevrons, triangles, and grecques are produced thus: First, the bottom is woven plain in the color of the material. In a great many pieces a row of plain weaving alternates with the twined weaving for economy. Then in the building up of the basket bands of plain color, red and black, are woven into the structure, having the same color on both sides.[a] Afterwards little squares or other plain figures made into designs are sewed on in

---

[a] See G. T. Emmons in the Memoirs of the American Museum of Natural History, New York, 1903. This paper is the result of twenty years' work among the Tlinkits by a patient observer, and should be studied with special care.

aresene, or what is here called false embroidery, that is, only halfway through, giving the most varied effect on the outside, while the inside shows only the plain colors and the red and black bands. Wild rye straws (*Elymus*) for coarse work and hair grass (*Deschampsia*) on fine work are used in this second operation, in plain rich golden color or dyed, being whipped over and over along the outer threads of the underlying woof. Other grasses for false embroidery are *Panicularia nervata, Calamagrostis langsdorfii, Cinna latifolia,* and *Bromus sitchensis.* (See Plate 145.)

No more attractive form and ornamentation are to be seen than those produced by the Indians of this Tlinkit stock.

The Tlinkit recognize five styles of weave, not including the fish-trap, the false embroidery in grasses and plant stems, and the plaited borders. These are all in twined weaving, the progress of the work being from left to right and the outer woof strand sloping downward. Lieutenant Emmons gives the native name of each as follows:

1. Plain close-twined weaving, Wush tookh á r-kee ("close together work"), which is perfectly water-tight and is the standard weave of fully three-quarters of all baskets made. It consists of the simple twining of two woof strands around each successive thickness of warp splints. The regular weave produces the vertical ridge-like appearance in the line of the warp, the polished exterior surface of the root forming the outside or ornamental face of the work.

An openwork work basket in this plain twined weaving is known as Khart ("a strainer," literally, "will not hold water"). It is used in trying out fish oil and in cooking and straining berries.

2. Twined and checker weaving, Khark gheesút ("between," "in the middle of"), from the introduction of a single woof strand in checker or wicker weaving between the lines of the regular twined stitch. It gives a broken, irregular effect from the exposure of the warp along the line of the single weft, as well as from the dull, fibrous surface of both of these strands, which are of the coarsest inner sections of the root. This weave is of a later origin; the plain weaving has been borrowed from the mainland and from the more southern people. It is characteristic of the cedar-bark work from Frederick Sound to the Straits of Fuca. It is wanting on the oldest specimens of Yakutat baskets. Its use is confined to the coarser work, such as the plaque-like berry, sewing, and workbaskets of the woman, the bottoms of the baskets and the unexposed tops of the covered basket. It is in great favor among the Chilkat, who make many large baskets. It is used for economy, both in the quantity and the quality of the material, as one woof strand is saved in every three and in the more valued exterior root section the saving is one-half. But its disadvantages are loss of strength, rigidity, and closeness of texture, and it does not admit of the embroidery in grasses and plant stems, which is the characteristic feature of Tlinkit basketry. (See fig. 140.)

3. Diagonal twined weaving, Hiktch hee há r-see (rough or uneven, like the skin of the frog's back, from its mottled character), is formed by the simple twining of two woof strands about pairs of warp elements. The weave separates the pairs in each superimposed line of woof, and breaks joints in the units of weave, just as in myriads of Attu and Ute baskets. (See Plates 96, 143.) It is, in fact, well-known twilled weaving. This weave was never extensively used among the Tlinkit, except as a skip stitch in conjunction with the ordinary twining (No. 1), whereby a number of geometric figures are produced which form the ornamentation of the Haida hat rim and the Chilkat basket border. As a weave it seems to have been confined to the double basket.

Shuck kuhk (strawberry basket) has erroneously been classed as a type of weave, but it is simply a variation of the regular twined weave (No. 1), in which the woof strands are of different colors, so that in both the vertical and the horizontal lines there is produced a variety of effects, supposed to resemble the seed-covered surface of the wild strawberry. This character of ornamentation is more commonly found in bands on the women's workbasket and on mats of basket covers. The flecking of the surface of twined ware with dark and light spots is not confined to the Tlinkit, but will be observed among all Western tribes that have this weave.

4. Crossed-warp twined weaving, Wark kus-ká rt ("eye holes" from the polygonal meshes of the openwork weave), in which the warp splints are drawn aside from the perpendicular at a fixed angle, the odd numbers trending one way and the even numbers the other. These cross each other successively in parallel series, just after which they are inclosed and held in place by the ordinary twining of two-woof strands. The size of the meshes is regulated by the distance apart of the spirals of the weave. This type was used for rather long, flat cases or bags, but more particularly for spoon baskets, which are fitted with a twisted root handle to hang them to hooks or pegs on the wall. In later years ornamental baskets are often made in this weave.

5. Three-strand twined weaving, Uh ta'hk-ka (twisted). This gives a longer winding, rope-like appearance to the weave outside, while on the inside the regular twining stitch in its ridge-like regularity is seen. It is strengthening as well as decorative and is often met with in circles at intervals near the bottoms of the larger, older baskets, which are required for the heavier work. It is in general use to-day as a single line of woof around the outer circumference of the cylinder basket, where the warp splints are bent upward to form the sides. Its more important use has been in the construction of the crown of the hat as well as of the cylindrical ornaments surmounting it, and other ceremonial headdresses among both the Haida and the Tlinkit.

The Tlinkit do not seem to have learned, or were forbidden by economy, in doubling the warp splints, to use strips from the outside of the root and to lay the wrong sides together so as to have both surfaces smooth. This is shown in the mixed twine and checker work on the bottoms of baskets.

Plate 146 is a collection of Tlinkit twined basketry made from the roots of the spruce and decorated in false embroidery with wild rye or hair grass, either in the natural color or dyed. It will be observed that the figures do not appear on the inside of the wallet. Attention is also called to the very fine workmanship on these old specimens, especially upon the large one in the middle. The ornamentation, in its symbolism,

FIG. 137.
TWINED BASKET WALLET.
Tlinkit Indians, Alaska.
Collected by J. B. White.

has reference to natural features and waterways. The composition of the ornament is in triangles and parallelograms.

Fig. 137, Catalogue No. 21560 U. S. National Museum, is a twined basket wallet of the Tlinkit Indians. It is of band-box shape when spread out, but here shown as folded for transportation. The bottom, warp, and twine is very roughly made of spruce root splints, the former radiating from the center. The boundary of the bottom is a single row of three-strand twine. This method of ornamenting and strengthening their work was used by the Tlinkits, not only at the bottom, but along the sides and near the top. The rest of the body is in stripes of natural spruce root color, in black and Indian red, done in false embroidery.

Figs. 138 and 139 illustrate the method of making false embroidery on the basketry of the Tlinkit Indians.   As the woman proceeds with her work she wraps the grass stem once around each strand of the regular twine when it comes outside.   On the inside, therefore, there is no appearance of ornament; the figure plainly shows how this work is done and it might be called a type of three-strand twined weaving in

FIG. 138.

FALSE EMBROIDERY.
Tlinkit Indians, Alaska.
Collected by J. G. Swan.

which one of the elements passes inside the warp.   Ornamentation on this ware is also produced by dyeing the filaments of which the basket is made.   This specimen is Catalogue No. 20726 in the U. S. National Museum, and was collected by James G. Swan.

Fig. 140, from the Tlinkit tribes about Fort Wrangell, in southeastern Alaska, is a carrying wallet for general purposes. It is an interesting and important specimen in that it forms the connecting link between common plain in and out weaving and twined work, both plain and twilled,

from the tribes immediately north and the Haidas.   The specimen is made of spruce root and the rows of weaving are alternately twined and wicker over the entire surface of the wallet.   In examples already described this combination of two weaves was seen on the bottoms, for economy, but in this piece the whole surface was thus covered.   The coarser type is shown in fig. 141 from the Tlinkit Indians taken from the bottom of basket work inclosing a bottle.   It will be

FIG. 139.

DETAIL OF FALSE EMBROIDERY.

seen that the first few rounds are plain twined work; after that the rows are far enough apart to allow an additional row of wickerwork or beading.

Specimen Catalogue No. 168163 in the U. S. National Museum was collected in southeastern Alaska by Herbert G. Ogden, and specimen No. 73755 was collected in Neah Bay, Washington, by James G. Swan.

Plate 147 represents a group of the Tlinkit Indian basket makers.

They were named Kolosch by the Russians more than a hundred years ago, because they wore labrets, or plugs in their lips. The woman

FIG. 140.
CARRYING WALLET.
Tlinkit Indians, Alaska.
Collected by Herbert G. Ogden.

on the left side of the picture has a modest one in her lower lip, but specimens in the National Museum measure as much as 3 inches in diameter. Owing to the broken condition of their island home and

FIG. 141.
TWINED AND WICKER WEAVE.
Tlinkit Indians, Alaska.
Cat. No. 73755, U.S.N.M. Collected by J. G. Swan.

the large ownership of personal property they are divided into innumerable villages or Kwans. The best known basket makers are

Chilkats, Hunahs, Sitkas, Takoos, Tongass, and Yakutats.[a] It will be noted in looking at the women in the group that the Tlinkits are a well-fed, vigorous race. The Russians spoke well of them, not only for their physical qualities but for their intelligence.

The group is a study in more respects than in basketry. They are all clad in trade goods. As to jewelry, one wears her rings on her fingers, but the chief woman has hers in the septum of her nose. Old forms of basketry are mingled with covered bottles and the ubiquitous can (Kanastron), formerly a basket both in Greek and Tlinkit, stands by the side of the genuine article. Before leaving the group it is worth while to recall that with thrifty tribes new tricks of handicraft are readily borrowed and too much stress must not be laid on the assumption of identity of race because of identity of art. It is worth while to linger here a moment. The Attu woman as well as the old time Algonquian tribes did suspend warp for baskets and matting, but here among the Chilkat is to be seen the pristine loom. It is not surprising when it is remembered that here the Rocky Mountain goat is at home.

FIG. 142.
WALLET.
Chilkat Indians, Southeastern Alaska.

On the main land of the northern Pacific slope the mountain goat (*Oreamnos montanus*) abounds. From the Chilkat Indians about Mount St. Elias southward to the Nez Percés of Idaho, blankets are woven from the wool. These fabrics are, in their manufacture, the transition from basketry to loom work. They are in twined weaving. The only shuttles are the skillful fingers of Indian women; the warp hangs down loose from a pole or bar, and the work of twine is upward, precisely as in Haida basketry. (See Plate 148.)

Vernon Bailey says of the material that the winter coat of the mountain goat is a dense piece of long, soft wool, with strong, coarse hairs scattered through it. In spring and early summer, when the wool is being shed, and hangs in loose strings on the goat, it catches on bushes and rocks and the low branches of timber line trees. On

---

[a] On the Ethnology of the Tribes of the West Coast, see Franz Boas, in the Proceedings of the British Association for 1884 and following years.

the slopes above timber line in May and June every bush and tall dry weed will be festooned with tufts of wool that could be picked off in handfulls.   In a good goat region the Indians might gather wool enough for a large part of their clothing without the trouble of killing one.

Fig. 142 is a section of a wallet made by the Chilkat Indians (Koluschan family) in southeast ern Alaska.   The material is the young root of spruce.   It is here introduced to show the effect on the surface of several kinds of weaving before described.   Beginning at the bottom of the drawing there are eight rows of alternate plain twined and checker weaving.   At the margin of this lower portion, and also at the upper margin of the drawing, will be found a row of twined work set on the regular twined weaving for

FIG. 143.

HAT IN FINE TWINED WEAVING.

Haida Indians, British Columbia.

Cat. No. 89033, U.S.N.M.   Collected by James G. Swan.

FIG. 144.

DETAIL OF FIG. 143.

strength and ornament.   The upper portion of the wallet is a mixture of plain twined work over one warp splint and twilled twine weaving over two warp splints, making a diagonal pattern on the surface.   The rope is made of the same material.

HAIDA BASKETRY

The Haida Indians live on Queen Charlotte Archipelago and adjacent islands. Their basket work is all in twined weaving and differs from that of the Tlinkits in artistic finish only, owing probably to the demands of trade. Their wallets of spruce are devoid of decoration, save here and there a band in plain black color, as would be the Tlinkit without embroidery; but hats made by these Indians are masterpieces in execution and ornamental weaving. The crown is in three strand or plain twined weaving of the most delicate workmanship, and the fabric is perfectly water-tight when thoroughly wet. Ornamentation is introduced into the brims by a series of diamond patterns in twilled weave covering the whole surface. This decoration is produced thus: Beginning at a certain point, the weaver includes two warp strands in a half twist instead of one; then makes two regular twists around single warp strands. The next time she weaves around she repeats the process, but her double stitch is one warp stem in advance of or behind its predecessor. A twilled effect of any shape may be thus produced, and rhombs, triangulated fillets, and chevrons made to appear on either surface. (See figs. 143 and 144.)

FIG. 145.

TWINED OPENWORK BASKET.

Haida Indians.

Cat. No. 88964, U.S.N.M.   Collected by James G. Swan.

The fastening off of the work is done either by bending down the free ends of the warp and shoving them out of sight under the stitches of the twisted web or a

FIG. 146.

DETAIL OF FIG. 145.

braid of four strands forms the last row, set on so that the braid shows outside and only one strand at a time shows inside. The ends of the warp splints are then cropped close to the braid.

Special attention should be paid to the fact that the ornamentation on these hats is painted and not woven. (See fig. 143.) Not far away, on the mainland, the same motives appear on blankets, woven into the texture. Figs. 143 and 144 show the head, wings, feet, and tail of the duck, laid on in black and red in the conventional manner of ornamentation in vogue among the Haidas and used in the reproduction of their various totems on all of their houses, wood and slate carvings, and the ornamentation of their implements.[a] Shells, beads, and feathers are often sewed on in profusion.

Catalogue No. 88964, collected by J. G. Swan, is a twined openwork basket of spruce root made by the Haida Indians. This piece of coarse workmanship shows both phases—the open and the close weave in rough inner splints. The handle is a twine of the same material fastened into the weaving while it is in progress. The border is effected by bending down the warp elements at the rim externally and sewing them in place with a row of twined weaving.

A square inch of this specimen taken near the top, where the open work and the close work come together, is shown. (See figs. 145, 146.)

Fig. 147 shows an unfinished Haida cylindrical basket. In order to explain the process of manufacture, the bottom is in plain twined weaving; at the border where this joins the cylindrical side is a row of three strand; and four rows of plain twined weaving of the body come next, the unfinished portion exhibiting the warp as it appears before weaving.

FIG. 147.
UNFINISHED BASKET.
Haida Indians.
Collected by James G. Swan.

[a] A very interesting instance of survival is to be seen in the rag carpets of these Indians. The missionaries have taught the women to save up their rags and to cover their floors with pretty mats. They are allowed to weave them in their own way, however, and the result is constructed on the ancient twined model, precisely as the weaving is done on the mats and hats.

Especial attention is here called to the sharpened stake which has a circular board on top. This is driven into the ground, and the woman seated works upward instead of downward, as in most cases. This specimen, Catalogue No. 89033 in the U. S. National Museum, was procured in Queen Charlotte Archipelago by James G. Swan. (See fig. 148.) It will be remembered that in an ancient drawing showing how the Virginia women made basketry the woman is seated in precisely the same fashion and is working from below upward.

FIG. 148.

VIRGINIA INDIAN WOMAN WEAVING A BASKET.

After W. H. Holmes.

Plate 149 represents old twined wallets of the Haida Indians, Queen Charlotte Island, British Columbia. The material is splints of spruce, some of which have been dyed simply by immersing in dark-colored mud. The Haidas used little color decoration other than black bands in their work, but they have learned the art of producing figures by including more than warp element in the twining. They also know the art of three-strand twined work, as will be seen on the upper border of the two larger wallets. The borders are finished off by false embroidery.

Plate 150 represents a company of Haida Indian basketmakers, photographed by J. G. Swan. They are in modern dress, but wear nose ring and labret common to their tribe.

THE FRASER-COLUMBIA REGION

Basketry is the most expressive vehicle of the tribe's individuality, the embodiment of its mythology and folklore, tradition, poetry, art, and spiritual aspiration.—NELTJE BLANCHAN.

The next general area for study will be the drainage region of the Fraser River and the Columbia River. The families to be visited will be the Chimmeseyan, Wakashan or Aht, Salishan, Shahaptian, and Chinookan. Other smaller groups are scattered around and will be treated at the proper place in the text. The transition from southeastern Alaska to this area is almost imperceptible in some respects and radical in others. The Tlinkit false embroidery will not disappear, but it will be remanded to a far humbler place. The roots and inner bark of the cedar will occupy the front rank. Coiled and imbricated work, unknown among the Tlinkits and Haidas, will bloom out in British Columbia and Washington. The semiflexible wallet will be replaced by the rigid cooking basket and the soft bags of hemp. The differentiation from the next area south of it will also be marked.

The small Chimmeseyan family, also called Tsimshian and better known as Nass, are the extreme northern of the group. Their basketry is of root and runs largely into the mixed twined, checker, and twilled.

Necessarily coming southward from the spruce-root country to the cedar area would have the effect to change much of the basketry from rigid surfaces to flexible and from twined weaving to checker and twilled work. The National Museum possesses no specimens of Chimmeseyan ware of striking individuality.

The Wakashan tribes occupy northern and western Vancouver Island, the coast of British Columbia, and a small point of land in the northwest corner of Washington. They are generally known by the name Aht or Nootka on Vancouver Island, and include Boas's Kwakiutl and the Bella Bella and Haeltzuk on the mainland. In recent years they have been studied by Boas, by Tolmie and Dawson, and by Swan.

A list of authorities will be found given by J. W. Powell[a] and by Boas.[b]

In addition to the matting, both checker and twilled, quite common throughout this region, the Wakashan tribes of Vancouver Island and Washington make a type of basketry which is called in this paper the bird-cage or wrapped twined work, in which one element of the weft remains inside of the basket, and the other element, which is more flexible, is wrapped about the decussations of the warp and the rigid element of the weft. It

FIG. 149.
DETAIL OF WRAPPED BASKET.
Clallam Indians.
Collected by J. G. Swan.

might also be called the "fish-trap" style, since without doubt the finer basketry is the lineal descendant of the rude wicker fish trap. Imagine a number of stakes driven into the ground pretty close together. A horizontal pole is laid against them in the rear, and by the wrappings of a withe around the pole and each upright stake diagonally on the outside and vertically on the inside a spiral fastening is produced. It is shown in the openwork basket, Catalogue No. 23480, U. S. National Museum, made by a Clallam Indian. This wrapping crosses the two fundamentals in front at an angle and the horizontal frame piece in the rear at right angles, and the lacing may always run in the same direction, or the alternate rows of lacing may run in opposite directions, as in fig. 149. As a matter of fact, in a soft and pliable material this operation pushes the uprights forward a little, giving to the fabric an appearance of the lathe work on the back of a watch. (See fig. 150.)

[a] Seventh Annual Report of the Bureau of Ethnology, 1891, p. 128.
[b] Reports to the British Association, 1889–1891.

The Wakashan weaving is not confined to this particular technic, but, as will be seen in the illustrations here shown (fig. 151), it is checker work on the bottom, three-ply twine between, separating the

FIG . 150.
WRAPPED TWINED BASKET.
Makah Indians, Cape Flattery.
Collected by James G. Swan.

checker work from the plain twine which completes the bottom.   The sides are built up of cedar-bark warp, both vertical and horizontal, and a wrapping of golden-colored grass stems.   These straws take different

FIG. 151.
BOTTOM OF MAKAH BASKET.

colored dyes readily, and so the Makahs have learned to ornament their baskets with geometric patterns in black, yellow, drab, red, blue, etc. The pattern, therefore, is alike on both sides, although the wrappings are, as in Clallam, Nez Percé, and other specimens, inclined on the outside and vertical on the inside. The rows of wrappings run at an angle of 45 degrees, which separate the elements, having a rhomboid appearance.

This specimen, Catalogue No. 23346 in the U. S. National Museum, was collected, with many others (Nos. 23343 to 23368), in Neah Bay, Washington, by James G. Swan.   (See figs. 149–151.)

In the Peabody Museum of Harvard University are eight old basket hats, supposed, by C. C. Willoughby, to have originated among the Southern Wakashan tribes, probably the Nutkas.   Lewis and

Clark described them as "made of cedar bark and bear grass inter-woven in the form of a European hat with small brim. They formed a a small article of traffic with the whites, and their manufacture is one of the best exertions of Indian industry." They say that "the only covering for their head is a hat made of bear grass and the bark of cedar interwoven in a cone form with a knob of the same shape at the top. The colors are generally black and white only, and the designs are squares, triangles, and rude figures of canoes and seamen harpooning whales." Captain Cook found the same form of head covering worn by the Indians of Nutka Sound. (See Plate 151.)

Mr. Willoughby[a] describes the hats in the Peabody Museum (Plate 151) as follows:

They are all in twined weaving, and are made principally of cedar bark and grass spires. The construction is double, as shown in the cross section (fig. 153). Each headpiece consists really of two hats, an inner and an outer one, joined at the rim, the

FIG. 152.

DETAIL OF NUTKA HAT.

After C. C. Willoughby, Peabody Museum.

FIG. 153.

CROSS SECTION OF NUTKA HAT.

After C. C. Willoughby, Peabody Musuem.

last few pairs of twisted woof elements of the outer hat inclosing also the ends of the warp of the inner. The inner hat, or lining, is coarsely but neatly woven of cedar bark, and only in one specimen is there a knob at the top of the lining correspond-ing to that of the outer hat. Upon the underside at about 3 inches from the rim each warp element is doubled upon itself, forming a loop about three-fourths of an inch long. Through these loops is run a strong double cord of Indian hemp. The loops are bound together by twined weaving (fig. 152), and form an inner rim edged with the cord of hemp, which fits the head snugly. To this is fastened the thong which passes beneath the chin of the wearer.

The exterior or outer hat is woven principally of grass spires and cedar bark. In most of the specimens a narrow strip below the knob is made of fine cedar roots. The warp appears to be formed of split roots, and is fine and strong. The grass of the woof was originally an ivory white, the selected cedar bark used in conjunction with it being usually stained a dark brown or black.

Each strand of the twisted pair of woof elements forming the design is composed of a grass spire overlaying a strip of cedar bark of the same width, the strand

[a] American Naturalist, XXXVII, 1903, pp. 65–68

thus formed being white upon one side and black upon the other. These double strands are used not only where figures appear, but throughout the groundwork of the design as well. The figures are principally black upon a white ground. In forming them the strands are simply reversed, the black sides which were concealed beneath the grass spires in the white background being carried outward. In some of the specimens the knob at the top is woven separately and afterwards joined to the hat. (See figs. 152,153.)

Comparing the descriptions with the technical processes worked out in this paper, it is evident that the Nutka tribes understood what is called overlaying. It is not the Makah wrapped weaving nor like the Nez Percé and other Shahaptian weave, but wiil be found in the Modoc and other California tribes as well as abundantly among the Salish. (See Plate 155, fig. 5.) The double hat is suggestive of the Orient, from which the royal Spanish fleet returned by way of Vancouver every year for two centuries (1570–1770).

The National Museum has an example of twilled weaving from Vancouver Island, which should be compared with Clallam ware. It is a large fish basket made from the split root of a cedar. Attempts at ornamentation are, first, in using alternately the smooth, natural wood and the inner, coarse surface of the splint, also by introducing strips in cedar root with the bark adherent, and finally, by laying on the outside certain strips the leaves of bear grass. With this variety of material, although the basket is as coarse as it can be, the effect is excellent. The finishing off is in three rows of twined weaving, in which black yarn and bear grass are laid on the fiber to give variety and color. The upright elements in the weaving are bent down on the inside and held together by a continuous row of buttonhole stitches. On the border is a scallop formed by a two-strand rope which passes underneath the border, back and through itself. Dimensions: height, 18 inches; width, 24 inches. Collected by G. T. Emmons. (See Plate 152.)

Plate 153 is a delightful mixture of two extremes in culture. Two Makah or Nutka women are clad in calico, woolen blanket, piano cover, bandana handkerchiefs, etc., not neglecting the latest patent in safety pins. They are seated on a mat of cattail (*Typha latifolia*) stems, sewed together in genuine aboriginal fashion, known before Columbus. And their fingers are following their conservative thoughts as though these cunning weavers had been born centuries ago. They are making from filaments of cedar bark and leaves of squaw grass the kind of twined weaving called wrapped in this paper (figs. 13, 14). The warp is plain, twisted from cedar bark. One element of the weft is of the same material and laid horizontally inside the warp; the other weft element, of squaw grass (*Xerophyllum tenax*), is wrapped in a continuous coil about the intersections of the other two elements. The photograph is from Capt. D. F. Tozier.

One of the largest families and most diversified, so far as industries are concerned, are the Salishan tribes, east and south of the Wakashan A small and detached body of them are to be found on Bentinck Arms, northern British Columbia, hemmed in on the east by Athapascan tribes and on the west by Wakashan tribes. The rest of the family are spread out in British Columbia and Washington, extending from Puget Sound northward, southward, and eastward across Idaho and even into Montana. A small body of the same family are on the Oregon coast, about the forty-fifth parallel.

Situated as these tribes are, in the midst of so many other linguistic families, it is not surprising to find a great variety in the types of their basketry. In the plates here shown (Plates 154 and 155) fig. 1 represents plain checker weaving; fig. 2, twilled weaving, in which both warp and weft pass over two; fig. 3, another form of twilled work, in which warp and weft pass alternately over two and under one. Figs. 4 and 5 show the methods of coiled and imbricated sewing in the bottom and on the body of a Thompson River or a so-called Klikitat basket. Especial attention will be called later to these types. Fig. 6 is plain twined weaving in openwork. Fig. 7 is an example of plain twined weaving in openwork over crossed warp of a special character in which every alternate one is vertical and the other inclined. It can be easily seen by looking at the figure that warps arranged vertically and parallel, every other one turns to the left and is caught, not in the twist just above it, but in the first one beyond. Figs. 8 and 9 show the outside and inside of latticed or bird-cage work; fig. 10, a form of twined work in which the tough fiber is overlaid by grass leaves or other colored fiber, adding to the ornamentation but not to the strength; fig. 11, false embroidery, in which the outer element of the twine is wrapped with an additional filament. Myron Eells, who has spent many years among them, and to whom Plates 154 and 155 are to be credited, asserts that styles of weaving peculiar to the stocks near by are practiced by a few women of Salishan tribes. This can be accounted for in two ways—women from these outside stocks may have married into the tribes under consideration, or, as is frequently the case, the Salish women, in order to learn something new, have taken up the methods of their neighbors.

Immediately south of the Haidas and Tlinkits, the bark of the white cedar (*Thuja plicata*) becoming common, the inner portion is quite tenacious, and since filaments of almost any required width and length may be obtained, checkerwork weaving is in demand for mats, sails, receptacles for all sorts of objects, parts of house furniture, and even of clothing. The figure here shown is a typical example of many hundreds of such baskets to be found in collections. The bottom and sides are in the same type of weaving. By an endless variety of real and proportional width of warp and weft and by coloring some of the strips an indefinite number of patterns may be produced. (See fig. 154.)

In many cedar-bark receptacles of this region the two sets of filaments—warp and weft—run diagonally; that is, they are not woven as in a loom, but the maker begins at the corner. Looked at vertically, the surface has a diamond rather than a checker appearance, but from the point of view of the maker the intersections are square. Again, but much more rarely, three sets of filaments are involved, two belonging to the warp and the other one to the weft. The warp elements cross at right angles or less, and the weft element runs across through the intersections, making a series of rhombs. This same technic is almost universal in Japan.

Fig. 154.
CHECKERWORK BASKET.
Bilhula Indians, British Columbia.
Collected by James G. Swan.

In addition to the oblique method of weaving the checker patterns in cedar bark, occasional diagonally or twilled weaving is to be seen in the same area.

A large collection of these were gathered by James G. Swan along the coast of British Columbia, and are now for examination in the U. S. National Museum.

Ornamentation in bark work is effected both by introducing different colored strands and by varying the width of the warp and the woof threads. In many examples the bottom of the basket is bordered and outlined with one or more rows of the twined or plaited style of weaving to give greater stability and definition to the form. Cedar mats of large size and made with the greatest care enter as extensively into the daily life of the Indians of this vicinity as do the buffalo robes into that of the Dakota Indians.

The Bilhulas made very neat baskets, called "Zeibusqna" as well as hats and water-tight vessels, all of fine cedar roots.

They boil the cedar root until it becomes pliable to be worked by the hand and beaten with sticks, when they pick the fibers apart into threads. The warp is of a different material—sinews of the whale, or dried kelp thread.

They also are expert in weaving the inner bark of the cedar.

It is not astonishing that a material so easily woven should have found its way so extensively in the industries of this stock of Indians. Neither should we wonder that the checker pattern in weaving should first appear on the west coast among the only people possessing a material eminently adapted to this form of manipulation. It is only another example of that beautiful harmony between man and nature which delights the anthropologist at every step of his journey.

Farther south in British Columbia a Salish people demanding careful attention are those formerly called Couteau or Knife Indians by the Hudson Bay Company's people. Their home is the southern interior of British Columbia, mostly east of the Coast Range, and is about 100 miles long and 90 miles wide. Their basketry is described by James Teit of Spences Bridge, British Columbia.[a] The basket work above Lytton is of birch bark, spruce bark, and willow twigs, and the rims ornamented with stitches made from the bark of *Prunus demissa*. The Indians on the lower division of the Thompson River and on the Upper Fraser make beautiful coiled and imbricated baskets of cedar roots (*Thuja plicata*) This type of basketry is also made by the Chilcotin and Lillooet, and Shushwap, who are said to employ spruce root.

William Arnott, of North Bend, gives the following Thompson River Indian names for baskets: Tsai, ordinary oblong style; spanach, small oblong and square; spa panach, very small; nikwoeten, round; spanikwoeten, small round; sklokw, very large.

Wallets are made of a twined weaving, the character of which is shown in Teit's fig. 132. Designs on these fabrics are in embroidery or by weaving colored grasses or bark twine into the fabric, as shown in the same figure. This style of weaving seems to have been acquired recently through intercourse with the Sahaptin.

The Lower Thompson Indians weave mats of strips of cedar bark of the same style as those used by the coast Indians (Teit's fig. 133).

At the present day rag mats or rugs are often made from scraps of cloth, calico, etc. The patterns on these are mostly the same as those on basketry.

The Thompson Indians also practice twined weaving in coarse bagging and in matting from tule (*Scirpus*), bulrush (*Typha latifolia*), and the twined weft of the bark of *Apocynum cannabinum*. These Indians also knew how to make mats by stringing them. The reed or stick is perforated at two or more places and a cord passed through the holes.

It is interesting to find among them also blankets made from twisted

---

[a] Memoirs of the American Museum of Natural History, II, 1900, pp. 163–392.

strips of rabbit skin used as weft and laid together by twined weaving. Attention is especially called to a method of ornamental overlaying among the Thompson River Indians that has not a wide distribution. An ordinary wallet is made of twined work from the fiber of *Apocynum cannabinum* and *Asclepias speciosa*. In the fabric these do not differ from the world-wide twined weaving, but in the ornamentation a strip of grass or other colored material—maybe corn husk—is wrapped around the twined work as it proceeds. Comparing this with the Makah wrapped work the twined weft takes the place of the strip laid behind the vertical warps, the wrapping is precisely the same, but in the Thompson River work the patterns are quite similar on both sides, only the elements are oblique on the outside and vertical on the inside.

The weaving of blankets by basketry processes was formerly an important industry among them. The coast Indians utilized both dog hair and goat hair in their manufacture, but the Thompson Indians seemed to have used the latter only. Sometimes the wool was made whiter or cleaned by mixing a quantity of baked white diatomaceous earth with it and beating the whole with a flat stick. The manner of making the thread is exactly the same as that described by Dr. Boas for the process employed by the Songish. The loom and spindle are also the same, excepting that both disk and shaft of the latter are of wood. The whole process of blanket making and the implements used are said to be exactly the same as those found among the Lower Fraser Indians. Most blankets had a fringe of tassels, 6 to 9 inches in length, along one end. Black bear's hair made into threads, and spun threads of goat's hair dyed either yellow with lichens or red with alder bark, were woven into the blankets in patterns similar to those used in basketry. The Indians of Spuzzum continue to make these blankets at the present day.

For making nets, threads of the bark of *Apocynum cannabinum* were used. A wooden netting stick (Teit's fig. 134) served for making the meshes of equal size. The meshes were tied with a square knot.

The Rev. Myron Eells states that the imbricated basketry is made by the Puyallups, Twanas, Snohomish, Clallam, Skagit, Cowlitz, Chehalis, Nisqually, Spokan, and Squakson who are Salish, as well as by the Yakima and Klikitat Indians of middle and western Washington who are Shahaptian. Only women and girls are basket makers; they use in securing material the ordinary root digger. Pieces of the desired length and about the thickness of a finger are buried in the ground to keep them fresh. When required they are taken out and peeled with a sharp stone or knife and hung up to dry. When needed they are split into long strips by means of the bone awl. The pieces of the desired width and thickness throughout are used for stitching; the others form the foundation of the coil, which in the weaving is kept of uniform thickness by adding fresh material. Foundations are also in narrow strips of wood. Mr. Teit makes the important assertion that the stitches of the preceding coil are intentionally split by the awl. Examples of this kind of work are common in collections. On the bottom and back as well as ends of the baskets ornamental strips are often overlaid or decorated by a process here called beading. In many examples strips of cedar and other woods are used as foundations. The method of ornamentation employed is imbrication, described on page 310, the material for the overlaying being a glossy yellow-white grass.

As soon as enough is known about the geographic distribution of this imbricated type of weaving a better classification can be made. The following characteristics will suffice as a general guide:

1. *Foundation.*—Either a bundle of splints, somewhat cylindrical in form, or narrow flat strips of wood usually laid in pairs.

2. *Sewing.*—All done in splints of root; in some baskets the stitch is carefully and systematically bifurcated on the outside, in others whole.

3. *Bottom.*—Either a flat spiral circular or elliptical in outline, as in most of the Washington varieties and in some of the farthest removed of the British Columbia specimens, or a series of straight rows of sewing. The bottoms of many of the baskets of this last type are receding, and even a border is built up outside of the structure of the basket. (Compare Plate 157 with Plate 163.)

4. *General shape.*—Either conical, rectangular, pyramidal, or fanciful.

5. *Decoration.*—Designs covering the whole surface; designs on the upper part of the surface only; and designs around the middle, leaving the top and bottom plain or separately figured. In some beading is mixed with the imbricated ornament. It may not amount to tribal differences, but some baskets are decorated in front with imbrications, and plain or beaded on the back and ends. It is impossible with the knowledge at present in hand to make a perfect ethnic chart of this wonderfully varied type of workmanship.

Plate 156 is a covered basket box in imbricated coiled work, from Douglas Harbor, British Columbia, now in the collection of Fred Harvey, Albuquerque, New Mexico. The foundation and sewing are of cedar or spruce root, and the imbrications are in squaw grass and cedar bark. The noticeable feature in this specimen is the coiled work. In order to diminish the amount of sewing, the basket maker has thought of the expedient used by the Mescalero Apache Indians of the south, and seen on specimens from other localities, of widening the foundation of the coil. In the Douglas Harbor examples, strips of wood take the place of two or more stems arranged one above another.

Plate 157 represents Thompson River and Fraser River coiled

baskets, showing both imbrication and overlaying with grass. The specimens shown in this plate are in the collection of Miss A. M. Lang, The Dalles, Oregon. They should be examined carefully with respect to the characteristics of foundation, stitch, shape, design, and quality mentioned above.

Fig. 155 is a precious old coiled and imbricated basket. The bottom is made up of fifteen foundation rods laid parallel. Each one of these is overlaid by a strip of bright yellow squaw grass. Thus prepared, these rods are sewed together by coil stitching, which are split or bifurcated, and some trifurcated in the operation. Again, while the stitching is solid on the inside, those in sight are from one-eighth to one-fourth of an inch apart on the outside, showing that every other stitch is under the straw. On the outside of this rectangular

FIG. 155.
COILED AND IMBRICATED BASKET.
Cat. No. 60235, U.S.N.M. Collected by J. J. Maclean.

bottom the regular coiled work begins and the body is built up, the stitches all being concealed by what in this treatise is called imbricated ornament or knife plaiting, carefully described and illustrated elsewhere. In this example the ornamentation is in squaw grass, cherry bark, and cedar bark, dyed black. (See figs. 52–55.)

The foundation of the coiled work is not a single rod, but a bunch of splints made from the cedar root. Catalogue No. 60235 in the U. S. National Museum was procured from Sitka, Alaska, Indians by J. J. McLean, to which place it had doubtless drifted in trade from the Fraser River region. Its length is 8½ inches and height 3¾ inches.

Mr. Hill-Tout reports that for boiling their food the N'tlaka pamuq tribe (Salishan family), on the Fraser and the Thompson River, always used basket kettles made like their other basketry from the split roots of the cedar. These roots are sometimes red and black, and very beautiful patterns are made from the three different colors. The red dye was obtained from the bark of the alder tree, and the dark stain was obtained by soaking the roots[a] in black slime or mud, or from the root of a fern (Franz Boas).

Dr. G. M. Dawson, in his " Notes on the Shuswap people of British Columbia," tells us that these baskets were made from roots of the spruce, and Dr. Boas, in his report on the Shuswaps, informs us that the basketry of the Shuswaps and N'tlaka pamuq always used the root of the cedar. As the N'tlaka pamuq were preeminent in basket making, it is possible that the information gained by Mr. Hill-Tout may be accepted as correct, although the cedar (*Thuja*) is not abundant in the Thompson River country.[b] So skillfully did the women make these baskets that they would hold liquids without trouble. In preparing food two kettles were used, one containing water for washing off any dirt that might adhere to the heated stones, and the other for holding the food. In boiling salmon for eating, the fish were tied up in birch bark to prevent breaking and falling to pieces.

The Washington or southern imbricated ware is far more true to the old type than the northern, as examples will show. It may be divided roughly between Salishan and Shahaptian. (See Plate 158.)

The Klikitat or Shahaptian basket (Plate 158, fig. 2) is thus made: The foundation consists of the roots of young spruce and cedar trees. They are macerated and split or torn into shreds and soaked for a long time. The materials for the ornamentation are thus prepared. Most of it is of squaw grass (*Xerophyllum tenax*). It grows on the east side of the Cascade Mountains and can be gathered only during the late summer, when the snow has melted and the grass has matured. The broad leaves are split into the requisite width and if they are to retain their natural color are soaked in water only. To be dyed they are soaked in mud and charcoal for black, in a dye from willow bark for brown, and a long time in water for yellow. In some cases cedar bast is dyed black instead of the grass, but it is not so durable, or willow bark takes the place of the grass, but the surface shrivels. With the three elements of structure around her, the Klikitat basket maker makes up a roll of root splints for the beginning of her foundation, which she wraps at one end for an inch with sewing splint. Doubling this she begins her over and over sewing, splitting, sometimes with exquisite taste and care, the wood of the stitch underneath. The ornamentation covering more or less the surface of every Klikitat basket, called imbricated work, is laid on in the process of manufacture. The woman (1) catches the end of a strip of grass or bark under a stitch, (2) bends the strip forward to cover the stitch, (3) bends it back on itself, leaving about

---

[a] According to Dr. Boas the black dye was obtained from the fern root. It is possible it was gotten in both ways.

[b] Report of the British Association for the Advancement of Science, 1899, p. 511.

one-eighth of an inch for the next stitch to rest on, (4) makes her stitch, draws it home, and bends the grass strip over and covers it. It is a kind of knife plaiting held down by coiled sewing and is an invention of this region.[a]

Plate 158, fig. 1, is an example of the Salishan or older type on the coast of Washington. It is specimen No. 2612, U. S. National Museum, collected by Capt. Charles Wilkes.

The imbricated basketry of Washington is divided by Mrs. Molson into two classes, by districts. The eastern slope of the Cascade or Yakima district belongs to the arid plateau of eastern Washington and the basket technic is heavy, staunch, and of good workmanship, but it shows the effect of climate. But the western or Cowlitz River district produced the perfect imbricated basket, with more coils to the inch, more stitches in the same space and also more beautiful designs.

I am indebted to Mrs. Harriet K. McArthur for copies of the old records relating to the southern imbricated baskets. The most absolutely beautiful and perfect baskets of this type were made on Cowlitz and Lewis rivers in Washington. These places are but a short distance from Portland, over in Washington. No imbricated baskets were ever made south of the Columbia, the finest and best are from west of the Cascade Mountains. The shaping is more graceful, being woven much finer, and the designs are far more intricate. They rarely have the openings around the top for lacing strings. Beautiful ones come from the Skokomish Reservation and from the coast, but they may have reached these remote places through the medium of trade.

Immersion in water, charcoal, and bark dyes is practiced. Cherry bark is employed much in British Columbia, and sometimes by the Klikitats who occasionally put in willow bark which shrinks and leaves an ugly stitch. The rare ones with colors—not the fine old brown, yellow, and black, but old rose and purple, are valuable because they are rare. The old rose is a berry stain and the purple is from a root; but they will never rival the old brown in beauty.

The typical coiled and imbricated baskets from west Washington, therefore, may be called the Cowlitz type. According to Dr. Boas most of them are made on the Cowlitz River and north to Fraser River. He also bears witness that the split sewing and the interlocking of stitches are both practiced. The Athapascans seem to have dwelt originally in this area, and it is just possible that they carried the coiling everywhere.

The so-called Klikitat baskets are now found on the Yakima Reservation, in Klikitat and Cowlitz counties, along the Columbia River, in the vicinity of The Dalles.

---

[a] Mrs. W. M. Molson, Basketry of the Pacific Coast, Portland, Oregon, 1896.

Plate 159 represents old Klikitat baskets, coiled and little imbricated, in the collection of Miss Anne M. Lang, The Dalles, Oregon. At once the difference will be seen between these conical and quite aboriginal forms and those of rectangular shapes farther north in the Fraser and Thompson River countries. The method of ornamentation is the same, but the borders are finished off with considerable skill and taste in braided work. In the National Museum are photographs of excellent old pieces in the Harvey collection in Albuquerque. For the sake of comparison, Plate 160 is inserted to show later and more highly embellished forms.

The baskets made in imitation of a trunk are used for a similar purpose and not for berries. The Hudson Bay and other people brought camphor trunks from the Hawaiian Islands, taken there from China. The work is wonderfully good in this as well as in others. The interesting part is that the weavers before this time had made baskets with rounded bottoms, and began, of course, with the coil in the center; but the oblong shape with corners was another matter, so a thin board was covered with cloth to form the bottom, and on the edge of this the bone awl was used to make perforations to fasten the first row on this bottom. Later baskets had an ingeniously woven bottom over a number of narrow slats, and the patient weaver subsequently mastered an oblong coil.

From a report of the Commissioner of Indian Affairs, Governor Isaac L. Stevens, 1854, the following statements are taken in order to comprehend the migrations of the tribe after whom imbricated ware has been popularly named:

The tribes of the Klikitat and Yakima inhabit properly the valley lying between Mounts St. Helena and Adams, but they have spread over the districts belonging to other tribes and a band of them is now located as far south as Umpqua.

The Klikitats and Yakimas in all essential peculiarities of character are identical and their intercourse is constant, but the former, though a mountain tribe, are more unsettled in their habits than their brethren. The fact is probably due in the first place to their having been driven from their homes many years ago by the Cayuses, with whom they were at war. They then became acquainted with other parts of the country, as well as with the advantages derived from trade. It was not, however, until about 1839 that they crossed the Columbia, when they overran the Willamette Valley, attracted by the game with which it abounded and which they destroyed in defiance of the weak and indolent Callapooyas. They still boast that they taught the latter tribe to ride and hunt. They manifest a peculiar aptitude for trading.

Under the term Walla Walla (p. 223) are embraced a number of bands, living usually on the south side of the Columbia and on the Snake River, to a little east of the Palouse.

The Tai-tin-a-pam, a band of the Klikitats already mentioned, living near the head of the Cowlitz, were called by their eastern brethren wild or wood Indian.

From the report of the Commissioner of Indian Affairs for 1858 (p. 225), Puget Sound Agency, T. Simmon, agent, is quoted:

There is a portion of the Indians of my district whose homes are high up on the river, principally on the Nisqually, Puyallup, and Snoqualmie. They are nearly related to the Yakimas and Klikitats by blood, and are sometimes called Klikitats.

R. S. Landsdale, agent, White Salmon Agency (p. 275), writes:

Many of the Klikitats were removed during the late war from their former homes, west of the Cascade Mountains, to this agency.

The home of the Klikitat Indians, says Mrs. Molson,[a] was along the waters of the Columbia and its tributaries, from the Cascade Mountains on the west to the Bitter Root Range on the east, and from 46 degrees 44 minutes north, to what is now eastern Washington and northern Idaho. They were not only rovers and marauders, but they went on annual expeditions to trade, carrying dried buffalo meat and robes, but also wild hemp, dried and twisted, to exchange for dried salmon and dentalia. They held the gateway between the East and the West, for the river was the only route of communication. South of the Columbia, along the ocean, is an old path known as the "Klikitat trail." They journeyed south by this route and returned north by the Klamath trail on the eastern side of the Cascades. There are no indications of their being basket makers. Their kindred, still in the old home, make no imbricated ware.

Plate 161 is a typical coiled and imbricated berry basket of the Klikitat Indians, from the collection of Mrs. R. S. Shackelford, from whom the following information is received: The inside walls, both foundation and sewing, are from splints of the root of the giant cedar (*Thuja plicata*), collected on the sides of Mount Hood. The ornamentation is the imbricated work described in detail on page 427, the materials being of the white Tooksi or squaw grass. Cedar and cherry bark are also used, and for color the yellow dye is procured from the Oregon grape (*Berberis nervosa*), the brown dye from alder bark, and the black from acorns soaked in mud. The meaning of the artistic terraced design is not known. Six months were consumed in making it. Catalogue No. 207756, U. S. National Museum. The following story was gathered from a basket maker by Mrs. Shackelford:

The Spirit told the first weaver to make a basket (tooksi). So she repaired to the forest and pondered over her mission. Gathering the plant yi, squaw grass, elk grass, pine grass, and the red cedar roots, noo wi ash (*Thuja plicata*), she began to weave, and after many toilsome days a basket was produced. She carried it to the lake and dipped it full of water, but it leaked, and the Spirit said to her: "It will not do. Weave again a tight basket with a pattern on it." She sat by the waterside, and as she looked into the clear depths of the lake the pattern (chato timus) was revealed to her in the refracted lines, and with new courage she repaired to the depths of the forest and worked until she wrought a basket on which the ripples of

---

[a] Basketry of the Pacific Coast, Portland, Oregon, 1896.

the lake were shown. Other women have learned the pattern all down the ages, but only very few are now left who can weave a faultless basket and a perfect imitation of chato timus.

The locality where the story was learned is Lummi Island, Bellingham Bay, Washington. The pattern referred to is similar to that shown in fig. 289, of the Sixth Annual Report of the Bureau of Ethnology.

Fig. 156 represents a fine old piece of Yakima coiled and imbricated basket, Catalogue No. 23872 in the U. S. National Museum, collected by James H. Wilbur. The foundation and sewing are in split root, probably cedar. The sewing is entirely overlaid and concealed by strips of squaw grass laid on in the manner explained on page 427. The border is especially interesting, connected structurally with

FIG. 156.
IMBRICATED BASKET.
Yakima Indians, Washington.
After W. H. Holmes.

examples from California and Peru (See Plate 248). It is in open coiled work, the foundation being wrapped, bent in a regular sinuous pattern and sewed down here and there. The design, according to Mrs. Judge Burke, represents a flock of geese migrating. Its height is 7½ inches. (See fig. 159 and Plate 35).

Fig. 157 is an old example of imbricated basketry from Washington, collected by Dr. J. L. Fox, U. S. Navy, of the Wilkes Exploring Expedition, Catalogue No. 2137. Such work is now generally called Klikitat, and the Indians of that stock are expert in the use of it; but the exploring expedition did not come in contact with tribes so far in the interior. The Salish Indians on Puget Sound make the same type of work, and it is known that the very best come from the Cowlitz country, so that this is probably a very old piece of Cowlitz basketry in this kind of weaving. The whole surface of it is covered with the imbrication or a knife plaiting, explained on p. 427, and illustrated in figs. 52–54.

Catalogue No. 2614, U. S. National Museum, shown in Plate 45, is an imbricated basket made by an Indian of Salishan family, in Washington. It is one of the oldest specimens in the National Museum, having been brought home by Captain Charles Wilkes more than sixty years ago. The material of the foundation and sewing is of cedar root. The surface is covered entirely with imbricated ornamentation, the body color being produced by strips of squaw grass. The figures are in cedar bark in natural color and dyed black by means of charcoal and mud. The golden color in the straw filaments is produced by longer immersion in water. The most interesting feature in this basket is the bottom, which is formed upon a strip of wood three-

FIG. 157.

IMBRICATED BASKET.
Cowlitz Indians.
Collected by Dr. J. L. Fox, U. S. Navy.

fourths of an inch wide and 6 inches in length. It is very closely wrapped or served with a splint of root. Upon the margin of this the coiled work begins, one round being made in plain stitches. Afterwards the patterns are attached immediately to this and extend outward to a black line on the margin, the body of the basket being completely covered with other figures, the ends different from the sides. The border is neatly finished off in false braid. There are about eight rows of coiled work and from twelve to sixteen stitches to the inch. On the outside the stitches are regularly split or furcated. Length, 8 inches; depth, 4¼ inches.

Fig. 158 represents a specimen of twilled work by the Clallam Indians and should be compared with Nutka example, Plate 152. It is made of flat splints of white wood, resembling birch. The bottom was woven first and all of the splints by being bent upward become the warp of the sides. Twilled effect is produced by passing each weft splint over two and under two warp splints. The fastening off of the upper border is done by bending down the warp splints and holding them in place by a whipping of the same material. The scallop on the upper border is formed by looping the middle of two splints under the rim, twisting both pairs of ends into a twine, passing one twine through the other, and doubling down to repeat the process until the whole is finished.

Illustrations of this method of making twilled work are shown in figs. 94–96, but, as will be seen, innumerable pleasing effects are produced by varying the color, the number, the width, and the direction of the splints that are overlapped in the weaving. Catalogue No. 23509, in the U. S. National Museum, was procured in Washington by James G. Swan. It is 15 inches in height.

Myron Eells, long a resident among the Sound tribes of Salish, has collected for the U. S. National Museum at different times many specimens of their basketry. It was he that first noticed the great diversity that exists in such small tribes as the Twana, or Towanhoosh.

FIG. 158.
TWILLED BASKET WORK.
Clallam Indians, Washington.
Collected by J. G. Swan.

They use in their work a knife for splitting material, a common awl, formerly of bone, in sewing their coiled ware. He has seen the woman using a small bone for pressing home her weft. This is rare, for the fingers are usually employed for this purpose.

Fig. 159 is a water-tight basket for cooking, marked Clallam. The foundation is the single flat strip type. Attention is called to the ornamental effect produced in this work by the splitting of the under stitch by the one above it. The noteworthy feature of this type of basket, however, is in the occasional overlaying of a filament of squaw grass or other material, which seems to be the first step toward imbrication. The grass lies over two stitches and is caught under the next stitch, passing under and over as in "beading." In other examples the straw is covered and revealed in the alternate stitches. It can be seen that a great variety of effects is possible in this manipulation.

A square inch from the surface of this specimen enlarged (fig. 160) will show more clearly what has been hitherto described—the interlocking stitches, the furcation of the stitches, and the overlaying with ornamental filaments.

Catalogue No. 23512, in the U. S. National Museum, was procured in Washington by James G. Swan.

FIG. 159.
WATER-TIGHT BASKET.
Clallam Indians, Washington.
Collected by J. G. Swan.

Charles C. Willoughby, who was agent among the Quinaielt or Quinault Indians in northwestern Washington, makes the following report of their basketry:

They have the cedar bark for the foundation of basketry and strips of the pine root for rigid work, hemp, rushes, and grass for the weft and ornamentation. The grass used in strengthening the borders of mats, rain cloaks, etc., grows on flat places. It is prepared like flax by soaking in water until the outer portion decays, when it is beaten with sticks until only the fiber remains. The yellow fiber of squaw grass used by Indians for the outside of baskets is a great source of traffic, as it is only found in this locality. The basket grass is gathered carefully, one blade at a time, to secure that part of the stalk that reaches about 6 inches under the ground before it meets the root. To prepare the grass for drying it is woven together at the ends with fibers of cedar bark. It is then spread upon the ground or upon roofs in the sun. When to be used it is moistened with water and split with two small knife blades, set in a stick in such a manner as to make the strips of the same width, the smaller portion being thrown away. The grass is kept moist with water while being made into baskets. The colored grasses are prepared by using aniline dyes. They were formerly colored by steeping the roots of plants that yielded a yellow coloring. A red dye was made from the bark of alder, and a paint was made of blue clay. [a]

Plate 162 shows a number of Quinaielt baskets in twined and overlaid weave in the collection of Miss Anne M. Lang.

Plate 163, top figure, is a wallet made from grass stems by the Quinaielt Indians. It is worthy of especial study, because the warp is horizontal and the weft vertical.

FIG. 160.

DETAIL OF FIG. 159.

Openwork figures are produced on the surface in a series of chevroned patterns by an ingenious but very simple process. At the point where the open effect is to be produced the two strands constituting the twine do not make a half turn, but pass above and below the warp, as in ordinary plain weaving, across one warp strand. In the next round the adjoining pair are similarly treated, and thus figures are produced. At the upper and lower margin two rows of horizontal twined weaving fasten off the ends, which are braided down. On the sides the warp strands are sewed into and concealed in a coarse braid of rushes. Width, 18½ inches; height, 14 inches.

Catalogue No. 151452, in the U. S. National Museum, was collected in Washington by Dr. Franz Boas.

Plate 163, bottom figure, is a Thompson River basket in the collection of J. W. Benham. It is introduced here for the purpose of showing how the Indian woman's mind struggled with the problem of starting the bottom of a rectangular coiled basket. It has been said that the Thompson River Indians do not understand this process, but many old Thompsons have coiled bottoms and this technic is older than the other. The work begins by wrapping a foundation of splints with the split root of spruce or cedar for 6 or more inches. This is

[a] Smithsonian Report, 1886, Pt. 1, pp. 267–282.

then doubled upon itself and the sewing begins and proceeds backward and forward, as in plowing, until fifteen rows are made; the coiling then actually begins, the sewing extending not only along the sides but across the ends, making a parallelogram, which is extended for ten rows farther outward, at which place the additional ornament begins.   So far it is plain coiled work with split stitches; afterwards it becomes a mixture of plain coiled work with upright bands of imbrication.   Its height is 13 inches, and its width at bottom is 9½ inches.

The twined baskets of Washington, with little animals around the margin, belong to the Skokomish and other Salishan tribes about Puget Sound.   When the tails turn up they are dogs or wolves; when they turn down they are horses.   Especial attention has been called to the varied and tasteful effects produced by the use of the rectangular element.

Plate 164 represents two carrying wallets of the Skokomish Indians living in Washington.   The examples shown are done in the style of weaving called here "wrapped twine" (figs. 21 and 22).

Plate 165 shows specimens of carrying baskets made by Salish tribes in Washington; the one in the center is Tillamuk, Catalogue No. 151149 in the U. S. National Museum, collected by Dr. Franz Boas. The others, Nos. 2709 and 23511, are very old specimens in the National Museum collection and are accredited to the Clallams.   The upper one on the plate is credited to the Wilkes Exploring Expedition, secured more than sixty years ago.   All of these are in plain, twined weaving with splint of root, probably spruce, made browner by soaking in mud.   The ornamentation is false embroidery in squaw grass.   The three methods of forming the border are noteworthy.   In the upper specimen stout cable is formed by "sewing" a small bundle of root splints with the same material.   This is sewed here and there to the upper margin of the wallet.   The other figures show the margin finished by braiding down; the loops of root were twisted in subsequently.   The animals on the margin are horses.

The specimen, Catalogue No. 23511, which is the lower one on the plate, was collected in Washington by James G. Swan.

Plate 166, upper figure, is an open twined wallet of the Tillamuk Indians, Salishan family, the remnant of which is living at Grande Ronde Agency, Oregon.   The bottom of this basket is rather ingenious. The warp splints of the sides pass across the bottom also and are held together there by courses of twined weaving.   At the edges of the end portions of the bottom the splints of the weft or twined work become the warp for the body.   At the upper border two rows of squaw grass are beaded in.   The braided border around the top is formed by the ends of the warp splints plaited together in a double row, additional material being used if necessary.

The lower figure is an open wallet of the Chinook Indians, Chinookan family, occupying formerly both sides of the Columbia River from the mouth to The Dalles, a distance of 200 miles. According to Lewis and Clark most of their villages were on the northern bank. To this family also belong the Clatsops and Wascos, to be mentioned later. The wallet illustrated in the plate is made of root in twined weaving with crossed warp. The bottom or foundation is a rectangular structure, about 4 inches square, made of double splints of root, securely lashed together backward and forward. From this central portion the splints spread out and the twined weaving begins. Additional warp elements are added from time to time as the structure widens. A coarse form of ornamentation is produced by overlaying some of the warp elements with squaw grass. The fastening off of the upper border is peculiar and on the outside imitates precisely a three-ply braid, but on the inside the structure is at once revealed. A strip of root is laid along the top of the warp elements and these are brought over in buttonhole stitch and tucked behind the strip, then cut off, making a a very rough appearance. It will be noticed that in the weaving of this wallet the half turns of the twine do not go around the crossings of the warp elements, but just below the crossings, so as to include each warp separately. On the outside of the warp splints here and there a strip of grass is regularly overlaid.

Catalogue Nos. 151447 and 151448 in the U. S. National Museum were collected by Dr. Franz Boas.

The Nez Percé Indians of the Shahaptian family, prior to the advent of the whites on the Pacific coast, made heavy and beautiful blankets of the wool of the Rocky Mountain sheep and of the hair of animals killed in the chase, dyed in different colors. The patterns are all geometric, and are, in fact, woven mosaics, each figure being inserted separately by twisting two woof threads backward and forward around the warp strands. Scarcely ever does the twine extend in stripes all the way across the blanket in a direct line.

The same Indians at present weave bags from the bast of the Indian hemp (*Apocynum cannabinum*) and from grass stems shredded. The figures are produced by overlaying the regular warp strands with corn husks or colored grass in false embroidery. In some examples (see fig. 161) the entire surface is covered with geometric figures; in others they are only partially covered. The Nez Percé are in the same family as the Klikitat and Yakima, but they make no imbricated baskets.

Fig. 161 is a twined wallet of the Nez Percés. The body weaving, both warp and weft, is of indian hemp. In the process of manufacture a sufficient number of warp strands were joined together in the middle by a row of twined weaving and probably suspended, the ends hanging down. The weaver filled this warp with the ordinary twisted work, proceeding from the bottom to the border. The ornamentation, in corn husk or other weak material, in the natural color or dyed, is laid on externally by what is here called false embroidery. The process was fully described and illustrated in speaking of Tlinkit weaving (fig. 139, p. 410). This specimen should be compared with the making of soft wallets among the Fraser River tribes, illustrated in Teit's monograph, where the corn husk, instead of being wrapped merely around the outer element of the twine, passes around both strands and the figure appears on the inside of the receptacle, which is not true of the Nez Percé example.

Fig. 162 will show a square inch of this wallet, the especial feature of which is that while the rows of plain twining seem to be vertical in the false embroidery, they are inclined to the right.

This specimen, Catalogue No. 9026 in the U. S. National Museum, was collected in Idaho by Dr. Storrer.

Plate 167 is an interesting collection of women's hats. Figs. 1 and 2 are Modoc twined baskets from the Benjamin collection, Catalogue Nos. 204258 and 204259; height, 5¾ inches. The foundation is of rush. The weaving is in the same material, the designs being formed by regular overlaying in step patterns, formed by piling rhomboidal figures upon one another. Strips of bird quill are introduced into these patterns, having been dyed a bright yellow, which gives life to the figures. It may be repeated that both of these specimens are in plain-twined weaving overlaid. All the other figures on the plate are in wrapped-twined weaving, as among the Makahs and other tribes of the Fraser-Columbia region.

Figs. 3 and 4 are women's hats of the Nez Percé and Walla-Walla Indians, Shahaptian family, Washington, Catalogue Nos. 23857 and 129680. The foundation is of hemp. The weft consists of strands of hemp on the inside wrapped around with a filament of squaw grass.

The process of this weaving is explained in figs. 21 and 22. Catalogue No. 23857, collected by J. B. Monteith, height 5 inches; 129680, collected by Mrs. Anna McBean, height 5¾ inches.

Fig. 5, Catalogue No. 9040, U. S. National Museum, is a woman's hat, called a wedding hat, and assigned to the Cascade Indians. It is doubtless Shahaptian. In every respect it is made like the Nez Percé examples described, being in wrapped-twined weaving similar to that of the Makah Indians. Height, 6½ inches; collected by Dr. James F. Ghiselin.

Figs. 6 and 7 are women's hats of the Nez Percé Indians, Shahaptian family, collected by F. W. Clark, 5 inches in height, and No. 23587, 5 inches in height, collected by J. B. Monteith.

The Cayuse (Waiilatpuan) and Umatilla (Shahaptian) make soft baskets in twined weaving. They are horse Indians and use their wallets for saddle bags. The material is rushes, wild hemp, corn husks, and worsted. The bottoms and undecorated portions are plain-twined work. In the figured parts the husks, split into narrow strips, are administered in four ways—by overlaying, not showing on the inside; by overlaying and twining so as to show on the inside; by false embroidery, wrapped about the weft twine elements on the outside, and by frapping the twined weft as in the Thompson River work (Mrs. McArthur).

FIG. 162.

DETAIL OF FIG. 161.

The soft wallets illustrated in Plate 168, often called "Sally bags," were made by Wasco Indians, who belong to the Chinookan family. At present they are on the Warm Springs Reservation in Oregon, and the Yakima Reservation in Washington. The wallet in the middle of the plate No. 9041 was presented to the U. S. National Museum by Dr. James T. Ghiselin in 1869; the others were collected by Mrs. R. S. Shackelford and Miss E. T. Houtz. They are all made in plain twined weaving over warp of rushes, the patterns being effected by overlaying the twine of hemp with strips of fiber that in structure resemble corn husks. On the newer specimens the designs are clearly shown, representing man (tillacum), elk (mowitch), sturgeon (pish), duck (culla-culla). By observing the men's faces in the newer specimens, it will be easy to detect the idealized faces on the fine, old wallet in the middle.

Prof. O. M. Dalton figures in "Man" (London), I, note 17, an old Wasco basket wallet with the image of a man in knee breeches on the surface. In the National Museum are a number of new wallets bearing this same figure, but the Dalton specimens show that it has been a motive in Wasco weaving for a long period.

Plate 169 represents twined wallets of the Wasco Indians, Oregon, in the Fred Harvey collection. The foundations are in native hemp in plain-twined weaving.   On the body of the wallets birds, beasts, and men are wrought in grass or husks of corn in corners.

Clatsops make flat mats and wallets of cat-tail rush.   The latter, with strap of grass and woolen to wear across the shoulders, are excellent for carrying fish.   They also construct a sack in open-twined work in roots.   The fine-twined small baskets in three colors are equal to any in Oregon (Mrs. McArthur).

THE CALIFORNIA-OREGON REGION

The human hand is so beautifully formed, it has so fine a sensibility, that sensibility governs its motions so correctly, every effort of the will is answered so instantly, as if the hand were the seat of that will.—Sir CHARLES BELL.

The California-Oregon basketry region has only one definite boundary, the hard coast of the Pacific; on other sides there is no sharp ethnic limit.   North, east, and south, it is full of turnstiles that move in one direction only.   Tribes from far away pushed through them into this region, but if they had desired to turn their backs on abundant game, fish, and vegetal foods, they would have been prevented by the column in the rear.

The ancient basket makers of this area knew nearly every type and technical process of the art, both in weaving and coiling.   They added at least one new technical process, the tee weave.   In ornamentation, imbrication is wanting as well as false embroidery, but there is quite enough else to make up the deficiency.   Within the California-Oregon area there are subareas, and the following list of linguistic families will help to unravel the tangle:

NORTHERN GROUP

Athapascan family: Hupa, lower Trinity River and Wailaki, western slopes of the Shasta Mountains.

Chimarikan family: Trinity River.

Copehan family: Wintun under many names, western drainage Sacramento River.

Kalapooian family: The Willamette Plains, western Oregon.

Kulanapan family: Pomo, under many names, in Mendocino and Lake counties.

Kusan family: Coos River and Bay, western Oregon.

Lutuamian family: Klamath and Modoc, Upper Klamath River or Klamath Lake.

Palaihnihan family: Pit Rivers; on Pit River to eastern boundary of the State.

Pujunan family: Concow (Konkau), Maidu, Nockum (Nakum), western drainage of the Sacramento River, south of Palaihnihan.

Quoratean family: Ehnek, Karok, middle Klamath River.

Sastean family: Shastas; middle northern boundary of State.

Takilman family: Lower Rogue River, Oregon.

Weitspekan family: Yurok, Weitspek, Lower Klamath River.

Wishoskan family: Wishosk, Eel River, and Humboldt Bay.

Yanan family: Nozis, north of Pujunan.

Yukian family; Ashochimi, Chumaya, Napa, Tatu or Potfer Valley, Yuki or Round Valley, in Potter and Round valleys.[a]

---

[a] For classification of these northern tribes on the concept of basketry, consult Roland B. Dixon, Basketry Designs of the Indians of Northern California.   Bulletin of the American Museum of Natural History, XVII, pp. 1–32.

SOUTHERN GROUP

Chumashan family; Santa Barbara, Santa Inez, San Luis Obispo, in Santa Barbara County.

Costanoan family; Mutsun; Pacific slope, west and south of San Francisco.

Esselenian family; Soledad, Eslen, and other missions close by on Monterey Bay.

Mariposan family; Yokut and many smaller tribes, Fresno River.

Moquelumnan family; Tulare, Upper Tulare River.

Salinan family; San Antonio, San Miguel, Monterey County.

Shoshonean family; Chemehuevi, Panamint and others intruded along the eastern border, more and more, from north to south, reaching the Pacific Ocean at the Santa Barbara Islands.

Yuman family; including Cochimi, Cocopas, Cuchan, Diegueños, Havasupai, Maricopa, Mohave, Waicuru, Walapai, and several missions.[a]

The location of the linguistic families in California is shown on the map. (See fig. 163.) A glance at the map will show how, in a general way, the State is divided into northern and southern portions by a line running from San Francisco Bay to the angle of Nevada, and also in the same manner the subdivision of the northern portion of the State into three vertical sections. A little difference exists between the nomenclature of this map and that of Powell. For instance, the Wintun are Copehan; the Maidu are Pujunan; the Yokut on this map correspond to the Powell Mariposen, but in Powell's subdivision of tribes the Yokuts are placed in the Moquelumnan family. With these slight amendments the map will be easily understood and of great importance in locating California basketry. It is interesting to note that, while the Powell map was made long ago from vocabularies only, the Dixon-Kroeber map is based on grammar, and yet the agreements are nearly complete. Especial attention is called to the vast area occupied by the intruding Shoshonean family from the interior basin.[b]

The western division of the north California area, including the coast of Oregon as well, may be divided into three locations, containing each different tribes. The most northern would be Athapascan and adjoining families; the middle division, those tribes associated in Round Valley; and the most southern of all, the Pomo.

The following list of plants carefully prepared by V. K. Chesnut, of the Department of Agriculture,[c] will apply to the Hupa, the Round Valley, and Pomo basketry:

Acer macrophyllum, Pal gun sche (Yuki), maple. The Yukis of California use the bark for their basketry. The Puget Sound Indians employ it in their textiles, and Rothrock says that from the inner bark the tribes of the Pacific slope weave baskets, mats, and hats waterproof.

---

[a] Seventh Annual Report of the Bureau of Ethnology, 1891, pp. 1–142.

[b] See Roland B. Dixon and Albert L. Kroeber, The Native Languages of California, American Anthropologist, V, 1903, pp. 1–26.

[c] Plants used by the Indians of Mendocino County, California. Contributions from the National Herbarium, VII, pp. 295–408, Washington, 1902.

Adiantum pedatum. The stems of maidenhair fern attain a length of 1 to 2 feet in the redwood belt of northern California, near the coast. They form the black strands in baskets and especially basket hats.

Alnus rhombifolia, mountain alder, Un se (Yuki); Juskiat' and Kus (Wailaki); Gashet'i (Pomo). The fresh bark is used by the Yukis, as well as the Hupa and Klamath Indians of California, to color their basket material.

FIG. 163.

LINGUISTIC MAP OF CALIFORNIA.

After Dixon and Kroeber.

Apocynum cannabinum, in Mendocino County, California, Indian hemp; Ma (Yuki); Po, in Concow; Masha (Little Lake); and Silimma (Yokaia) yields the common Indian fiber. The inner bark, collected in the fall, is soft and strong for thread, twine, ropes, and nets.

Asclepias eriocarpa, Go to la (Little Lakes); Bo ko (Concow); Machal and Chaak (Yuki), poisonous milkweed. The inner bark is used by the Eel River, Concow, Potter Valley, and Little Lake Indians for strings, nets, and other textiles.

Butneria occidentalis, Sai ka lé (Pomo), spice bush or calycanthus. Both the wood and the bark from fresh shoots are used in basket work.

Carex, Tsu wish (Pomo), blackroot sedge. Used by the Pomo in their coiled basketry for decorating in black.

Carex sp. The long, tough rootstocks of several and perhaps most of the sedges (saw grass) in Mendocino County, California, are used by the basket makers. Great patience is exercised in tracing these from 2 to 5 feet through sand and mud and in preparing the splints. The baskets made from them are called "root baskets." Sedge rootstocks are the most important underground material, and the baskets made from them are the strongest, most durable, and most costly. Special characteristics belong to the different species.

Carex barbarae, Dewey, Kahum, (Pomo for water-tight baskets). The rootstocks furnish the splints for the white or creamy groundwork of most Pomo baskets. They are dug out with clam shells and sticks aiding the hands and feet.[a] One end of the stock is grasped by the first and second toes, the clam shell serves for scraping away the soil, and the stick for prying out stones and loosening the ground. A woman will secure 15 to 20 strands a day. They are placed in water over night to preserve the flexibility and to soften the scaly bark, which is removed in the morning by the women. The end of the stick is chewed until the bark is separated. The wood is then held by the teeth, the other end of the stock is held taut by the first and second toes, and the bark is scraped away, leaving a tough white or tan-colored strand about one-half the original thickness. These are done up in small coils and carried by the women to the camp. Mr. Coville draws attention to a bit of primitive agriculture in this connection. The Pomo women insist that the toughest and finest roots can be obtained only at certain spots. Unconsciously they have been making this true by means of their digging sticks and clam shells, during all the years loosening the ground and removing weeds.

Carex sp., Ta tet el (Wailaki), sea grass or sedge. The roots and leaves used in basketry, especially for hats and cheap semiflexible baskets.

Ceanothus integerrimus. The Concow squaws gather the young and flexible shoots of the California lilac, Hibi, for the warp of their baskets.

Cercis occidentalis. The bark and the wood from sprouts of the redbud, Cha-ba, in Yuki; Mula, in Little Lake; Kala-a-kala, in Yokaia; and Dop or Talk, in Concow, are used in finer baskets as foundation, as weft in twined ware, and as sewing material in coiled work. The Indians produce a variety of results in *Cercis.* The stems are sometimes cut in winter and early spring to insure material for the next fall. The color of the bark is then slightly red, which may be darkened by exposure to smoke and blackened by soaking in dirty water, in water and ashes, or in a decoction of oak bark to which scraps of iron have been added. The bark to be used in sewing coiled baskets is separated by steaming. In twined basketry some of the white wood is left adhering to the bark, in which case designs in two colors are produced, since the willow and carex are both much darker.

Corylus californica. The slender stems of the Hazelnut, Olmam, in Yuki; Gom he ni, in Concow; Ch' ki, in Wailaki; Cha-ba, in Little Lake, are commonly used in place of willows in Round Valley for coarse sieves and fish traps and as warp in saw-grass baskets. A baby-carrying basket at Ukiah was made from the same material. The Calapooias make the finest openwork twined basketry of hazel sticks. The Coos and Roque river ware resembles the Shasta, the latter produce excellent work in hazel stems (Mrs. McArthur).

---

[a] J. W. Hudson, Overland Monthly, XXI, 1893, pp. 561–578.

Covillea tridentata, Tah sun up (Paiutes), creosote wood. It is one of the commonest industrial plants in southern California, Arizona, and southern Utah. The gum is used by the Apaches for cement. It is also used to produce a greenish-yellow dye. Owing to the odor emitted when heated, the plant is called creosote wood.

Gymnogramma triangularis, Gold-back fern. Common on open brushy hillsides throughout Mendocino County. As in the case of the five-fingered fern, this plant grows much more thriftily near the coast. The stems are also used there in the making of baskets.

Juncus effusus Linnæus. The stalks of wire grass. Lolum, in Yuki; Cha-ba, by the Potter Valley, Little Lake, and Yokaia Pomos; and Sito by the Wailaki, are used in Mendocino County for making temporary baskets. With them also children are initiated into the art of basket making, and rackets used in gathering pinole seed as well as fish traps are woven.

Lonicera interrupta, Hai wat (Yuki), honeysuckle. The Yukis employ the flexible stems slightly for hoops in basket borders.

Philadelphus gordonianus, Ka kuss (Wailaki); Shon a hi (Little Lakes); Hawn li (Yukis), arrowwood. A species of syringa or mock orange. The pithy stems are valued on account of their lightness for the manufacture of baskets used by women for carrying babies.

Pinus sabiniana, Pol cum ol (Yuki) nut or digger pine. Used for basketry. The more pliable wood from the root is the chief source of material used in making large V-shaped baskets, which Little Lake Indians use for carrying acorns. The root is warmed in hot, damp ashes, and strands are split off before cooling. They are brittle when dry, but after being soaked in water they are easily manipulated in the more simply woven baskets, which are made by passing the strands out and in through the numerous vertical withes that make up the skeleton. They are not sufficiently pliable, as sedge roots are, to be used like thread in wrapping round and round a horizontal withe.

Pseudotsuga mucronata. The smaller roots of the Douglas spruce, Nu, in Yuki language, are used in fine Pomo baskets. They are found in sections 8 to 10 feet long, uniform in thickness, and about the diameter of a lead pencil (quoting Hudson).

Pteridium aquilinum, Bis (Calpella Pomo); Bebi (Little Lakes); Sulala (Concows); Dos (Nomelakkis); Ma orda-git (Yokaias), the bracken fern. The hard wood is easily split into flat bands, which are sometimes used by the coast Indians for the black strands of their cheaper baskets. They are much less frequently used for this purpose by the Indians of Round Valley and Ukiah. Because susceptible of a fine polish, they are far weaker and more brittle than the saw-grass roots which compose the weft of their choicest baskets. The black color is imparted by burying in mud.

Quercus lobata, Ky am (Yuki), white oak, acorn. The bark is used to a very slight extent by the Concows to blacken strands of the redbud for use in basketry. Rusty iron is added to the water extract of the bark to produce a black solution in which the strands are allowed to remain for some time.

Rhus diversiloba. For dyeing the splints with which some Pomo baskets are sewed. Dr. Hudson is quoted as saying that an intense black is produced by applying to them the fresh juice of poison oak in Pomo, Matuyaho; in Wailaki, Kots ta. The slender stems are also worked into the foundation of coiled basketry. *Rhus aromatica*, says Purdy, was formerly used by tribes eastward from Ukiah, as redbud is used by Pomos.

Salix argyrophylla. The white-leaved willow, Bam Kal é, in Pomo; Kalalno, in Yokaia, is considered the best for coarse baskets. It is common along Russian River, in California. It is not found at Round Valley, so these Indians would carry back small supplies of the slender stems when they returned from hop picking near Ukiah. The roots are also highly valued in making certain baskets.

Scirpus sp. The most valuable of the sedges for basket splints in Mendocino County is an unidentified species of the bulrush, *Scirpus* sp., Tsuwish, in Pomo. It is an article of commerce. Being rare near Ukiah, it is purchased at a cent a root from plants collected by Clear Lake Indians and in parts of Sonoma County or along the seacoast. The rootstocks, about one-fourth of an inch in diameter, consist of three distinct tissues—the outer, brown, like parchment; the middle; and the heart, a tough, woody structure. The outer surface of this woody tissue, which makes up the great bulk of the black fiber in the finest Pomo baskets, is slightly ribbed and varies from light brown to nearly jet-black. The interior is more or less white. Some of the dark splints are used just as they are, while others are blackened with the juice of poison oak, *Rhus diversiloba*, or by burying them with charcoal, ashes, and earth for about eighty hours.

A detailed account of the manipulation of these rootstocks at Round Valley is given.[a]

Smilax californica Gray, the only species of smilax in California, does not occur in Mendocino County, but is common along the headwaters of the Upper Sacramento. The fine, long trailing limbs are exceedingly strong and are used to some extent in Round Valley and perhaps at Ukiah for basket making. The Indians say that the strands have a brownish-black color.

Tumion californicum. Splints from the roots of the California nutmeg, Kahe in the Yokaia language and Ko'-bi in Pomo, are said to be used by the Pomo in some of their fine baskets.

Vitis californica. She in (Pomo); Mot mo mam (Yuki); Kop (Numlaki); wild grape. The native wild grape of the region climbs over trees in canyons and in damp places to a height of 30 feet or more. The smaller, woody parts of the vine are extremely flexible and are very considerably used by the tribes for the rims of their large, cone-carrying baskets. It is gathered at almost any time, soaked in water and hot ashes, after which the bark is removed and the wood split into a couple of strands, which, although very coarse, are used substantially as thread. The tribes of California make ropes and various household articles from the vine.

As a connecting link between the Salish and other basketry north of the Klamath River and the true California types there is here shown the figure of an old piece of basketry brought from Oregon more than sixty years ago (fig. 164). It is the ordinary coiled weave of the West Coast, covered with red and white feathers. The feathers are caught by their stems under the stitches as the work progresses, just as in the Pomo and other California tribes of to-day. It is interesting to find this type of work so far north. It points to the fact that many of the gaps which occur in this study could have been easily filled when the Indians were in their native situations. Holmes has other figures in the same type of basketry, only the feather work is combined with the ornamentation in the weaving on the surface. Attention is called again to the fact that the imbricated ware stopped short at the Columbia River. The plaits of grass or bark overlie one another just as feathers do in the feather work, and the stem of the feather is doubled under the stitches in the same way. To be especially noted are the groups of vertical stripes on the margin and the chevroned design at the bottom. Whether there was genetic relation-

---

[a] Plants used by the Indians of Mendocino, California, p. 317.

ship between the two remains to be studied out.   The specimen Catalogue No. 2138 in the U. S. National Museum, was collected by
Dr. J. L. Fox, U. S. Navy, of the Wilkes Exploring Expedition.

The Pacific slope branch of the Athapascan family is found in the
northwestern corner of California and far northward into Oregon.
On the Hupa Reservation were placed, in 1864, a number of bands
scattered around Trinity River, the names of which may be found in
the Smithsonian Report for 1886, Part 1.   As late as 1850 the Hupa
are said to have lived in pristine simplicity.   Autumn supplied the
all-important acorn, large quantities of which were collected and kept
in store for use during the winter and spring.   The vegetable food is
gathered chiefly by the women.   The outfit of the primitive gleaner,
miller, and cook was chiefly in basket work.   While no edible root or
food was despised, the oak furnished the chief breadstuff.   The acorns
were gathered in an osier hamper about 16 inches high and 20 inches

FIG. 164.
OLD FEATHERED BASKETS FROM OREGON.
Collected by Dr. J. L. Fox, U. S. Navy.

in diameter, made in twined weaving.   It was used by the women in
carrying loads, supported by a band across the forehead.   Filled with
acorns, this hamper was placed on the back and held in position by
means of a carrying pad consisting of a disk of mat 5 by 4 inches.
About the middle of October the Indians beat the acorns from the
trees with long poles and carry them home in these baskets.   The
squaws remove the hull by giving it a slight tap with a pestle.   The
nuts were then dried and beaten to powder in a mill with a basket
hopper.   The flour was soaked in a hollow scooped in the sand and
cooked into a kind of mush in baskets by means of hot stones and
were baked into bread in an underground oven.

If the harvest were of seeds instead of acorns, they were winnowed
in another basket of close-twined weaving which the good woman
had not failed to decorate with graceful patterns, following that
unconquerable artistic instinct which is the heritage of all the peoples
who breathe the air of the Pacific Ocean.   Under the heading of

uses a multitude of functions for the Hupa basket will be described in detail.[a]

Dr. W. L. Jepson has determined for Dr. P. E. Goddard the materials used by Hupa in baskets. The burden basket, the baby basket, and the salmon plate are made entirely of the shoots of *Corylus rostrata* var. *californica*. Hupa name is mûk-kai-kĭt-loi. These shoots form foundation or warp of all other baskets except the finest hats and the covered bottles. For these shoots of willow are used, of which *Salix sessilifolia* and *S. fluviatilis* var. *argyrophylla* are indicated. These willows are not common in Hupa Valley. The warp stems while slimmer than those from the hazel, are said not to be so durable. They are fastened at the origin of the basket and at the beginning of the body by rounds twined with the root of certain deciduous trees. This material is called indiscriminately "kût." The roots of the more common willow as well as the two mentioned are used besides the root of *Alnus oregana*, *Vitis californica* and *Populus trichocarpa*. The principal weft of all close-woven baskets is composed of the root of *Coniferæ*. Of the trees growing in or near Hupa the roots of *Pinus ponderosa*, *P. sabiniana*, and *P. lambertiana* are used. The selection of the species and of the individual trees depends on their readiness to split properly. These roots are roasted in the ground. Besides these the Hupa import from the coast, material from *Sequoia sempervirens* and *Picea sitchensis*. These root materials are called "xai." The root of the wild grape, *Vitis californica*, is used in place of the coniferæ roots in fine hats for the woof. For decorative work the leaves of *Xerophyllum tenax* serve for white, and the bark of the stems of *Adiantum pedatum* for black. A reddish brown is obtained by dyeing the inner part of the stem of *Woodwordia radicans* with the bark of *Alnus oregana*. The primitive method of dyeing was to chew the bark and draw the splint through the mouth just before introducing it into the woof. The alder dye is now sometimes applied by steeping in a dish but the results are said to be not so certain. Yellow is obtained by dipping the leaves of *Xerophyllum tenax* into a decoction of *Evernia vulpina*. The setting of this dye is difficult and many women do not use the yellow in basket making. Porcupine quills are dyed with this lichen giving a brighter effect. Their use is not common. A few women are now employing the "Oregon grape" for dyeing the xerophyllum leaves. Baskets are sometimes collected for Hupa work which are made by the Tolowa in Del Norte County. These have a steel-gray color obtained by dyeing the root of the tideland spruce with rusty iron. The root and iron are buried in the damp ground for some time.[b]

---

[a] The Ray Collection from Hupa Valley, Smithsonian Report, 1886, pp. 205–239.

[b] P. E. Goddard, The Life and Culture of the Hupas. Publications of the University of California, I, 1903. Anthropology.

Plate 170 represents three granary baskets of the Hupa Indians in the Harvey collection. The figure shown on the right is used as a cover for the granary. These baskets furnish excellent examples of form and decoration, as well as technical processes, among this Atha-pascan group. It has been mentioned before that we have here an example of acculturation through women of an art created by the conservative sex. If a number of Hupa men of Athapascan stock broke into this area and took to themselves wives of the country the weaving processes would not be changed, so that in any one of these baskets will be found, beginning at the bottom, three-strand twined weaving; above that two-strand plain-twined weaving, and over the surface decoration in overlaying. On the granary baskets the trian-gular and rectangular elementary forms are worked into vertical stripes, the basis of which is the bent line, or zigzag, forming the ornamentation, the leaves of grass alternate with the foundation color by laying a strip of the former on the latter and exposing it or turn-ing it under at will. Dr. Goddard, in his paper published by the University of California, gives the following symbolism:

The isosceles triangle the Hupa calls "rattlesnake's nose" (Lūwminchwūw); right-angled triangles made with a horizontal line meeting a vertical line are called "sharp and slanting" (chesLinalwiltchwel). Oblique-angled parallelograms are very frequently used. The name given them is "set on top of one another" (niLkut-dasaan). Another design, which lacks beauty on account of its jagged appearance, is called "grizzly bear his hand" (mikyowe mila). Another figure is called "frog his hand" (tewal mila). A third design has angles projecting upward with the vertical lines on the outside of the figure and the oblique lines sloping inward and downward. This pattern is called "swallow's tail" (teschechmikye) or "points sticking up" (chaxcheuñeL).

When the isosceles triangles (called Luwminchwuw) are grouped one above another they are called Luwminchwuw nikutdasaan ("snake's nose piled up"). When these figures come back to back so as to form diamonds alternating with the background they are called Lokyomenkonte ("sturgeon's back"). When the figure apex is superimposed on a trapezoid the name cha is given to the design. These figures are nearly always so connected as to encircle the basket, when the name LenaLdauw is given to it, signifying "it encircles." A design which seems to be the trapezoids superimposed is called LekyuwineL ("they come together"). The conception of the design seems to be that of the second variety of triangles back to back. A series of rectangular parallelograms superimposed so that each higher one projects to the right of the one below it, the whole being bordered by a double line conforming to the outline, is called kowitselminat ("worm goes round" or "worm's stairway"). The oblique-angled parallelograms in pairs, with the upper one at the right, are the designs most frequently found on the hats. They are found in series on the storage baskets (djelo). Usually even numbers are employed, pre-serving the symmetry of the zone. Designs in red often have horizontal lines in black. Oblique lines in white often run across the design. When such lines run through the oblique-angled parallelogram they are called niLkutdasaan mikiteweso ("one-on-the-other its scratches").

Plate 171 represents a basketmaker from the Hupa Reservation in northern California, wearing one of the beautiful twined basket hats, so called among this tribe. She also has about her, as a garment, a deerskin decorated with long fringes of false braided work in straw, the work done in a single strand. This photograph was taken by Governor John Daggett, of Black Bear, California.

Plate 172 is a portrait of Mary or Sheretta, a Klamath Indian woman, using different forms of basketry in the milling and cooking industry. Acorns are picked in a gathering basket, brought home in a carrying basket, ground in a mill with a basket hopper, the bitterness leeched out of the acorn mill fixed in a bed of sand, dipped with a basket ladle into a basket where it is cooked by means of hot stones, and afterwards served in dishes of basketry. This was also photographed by Governor Daggett.

The lower figure is a Wintun woman on McCloud River, in northern California, making a basket. The utter wretchedness and lack of inspiration from the environment could not possibly be worse. The Wintuns belong to the Copehan family.

From Governor Daggett comes the information that the California Indians about him make the frame of the coiled baskets of hazel twigs skinned. The weaving is done with split pine root. The ornamental patterns are produced by sour grass and maidenhair fern. The white splint is dyed by being chewed in the woman's mouth together with alder bark, making a kind of animated vat of herself. For the conical carrying basket, the Hupa Indian name is As tim num. Papoose basket, locks too; soup cooking basket, sal am poki; soup eating basket, pas tarrum; large storehouse, sip nook; cover to same, ash roos; mortar basket with hole in bottom, kraam num; acorn sifter, a flat disk, ten na bra; acorn bowl, moo roch.

South of the Hupa Indians is the Round Valley Reservation with the following-named tribes: Concow (Pujunan); Little Lakes (Kulanapan); Redwoods and Yukies (Yukian); Wailakis (Athapascan); Pit Rivers (Palaihnahan), and the Nomelakis (Copehan or Wintun family). A moment's thought will show why it is that varieties in basket types come from this reservation. The Indian tribes of the neighborhood are mixed with those of the Sacramento Valley and Maidu or Pujunan people east of the Sierras. With biological mixture there has been corresponding fertilization of ideas.

N. J. Purcell, for a long time agent among the Round Valley Indians, describes the gathering basket as coarse meshed and roughly constructed. He has sent to the National Museum an example made by the Little Lake tribe. It is woven of sticks with the bark on, and is very quickly made. It has a buckskin string attached about the center, by which it is carried. It is used for gathering acorns, nuts, grain, etc. When filled, this basket is emptied into a large carrying basket, this being repeated until the larger basket is filled.

The large carrying basket is always put in some convenient place and a smaller one is used for picking of nuts or grain. Several of the other tribes there use the same basket, though it seems to have originated among the Little Lake Indians. The willow of which it is composed is of the ordinary kind which is seen along nearly all the creeks in the East and is equally as plentiful here.

The sticks are generally used while green, though they are frequently gathered in quantities, allowed to dry, then soaked in water as they are required for use.

The carrying sack is made like an ordinary hunting bag and about the size. It is manufactured by the Concow Indians only. The buckskin string attached is thrown across the shoulder, allowing the sack to swing by the side, as we carry the hunting bag. The material of which it is made is from a weed-like plant that grows from 3 to 5 feet high, found in but one place in this country. At the foot of the Black Butte, about 7,000 feet above sea level, it grows in great quantities. This plant, bo-coak, bears a large white flower, which is filled with seed and has quite an agreeable odor. The leaves are large and long, tapering at the points. In winter the stalks die and become hard and dry, and are gathered in great quantities by the Indians. The bark is carefully taken off and the material from which the twine is made is stripped from the inside of the bark. This flax-like material is as white as cotton and seems much superior in strength. In making his twine the Indian seats himself, after first removing his trousers, takes enough of this flax to twist into about the size of No. 10 cotton in his left hand, lays it across the fleshy part of his right leg, licks the palm of his right hand, places it upon the flax and twists it. In this way they make twine of all sizes, from that of the coarse sewing thread to that of a half-inch rope.

In early times all the sewing they did was with this thread, using a sharpened bone for a needle. The larger size twine was for making fish nets, bird nets, carrying sacks, snaring deer, etc.

The mortar basket is used for pounding acorns, grain, all kinds of nuts and seeds. It is made of tough roots of the fir, which are usually gathered in spring or winter, when the ground is soft. Roots of the small saplings are preferred, being tougher than those of the old tree. The size of the roots gathered varies from one-half to 1½ inches. These are now buried under hot ashes and are allowed to remain thus for an hour. They are then taken out, not burned, but very hot. This steaming process toughens them and makes them split more easily, besides seasoning them to some extent. The squaw now takes this hot root in both hands, seizes it near the end with her front teeth, throws her head back and her hands forward, and the root is split exactly in the center in less than half a minute.

The two halves are again split in like manner and so on until the pieces become about twice as large as required. The craftswoman is now more careful, and the last piece is sometimes started with a sharp rock or knife, but usually with the teeth. One end of the splint is caught in the right hand, the other being kept between the teeth. The thumb and forefinger of the left hand are clinched tightly on the stick below the mouth. The head and right hand are now pulled slowly from each other. As the operation proceeds the finger and thumb of the left hand are slowly slipped down in front of the split part. Thus this last piece is divided accurately in the middle. The splints are not used at once, but are tied up in large circular coils and allowed to season, which, however, does not take long, as they are thin and the heating process aids in seasoning them very quickly. Being now prepared to make a basket, the woman uncoils the splints and throws them into a pan or basket of water, which renders them pliable and easy to be worked. The ribs of the basket are willow switches with the bark scraped off. In beginning the basket two of the splints are taken from the water and attached to one of the ribs with a kind of wrapped knot, so fastened as to allow one splint to stand toward the weaver and one directly from her. Another rib is now set close to the first one, and the splints are reversed; that is, the outside is pulled toward the weaver and the inside one is put from her; this forms a half turn around each side of a rib, the splints crossing or twining between the ribs. The same weave is used in the construction of the whole basket. Around the extreme top of this basket is a half-inch stick usually wrapped or stitched on with small vines split in the center. The dark red material used occasionally in this basket (*Cercis occidentalis*) is found in the mountains and is an undergrowth never attaining a size larger than one's ankle. The Indians call it "mo-lay." It bears a red blossom and small slender switches grow up at the bottom of the larger bush which are of a dark red color. These are split open in the middle in the same way as the fir root, save that they are not heated. The stitches represent half the size of the stick, as it is split only once. The wood with bark off is snow white.

Mr. Purcell, in describing a pretty little basket of grass root covered with red feathers, made by the Little Lake Indians, says every mother in this tribe presents one of these baskets to her child when it is about 7 years of age with the admonition to take care of the gift. They have a superstition that if the basket is lost some evil will befall the child. It is impossible to obtain one of these from the Little Lakes, the specimen described having been secured in the Concow tribe.

Under the name of Pomo are included a great number of tribes or little bands, thirty, according to Hudson, Purdy, and Wilcomb— sometimes one in a valley, sometimes more—clustered in the region where the headwaters of the Eel and Russian rivers interlace, along the latter and around the estuaries of the coast. In disposition the

Pomo are quite different from the Yuki and their congeners, being simple, friendly, peaceable, and inoffensive.   They are also much less cunning and avaricious and less quickly imitative of the whites than the lively tribes on the Klamath, to whom they are inferior in intellect.   As to their physique, there prevails on the Russian River essentially the same types as that seen in the Sacramento Valley. When first occupied by the European, the valleys inhabited by the Pomo teemed with wild grasses and the streams were hedged in with carex and willow.   The native grasses have almost disappeared, while the carices have given place in the lowlands to hops and alfalfa. Many ranchers forbid an Indian to dig on their lands, thus limiting the weaving-material supply to outlying canyons or compelling a substitution of inferior material.   Sometimes an indifferent worker will use but one character of material in a basket; for instance, the redbud shoots for warp and the two contrasting sides of the cortex for pattern.   This method, called bi-to'-i, effects looseness of weft and warp, incongruity of colors, and instability of the vessel, and is strongly condemned by an expert.   Some weavers will conscientiously refuse to work rather than substitute hai (woody material) for ma-yem' (roots).   The following notes by J. W. Hudson accompanied his collection to the National Museum:

Vegetal materials for Pomo basketry

Indian name.	Scientific name.	Common name.	Parts used.
Ka-hum'	*Carex barbaræ*	California sedge	Prepared root.
Tsu-wish'	*Carex*	Black-rooted sedge	Dyed root.
Shi-kŏ'	*Salix sitchensis*	Sitka willow	Prepared root.
Băm	*Salix sessifolia*	Hinds's willow	Prepared stems.
Ma-ló-ma-ló	*Salix nigra*		Prepared inner bark.
Ka-lĭ'-she	*Pinus sabiniana*	Nut pine	Split root
Ka-wă'	*Pseudotsuga taxifolia*	Douglas spruce	Root.
Bĭs	*Pteridium aquilinum*	Brake or bracken	Prepared root.
Mu-lé	*Cercis occidentalis*	Redbud	Bark of shoots.
Pshû-bă'	*Corylus californica*	Beaked hazel	Stems.
Băm-tú	*Vitis californica*	Grape	Vine.
Ma-shă'	*Linum californicum*	California flax	Prepared stems.

Wilcomb finds black designs sewed in tule root and fern roots also.

Animal materials for Pomo basketry

Indian name.	Scientific name.	Common name.	Parts used.
Ká-ya	*Saxidomus gracilis*		Prepared shell.
Ká-ya	*Cardium corbis*		Prepared shell.
Tĕm	Haliotis		Prepared shell.
Ka-tăte'	*Melanerpes formicivorus*	Woodpecker	Throat and scalp feathers
Ju-shĭl'	*Sturnella magna*	Meadow lark	Breast feathers.
Chi-ká-ka	*Lophortyx californicus*	Crested quail	Crest.
Ka-yăn'	*Anas boschus*	Mallard	Scalp feathers.
Tsă-wá-lû	*Cyanura stelleri*	California jay	Neck feathers.
Ba-chí-a	*Colaptes cafer*	Mexican woodpecker	Quill splittings.
Shai-i	*Aquila chrysaetos*	Golden eagle	Tail and pinions.
Tsu-lí-a	*Agelaius gubernador*	Tricolored blackbird	Elbow feathers.
Kai-yó-yo	*Icterus bullockii*	Bullock's oriole	Neck and breast.
Pö *a*	Magnetite	Magnetic iron ore	Burned, prepared cylinders.

a Mineral.

Ka-hum' is split into strings or flat splints and kept wet during the process of construction. Color, light tan or white. Used in sewing coiled basketry.

Tsu-wish' is buried with ashes for about eighty hours, thus dyeing to shades of black; then split into splints like Ka-hum'.

Shi-kó, split into splints. Whole stems are used for fish weirs; color, cream.

Bam. 1. Young shoots decorticated and polished for foundation of coiled basketry; color, straw.

2. Splittings from bark of young shoots.

3. Splittings of young shoots.

Ma-lo-ma-lo. Inner bark strips; color, dark tan

Ka-li-she. Split root; color, buff.

Ka-wa. Split root, trimmed limbs; color, gray.

Bis. Chewed and cleansed root, split; black.

Mu-lé. Bark of shoots, split into tape with a bit of wood adhering; burnt-sienna color. Used in sewing coiled basketry.

Pshu-ba. Trimmed stems.

Bam-tu. Vine, used rough or decorticated.

Ma-sha. Crushed, hackled, and combed.

Ka-ya. Manufactured from clam shells; current among the Indians as "Indian silver." Monetic base.

Po. Magnetite, mined in Lake County, California. Heated dull red, then tempered in hot water. Knapped and scoured into cylinders.

Bored. Current as Indian gold. Monetic base.

All prepared vegetals turn dark with age, and especially by the smoke from the open fires in Indian huts.

Tsu-wish ranks first in value; a bunch equals 100 Ka-ya. A bunch of Ka-hum equals 65 Ka-ya; Mu-le, 20 Ka-ya.

Plate 173 illustrates a coiled basket of the Pomo Indians left unfinished to show the workmanship. The foundation is in the style called Tee weaving, twined work, described and illustrated on page 239 and in fig. 27. These structural features are clearly set forth in the plate. In the foreground the vertical and the horizontal warp, as well as the twined weft, appear in their true association. The body sewing is done with white splints of mu lé or redbud (*Cercis occidentalis*); the figures, representing mountains, are wrought with brown splints of cercis. It is 10 inches in diameter, collected by Dr. J. W. Hudson, and is Catalogue No. 200013 in the U. S. National Museum.

In feather work, each feather is plucked from the prepared skin of the bird and neatly caught under a stitch, which is then drawn tight. They are used either to heighten the color without aiding the design or the design is in the feathers and not in the stitches. For the former quail plumes and the red feathers from the woodpecker's head are employed. The red feathers are placed regularly but thinly on the stitches of the upper half of the basket and the quail plumes scattered, or below three rows of shell disks (kaia) on the upper edge of the basket. In the feather basket proper there are two varieties called "tapica" and "epica." The tapica is the so-called sun basket; but Purdy insists that the word means "red basket." The oldest specimens are saucer-shaped baskets, covered with red feathers, decorated with pendants of kaia and abalone, with circles of shell money. The use of other feathers than red is a charming innovation. The Ballo kai Pomo name for feather baskets in any other shape is "epica." When the Pomo use shell disks (kaia) to decorate coiled basketry, a thread is carried along under the stitches and the disks threaded on as needed. Beads are usually applied in the same way, but in some examples they are threaded on the sewing filaments. (Carl Purdy.)

There is no more interesting group of Indians in America than the Pomo with respect to the variety of technical processes in basketry. They not only understand many of the processes common among other tribes, but have introduced one or two types of manipulation peculiar to themselves. The following classification, prepared by J. W. Hudson and Carl Purdy, shows the variety of basket work made by them:

TWINED WORK (TSHAMA)

1. Pshukan (Shakan, Purdy), coarse twined work of shuba or hazel.
2. Pshutsin, wrapped weft, happily called backstitching by Hudson.
3. Bamtush, plain twined weaving.
4. Shuset, twine over two warp rods, diagonal.
5. Sheetsin, three-strand braid or twine.
6. Lit, Makah style, wrapped weft twined (figs. 20, 21).
7. Tee, twined weaving over lattice foundation.

COILED WORK (SHIBU)

8. Shailo, foundation of splints (Shailo, Purdy).
9. Tsai, foundation of one rod.
10. Baumko, two-stem foundation laid vertically.
11. Bamshibu, foundation of 3 rods.
12. Bamteck, four-stem foundation.
13. Tsawam, the half-hitch work on cradles.

Purdy adds ringed and sewed; each circle of foundation complete. These names are from Yokaia, Upper Yokaia, Calpella, and Potter Valley. The word for basket in Potter is Pika; at Upper Lake, Sitol; at Lower Lake, Kolob; at Cache Creek, Kawah.

1. Pshû-kăn' (fish weir) in its simplest form is the binding of a row of upright warp rods by means of pairs of hazel or willow shoots passing them horizontally with a half twist in each space. Undressed material is the rule, but in more delicate household vessels the willow is decorticated, even polished. Hazel (Shu ba, the fisherman) was the original material. It is nothing more than a very coarse open twined work, passing now and then into three-strand twine. (See fig. 20.)

2. Pshutsin, a very substantial means of framing a large, heavy structure, such as granaries, sheathing for thatch, game fences, etc. It is in effect wrapped twined weaving, seen also in Mohave carrying frames. From the periphery a strand of grapevine loosely encircles two ribs, passing to the left over four ribs, then backward, catching two or more and repeating gradually, back two, forward four, inward to the center or apex. A second vine catches a rib at the bottom of the roof passing to the left over four ribs, encircling two, thence zigzags parallel with No. 1 to the top. This is repeated till spaces are covered. Pshutsin effects in house building a coarse mesh at the foundation, but gradually closed in at the apex, where most needed. In granaries the conditions are reversed, but the effect is the same. Fences require an additional top vine. (See fig. 13.)

3. Bamtush (Bamtu, grapevine) plain twined weaving. Pattern and æsthetic art were here born, the brown bark of the vine contrasting with pale yellow of the inner vine splittings. The grape has long since been discarded for stronger and more polished material. Bamtush is the strongest weave and is used in carrying baskets, acorn baskets, and very large, heavy mush baskets. There is a warp of willow or other stems radiating from the bottom. On this the warp is laid in pairs, the two splints being twisted a half time in passing a warp stem. The effect is that of ribbed cloth or corduroy. The ornamentation is usually in bands. (See fig. 15.)

4. Shuset is twining over two warps and alternating from round to round and affords the amplest opportunity for artistic display. It is called diagonal or twilled-twined work, as its surface is the smoothest

of Pomo weaves; the patterns are bold and clear and cover the whole area. It is the only weave whose pattern is not woven through. It has also the mode of delicate structure. It is used in large acorn baskets, also in mush baskets, being strong, smooth, and moderately close. Some fine gift baskets are also in this weave, and it seems to be susceptible of much more elaborate ornamentation than the plain twined work. The word Shuset, says Hudson, is understood only as far south as Ukiah City, the Yokaia term for diagonal twine being Bam tsai. (See fig. 20.)

5. Sheetsin is a style of three-strand twined weaving in which at each third of a turn one weft filament is carried behind a warp stem. It will be seen at once that when the bundle of weft filaments has made a whole revolution, each one of them will have been carried behind the warp. On the inside this basketry does not differ in appearance from common twined weaving, but on the outside each weft element passes over three warp stems and under one.

There is a peculiar type of Sheetsin used chiefly to start the foundations of twined baskets. It is a three-strand weft in which a braid is formed instead of a twine, one of its elements passing over each warp, the other two remaining outside. On the inside the effect is of plain twined weaving, while on the outside the effect is diagonal. (See fig. 28.)

6. Lit is a style of twined weaving in which one of the elements remains on the inside of the basket and the other is wrapped around the checks formed by the crossing of this horizontal element with the vertical warps. The Makah Indians, of Cape Flattery, employ this technic almost exclusively, but Hudson says the Kulanapan tribes used it only to give variety to a surface in which plain twine and Shuset are used. On the same authority, this word Lit is known among all the Pomo tribes, even among the Tsawalu Pomo, near Guernerville. (See figs. 21, 22.)

7. Tee (intricate) is a double structure, a Bamtush reinforced by horizontal warp across the outside of the vertical. On the inside this ware is undistinguishable from plain twined work. Its characteristics are great strength, the closest mesh, and a pattern dim and impressional. It is the most difficult and highest priced of the Tshama weaves. The openwork basket trays in tee weave are called by Dr. Hudson psher kom, or fish plate. (See fig. 27.)

The name Shi bu, or Tschibu, applies, says Purdy, in reality to only the three-stick coiled baskets. The full name is Bam shi bu, or Bamsibu, sticks three. No branch of the Pomo use it except for three-stick baskets and only the Calpella, Kalshe, and Ballo bai Pomo use it at all as a basket name. One-stick baskets in Calpella, Kalshe, and Ballo bai Pomo are bam cha, stick one, or tishais. The filaments of Pomo Shibu coiled basketry are shaved down to uniform width and thickness with the greatest care.

8. Shailo, suggested by the spiral rib of Tee, was constructed of a spiral coil of fir-root fibers bound to its adjacent coil below by a single strand of the same material catching in the lower coil fibers or the tops of its lacings. This method, the Protean Shibu, developed and considered by other California Indians, notably Yokut, as the acme of art, has long since been discarded by the Pomo as inadequate to the demands of even close weaving and pattern. However, it proved the coil to be practicable and from it evolved Tsai.

9. In the Tsai (bam-cha, one rib) or single-rod coiled basketry the foundation is a single willow shoot of uniform thickness throughout, seasoned and smoothed, spiraling from base to rim and sewed down with narrow splints of various materials. Two rods are inclosed in each stitch which passes beneath the rib of the previous turn, the stitches interlocking. This structure is quite light and elegant, permitting the most delicate treatment, both in stitch and pattern. Specimens frequently average 60 stitches to the linear inch. (See fig. 46.)

10. Baumko is the Pomo name for coiled basketry on a foundation of two stems, one above the other. It is an economical method of work, for it widens the coil and to that extent diminishes the amount of sewing. (See fig. 47.)

11. Bamshibu or bamtsuwu (tsu-ba, three) consists of a three-rod warp or coil bound down by its lacings, catching in the lacings and one stem of the next lower coil. This is justly regarded by the Pomo as the highest type of basket art. Its materials require the most careful tests of evenness, pliability, and color. The legitimate function of treble ribs besides solidity is its adaptability for retaining the bulbs of feathers, and was doubtless created by an incentive for this rich ornamentation. Comparison with other styles of work reveals the fact that by reason of fine material and pressing together of the stitches the sewing conceals the foundation, while in the varieties before mentioned the latter is visible between the stitches. (See fig. 50.)

12. Bamteck is scarcely to be looked upon as a separate style of weaving. It is simply a variety of No. 11. The manipulation of the stitches is precisely the same in both.

13. Tsawam. This is an application of the backward and forward braiding or false braiding found on the margins of many baskets and described in the proper place in this work. The rods of the cradle are held together by a coarse cotton string obtained from the traders, formerly, no doubt, made of splint. Carried across the warp rods the weft material passes forward four, backward two, right; forward four, backward two, left—and so, alternately backward to the right or left, forms a very neat braid on one side of the basket, and what looks like two rows of twined weaving on the other.

The making of a fine coiled basket requires an infinite amount of patience. The rootstocks carefully gathered during the summer and

early autumn are split into fine strands for direct use. At Round
Valley the process is as follows: The rootstocks, denuded of their outer
coverings, are thoroughly soaked in warm water, and one end of a root
is divided through the center, by means of the finger nails, into three
parts. One of these parts is held firmly between the teeth, while, by
means of the fingers, the whole root is carefully and very evenly split
into three sections. Each of these sections is again separated into
three parts in the same manner, and the same process is carried out
until the strands are as fine as may be desired, the value of the basket

FIG. 165.
TINY COILED BASKET.
Pomo Indians.
Collected by C. P. Wilcomb.

depending in great measure upon the fineness of the strands used as
well as the general beauty of the finished fabric. These strands are
used not like those from the pine root in twined work, but for thread
for sewing coiled ware. In beginning the basket, three very pliant
stems are so selected that when placed together their combined cross
sections will be nearly circular. The use of three "sticks" instead of
one, as is sometimes the case in less costly baskets, gives much more
elasticity and greater strength to the basket. The strand is wrapped
tightly about one end of the compound withe, and as the wrapping

FIG. 166.
TINY COILED BASKET.
Pomo Indians.
Collected by C. P. Wilcomb.

progresses, the wand is bent into a minute circle; the central hole is
filled in by stitching over and over again, and with this as a basis the
little plaque is gradually built up by coiling. The general shape and
plan of the basket must necessarily be carried in mind, for there is no
skeleton to serve as a guide. Infinite care must therefore be exercised, not only in preserving the symmetry of shape, but also the
symmetry of the designs which are worked in with the black and white
strands. It requires many months, sometimes years, of leisure work
to complete a first-class basket. Some of the very best are more or
less individual in their shape and pattern. (Chesnut.)

Fig. 165 is a coiled basket of the Pomo Indians (Kulanapan family) in a style of sewing called Bamshibu. The foundation consists of three stems or rods. The stitches pass over the foundation and interlock with those underneath, giving a ribbed appearance to the fabric. This tiny object is a little over one-half an inch in diameter and passes easily through a lady's finger ring. In the foundation, the uniform width of the coil and of the stitches, and the neatness of the sewing, it would be difficult to find a more charming piece of Indian handiwork.

Fig. 166 is a coiled basket of the Pomo Indians in a style of weaving called tsai, in which a single rod is used for the foundation, the

FIG. 167.
COILED BASKET.
Hoochnom Indians, California.
Cat. No. 21371, U.S.N.M.   Collected by Stephen Powers.

stitches passing both over the rod of the course in progress and under the rod of the foundation of the course beneath. These small pieces represent fairly the best Pomo workmanship.

These two baskets are in the collection of C. P. Wilcomb, curator of the Golden Gate Park Museum, San Francisco, California, and were made under his supervision.

Fig. 167 is a coiled basket of the Hoochnom Indians, Yukian family. It is made in a style of coiled weaving called rod and welt. In this method one or two small rods or stems of uniform thickness constitute the body or foundation of the coil. Over this is laid a thin filament or strip of material, and the stitches of each coil pass over the foundation, under the splint, and interlock. The work of the Hoochnom Indians is of excellent character, the coils about the same width of the number of stitches to the inch, uniform. In the example here shown the coils are one-eighth of an inch in diameter, and there are twenty stitches to the inch. The ornamentation appears to be the usual California combination of mountain and coil plume. The use of light and dark filaments and the alternation of triangles and rectangles on the two sides of the open space form a very attractive ornament. The use of shell disks improves the appearance of the object. Feathers

are also employed on some specimens from this locality.

A square inch shown in fig. 168 illustrates more definitely the description here given.

This specimen, Catalogue No. 21371 in the U. S. National Museum, was procured in Eel River, California, by Stephen Powers.

Leaving the west coast peoples, the next group of basket makers will be found in the Oregon tribes belonging to the Lutuamian family, namely, the Klamath and Modocs, and the Shastas, also various bands

FIG. 168.
DETAIL OF FIG. 167.

of Wintun belonging to the Copehan family. The basket work of this middle region is largely twined work with overlaying. The designs have been studied by Roland B. Dixon and will be found illustrated in Plates 18 to 24 in his paper on the basket designs of northern California.[a] In the work here mentioned it is interesting to find that the movement has been eastward, for quite a number of these specimens figured as Maidu are very surely made under the influence of tribes here mentioned.

The Klamath Indians have their home upon the Little and Upper Klamath Lake, Klamath Marsh, and Sprague River, Oregon. Their name in their own language is E-ukshikni (Klamath Lake people). The Modoc are termed by the Klamath *Modokni* (southern people).[b]

Fig. 169 is a twined flexible basket of the Klamath Indians. The body is in plain twined weaving; the three elevated bands on the outside are in three-ply twined weaving, the effect being that of hoops placed on wooden vessels for the purpose of strengthening them and is very pleasing. By choosing straws or stems of different plants for these three-ply bands the artistic impression is heightened. By twining dark and light colored straws in the texture and by varying the number of monochrome or dichrome twines, charming effects in endless variety may be produced.

[a] Bulletin of the American Museum of Natural History, XVII, pp. 1–32.

[b] J. W. Powell, Indian Linguistic Families, Seventh Annual Report of the Bureau of American Ethnology, Washington, 1891, pp. 1–142.

A square inch shown in fig. 170 makes clear the manner in which the plain twined and three-ply twine may be combined and also that of using different colored materials. The rows in both cases, however, are monochrome. If the alternate meshes were dark and light, the beauty would be enhanced. The using of dichrome twine is rather limited to this particular area—northern California and southern Oregon.

This specimen, Catalogue No. 24124 in the U. S. National Museum, was procured in Oregon by L. S. Dyar.

FIG. 169.

TWINED BASKET BOWL.

Klamath Indians, Oregon.

Cat. No. 24124, U.S.N.M. Collected by L. S. Dyar.

The following names for baskets were collected from the Hot Spring Valley Indians, Modoc County, California:

Indian name	Basket work
Doch jäm′ä	Papoose basket.
Po lu′ lu	Boat shaped, used to hold trinkets and small articles.
Bä po′ kä	Storage basket, also used for cooking, also applied to any basket where the top curves in toward the center.
Shute′ pä	Soft plaque used for gambling and winnowing.
Tä wi y′ä	Hard plaque used for gambling and winnowing.
Clowä′	Coarse basket with hole in bottom for grinding meal.
De le′ mä che	Cone-shaped burden basket.
Shu′ wä	Squaw's cap.
Da lu′ ti ä	Coil weave. A coiled weave storage basket is called dalutia bapoka and is greatly prized, also the plaques in dalutia weave.

Plate 174 represents two Klamath Indian baskets in the collection of Dr. C. Hart Merriam. The interesting feature in them is that the entire structure is in three-strand twined work. The border resembles closely one of the simplest among the Tlinkits, namely, the warp strands are turned down and held in place by a row of twined weaving. All the Indians of this area practice the three-strand work, but do not cover the whole basket with it. This weave is reserved for strengthening weak places and for ornament. It has the disadvantage of being wasteful of material.

FIG. 170.

DETAIL OF FIG. 169.

South of the Klamath and Modoc tribes and closely associated with them live the Shasta Indians (Sastean family, formerly on the Klamath River from Bogus Creek to Scott River; on the Shasta River, Little Shasta and Yuka Creek; and in Scott Valley, to which has been added the Upper Salmon and a part of Rogue River in Oregon). Stephen Powers commends the strength and beauty of the Shasta women. With their basket hats fitting tight on their round heads and walking with a grenadier stride, they present quite an Amazonian appearance.[a] The specimens of Shasta Indian baskets in the U. S. National Museum are not to be distinguished fundamentally from those just described. They are in twined weaving with overlaying in straw. Their special marks are in the designs or symbols.[b]

Plate 175, top figure, represents a twined basket of the Pit River Indians, Copehan family, in Shasta County, California. In Dixon's paper precisely the same symbols are seen on a basket labeled Yanan (Plate 25). The warp and weft on the bottom are of some kind of rush. The weft on the body is in stems of the squaw grass. There are twelve twists and twenty rows of twined weaving to the inch. The color of the body is a beautiful old gold produced by age. The ornamentation is in three sets of three rhombs, each done in black material, perhaps fern stems. Crosses and diamond patterns are employed to

[a] Powers, Contributions to North American Ethnology, III, Chap. XXVI.

[b] Shastas, Rogue Rivers, and Calapooya tribes on Grand Ronde and Siletz Reservations, Oregon, make excellent openwork twined baskets from hazel (*Corylus californica*) sticks cut in May, peeled. Those cut in autumn are toasted, then soaked and peeled. Charming effects are produced in the seasoning of the wood. Rarely stems dyed black by soaking them in mud are used in weaving. Besides the old-time plaques, baby frames, and conical burden baskets, the latest willow ware is being freely imitated in hazel for all domestic and industrial uses.—MRS. HARRIET MCARTHUR.

decorate the centers. The margin is formed by braiding down the unused warp stems. Height is 3¼ inches; diameter 5¼ inches. Catalogue No. 19283. Collected by Livingston Stone.

The middle figure is said to have been made by the Pit River Indians, the warp and bottom being in soft rushes. The weft of the body is in strips of rushes over which thin filaments of squaw grass have been wound. The delicate figures are in black fern stems. Design, lizard's feet, three in number, with festoons of short lines between. The border is formed by braiding down the ends of the warp and holding them in place by a row of twined weaving. This is a very common method of treatment throughout this country. Its height is 3 inches and diameter 5½ inches. Catalogue No. 204910, U. S. National Museum. Collected by Harry F. Liston.

The lower figure represents a basket from the McCloud River Indians, Copehan family. The warp is in small rods, perhaps of hazel. The weft in twisted root of dark brown color. The first few rows of twining, and here and there another row around the bottom, are in three-strand, the rest in double twining. The body is in the same brown material wrapped with squaw grass, the figures showing on both sides. The ornamentation consists of four rows of double rhombs in black fern and one single row. Around the bottom is a double row in two colors. The border is finished in one row of three-strand twine weaving, the ends of the warp showing. Its height is 4½ inches and its diameter 5 inches. Catalogue No. 19349, U. S. National Museum. Collected by Livingston Stone.

Fig. 171 is a carrying basket of the McCloud River Indians, Copehan family. The tribes of this family are described by Powers under the general name of Wintun. Those living on the McCloud Fork are named Winnimin, the meaning of which term is North River. The similarity of the McCloud River basketry with that of the Pit River people will be apparent. The technic, poorly shown, is in twined weaving with a foundation of stems. The noticeable feature is the overlaying of the filaments with grass stems or fern stems to produce the ornamentation. The strength of the basket is in the weaving. The bottom is cup-shaped, and for 3 or 4 inches is in three-strand twined weaving. The rest of the workmanship is in the ordinary two-strand twine. In order to strengthen the basket a coil of rods is sewed around the bottom for about a foot. The border is a strong hoop attached to the warp stems by bending down the latter and sewing them in place with splints, forming a single row of coiled work. The overlaying passes to the inside, so that the figures are the same without and within the basket. On the body the rhomboid figures forming triangular ornaments are named in Mr. Dixon's paper "leaves strung along."

Plate 176, Catalogue Nos. 19297 and 19281 in the U. S. National

Museum are labeled McCloud River Indian baskets. They were collected by the superintendent of the United States fish-hatching establishment in northern California many years ago and doubtless were procured from the McCloud River Indians.

The upper figure is an example of two-colored design in plain twined weaving by simply hiding every alternate twist of the weft strands. The lower figure is made in the same fashion with broken bands in two colors, brown and yellow, but the border is finished off by bending down the warp stems and sewing with thread.

Plates 177–178, show the work of the Hat Creek Indians, Pakamalli, who live on Hat Creek, a branch of Pit River in northeastern Cali-

FIG. 171.
CARRYING BASKET.
McCloud River Indians, California.
Cat. No. 19290, U.S.N.M. Collected by Livingston Stone.

fornia. They belong to the Palaihnihan family, which Mr. Gatschet believes to be related to the Sastean or Shasta tribes. Dixon (1902) places the basketry of these tribes in his northeastern group of California tribes associated with the Klamath and Modoc (Lutuamian), Shastas (Sastean, but probably Palaihnihan), Pit Rivers (Palaihnihan), Yana (Yanan), Wintun (Copehan), and Maidu (Pujunan). Powers[a] characterizes the Hat Creek Indians as the most warlike in all the Pit River Basin, and the one most dreaded by the timid aborigines of the Sacramento Valley. These specimens are in the collection of H. E. Williams.

---

[a] Contributions to North American Ethnology, III, 1877, p. 274.

The eastern portion of northern California, as before mentioned, is largely divided between the Palaihnihan, Yanan, and Pujunan linguistic families. It might be easily supposed by one who had no knowledge on the subject whatever, that the coiled basketry of the interior basin would obtrude itself here and either push backward the tribes making twined work, or at least the latter would be forced to a very subordinate position. Dr. Roland B. Dixon has published in the American Anthropologist, but more extensively in the Bulletin of the American Museum of Natural History,[a] the result of accurate studies in the basketry of the eastern tribes. The most extensive researches of Dr. Dixon are on the basketry of the Maidu Indians described by Powers. On Powell's linguistic map these Indians are assigned to the Pujunan family. Their country lies east of the Sacramento River and extends as far as the Nevada line, stretching north and south from the southern line of Lassen and Tehama counties to the Consumne River. A number of examples of Maidu basketry have already been described, and illustrated in Plates 56 and 57. The specimens are in the U. S. National Museum.

The body is either in splints of willow or other wood and a species of root. At the time of this writing Mr. Coville was not quite sure as to the species employed. The designs on the body of the basket are in the splints of *Cercis occidentalis*, the bark and young shoots remaining in place. An inspection of a number of Maidu baskets together leaves the impression of distinct individuality. They belong to the three-rod variety of coiled weaving and the sewing passes over the foundation, under one of the rods of the foundation beneath, the stitches interlocking. Frequently on the inside they split, which enables the sewer to give each stitch on the outer surface a vertical position. The material used in the sewing is hard and is not driven tight home, each stitch being wide below and narrow above. After a study of one of these specimens, its colors and patterns, the investigator will have no trouble afterwards in identifying a Maidu basket.

Dr. Dixon, who has given most attention to the lore in Maidu baskets, divides the symbols into three classes, namely: Natural designs, plant designs, and those representing natural or artificial objects. His plates 1 to 17 are devoted exclusively to Maidu basketry. Among them will be seen a few in twined weaving, principally conical burden baskets. A comparison of these among themselves and also those of the Pit River Indians and tribes living in the Sacramento Valley indicate acculturation of some kind, borrowing ideas, or may be women, ideas and all. A number of Maidu baskets in the U. S. National Museum were collected by W. H. Holmes.

A suggestion might be made in this connection that the so-called

---

[a] Vol. XVII, pp. 1-32.

feather design on the Dixon baskets[a] may be those on arrows, which in some California tribes are notched.   This is only a suggestion.   One of Dixon's most intricate feather patterns has narrow lines between, resembling the letter H, which might be either the rib of the feathers or the owner's mark on the shaftment of the arrow.   The association of this notched half feather design with the symbol for arrow points would be in harmony with this view.   No other artificial object enters so profoundly into Indian art, gaming, lore, and ceremony.

On the map of California, covering a small spot at the angle of the eastern border, are the Washoe Indians (Washoan family).   They extend into the parts of Nevada adjoining, occupying the mountain region in the extreme western portion of the State about Washoe and Tahoe lakes and the towns of Carson and Virginia City.   They formerly extended farther east and south, but were driven back by the Paiute, who conquered them and reduced them to complete subjection.   Their basketry is the same general type as the Maidu, just north, but in execution it is far above.   The material is willow, Datill-yah-wee; the brown or reddish tint is that of the bark of mountain birch (*Cercis occidentalis*), Et-ba-sha, and the black is from the root of a mountain brake (*Pteridium aquilinum*), mes-a-weg-a-see, all of lasting quality, and they acquire with age a richness that makes them incomparable.   The sewing is faultless.   Stitch after stitch, over and over, increases in width and length with the swelling and shrinking of the basket like a harmony in music.   The form of the specimen is charming, and the ornamentation ideal.   The recognition of worth in the Washoe basketmaker is encouraging, for the price of a few pieces reaches into the thousands of dollars.   The author heartily acknowledges the aid of Mrs. A. Cohn, of Carson City, Nevada, for information about the Washoes and for photographs.

The tiny Washoe offering or gift basket (Sing-aru-mi), when used to propitiate the harvest spirit, is filled with choicest grain or seeds or acorns from the last crop to insure a future good harvest.   One or two of the large storing or household baskets (Da-gee-coop) will hold the winter supply of grain or nuts.   The flat cradles (Bicose-modi-mi-odi) are for the papooses (now-gung).   If the child's father is a famous brave or chief, the basket is covered with buckskin and gaily decorated with beads, trinkets, tasseled fringes, or feathers.   The ornamentation of the little sheltering cover for the head tells the sex of the occupant.[b]

Plate 179 represents three basket bowls in the U. S. National Museum labeled Washoe.   They all show the characteristics of uniformity and plain ornamentation referred to.   The lowest in the series has also a margin of feather work which allies it with the type of the

---

[a] American Anthropologist, April–June, 1900, pp. 266–276.
[b] Clara MacNaughton, Out West, XVIII, 1903, p. 438.

tribes farther west. Catalogue Nos. 204846, 36244, 35435, U. S. National Museum.

Plate 180 is one of the best specimens in Mrs. A. Cohn's collection in Carson City, Nevada. The symbol on the surface is a collection of points meaning "clear skies, good weather." Mrs. Cohn finds variations in these, the number of points ranging from three to seven. In some examples they are contiguous; in others separated by narrow spaces.

Plate 181 is a picture of Datsolallee, the maker of the finest specimens of Washoe basketry. She is holding in her left hand the bowed stick in shape of a racquet, with which hot stones are taken from the fire to be placed in the basket of mush in order to cook it. The symbols shown on the various baskets at her feet represent men, women, snakes, arrows, wind, weather symptoms, morning, and migrating.

Plate 182, upper figure, shows a basket bowl of the Washoe Indians, collected by Eugene Mead. The foundation is the three-rod style in willow. The sewing is done in splints of the same material. The ornamentation on the bottom is a many pointed star in brown cercis. On the body there are three circles made up of isosceles triangles in the same. Two of the rows on the body of the basket are so arranged as to have a narrow belt of white between them, the points of one being downward and the other upward. This form of ornamentation is suggestive of the patterns on the sewed coils of the Navaho basket bowls. The border is plain coiled sewing. Its diameter is 8¾ inches, and height 3½ inches.

Plate 182, lower figure, is a basket bowl, Catalogue No. 204852, U. S. National Museum, coiled work from Inyo County, California, tribe not positively known. There are four sets of ornamentation on the side in step pattern in threes, done in sewing splints dyed black. The most interesting feature of the basket is the border, which is in false braid, made of a single splint wrapped over the upper foundation, forward, under, and back, over again and down beneath the two foundation rows, making a figure 8.

The southern portion of the Oregon-California basket area is bounded on the west by the Pacific Ocean and there was little encouragement to venture beyond the shore line except in San Francisco Bay and around the Santa Barbara Islands. On the north of it are the Maidu, Copehan, and the Yukian families. On the south and forming a part of the subarea itself are the Missions, some of which belong to the Yuman family, the southern boundary of the area. The great Shoshonean family has pushed across the drainage of the interior basin to the coast at Santa Barbara. This southern region is a long rectangle inclined toward the west. Its axis would be a meridian through diagonal corners. The eastern portion is Shoshonean territory. The western portion belongs to the following linguistic families: Moquelumnan, Costanoan, Mariposan, Esselenan, Salinan, and Chumashan. Along the median line of this subarea are Mono, Fresno, Inyo, Tulare, and Kern counties—another basketry Caucasus or Babel. (See fig. 163.)

Those who have made collections from this part of California will bear witness that the exchanging of baskets and of women who make baskets from stock to stock has rendered it almost impossible to identify forms ethnically. Here blood and speech and industry are apt to be confounded. At least, it is too early in the investigation to be positive on the subject.

Another difficulty arises in this study from the fact that language groups, tribal names, and county names are also mixed up. For instance, a basket may be called Tulare because it was purchased in that county of California, having no reference to the Indian tribe. A specimen made by the same woman will bear the name of the tribe of which she is a member. Still another one of her productions might be called from the group of languages to which her own belongs. At present the confusion extends beyond form and design to the substances and technical processes. The author acknowledges his obligations to E. L. McLeod, of Bakersfield; C. P. Wilcomb, of Golden Gate Park Museum, and Dr. C. Hart Merriam, of Washington, for the information here given. Each of these has given most careful study to this cosmopolitan basket region. Dr. Merriam has devoted special attention to the plants used.[a]

Of this ware Dr. Merriam says that most of the coiled baskets made by the Indians inhabiting the lower slopes of the Sierra from Fresno River south to the Kern are celebrated for excellence of workmanship; beauty of form, elegance of design, and richness of material, which differs in tone and texture from that used by the tribes north and south of the region indicated. When fresh, its color is brownish buff; with age it becomes darker and richer. By careful selection a handsome dappled effect is produced. It is made from the root of a marsh plant which the Indians traveled long distances to procure, identified by Miss Alice Eastwood, botanist of the California Academy of Sciences, as *Cladium mariscus*. The foundation consists of a bundle of stems of a yellow grass, *Epicampes rigens*. The black in the design is the root of the "bracken" or "brake fern," *Pteridium aquilinum*. The red is usually split branches of the redbud, *Cercis occidentalis*, with the bark on, gathered after the fall rains, when the bark is red. The tribes making the *Cladium* baskets are the Nims, Chukchancys, Cocahebas, Wuksaches, Wiktchumnes, Tulares, and perhaps one or

---

[a] It is too early to complete a plant synonymy for the Inyo-Kern and Tulare basketry. The list of Coville (pp. 199–214 of this paper) and the following paragraphs from Merriam will be helpful.

two others. Besides these, the root is sometimes used by certain squaws of the Mewah tribe living north of the Fresno and by the Pakanepull and Newooah tribes living south of the Kern; but among these its use is exceptional.

Another material which has proved a stumbling-block to collectors is the red of the design in the handsome baskets made by the Kern Valley, Newooah, and Panamint Shoshone Indians. This material is often called cactus root. It is the unpeeled root of the tree yucca (*Yucca arborescens*), which grows in the higher parts of the Mohave Desert, pushes over Walker Pass, and reaches down into the upper part of the valley of South Fork of Kern. The so-called Tejon Indians obtain it in Antelope Valley, at the extreme west end of the Mohave Desert. The yucca root varies considerably in depth of color, so that by careful selection some of the Indian women produce beautiful shaded effects and definite pattern contrasts.

Some of the Panamint Shoshones inhabiting the desolate desert region between Owens Lake and Death Valley use, either in combination with the yucca root or independently, the bright-red shafts of the wing and tail feathers of a woodpecker—the red-shafted flicker, *Colaptes cafer collaris*. These same Indians use two widely different materials for their black designs—the split seed pods of the devil's horn, *Martynia*, and the root of a marsh bulrush, *Scirpus*. The *Martynia* is a relatively coarse material, and when properly selected yields a dead black. The *Scirpus* root is a fine, delicate material, which, by burying in wet ashes, is made to assume several shades or tones, from blackish brown to purplish black, or even lustrous black.

In parts of the Colorado Desert in southeastern California the Coahuilla Indians use split strands from the leaf of the desert palm (*Neowashingtonia filamentosa*) as a surface material for their coiled baskets. The design is usually black or orange-brown, and is a rush (*Juncus*).[a]

The following list gives the families of the tribes in Tulare, Kern, and Inyo counties, using the plants named in the first part of this description: 1. Chukchan cys Chukchan si (Mariposan); 2. Cocahebas; 3. Mewah (Moquelumnan); 4. Newooah; 5. Nims; 6. Pakanepull; 7. Tulares (part of Olamentke div., Moquelumnan); 8. Wiktchumnes, Wikchumni (Mariposan); 9. Wuksaches, Wiksachi (Mariposan).

The elements of ornamentation are lines direct and crooked, in shapes as varied as the margins of leaves, and they might without affectation receive the same names—dentate, serrate, sinuous, etc. These simple lines are combined in parallels, herring-bone, chevrons, crenellations, and many more patterns. The triangle, the rectangle, the rhomb, and the polygon are used in great variety. Out of these elements the designs on this basketry are separate, concentric, or radiate.

---

[a] C. Hart Merriam, Science, May 23, 1903.

The separate designs are, after all, subservient to the others. Very little of this ware shows entirely free and scattered patterns. The plume or L-shaped, the white and colored rectangles associated, the groups of marks on the border, and chiefly the rectangles in two colors with hourglass middle are most common.

Concentric designs are narrow or wide bands, whose middle portion is decorated with crooked lines and geometric figures in endless variety of combinations. Most of the bands have entire margins, but projecting margins are not unknown. The most noteworthy is Merriam's "butterfly flight design." (See Plate 194.)

The radial designs are straight or spiral. The composition of each ray is a study in itself. But a glance at a large number of baskets from this central region shows the predominance of the cuneate motive. These truncated wedges spring out of a central, circular pattern and widen toward the margin. Their surfaces and their margins are seldom entire. The spiral designs are also frequently wedge-shaped, but the manner of their composition is of the greatest interest. Lurking in them all is the stepped motive in which herringbone or jagged lines and simple geometric figures follow one another by echelon. This on a roundish surface gives spirals of any amount of curvature. By widening and lengthening the rectangular elements the wedge-shaped interspaces are filled with the spiral pattern and the whole surface is covered with a single design. This charming decoration is peculiar to the Santa Barbara baskets. (See Plate 49.) In outward form the baskets of the area here considered vary from round, flat gambling mats, through trays and bowls of various depths, and hats of conical shape, to narrow-mouthed vases, or "bottle-necks" as they are called. Some of these are low and broad and closely resemble the best of ancient Arizona pottery.

The basketry of the Panamint Indians (Shoshonean) living in Death Valley, Inyo County, says Coville, is made by the squaws at the cost of a great deal of time, care, and skill. The materials are very simple. They consist of the year-old shoots of some species of tough willow, splints from *Salix lasiandra*, the year-old shoots of the aromatic sumac, *Rhus trilobata*, the long, black, slender, flexible horns on the mature pods of the unicorn plant, *Martynia louisiana*, locally known as devil horns, and the long, red roots of the tree yucca, *Yucca arborescens*. These materials give three types of color—that of the willow and the sumac, the black of the devil horns, and the red of the yucca roots. This last material, although it has a strong fiber and a pretty red color, is rarely used, for it is too thick to pack closely and the resulting fabric is full of interstices.

Sumac and willow are prepared for use in the same way by the Panamint Indians. The bark is removed from the fresh shoots by biting it loose at the end and tearing it off. The woody portion is scraped to remove bud protuberances and other inequalities of the surface and is then allowed to dry. These slender stems serve as foundation. The sewing material is prepared from the same plants. A squaw selects a fresh shoot, breaks off the too slender upper portion and bites one end so that it starts to split into three nearly equal parts. Holding one of these parts in her teeth and one in either hand, she pulls them apart, guiding the splitting with her fingers so dexterously that the whole shoot is divided into three equal even portions. Taking one of these, by a similar process she splits off the pith and the adjacent less flexible tissue from the inner face, and the bark from the outer, leaving a pliant, strong, flat strip of young willow or sumac wood. Both stems and splints may be dried and kept for months and probably even for several years, but before being used they are always soaked in water.

The pack baskets and some, at least, of the water baskets are made of these splints and rods in twined work. The women begin at the bottom with two layers of rods superimposed and fastened by their middles at right angles. The free ends are bent upward, and in and out between them the strands are woven, new warp rods being inserted as the basket widens. An attempt at ornamentation is frequently made by retaining the bark on some of the strands or by staining them and by slightly varying the weave. A squaw commonly occupies an entire month constructing one such basket.

Starting from a central point to make a coiled basket, a bundle of two or three grass stems and one very slender rod is wrapped with a willow splint. At the proper point the foundation is drawn more tightly, so that the remainder of the spiral forms the sides of the basket. The wall has the thickness, therefore, of one of these bundles, and is composed of a continuous ascending spiral. The willow rod furnishes a strong hold for the stitches, and the punctures are made with an iron awl. When such an instrument can not be obtained an admirable equivalent is substituted in the form of a stout, horny cactus spine from the devil's pincushion, *Echinocactus polycephalus*, set in a head of hard pitch. The grass stems, when the stitches are drawn tightly, make a perfect packing, and the basket when finished is water tight.

The pack baskets of the Panamint Indians have the form of a funnel, from $1\frac{1}{2}$ to $2\frac{1}{2}$ feet high and not quite so broad. The loaded basket is held against the back between the shoulders, either by the hands grasping its rim, or by leather or rope throngs passed around the forehead, the body meanwhile bent forward.

The plaques are small, flat, circular pieces of closely sewed coiled work, usually 9 to 12 inches in diameter. They are flexible and sometimes slightly saucer-shaped, and are used not only as plates and pans, but also as substitutes for sieves. The material to be sifted, composed of ground seeds, is placed upon the plate and the chaff winnowed out.

The pot basket of the Panamints is in coiled work and has the shape of a rather deep bowl with curved sides and a deep bottom, and has a capacity of about 3 pints. The squaw uses it as a general measure, as a bowl for dry food and for soup, and often, when in the sunshine, as a hat. Most of their starchy food is roasted dry by mixing seeds, before they are ground, with hot coals and stirring them in the basket. This process is still largely used.

The water basket has a capacity of 2 or 3 gallons. Its outline is that of an urn with a narrow neck and a rounded, conical bottom. The entire inner surface, and frequently the outside, is coated with pitch. Woven into the shoulder of the basket on one side are two loops of horsehair, or other strong material, to which is attached a thong. In carrying, this thong is passed around the forehead, while the basket is rested on the back between the shoulders.

All the Shoshonean types of weaving, all their forms of baskets, and most of the patterns on them are ancient. The canyon walls of the upper tributaries of the Colorado are honeycombed with cliff and cave dwellings. From them came inexhaustible treasures of basket work.[a]

In the collection of Dr. C. Hart Merriam in Washington City there are most excellent examples of the Panamint (Shoshonean) Indian basket work in which the ornamentation has been a matter of especial study. Plate 183 illustrates five examples from Dr. Merriam's collection, which I am allowed here to reproduce. Before speaking of them it will be at once noticed that these Indians, whose origin, or at least most numerous kindred, are in the Interior Basin, have been in contact with well-known California tribes and have been subjected to their influence. (See also Plate 185.)

Fig. 1 will be recognized at once in its relationship with the Tulare tribes. The ornamentation consists of four cycloidal radii made up of rectangles in black, arranged in stepped pattern. Each one of these rectangles is ornamented with two double chevron patterns called hour-glass designs by Dr. Dixon. In some examples the color is mixed red and black. Collections of short and parallel lines on the border terminate the patterns.

Fig. 2, another Panamint bowl, has the center ornamented with groups of small rectangles in threes. The first band near the bottom has for decoration a design which resembles a barbed harpoon head with unilateral prongs. The principal band on the body is decorated with a series of rhombs in black, containing white and black designs within. In some of the Californian eastern tribes this design represents the eye, but until the symbol is surely known, denotive names are better. The border is decorated with groups of short marks in threes.

---

[a] See F. V. Coville's account of the Panamint Indians of Death Valley, California, American Anthropologist, V, 1892, pp. 351–361.

Fig. 3 is a bowl with plain center, excepting a short owner's mark, and on the body are two bands, each one decorated by a threefold chevroned pattern.   It will be noted that the offsets in the three boundary lines of the designs are exactly in line with the finishing off at the upper border.   This feature is often mentioned by basket collectors among other tribes.

Fig. 4 is another Panamint bowl, the interior decorated by plain rings in black.   From the bottom project four equidistant wedge-shaped designs decorated on the surface with rhombs in white.   On the border, the pattern shown in fig. 1 appears rectangular in form with eight single chevroned designs on the surface.   One of the patterns is abbreviated, and between the two wedge-shaped designs on the right side of the figure is an arrow motive which may represent arrowheads strung or the feather of the arrow notched.

Fig. 5 is another Panamint bowl, with five wedge-shaped designs on the body, proceeding from a dark ring bordering the bottom.   Each design has outside edges bordered in white, with serrate edges in brown and straight venations in white on the middle portion.   The little groups of marks in threes on the border have nothing to do with the radiate pattern.

Plate 184 is introduced here for the purpose of showing how the colors mentioned in the foregoing pages are used in giving variety and beauty to the surface of the ware in this area.   The yellow golden color is that of the usual sewing material.   The black is produced by the use of martynia.   The red is from the *Yucca arborescens*.   In the ordinary photographic plate the effect of these colors is lost, but in the illustrations here given the full effect is brought out.   Attention is called also in the lower figure to the union of two methods of sewing. In the figured stripe in the middle, open sewing is shown, while on the rest of the body the stitches are packed close together.   It has Panamint designs.   On the upper bowl they are Yokut, but the materials of both are Panamint.   The open weaving also and the shred foundation point in the same direction.

The following information concerning the basket tangle in this area is from Mr. C. P. Wilcomb, of the Golden Gate Park Museum, San Francisco.   The Inyo and the Kern (Inyo-Kern) basketry are virtually undistinguishable, the tribes are Paiute (Shoshonean).   The Tulare County basketry is that of the Yokuts, and is identical with that of the Yokuts of Fresno County and of the Monache or Monos (Shoshoneans inhabiting the headwaters of the San Joaquin and Kings rivers).   The Monache and the Fresno work are somewhat coarser than that of the Tulare tribes, but in materials and shapes are identical. The Kern tribes are mostly on upper Kern River in the vicinity of Kernville.

The distinction between the two groups seems to rest on a geographical basis, inasmuch as the Inyo-Kern tribes are all east of the Sierra-Tehachapi range, and the other group, both Yokuts and Shoshonean Monache, west of the main divide.

The Tulare-Fresno foundation is made of grass stems (*Sporobolus vilfa*, or *Epicampes rigens*). The Inyo-Kern foundation is of willow (*Salix lasiandra*) or sometimes of the root of sumac (*Rhus trilobata*). For the Tulare sewing, roots of slough-grass (*Cyperus virens*, or *Cladium mariscus*) are used, while in the Kern, willow is usually employed. For the red of their patterns the Tulare-Fresno women employ the redbud (*Cercis occidentalis*), which is coarser than the root of the *Yucca arborescens*, used for the same purpose by the Inyo-Kern and Panamint. The Yucca root is of light yellowish red like willow bark, but is sometimes as dark as cercis. In some of the burden baskets and winnowing trays willow bark is used for red. The Paiutes do not use redbud. For black the Tulare-Fresno women use the common fern root (*Pteridium aquilinum*), while in Inyo-Kern and Panamint the heart of the tule root (*Scirpus nevadensis*) and Martynia are employed. In Inyo-Kern ware quail tips and red wool are rarely used on baskets as they are on Tulare; but small private marks and symbols are wrought with split pink quills from the woodpecker known as redshafted flicker. The Tulare make many large bowl-shaped baskets. In Inyo they are small, if of this shape.

Plate 185 will emphasize the difference hinted at in the foregoing text between the coarser and finer weaving in the same area. The upper figure in the plate is a Tejon bottle-necked jar in the collection of E. L. McLeod, of Bakersfield. The ornamentation is the striped pattern well known among the different tribes in this area. The foundation is laid up rather wide for the size of the basket and the sewing far apart, the stitches not being crowded home. Compare this with the specimen which follows.

Fig. 2, catalogue No. 204851, U. S. National Museum, is a fine coiled basket bowl collected by Eugene Mead. The foundation is of the three-stem type. The sewing is in splints of *Cladium*. The ornamentation is in the black fern root (*Pteridium aquilinum*). There are nine rows of sewing and thirteen stitches to the inch, but the most remarkable feature in this large bowl is that the three rods foundation and the sewing together make a fabric not an eighth of an inch in thickness. The designs are two serrated lines in black. On either side is a combination of symbolic figures which almost resemble letters of the alphabet. There is no exact history of this basket, but it is pronounced by Dr. Merriam to be the Fresno type of Yokut basket. It is an intrusive form among the Owens Valley Paiutes, captured by them on a raid into the interior side of the Sierra Mountains a long time ago. Its height is 7¾ inches, and diameter 15 inches.

Plate 186, one of the interesting specimens in Mr. Wilcomb's collection, is an Inyo basket, made in Inyo County by a Tulare (Yokut) squaw. It is 13 inches in diameter. The ornamentation outside the plain center is radial in two bands of stepped patterns, the inner band of six, the outer of thirteen. Each one of the latter having five parallel elements, there are with the interspaces seventy-eight elementary stepped designs in the band. The border is the oft-recurring bunch of colored stitches in groups.

Plate 187 represents baskets in the collections of, Powers and Gavin and Leonard. They are Tulare, but an examination shows what has heretofore been alluded to, the difference between the open and rather coarse texture of the Tulare basket mentioned by Mr. Wilcomb and the very much more refined type of the Inyo-Kern makers as in the lower figure. One characteristic worthy of observation is the use the weaver has made of small differences of shade in the splints for sewing, giving a clouded effect to the surface.

From the Tule River country, says E. L. McLeod, we have the fine flexible work, an improvement on their more northern sisters in Fresno. But the women of the Tejon and adjacent mountain tribes certainly excelled in their basket work. Their choice ware is much more beautifully finished, their patterns much more numerous, and here is where they show the influence of both north and south in the number and diversity of their patterns, also in the trading of materials. Old baskets have been taken from the caves in the Tejon where the bottom was Mission and the top beautiful, fine Tejon; also examples brought from caves in Santa Barbara County that were made over in the Tejon, as the stitch, texture, and all general appearance go to show that they were carried about by the Indians with them.

An excellent example of moving about of basket makers is given by McLeod. A woman was born at San Gabriel Mission, where she was baptized as Maria Narcissa, and is now about 70 years old. She was brought to the Tejon Canyon while a young child about 9 years old, and she still remembers much of the language and customs of her native people. Her uncle Sabastian was General Fremont's guide into the San Joaquin Valley through the Tejon Pass. Maria Narcissa not only learned the language of her adopted people, but many of the dialects of the surrounding tribes. Between forty and fifty years ago she was taken as wife by a young American of English-German parentage. They were the parents of a large family of children, and he gave them all as good an education as possible, especially the eldest daughter.

She was not able to give much light on the general family relation. The tribes from the north as far up as Tule River used to come down to the Tejon for some purpose, either religious or social. She tells of great feasts and dances and great gaming baskets where they used to play games of chance. But far the longest travel was from San Fernando, San Gabriel, Ventura, Santa Barbara, and Santa Inez. Many came from there every year to the Tejon, and we find unquestionable evidence in the meeting of all these streams in their basket work.

In a translation from Costansó (1769)[a] occurs this account of the Santa Barbara basket makers:

These are [the Indian women] who make the trays and vases of rushes, to which they give a thousand different forms and graceful patterns, according to the uses to which they are destined, whether it be for eating, drinking, guarding their seeds, or other ends, for these people do not know the use of earthenware as those of San Diego use it. * * *

The large vessels, which hold water, are of a very strong weave of rushes [junco], pitched within, and they give them the same form as our tinigas [water jars].

Plates 188 to 195 are taken from baskets in the McLeod collection and cover the subjects of form and design in the Inyo-Kern and Tulare-Fresno area. They furnish an excellent opportunity of seeing how far a few simple geometric elements combine in kaleidoscopic effects in the hands of the skillful Indian woman. Some of these specimens are of exceeding delicacy, and it is a matter of wonder how so many little stems of uniform diameter could be gathered together. Gauges are out of the question.

Plate 188, fig. 1, crenelated and chevroned designs; color, cream, black, and red; diameter, 12 inches; depth, 9 inches.

Fig. 2 is a very different pattern, resembling a pine tree; color, two shades of brown, black, and cream; diameter, 13 inches; depth, 10 inches.

Fig. 3, diameter, 11½ inches; depth, 8½ inches; 24 stitches to the inch; very rich shades of brown, mottled, cream, and black. Pattern very peculiar; so flexible it has been bent together; a most beautiful specimen.

Fig. 4, diameter, 11½ inches; depth, 7¼ inches; 15 stitches to the inch; body, brown; design, black and cream; very rare.

Fig. 5, diameter, 11½ inches; depth, 7 inches; 22 stitches to the inch; color, red, black, and cream.

Fig. 6, diameter, 13½ inches; depth, 9½ inches; 24 stitches to the inch; color, cream, and two shades of brown.

Fig. 7, diameter, 11½ inches; depth, 7¼ inches; 18 stitches to the inch; colors, red, black, and cream; very old; used to cook grubs.

Fig. 8, diameter, 10 inches; depth, 7 inches; 20 stitches to the inch; color, black, brown, red, and cream.

Fig. 9, diameter, 21½ inches; depth, 15 inches; 12 stitches to the inch; color, cream and brown. Very effective; thread even, well made, but not closely woven; the spirals are built up by elongating the little rectangles.

---

[a] Land of Sunshine, XV, 1901, p. 39.

Plate 189, Tulare baskets, fig. 1, diameter, 22 inches; depth, 13 inches; stitches to the inch, 30; wood mottled, dark and light brown, and red. One of the very old style of flexible gambling baskets. It would be possible to bend it together. The variety of effects here shown by the mere use of the broken line must be noted.

Fig. 2, bottle, diameter, 8½ inches; depth, 3¾ inches; diameter of neck, 2¾ inches; 17 stitches to the inch; color, black, red, and wood dark with age.

Fig. 3, diameter, 9 inches; depth, 5½ inches; 22 stitches to the inch; color, brown, red, and white.

Fig. 4, diameter, 8 inches; depth, 4½ inches; neck, 3¾ inches; 22 stitches to the inch; color, cream, red, and brown. Red wool and quail plumes.

Fig. 5, diameter, 9 inches; depth, 6 inches; 14 stitches to the inch; color, black and natural-wood color; very old. The white woman from whom Mr. McLeod purchased this basket had owned it for fifty years.

Fig. 6, diameter, 15 inches; depth, 9 inches; 14 stitches to the inch; color, brown, red, and mottled wood.

Fig. 7, diameter, 8 inches; depth, 8 inches; 22 stitches to the inch.

Plate 190, group of baskets from Tejon, Kern County. Fig. 1, diameter, 13 inches; depth, 7½ inches; 18 stitches to the inch; color, cream, black, red, and brown.

Fig. 2, mortar basket; diameter, 17 inches; depth, 8 inches; color, cream.

Fig. 3, diameter, 12½ inches; depth, 7 inches; 24 stitches to the inch; color, black, brown, red, and cream; very old and fine specimen.

Fig. 4, diameter, 7 inches; depth, 3¾ inches; 20 stitches to the inch; color, black, brown, and cream, with spots of yellow-hammer quill.

Fig. 5, diameter, 4½ inches; depth, 3½ inches; 30 stitches to the inch; color, cream and brown; very old and most beautifully made.

Fig. 6, oblong; length, 13 inches; width, 12 inches; depth, 6 inches; 18 stitches to the inch; color, brown and cream. A very peculiar basket, as the pattern is so allied to those of Arizona and New Mexico.

Fig. 7, diameter, 5 inches; height, 3 inches; 24 stitches to the inch; color, dark wood, cream, brown, and white, with dots and rim of red wool. This was a birth-gift basket, being presented filled with silver coins to an Indian woman from whom it was purchased at the birth of one of her daughters, who is now 40 years old. The giver was Sabastian, General Fremont's guide.

Fig. 8, diameter, 6½ inches; height, 5¼ inches; 21 stitches to the inch; color, black and cream; very old.

Fig. 9, diameter, 12 inches; circumference, 38 inches; depth, 7¼ inches; 15 stitches to the inch; color, black, brown, cream, and mottled wood.

Fig. 10, oblong; length, 4 inches; width, 3 inches; height, 3 inches; 22 stitches to the inch; color, cream and brown.

Fig. 11, diameter, 20 inches; depth, 12 inches; 24 stitches to the inch; color, cream; pattern, black.

Plate 191, baskets from Kern and Tulare counties. Fig. 1, Kern County; diameter, 18 inches; depth, 12 inches; 17 stitches to the inch; color, cream, brown, and red. A very dark basket. The vertical row of triangles and the human figures must be observed.

Fig. 2, diameter, 8½ inches; depth, 6 inches; diameter of neck, 3¾ inches; 22 stitches to the inch; very fine in weave, shape, and finish; color, rich cream, black, and red; very old; made at Tejon.

Fig. 3, diameter, 6 inches; depth, 4½ inches; neck diameter, 2¼ inches; 17 stitches to the inch; made at Tejon. Top is brown; bottom and pattern are white with black markings. This design is the "Sachem dancing about the funeral baskets," which they string on poles erected at their burial places.

Fig. 4, diameter, 15½ inches; depth, 9 inches; 18 stitches to the inch; color, cream and three shades of brown.

Fig. 5, Kern County squaw cap; diameter, 8 inches; depth, 5 inches; 26 stitches to the inch; color, cream, black, and red.

Fig. 6, Kern County basket; diameter, 20 inches; depth, 12½ inches; color, cream, brown, red, and black.

Fig. 7, Tulare basket; diameter, 30 inches; depth, 17 inches; 14 stitches to the inch; color, dark wood, red, and black. Braided edge; very beautifully woven and finished. The thread is regular but wide. The squaw was one year in making it.

Fig. 8, diameter, 7¾ inches; depth, 5 inches; diameter of neck, 4 inches; 20 stitches to the inch; made in Kern County; colors, body in brown; pattern, in black and white.

Fig. 9, Tulare basket; diameter, 7 inches; depth, 4 inches; 30 stitches to the inch; color, wood, black, red, white, and dark brown, and red wool; a beauty.

Plate 192, group of baskets from South Fork Caliente Creek and Paiute Mountain (McLeod's Plate 11).

Basket No. 1, diameter, 24 inches; depth, 15½ inches; stitches, 14; colors, cream, black, red, brown. The noteworthy features are the simple, undecorated crenelations. Compare fig. 9.

No. 2, diameter, 21 inches; depth, 15½ inches; stitches, 17; color, body, mottled wood shades; pattern, cream, black, and dark red. This is a very choice specimen. The design is one that they use when they make a basket for a special friendship gift and is highly prized. I was five years in getting the squaw to part with this basket.

No. 3, described on another plate.

No. 4, diameter, 18 inches; depth, 13½ inches; stitches, 17; color, body, wood shades; pattern, cream, black, red; a very beautiful basket.

No. 5, described on another plate.

No. 6, diameter, 7½ inches; depth, 6½ inches; stitches, 19; color, cream, red, and black; a very fine squaw cap.

No. 7, diameter, 8 inches; depth, 6 inches; stitches, 17; .color, cream, black, and brown.

No. 8, diameter, 15½ inches; depth, 11½ inches; stitches, 14; color, cream, red, and an unusual amount of black. This design with some is the tail of the rattlesnake and with others the arrowhead. The administration of radial patterns is a striking feature in this plate. The forms of the radii, but chiefly the varied markings on them, are most effective.

No. 9, described on another plate.

No. 10, diameter, 11½ inches; depth, 9 inches; stitches, 22; color, black, brown, and cream, with yellow-hammer quills; a very odd shape and good pattern.

No. 11, diameter, 15 inches; depth, 11 inches; stitches, 15; color, rich red, brown, black, and cream. A very striking example and unusual for so much dark color.

Plate 193 is a fine coiled basket of the Kern County Indians, who belong to the Shoshonean family. It was made in Canebrake Canyon by the last old basket maker of the tribe, who was swept away in a flood in August, 1901. The decorative patterns are ideal. Nine vertical stripes in black and red, with stepped borders and diamond figures on the interior, rise from the plain bottom and extend to the lower edge of the rim. The latter has its own fine-checkered, sloping designs, with no relation to the decoration on the body. Circumference, 29 inches; diameter, 9 inches; height, 5 inches; stitches to the inch, 32; colors, red, black, and cream. A design of quail plumes is shown on the border.

Plate 194 is a coiled bottle neck from Cane Brake Çanyon, Kern River, Kern County. Diameter, 9 inches; height, 6 inches; stitches to the inch, 24; color, cream, black, and brown. This and Plate 193 were both made by the same squaw, who was supposed to be about 85 years of age, and was the last really good weaver in Kern County. The ornamentation on this basket consists in a band of dentate figures on the bottom and three bands of crenelated ornament on the body and top. The dentate figures also occur on the outer projection of the crenelles on the body. Dr. Merriam has found this pattern symbolizing the spasmodic flight of a butterfly. Below the border of the lower band are rhombs in pairs, and there are five checker oblique patterns about the rim.

Plate 195, McLeod collection, is a Kern County basket from Paiute Mountain, called by him the apostolic basket, from the human figures on the top. Diameter, 15 inches; height, 12 inches; stitches to the inch, 28; colors, red, brown, black, and cream. The owner speaks of this as the most beautiful specimen in his collection. The woman was three years at work on it, and it is at least 60 years old. The ornamentation consists of discrete figures of five rectangles, thirteen men on the upper part, but chiefly of seven radial patterns ascending to the mouth. Each is made up of a continuous series of rectangular figures touching and by echelon. This pattern will be seen frequently, and the specimen may be taken as a type of that particular design.

Fig. 172 is a grasshopper basket of the Wikchumni Indians (Mariposan family), in a style of technique which may be called interrupted coiled work. The foundation is a small bundle of stems or shreds. The sewing consists in wrapping the foundation from five to ten times with the splint, and then catching this under one or two turns of the coil below in the form of stitches, the only bond which holds the fabric together being these few stitches. Another example of this sort of interrupted work in North America is shown in Plate 126, illustrating basketry from the Eskimo of Hudson Bay.

FIG. 172.
GRASSHOPPER BASKET.
Wikchumni Indians, California.
Cat. No. 215586, U.S.N.M.

The existence of this type of basketry in a restricted area among the Mariposan family raises interesting questions about the cause of its occurrence here. The ornamentation consists in rows, hourglass patterns, and figures resembling the letters of the alphabet, done in brown material, like cercis or fern stems.

FIG. 173.
DETAIL OF FIG. 172.

The detail of this interrupted work is well shown in fig. 173, where the wrapping is plainly illustrated, and also the methods of joining. By bringing the stitches one over another, geometrical patterns are produced. As the work widens, new rows are introduced, as will be seen in the principal figure.

This specimen Catalogue No. 215586, in the U. S. National Museum, is a gift from C. P. Wilcomb, of California.

Mr. McLeod, who has the largest collection of the grasshopper baskets, says of them that they have no such function. They are all made by two families, the Butterbread and the Williams, living in Kelsey Canyon, Kern County, California. The sewing and wrapping are faultless. The ornamentation is chiefly in plain lines and rectangles. On one of them, fig. 10, the chevroned design is attempted with doubtful success, but figs. 2 and 3 have the stepped radial patterns well carried out, and on fig. 9 the human conventional figure is cleverly executed. (See Plate 196.)

Mission Indian basket makers belong to the Shoshonean and Yuman families. They receive their several names from the Franciscan missions of southern California, into which they were gathered, and where their tribal identity was lost. In the present state of knowledge it is not possible to distinguish the linguistic family by the shape, technic, or designs of basketry.

The material of Mission Indian baskets differs according to locality. A rush, probably several species, is used for the sewing; the best known to Mr. Coville is *Juncus lesnerii*, the Techahet Indians using it almost exclusively. This plant is collected and dried, and what are often thought to be brushes by strangers are merely bunches of this rush prepared for the weaver's use. A tall, thin grass, *Vilfa rigens*, is used as the body of the coil, about which pieces of the *Juncus* are wound. Such of the latter as are intended for ornamentation are dyed black by steeping in water portions of *Sueda diffusa*, and a rich yellowish brown is produced in a like manner from the plants *Dalea emoryi* and *Dalea polyadenia*. The bottoms of large baskets are often strengthened by the introduction of twigs of *Rhus aromatica* or three-leaf sumac. Dr. Merriam finds that latterly the leaf of a palm (*Neowashingtonia filamentosa*) is used for sewing. The work resembles that done in rafia.

In beginning a basket a central foundation is made and the rush wound about it and coiled, fastened by fibers passing through holes made for the purpose with a pointed bone or metal awl. This is the commonest method employed.

To assist the student in understanding the relationship of arts in southern California, the following account of tribes from Dr. Barrows will be helpful. The Indian tribes south of Santa Inez Mountains on the coast and San Joaquin Valley in the interior fall into three divisions: (1) Tribes of Santa Barbara channels and islands covering the coast of Ventura County; (2) Serranos; (3) Coahuillas.

The Serranos live on a small reservation at San Bernardino and on the Morongo Reservation in the San Gorgonio pass in southern California. They are called Takhtam by Loew.

The Coahuillas live in the Colorado Desert and the San Jacinto Mountains. The word is also spelled Kauvuyah by Gatschet after Loew. Dr. Barrows thinks this to be only the German spelling for Coahuilla (pronounced Kau-vü-yah).

With them he joins by speech the Indians of the missions northward, making a Coahuillian linguistic family; perhaps it were better a subfamily.

Coahuillian subfamily

1. Coahuillas. Colorado Desert and San Jacinto Mountains.
2. Gaitchim. Oscar Loew's name for Netela.
3. Kechi. Missions of San Luis Rey.
4. Kizh. San Gabriel Missior
5. Luiseños. (*See* Kechi.)
6. San Fernando Mission.
7. Serranos.
8. Takhtam or Takhtem, Loew's name for Serranos.
9. Temeculas. At Pechanga, 8 miles north from Luiseños.
10. Tobikhar. Loew's name for Kizh.

Barrows narrates that the Coahuilla basketry and that of the Diegueños as well as Luiseños is of the one California type, namely, coiled ware, and fragments of similar technic have been found by Schumacher in the graves of the Santa Barbara channel. He quotes Humboldt to the effect that the Indians presented the Spaniards "with vases curiously wrought of stalks of rushes and covered within with a very thin layer of asphaltum that renders them impenetrable to water." Lumps of the material are said to have been put into the basket with hot stones and shaken with a rotary motion to distribute it. The foundation of the coil is a bunch of grass, su-ul (*Vilfa rigens*). The sewing material varies according to the color desired. The three-leaf sumac (*Rhus trilobata*) gives a light straw color; these are dyed black in a wash, made from the berry stems of the elder, hun kwat (*Sambucus*). The other sewing material is a bulrush or reed grass (*Juncus lesnerii*, or *Juncus robustus*). The scape and leaves are 2 to 4 feet high or more, stout and pungent. A supply of these is gathered by the basket maker and cut into suitable lengths. The woman then with her hands and teeth splits the scape carefully into three equal portions. Near its base the reed is of a deep red, lightening in color upward, passing through several shades of light brown, and ending at the top in a brownish yellow. For dyeing black, ngaial (*Sueda diffusa*) is also employed, and Dr. Palmer also mentions a dahlia (*D. polyadenia*) as furnishing a yellowish brown dye.

The Techahet, use the reed grass (*Juncus robustus*) or the *Rhus trilobata*, and the tall thin grass (*Vilfa rigens*) in a dried state for making basketry, the first two for binding material, the latter for the body. The reed grass is split, some of it dyed, usually brown. The basket is begun at the center of the bottom, the thickness of the coil of grass depending upon the size of the basket to be made. A bone pricker is used. The coil is begun by laying one end of the filament upon the bunch of grass and taking a few wraps about it to hold it down. This is bent double and the sewing progresses by catching the filament over the bunch of grass through the coil of the sewing filament made at the last turn.

Basket making among the Coahuillas belongs to the old women. They sit flat on the ground with the feet thrust out in front. The deft artist holds her work in her lap, at her right lies the grass for the foundation, on her left, soaking in a pot of water, her variously colored splints. Her only tool is her awl, " wish," anciently of bone or a cactus spine set in a piece of asphaltum; but now a nail serves the purpose, one end pointed, the other in a handle of manzanita wood. The sewing materials are named according to colors—the scapes of *juncus* se il; the red portion, i i ul; dyed black they are se-il-tu-iksh. Splints from sumac are se-lit and the grass of the foundation suul. No model or pattern is ever used. The border is finished by simply cutting the sewing material close on the inner side. The most common form, se-whal-lal, of Coahuilla basket has a flat bottom and gently flaring sides, a depth of from 4 to 7 inches and a width of from 13 to 20 inches. These are for holding foods, including seeds, grains and fruits, household utensils, and basket materials. Small, globular baskets, with bulging sides and rather wide mouths, 5 to 10 inches in diameter, are called te-vin-ze-mal. They are the prettiest and the most carefully ornamented and are used to hold trinkets and sewing materials. The deep packing baskets, se kwa-vel-em, are about 18 inches deep and are used for packing loads. Rawhide strings, ka wi ve, are tied to opposite edges to pass around the forehead, but usually the basket is sustained in a net. They are used not only for food gathering, but on the threshing floor for storing foods. The chi-pat-mal is a round, almost flat basket, 16 to 18 inches in diameter and one or more inches deep, used for harvesting. The woman beats it full of grass seeds or fills it with elder berries or cactus fruit, and transfers the contents to the packing basket on her back. It makes a good tray, platter, fruit dish, or receptacle for meal, and is exclusively the winnower.

The basket hat, yu-ma-wal, shaped like a truncated cone, is worn by women especially to protect the head from the carrying band. It serves also for a water dipper or mixing pan. The chi-pa-cha-kish, holding about 2 quarts, is an openwork basket of network, made from the unsplit, flattened scapes of the se-il, or Juncus. They are often provided with a bail and hung up in the house or ramada to contain fruit or vegetables.[a]

Fig. 174 is a coiled basket of the Coahuilla (Shoshonean family). The foundation coil is of stems of grass; the sewing is in splints of sumac (*Rhus trilobata*). The ornamentation is in stems of rush dyed black with sea blite (*Sueda diffusa*).

No special study has been made of the meaning in the designs upon the Coahuilla basketry. It is impossible, therefore, to guess what the combinations of parallelograms may mean. From the point of view of elementary forms in design, it is interesting to note what diversities of effects may be produced by variations in the form and composition

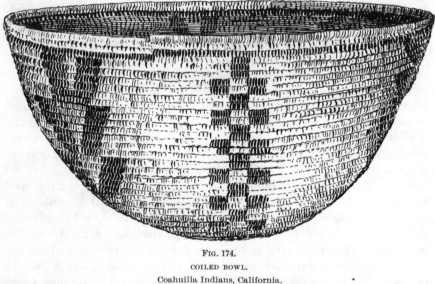

FIG. 174.
COILED BOWL.
Coahuilla Indians, California.
Cat. No. 21787, U.S.N.M. Collected by Edward Palmer.

of simple geometric patterns. Five of the figures on the example here shown are built up of rhomboidal elements and a single one is the composition of rectangles in quincunxes.

Fig. 175 is a view of the inside of the bowl, showing the ornamentation. A square inch of coil foundation, made up of straws or small filaments, is shown in fig. 176. This specimen, Catalogue No. 21787 in the U. S. National Museum, was procured in southern California by Edward Palmer.

Fig. 177 is an inside view of another specimen from the Coahuilla tribe and made of the same material. It is possible that some of the specimens from this tribe are sewed with splints of willow. It is dif-

---

[a] David Prescott Barrows, The Ethno-Botany of the Coahuilla Indians of Southern California. Chicago, 1900. Chapter IV (quoting Paul Schumacher, Humboldt Hugo Reid, Edward Palmer).

ficult in the dried form to distinguish the two materials. The pretty, attractive design on this specimen is simplicity itself. Small triangles are arranged in two rows, half of them joining outward and the other

FIG. 175.
INSIDE VIEW OF FIG. 174.

half inward from the base, forming a continuous circle. One row is so suggested with reference to the other that the white space between forms a continuous chevron. It is a little difficult to say whether the whole meaning of such a result from simple processes was in the mind

of the basket maker. While not wishing to deprive her of all the credit due to her for this beautiful work, one can scarcely refrain from thinking that the total effect was not comprehended by the artist.

This specimen, Catalogue No. 21786 in the U. S. National Museum, was collected in southern California by Edward Palmer.

Plate 197 is the portrait of Mercedes Nolasquez, the mother of the capitan of the Mission Agua Caliente in San Diego County, southern California. The Mission Indians of this reservation belong to the great Shoshonean family. A portion of her house is shown in a coiled bowl filled with acorns. In her hands she is holding a partly finished coiled basket, the foundation of which is a number of stems

FIG. 176.
SQUARE INCH OF FIG. 174.

of grass. The sewing is done with split martynia pods giving the black color, and split stems of rhus giving the white color. The only implement used in the manufacture is a fine awl for making holes to accommodate the stitches.

It is to be noticed that Mercedes is not holding the bowl in the position for sewing, but has turned it down and around in order to show her work. Photographed by George Wharton James.

Plate 198 represents a Saboba basketmaker near the mission of San Jacinto on the Mission Indian Reservation in southwestern California, sitting at the door of her rude home and studio. She is the

FIG. 177.
COILED BOWL.
Coahuilla Indians, California.
Cat. No. 21786, U.S.N.M.   Collected by Edward Palmer.

wife of Jose Pedro Lucero, of Shoshonean family, and is now one of the few makers of Mission Indian coiled baskets left at this point. Specimens of her work are shown in the adjoining illustrations. Photographed by George Wharton James.

Plate 199 is a coiled bowl made by the Mission Indians of California, illustrating the technic with splint foundation. The sewing of the Mission baskets is sometimes in bullrush and at others in splints. The dark mark near the center is said to be the signature of the maker. The colors in the ornament around the border are produced by sewing natural material of different shades.

Plate 200 represents a Havasupai or Coconino woman making a

coiled basket.   In Powell's Indian Linguistic Families the Yuman tribes include the Coconino, Cocopa, Kutchin or Yuman proper, Diegueños, Havasupai, Maricopa, Mohave, Seri, Waicuru, and Walapai. The Yuman tribes occupy the peninsula of Lower California, and are are also mixed with other tribes in southern California and in western Arizona, especially along the Colorado River.   Many of the bands of Indians called missions belong to this linguistic division.   The types of basketry made by the Havasupai are shown in the following illustration.

Formerly the only implement of the basket maker was a bone awl replaced in this instance by one of metal.   It is noteworthy that she is working toward her left hand, the wrong side of her basket being inside.   After the work is done the projecting ends are carefully clipped by means of scissors.   Photographed by George Wharton James.

Plate 201 presents two very ancient tray-shaped baskets or plaques from the cave in San Martin Mountains, Los Angeles County, California, which were collected by Stephen Bowers. The Catalogue No. is 39245, in the Peabody Museum, Cambridge, Massachusetts. (See also Plate 202.)

FIG. 178.

TWINED BASKET.

Dieguéños Indians, California.

Cat. No. 19742, U.S.N.M.   Collected by Edward Palmer.

The upper figure is a fine old example of coiled weaving in the three-rod type, the stitch interlocking with the upper element.

The lower figure is an example of the same kind of coiling, but the surface has been covered with asphalt, so that the texture is almost totally obliterated.

Twined weaving is not so common as coiled work in southern California.   One could scarcely conceive a more primitive specimen, however, than is shown in fig. 178, from the Dieguéños Indians (Yuman family) living about San Diego, California.   The specimen is a basket for cactus fruit.   The warp is gathered singly or in pairs in the twists of the weft.   Old specimens of twined weaving from the region, on the contrary, are finely wrought.

Plate 203 represents a sack in twined weaving, collected at Mesa

Grande, on the Mission Indian Reservation, in southern California, by Mrs. Watkins, the Government teacher there, and sent to the National Museum by Miss Constance Goddard DuBois. The dark threads are said, by Mrs. Watkins, to be made from the inner bark of *Asclepias vestita* and the lighter threads, in which the decorative bands are worked, from *Asclepias ascicularis*. It is a very ancient piece, the only one that had been seen in those parts. Narciso Lachapa, whose father owned it, says it was old when he was a boy.

The majority of baskets from the Mission region are in coiled weaving. A few examples of twined weaving from this area have been seen in collections, but none equalling this in size and beauty. Its height is 29 inches.

THE INTERIOR BASIN REGION

Not the hands, but reason teaches mankind arts; but the hands are the instruments of arts, as the lyre is of the musician and the forceps are of the mechanic.—GALEN.

Leaving now the Pacific slope we may examine the basketry of the Great Interior Basin, bounded on the east by the Siouan, Kiowan, and Caddoan families beyond the Rocky Mountains. The Siouan tribes, together with the western Algonquian and other tribes wedged in among them, borrow coiled gambling baskets and substitute the convenient buffalo hide for textiles; but the Caddoan (see figs. 124, 125) were excellent workers in twilled weaving.

On the north, this basketry area merges into the Fraser-Columbian group, Salishan and Shahaptian tribes chiefly, who are especially skillful in twined work of peculiar types. The soft hat in wrapped twined work and most of all the twined wallet overlaid predominate with the Shahaptian, but the Salish have a wide range of technic.

On the west there is no sharp boundary line as will be soon shown, the Interior Basin area and the Oregon-California fitting into and invading each other as shore and water line on an irregular coast. This will be especially noticeable with coiled work, the three-rod foundation of California being adopted by some Ute tribes.

The same is true of the southern boundary, the linguistic families dovetailing into those of Mexico. The Apache cross the boundary southward, the Yuman and Piman tribes also reaching northward and excelling in coiled ware with fine grass foundation.

The tribal or ethnic groups in this area are chiefly the Shoshonean and the Athapascan. The first named is a vast linguistic family reaching from near the forty-ninth parallel to Costa Rica, the latter, quite as widespread, extending between 30° and 70° north. Care must again be taken to separate the classific concept of language from that of blood kinship or of arts. Where peoples live contiguous and have the same speech, their blood becomes mingled as a matter of course. Arts will also be communicated. Especially is this true of the one here considered, being a woman's craft. The Athapascan occupies the southern portion of the Basin, and the Pueblos are most of them in northern Arizona and New Mexico.

SHOSHONEAN AND PUEBLO BASKETRY

By far the largest part of the Interior Basin is Shoshonean. The tribes also spread out far to the north in the drainage of the Snake River; have pushed themselves across the Rocky Mountains on the southeast into the drainage of the Gulf of Mexico, and on the western side occupied a large part of southern California as was shown. The basket-making tribes are the Shoshoni in Idaho; the Ute, with many subdivisions, in Colorado and Utah; the Paiute in western Nevada and California adjoining. As before intimated, both exclusions and inclusions of the term are undefined.

This great stock of Indians employ both structures, the woven and the coiled. The twined weave of all kinds is used in the conodial basket hats, the baskets, jars and bottles, the roasting trays and wands. The coiled and whipped structure is used in pitched water bottles, trays, and bowls. The hat is a conical basket made of splints, the warp radiating from the apex, the woof splints being carried around and twined in pairs, generally in diagonal weave. The woof is not so thoroughly driven home as in softer and more pliant material, but remains open so as to have the appearance of the osier weaving of the East. Simple ornamentation is produced by using one or more rows of red or black splints in elementary geometric patterns.

Roasting trays are shaped like a scoop rimmed with a large twig. The warp is made of parallel twigs laid close together and held in place by diagonal twining. The Shoshonean tribes place seeds of wild plants in these trays with hot stones, and thus roast them. Some specimens are much charred on the upper side. In the Ute country could be seen Indian women gathering seeds in conical baskets, beating the heads with a spoon-shaped wand toward the basket held in the left hand with its mouth just under the plants. These baskets are constructed in every respect like the conoidal hats and the fans are made of twigs coarsely woven on the same pattern.

The water bottles of the Shoshonean tribes on the other hand belong to the coiled and whipped structure. As before mentioned, this style can be made coarse or fine, according to the material and the size of the coil and the outer thread. If twigs not of uniform thickness are carried around in the coil, the stitch will be hatchy and open; but if one is larger than the other, or if yucca or other fiber replace the upper and narrower sewing material be used, the texture will be much finer. These bottles differ in shape—one class has round bottoms, another long pointed bottoms; one has wide mouths, another small mouths; one class has a little osier handle on the side of the mouth like a pitcher, but the majority have one or two loops of wood, horsehair, or osier fastened on one side for carrying.   All of them are quite heavy, having been dipped in pitch.   The same form is found among the Apache, Mohave, Hopi, and Rio Grande pueblos, but it is not improbable that they were obtained from the Ute.   These bottle-shaped baskets are used for small granaries as well—to hold seed and keep them away from vermin.

The basket trays of the Ute do not differ essentially in general style from those of the Gila River or California tribes, but they are much coarser.   Among the coiled basket trays in the collection accredited to the Ute are indeed two styles, but one of them resembles so much those of their Apache neighbors on the south as to raise the suspicion that they were obtained by barter.

FIG. 179.
WOMAN'S HAT.
Ute Indians, Utah.
Cat. No. 11838.   Collected by J. W. Powell.

The typical styles here mentioned, as well as interesting variations, will be best understood from examples.

The National Museum has a rare old collection of Ute or Shoshonean material, of which A. H. Thompson writes that of the baskets and other articles of Indian manufacture gathered by the Powell expeditions between 1870 and 1875 the greater part, probably nine-tenths, were secured from the Kaivavits at Kaibab and the Shivwits about St. George, southern Utah, and the Moapas about St. Thomas, southeastern Nevada.   These clans all belong to the Paiute Nation.   The articles secured from the Ute were from the Gosiute about Deep Creek in western Utah and the Uinta Ute on the Uinta Reservation. By far the larger part of the Paiute collection was from the Kaivavits.   Much of the clothing (buckskin and rabbit fur) and many of the baskets were made by the Indians working under the direction or rather observation of Mrs. E. P. Thompson, the endeavor being to have the work done by the methods employed before the coming of the whites and by the older people of the clan.

Fig. 179 is a hat of a Ute Indian woman, in diagonal twined work. The warp stems converge at the top and additional ones are added as the texture widens. The weft splints are twined so as to include the vertical warp twigs in pairs. On the next round the warp elements are again inclosed in pairs, but not in corresponding ones to those of the row underneath. The lines of weft elements ascend diagonally and a twilled effect is produced on the surface. This form of twining must not be confounded with three-ply twine around the border which has a somewhat similar appearance, but is so close that the warp stems do not show. The border of this Ute basket is ingeniously made. First, the projecting warp elements were bent and whipped in place with splints to form the body of the rim; on the top of this the weaver has sewed an ornamental false braid catching the splint into the bent warp stems underneath. The ornamentation on the outside is produced by three-strand monochrome or dichrome weaving. The Utes are skillful in various methods of technic, but the materials in which they work are coarse and rigid, giving a rough appearance to the surface. The hats are used also as receptacles, so that the terms top and bottom are only relative to function.

Fig. 180 is a harvesting fan of the Paiutes made of small stems, split or whole, and bound together with various fiber, the manual portion being wrapped with softer material. This very coarse specimen is represented in other tribes,

FIG. 180.
HARVESTING FAN.
Paiute Indians, Utah.
Cat. No. 11823, U.S.N.M. Collected by J. W. Powell.

especially on the western side of the Sierras, by finely woven, spoon-shaped harvesting wands. It is Catalogue No. 11823 in the U. S. National Museum, collected in Utah by J. W. Powell.

Fig. 181 is a pair of harvesting fans of the Paiute Indians in southern Utah. A bundle of rods is fastened together to form the grip of the fan, the other ends of these rods are then spread out and afterwards brought together to a point, at the same time bent downward in spoon form for a warp. These are held in place by a continuous twined weaving backward and forward, the rows being at irregular intervals. Near the end the points are held together by compact twined weaving. The border is made by coiled work built up on a pair of strong rods. These interesting objects are not confined, as will be seen, to the Ute Indians, but all the tribes in California, Nevada, and Arizona that depend upon the smaller seeds for their sustenance have the same method of beating the ripe grass into a conical carrying basket. The fans of this type, perhaps, form the very earliest harvesting device.

Associated with the harvesting fan is the gathering and carrying basket and the roasting or winnowing tray.

Catalogue Nos. 11817, 11822 in the U. S. National Museum, procured in Utah by J. W. Powell.

FIG. 181.

HARVESTING FANS.

Paiute Indians, Utah.

Collected by J. W. Powell.

Figs. 182 to 184 illustrate a gathering basket of the Paiute Indians. The first, fig. 182, represents the entire structure which is at basis open-twined work. The noticeable feature about this piece is the treatment of the warp, which, instead of rising perpendicularly from the bottom to the top, is twisted to the left, each radial element of the warp making about one-fourth of a turn from the vertical. Again, the technic is diagonal weaving in twined work. The diverting of the warp from the vertical is not common in twined weaving, but occurs quite frequently in this area and among this family.

Fig. 183 gives a good notion of the way in which the bottom is started. Four pairs of warp stems constitute the base. These are held in place by very coarse twined weaving. The ends of the stems are bent up to become the warp of the body. The upper border of the basket shows how the warp stems are bent down to the left; a bundle of splints laid on top and sewed as in coiled weaving (fig. 184). On the top of this a stout rod is sewed by another turn of the same process, so that both coiled work and twined work are to be seen in this coarse bit of everyday ware.

This specimen, catalogue No. 14688 in the U. S. National Museum, was collected in Utah by J. W. Powell.

Fig. 185 is a harvesting and carrying basket of the Paiutes in diagonal twined weaving, precisely as in fig. 179 representing a Ute woman's hat, and fig. 180 the fanning tray. The bottom is covered with hide to protect it and on the side is fastened a headband used in carrying. The ornamentation on many Ute specimens seems to have been effected by charring, since the figures do not appear on the inside at all.

FIG. 182.

GATHERING BASKET.

Paiute Indians, Utah.

Cat. No. 14688, U.S.N.M. Collected by J. W. Powell.

The Ute Indians make use of many kinds of seeds in their dietary. The women go out into the plains with this carrying basket and the fan, illustrated in fig. 181. The apex of the carrying basket is rested on the ground and the seeds are beaten into it by means of the gathering fan. When the basket is full the woman places the band across her forehead, rests the receptacle on her back, and trudges home with her load.

Catalogue Nos. 14667 to 14746 in the U. S. National Museum were procured in Utah by J. W. Powell.

FIG. 183.

BOTTOM OF FIG. 182.

Fig. 186 is called a roasting or fanning tray of the Paiutes, being used for the purpose of separating the chaff from the seeds which have been gathered either by blowing or roasting. The warp is a lot of twigs spread out like a fan. The weaving begins at the inner or manual end, which is the bottom of the illustration, with short curves and progresses by ever widening rows to the outer margin. The rim is produced by a double row of coiled and whipped work. The whole surface is very rough by reason of the nature of the material which these people living in a desert region have to use.

FIG. 184.

BORDER OF FIG. 182.

This specimen, catalogue No. 11857 in the U. S. National Museum, was collected in Utah by J. W. Powell.

Fig. 187 is a coiled seed jar of the Paiute Indians. It belongs to the type of coiled work called two-rod; that is, the foundation of the

FIG. 185.

CARRYING BASKET.

Paiute Indians, Utah.

Cat. No. 14667, U.S.N.M.   Collected by J. W. Powell.

coil work consists of two stems, one above the other, the stitches pass around these two and under one of the foundation underneath and interlock. Baskets of this kind are frequently dipped into hot gum or pitch of some kind, varying in different localities. The peculiar effect of this sort of weaving is to hide one of the rods in the foundation and to reveal the other. Frequently, the upper one in each pair is smaller, and by driving the stitches close home a tolerably close and very enduring structure is the result.

Pottery was made by the ancient Utes, but is not now common. The basket bottle is much more useful and enduring. A square inch from the surface of this bottle is shown in fig. 188.

Catalogue No. 11262 in the U. S. National Museum was collected by J. W. Powell, together with Nos. 11249 to 11261.

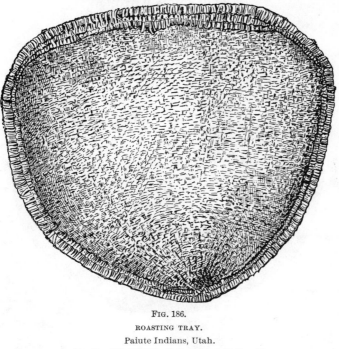

Fig. 186.

ROASTING TRAY.

Paiute Indians, Utah.

Cat. No. 11857, U.S.N.M. Collected by J. W. Powell.

Plate 204 presents two figures from different localities, but having essentially the same form, structure, and function. That on the left, catalogue No. 19029 in the U. S. National Museum, is a fine old water jar made by a Coyuwee Paiute woman, Pyramid Lake, Nevada, secured by Stephen Powers. It is a model of uniformity in technic. The twilled weaving in twined technic is laid up as regularly as brickwork. There is no attempt at ornament, either in color or variety in weaving. The pine gum is applied so carefully that it does not hide but emphasizes the workmanship. The lugs are of braided horsehair. Its height is 15 inches.

The right-hand figure, No. 2610, is labeled "Pueblo Indians," but it was evidently made by a Ute woman. The pitch has worn off sufficiently to reveal the process of making the other. Note, first, the twilled weaving in openwork. The twists of the weft each include two of the warp stems. On the next round the same two are not included; they are separated to be joined again in the next row above. Now, if the woman had pressed her weft close home, she would have produced exactly the same effect as may be seen on the left-hand figure, a close twill. Observe, however, that at the widest part of the body she has introduced one round of three-strand twine. Two rows

FIG. 187.

COILED JAR.

Paiute Indians, Utah.

Cat. No. 11262, U.S.N.M. Collected by J. W. Powell.

of the same form the lower boundary of the neck, which is done carelessly in plain weaving. Collected by W. L. Hardesty.

Nordenskjöld found in the cliff dwellings of the southwestern United States:

1. Checker work in heavy, coarse sandals.
2. Wickerwork. This may be seen also in Hopi basketry.
3. Diagonal or twilled weaving, common in Hopi pueblo especially.
4. Matting of rod strung on twine. Apache now use it. (See fig. 103.)
5. Braiding in the round. In lariats.
6. Twined weaving in many forms.

7. Three-rod coil foundation (Bam-shi-bu).

8. Coiled network, the spirals twisted on themselves. (Compare Muskemoot, Plate 102.)

9. Sandals with knots of various patterns in the lacing.

In a paper by Dr. George H. Pepper,[a] attention is called to a cliff people formerly living in Grand Gulch region of southeastern Utah called the "Basket Makers." They are shown to have worn beautiful robes of feathers and of rabbit skins woven, and sandals of yucca fiber squared in front, and to have had little or no pottery. They fought with "atlatls" rather than bows, and hunted with the Hopi rabbit stick. Most interesting of all, they lived in caves, but not in stone houses. In some of the caves the houses of the Cliff Dwellers have been found overlying the remains of the earlier Basket Makers. Finally, the bodies of the dead were doubled up, placed at the bottom of potholes or granaries, some of which were lined with baked clay, covered with robes and finally with baskets, either several small ones or one large carrying basket. The last-named feature is said to have been almost invariably in evidence, and it is to this that attention is here given. The material is willow, the designs on the baskets being in splints of black or a peculiar dull red. The bottoms of the carrying baskets were reenforced with heavy yucca cord.

FIG. 188.

SQUARE INCH OF FIG. 187.

The borders were finished with the ordinary coiled stitch, but in some the last inch or two are finished off with false braid or herringbone.

One example of Dr. Pepper's, called openwork or sifter basket, has a single rod foundation and the wrapping at one turn passes around the foundation only; at the next it is drawn under the rod in the coil below and returning is wrapped about itself or "the standing part," as the sailors say. The ordinary Japanese lunch baskets, Samoan basket work, and those from the Straits of Magellan are on the same plan. But it is certainly a rare sight in this part of the world. (See Plate 317.)

Plates 205 and 206 are from the Pepper collection of coiled basketry from the caves of the ancient Basket Makers. The particular specimens will be described under separate photographs of each one, but the group shows both the forms and functions of the material gathered in this interesting locality.

---

[a] The Ancient Basket Makers of Southeastern Utah, Guide Leaflet No. 6 of the American Museum of Natural History, New York, 1902.

Plate 207 is a coiled tray, having as design two circles of figures resembling aquatic birds floating on the water. This is an excellent opportunity to speculate about the relation of this desert region with prayers to the water god.

Plate 208 is another coiled tray from the cave dwellers, with an ornamental design, showing two sinuous rings in black.

Plate 209 contains two bowls apparently with the three-rod coil; such is now common among the best basket makers of California. The ornamentation is also suggestive of the same locality. On the upper figure are four radial designs triangular in outline, two having their bases at the bottom and two on the outer border, each pattern made up of fringe work of triangles, reminding one of the strings of arrowhead patterns mentioned by Dr. Dixon in his pamphlet on the Maidu. The lower figure is similarly constructed in coiled weaving, the ornamentation being in circular patterns; the bottom is plain; then follow narrow rings in black, a broad ring in white, a broad band with seven triangular rays, a narrow band in black, and a broad band in the natural color of the wood.

Plate 210 is interesting as showing the function of the baskets which were found in the Utah cave. All of them have relation to food. They are in twilled and coiled weaving and show how in ancient times the basket entered into the service of these agricultural Indians.

Plate 211 shows a mortar basket of the ancient basket makers in coiled weaving on splint foundation. It is not possible to determine the material of the stitches. It is 13 inches in diameter and $3\frac{1}{2}$ inches deep. The interior is coated with meal and the surface of the sewing is worn through from long use. Mortar baskets are common among the California tribes, both in twined weaving and in coiled work. A specimen quite similar to the one here shown in the U. S. National Museum has a coiled basket top, cemented to the shallow mortar stone underneath by means of pitch. The specimens are in the collection of the American Museum of Natural History.

Pepper describes four varieties of sandals among the ancient Cliff Dwellers—thin soles in twilled weaving from narrow leaves of yucca; those made of broad leaves split; a padded variety made from the same leaves shredded; and an exceedingly fine kind, of spun fiber and worked into elegant patterns. In these last the warp is in two or more layers or plies, so that the body is thick and durable. He quotes Richard Witherill to the effect that while the chamber-building Cliff Dwellers wove the sandal with pointed toes and a jog or step a few inches from the toe, those of the Basket Makers were square in front. McLoyd and Graham [a] assert that square-toed sandals were made by the people that inhabited the underground rooms, since they are found only with

[a] Guide Leaflet, No. 6, of American Museum of Natural History, New York.

mummies of that race.　No square-toed sandals are found in caves where remains of the basketmakers do not exist.

The term Pueblo basketmaker is far from specific.　It applies to women of all the settled villages in New Mexico and Arizona, from Taos on the Rio Grande, in the former, to the Hopi in Arizona.　The peoples belong to the Tañoan and Keresan families on the Rio Grande, to the Zuñian in western New Mexico, and the Hopian or Shoshonean in Arizona.[a]

Far back in time those structures whose ruins furnish inexhaustible supplies of pottery and some textiles have to tell the tale as to the ancient types of basketry.　At the present moment great confusion exists concerning the ethnic significance of basketry in the pueblos. Beautiful old pieces came twenty years or more ago from these villages about which there is little information.　James Stevenson wrote then that the women of the villages were fond of securing in trade and hoarding rare forms and weaves.　The best that can be now done is to classify Pueblo basketry as follows:

(1) What the women are actually making and old material precisely like it.

(2) Specimens dug from sites of old pueblos and carefully labeled.

(3) Old materials stored up in the modern pueblos, handed down from the past, whose authorship is not known.

If all this material could be assembled a variety of technical processes would be revealed, some of them common over wide areas and a few characteristic of the pueblo culture.　The following weaves are among the list:

(1) Checker weaving, rare.

(2) Wicker weaving, coarse and fine.

(3) Twilled work, in hard stems and in yucca.

(4) Twined work of many kinds on old baskets.　Thought to be intrusive.

(5) Coiled work with foundation of stems, splints, grass, and shredded leaves.　The fine wicker and the thick coiled plaques are peculiar.　The great variety mentioned is quite as much between pueblos as between these and tribes outside.　The Hopi are noteworthy in this regard, having in their hands the making of the two unique kinds of weave in their sacred meal plaques.　A better insight into these differences will be gained by an examination of specimens.

Plate 212 represents two ancient coiled basket jars collected at the pueblo of Sia, on the Jemez River, a tributary of the Rio Grande in New Mexico.　The Indians of this pueblo belong to the Keresan family.　The characteristics to be observed and studied on these speci-

---

[a] For a list of pueblos see Seventh Annual Report of the Bureau of Ethnology, under the words Keresan, Shoshonean, Tañoan, and Zuñian; for ruins see bibliography under Fewkes, Hough, Keam, Mindeleff.

mens are the following: The foundation is of splints, the sewing is done with willow or rhus, and the stitches are just barely carried around a small portion of the foundation underneath where they are interlocked. Note also that the ornamentation—an ascending spiral—is in one case a rhombic figure and in the other is built up of little rectangles formed by counting stitches, which may be few or many, as the curve on the body of the basket expands or contracts. This mingling of very simple elementary forms is capable of an infinite variety in treatment.

The attention of the student is especially called to the margins of these baskets, which appear to be in a three-strand plait; but they are really done in a single splint which passes backward over the foundation, then under and forward, inclosing the rod underneath, forming a figure of 8, and the multiplication of this produces on the surface the braided appearance. For detail, see page 276, fig. 87. Catalogue Nos. 134214, 134215. Collected by James Stevenson.

Although there may be seen at the pueblo of Zuñi all sorts of baskets, the most of them include pitched bottles for water, coiled and whipped trays, Hopi-coiled and wicker-basket trays, but it is not to be understood that they were necessarily made there. The only work made by the Zuñi nowadays is their small, rough peach baskets, of twigs and wickerwork, hardly worthy of notice except for their ugliness and simplicity. Those who are familiar with this interesting tribe of Indians say that trading is a passion with them, and that through their agricultural products and their refined loom work they are able to gratify this taste among the surrounding tribes for old basketry.

Plate 213 shows some old so-called Zuñi ware, collected for the Bureau of American Ethnology by James Stevenson in New Mexico long ago.

Fig. 1 is a wicker basket, globular form. The warp consists of a number of stems of *Chrysothamnus* laid flat. The weft of the same material is in wickerwork, the border being fastened down in coiled sewing with yucca leaf. Handle, a rawhide thong. Used by these Indians in gathering fruit and other food substances. Height, 8 inches. Cat. No. 68603, U.S.N.M.

Fig. 2 is a jar-shaped basket of *Chrysothamnus* (*Bigelovia*) splints. The warp is radiating at the bottom and parallel on the body; the whole basket is made in twilled style of twined weaving over two. The border is not finished off. The handle is a rawhide thong around the neck. This is a very coarse specimen of twined work. The height is 8 inches. Cat. No. 68480, U.S.N.M.

Fig. 3 is a rare and interesting specimen of twined basket jar. The bottom has radiating warp and is in coarse twilled weaving, but the body from the bottom to the upper margin is plain, twined weaving, without variation. There is not in the National Museum collection from this Pueblo region another basket in which the whole body is treated in this monotonous manner. Its height is 8½ inches. Cat. No. 68513, U.S.N.M.

Fig. 4 is a water-tight jar from the Zuñi Indians. The whole surface of the object is in twilled type of twined weaving and well saturated in pitch. The characteristic feature is the lugs of wood on the side for the carrying strap, and flattening of the surface between these lugs, as in a canteen. This is partially shown in the photographs, but is quite apparent on the jar itself. Its height is 9 inches. Cat. No. 68515, U.S.N.M.

Fig. 5 is a water-tight basket jar constricted in the middle for the attachment of a carrying strap. The whole surface is in coarse twilled weaving in two-strand twine with the exception of one row between the bottom and the body, which is in three-strand. The constriction of the body is said to be an imitation of a custom of tying rag around the young gourd so as to stop its growth, which results in a modification, useful for holding the carrying strap. Its height is 9 inches. Cat. No. 68541, U.S.N.M.

Fig. 6 is a water-tight basket jar from the Zuñi Indians, symmetrical in outline. It is in the twilled type of twined weaving, with wooden lugs on the side and no flattening of surface between them. Its height is 7½ inches. Cat. No. 68502, U.S.N.M.

Fig. 7 is a gathering basket from the Zuñi Indians. The weaving on the bottom and the body is in the twilled type of twined work; the neck, on the contrary, has about an inch of plain twined weaving and is finished off with four rows of three-strand twine. The border is in coiled sewing of yucca. This specimen, like the preceding, is made from the stems of *Chrysothamnus*. Its height is 7½ inches. Cat. No. 68491, U.S.N.M.

Fig. 8 is a gathering basket from the Zuñi Indians. The bottom is in twilled twined work; the body is in plain twined work relieved at varying distances with single rows of three-ply weaving; border finished off with coiled work in yucca. Its height is 6 inches.

The Zuñi pueblos in western New Mexico lie in the very heart of the desert region. On the east are the Rio Grande pueblos, on the northwest the Moki, and far to the south the Gila River. Beside the settled communities long inhabiting this region, the Navaho and Apache are close at hand on every side, and the Utes are not far away. There is no surprise, therefore, in finding on the same plate illustrations of wickerwork, twined work in its many varieties of plain twilled and three-strand work, and all of these at times on the same piece of basketry.

Plate 214 shows a rare lot of old coiled baskets, chiefly from Zuñi and Sia, in New Mexico, collected under the direction of Major J. W.

Powell, by James Stevenson, of the Bureau of American Ethnology. They appear to be of the three-rod variety, though splints may take the place of rods in some of them. They are catalogued as follows in the order named:

Top row—

1. No. 68471, Zuñi, James Stevenson; length, 9½ inches.
2. No. 68550, Zuñi, James Stevenson; height, 4¼ inches.
3. No. 68474, Zuñi, James Stevenson; height, 7 inches.
4. No. 68472, Zuñi, James Stevenson; height, 4¾ inches.
5. No. 42140, Zuñi, James Stevenson; height, 4¼ inches.

Bottom row—

1. No. 68489, Zuñi, James Stevenson; height, 4¾ inches.
2. No. 166800, Apache, James Mooney; height, 8¾ inches.
3. No. 134215, Sia, James Stevenson; diameter, 11½ inches.
4. No. 134214, Sia, James Stevenson; height, 12 inches.
5. No. 42168, Zuñi, James Stevenson; height, 4 inches.

A jar-shaped coiled basket attributed by the collector to the Zuñi Indians is shown in fig. 189. It is a very beautiful and smooth piece of coiled ware, to which justice is not done by the drawing. In regularity of stitch, symmetrical shape, and ornamentation it is almost without fault. It belongs to the class of technic termed in this treatise rod and welt. The foundation consists of a single rod, over which is laid a thin splint, perhaps of the same material. The stitch passes over rod and welt in the row that is in progress of manufacture, and not only locks with the stitch underneath but in each case takes up the welt. This forms an excellent packing. The stitches are crowded so closely together that in the original those of the different rows lie practically one over the other, with a slight inclination from the perpendicular. On the bottom, not shown here, it has a circle in black from which radiates six spiral rays. On the body the ornamentation is as shown in the figure. It is made from the pod of *Martynia louisiana*. On the shoulder two lugs of leather are sewed for the purpose of carrying the jar, being intended, doubtless, for the transportation of food or water. It is customary to attribute such ware to the Apache Indians, although in the National Museum there are quite a number of very old coiled jars of this type and fine workmanship purporting to come from the Zuñi Indians. This specimen was gotten by Major Powell, one of the most careful collectors, so that there is no doubt of the location. It is possible, however, that the Zuñi, since they are potters, may have acquired this coiled specimen in traffic.

The detail of this texture, both in its sewing and ornamentation, is illustrated in fig. 48, also by Cushing [a].

---

[a] Fourth Annual Report of the Bureau of Ethnology, 1886, p. 486.

This specimen, Catalogue No. 68546 in the U. S. National Museum, was procured in New Mexico by James Stevenson. Its width is 9 inches and depth 10 inches.

The Hopi pueblo settlement, called also Moki, in the ancient province of Tusayan, is made up of the following-named villages, in order from east to west: Walpi, Hā′no or Tē′wa, Sichōmōvi, Shipaulovi, Mŭsh-ŏngŭnŭvi, Shumōpavi, Oraibi. Here in these seven old towns are

FIG. 189.
COILED BASKET JAR.
Zuñi Indians, New Mexico.
Cat. No. 68546, U.S.N.M. Collected by J. W. Powell.

made all kinds of basket work. From Dr. Walter Hough the following information is received: The thick North-African-like coiled plaques are from Mŭshŏngŭnŭvi, Shipaulovi, and Shumōpavi, all on the middle mesa, and nowhere else in the Western Hemisphere. The material for the foundation is stems of Takashu (*Hilaria jamesii*), gathered in October. The sewing is done with narrow strips from the leaves of Mohu (*Yucca glauca*) in the natural color of the outside or the interior, or nowadays dyed in aniline colors. Formerly vegetal dyes were employed, red brown Ohaishi (*Thelesperma gracile*); dark blue from seeds of Akaushi (*Helianthus petiolaris*); yellow from Asapzrani (*Carthamus tinctorius*); green or blue, rarely seen on old baskets. The following are their terms for basketry.

Apa, blanket mat. (Anciently made in checker weaving.)

Chu ku pö eta, also Chu ku böt se buh, Havasupai.

Shio eñ ya puh, Oraibi wicker tray.

Du tsi ye, or Du tsai ya, sifting basket.

Hó a pūh, carrying basket (wicker over frame of bent sticks crossed).

Kŏm che, awl of bone.

Hush tush shum pi, or Ko tuc, basket for parched corn.

Kwakü ütshpi (hay cover), twined mat for kiva hatch.

Pek ech be, piki tray (food tray).

Pö eta, basket plaque (coiled).

Se boch be (Oraibi basket).

Tümni, flat basket in Soyalana rites.

Wiko zhro, pitched bottle.

Plate 215 is the portrait of Kuchyeampsi, the Mŭshŏngŭnŭvi weaver of coiled plaques. Figures and colored plates of this ware are shown. (See Plates 30, 47, 85, 93.) Photographed by George Wharton James.

Wicker baskets are made at the Hopi pueblo, Oraibi. The radiating framework is of slender shoots of sübi, *Rhus trilobata*. The interwoven element is of branches of hanoshivapi, *Chrysothamnus graveolens*, also called *Bigelovia*, carefully smoothed and dyed, as in the coiled baskets, red brown, red, yellow, dark blue, purple, green, blue and white, the latter with kaolin.

The white of the background is applied after the basket is finished. The edge of the basket is finished with a winding of yucca over the several rods of rhus bent down after the basket has reached the size required. This edge is often painted with red ocher (Hough). The framework consists of two cross sets of twigs, four or more in a bar of the cross. These are firmly held together at their intersection by weaving. They are then spread out radially, the space being from time to time supplemented by additional stems. The worker provides herself with bunches of white, yellow, orange, purple, black, blue, and green twigs only a few inches in length. These she proceeds to weave into patterns of the greatest beauty, even imitating cloud effects seen on Japanese screens, using long or short twigs as the occasion demands, hiding the ends between the ribs and the filling of the preceding coils. (See Plate 216.)

The variety of ornament created with these poor appliances is marvelous. In no other tribe of Indians and in no other type of basketry are more striking effects realized. It seems almost as though the women had set themselves the problem of producing with the least pliable materials the most versatile of effects, in which are embodied the symbols of an intricate ritual, in all grades of symbolism from the pictograph to the mere conventional mathematical scene. Both, however, represent the same ideas. Under the influence of trade the ancient patterns are really mosaics and could be picked out. It will be easily seen that the figures on the back and front do not exactly conform, the corresponding square on the back being always one space to the right or left of the same in front.

Attention is called at this point to the ornamental beginning of the wicker plaque, or sacred meal baskets. In the chapter on structure attention is directed to the methods of holding the central warp stems together before bending them apart radially. Two methods are resorted to. On one, half a dozen or more stems are laid side by side and wrapped together by a process shown in fig. 38, after Miss White. The same number of stems are similarly joined and laid under this at right angles, the whole twelve being bound together by one or two rows of wicker weaving. From this central point the twelve or more wrapped stems are bent apart at equal distances and the regular wicker weaving proceeds. At a certain distance outward new warp stems are added between each pair of those already in use, and from this circle the weaving proceeds to the margin.

With the same number of warp stems quite a different process is sometimes employed, by which the two sets of the upper and lower are held together in pairs by wicker weaving, and at an inch from the center the whole series are bound together as before and widening and weaving proceed in the same manner.

Fig. 190 is a coarse wicker tray of the Hopi Indians of northeastern Arizona, and is introduced for the purpose of illustrating the method in which the much finer work on the sacred meal trays is done. Here may be seen the plan of starting out with a few stems crossing each other at right angles for warp; the method of hiding the large end of the weft stems to become a portion of the warp, and the method of adding new warp stems as they are needed. Especial attention is called to the way in which several stems for weft are introduced at the same time and worked along in sets or series. The common method of working out the twill would be to introduce a weft stem, carry it as far as it would go, and then insert a new weft stem, but in this case the series of half a dozen stems are all worked at the same time. Compare description of a Mexican wicker basket, on page 527.

The modern twilled basketry is as rough as it can be. The same is true of the flat mats used about their dwellings; in fact, the mat and the basket are identical in weaving. The basket is formed by bending the mat over the edge of a hoop and sewing down with a row of twined weaving.

Plate 217, from a photograph the gift of G. Wharton James, represents an ancient basket maker of Oraibi. The picture is interesting beyond the mere twilled basket which she holds in her hand in the act of mending a broken strand.   The corn, the mixture of objects belonging to civilization and savagery, the homespun and woven clothing on herself, and the maiden at her side are all a study in the culture of the region.   The adobe and stone wall and the coarse beams of wood inset must be included.   It is an excellent picture of very little modified savage life.   Yucca baskets and trays are made by the Hopi in plain checker; although the material is coarse, quite pleasing effects are produced by means of the two sides of leaf and different shades of the same size.

The twined ware of the Hopi are a few peach baskets and other domestic utensils, made in the same manner as the Ute hats, but there

FIG. 190.
COARSE WICKERWORK.
Hopi Indians, Arizona.

is enough dissimilarity of form to give the Hopi the credit of inventing this peculiar style.   (See Plate 218, figs. 4 and 7.)

Plate 218 shows a collection from Oraibi, the westernmost of the Hopi pueblos in northeastern Arizona, gathered by Colonel James Stevenson and Cosmos Mindeleff.   The three types of work always in mind when Oraibi and the pueblos of the adjoining mesa are mentioned, to wit, twilled, thick coils, and wicker, are utterly wanting here.   The cosmopolitan character of the Hopi is further attested by the varieties of technic in the plate.   The baskets on the upper row are as follows, from left to right:

1. Water-tight coiled jar, with foundation of rods, sewing material of willow splints, the stitches interlocking, but not taking in any of

the foundation below. Catalogue No. 42106 in the U. S. National Museum. Height, 7½ inches. The lugs on the side are of horsehair.

2. An old flat coiled dish, No. 41227, said to have come from Zuñi, in western New Mexico, 7¼ inches in diameter.

3. A delightful old gathering basket, No. 42126, from Oraibi. It is of the three-rod coiled variety and might be taken for the original elegant Pomo Bamtsuwu. Each stitch passes over three rods of the current foundation and under the upper rod of the coil underneath. Its height is 7¼ inches.

4. A gathering basket in twilled twined technic. On the bottom is a projection whose function is not known. Notice on the shoulder three rows of twined work over two warps. The difference between this and twilled work lies in this, that the weft elements embrace the same pairs of warps and are superposed. The border is finished off with a neat herringbone stitch. Catalogue No. 83977, U. S. National Museum. Its height is 6 inches.

The old pieces on the lower row are equally interesting.

1. A globose coiled jar in three-rod foundation. The workmanship is coarse, but the form is suggestive of old pottery. This specimen is No. 84596, U. S. National Museum, and is 7 inches in height.

2. A water jar in three-rod coil, modern, with lugs of horsehair on the side for carrying. The border is fastened off with a kind of sewing, here called false braid. The material for making the vessel water-tight is pine resin. Catalogue No. 42107, U. S. National Museum. Its height is 10 inches.

3. This interesting piece of water-tight twilled twined work is strengthened by an interior framework similar to that seen often in the large Zuñi packing baskets for donkeys, and suggests the possibility of transporting water in the same fashion. The weaving is rude, but all the better for holding pitch. The border, however, is neatly done in false braid. Catalogue No. 68506, U. S. National Museum. Its height is 15 inches.

4. The water jar constricted in the middle might with propriety be called a canteen. Frequently the savages in this arid region tie a bandage around a young gourd which afterwards takes the shape here shown. The foundation of the coil is more like that of Apache, the stitches interlocking. Indeed, the piece is labeled "old Apache" by the collector. It is numbered 40109 and is 8¼ inches high.

5. A water jar or pitcher in three-rod coil. It should be compared with No. 1 in the same row, secured in Oraibi by the same person. It is Catalogue No. 84596, U. S. National Museum. Its height is 8½ inches.

Fig. 191 is an ancient miniature gaming wheel used frequently in the ceremonials of the modern Pueblo Indians. Then, as now, the hoop of wood was made and a series of half-hitches passed around the inner side, done in yucca fiber.   This process was repeated upon the loops thus constituted until the center of the wheel was reached.   It is in effect a kind of coiled work in which the foundation is absent. Collected by James Stevenson.

Dr. J. Walter Fewkes was so fortunate as to recover from the Chevlon ruin, 15 miles from Winslow and in sight of the station Hardy on the Santa Fé Railroad, fragments of ancient basketry, shown in the accompanying plates.   The custom of burying baskets with the dead is still preserved in the Tusayan towns, and from the specimens here figured, it has been inherited from ancient times. Baskets, says Fewkes, are not now made at the east mesa, and the craft is confined to the middle mesa and Oraibi.

FIG. 191.
ANCIENT BASKETRY GAMING WHEEL.
Pueblo Indians, New Mexico.
Collected by James Stevenson.

The wicker baskets from several graves at Chevlon were identical with those made to-day in the pueblo of Oraibi.   Some of these specimens were painted on the surface a green color with malachite, or blue with azurite.   In other examples the small stems had been stained before they were woven.   Plate 219 represents a segment from a wicker basket made from the stems of *Chrysothamnus graveolens*. The warp consists of small bundles of stems; the weft, of the same material barked and smoothed down, in some places dyed.   The interesting feature of the specimen is the increasing of the number of warp elements as the basket enlarges.   At first in the drawing there are five bundles of stems; about 2 inches lower down the number is increased to seven, and near the bottom, by the introduction of new stems, ten warp elements are provided for. As in the modern basketry, in this ancient example the weft is soaked and woven in that condition and pressed home so effectually that the warp is invisible.

In Plate 220, fig. 1, is shown a specimen of ancient matting in twilled weaving. The work is done in split yucca leaves, just as to-day, and in certain places the figure shows where the leaf was stripped from the stalk. Examining the thousands of mats and soft baskets from the same pueblo reveals the identical method of doing the twilled work, but in a great many of the modern examples regular diaper patterns are introduced. In the same plate (fig. 3) is an ancient example of coiled basketry, having foundation of three stems or rods. By referring to the California basketry it will be seen that this foundation is the same. This makes a very smooth surface, easily distinguishable from the rugose condition of Apache basket built on a single rod.[a]

These specimens are Catalogue Nos. 157912, 157915, 157918 in the U. S. National Museum, and were procured at Chevlon, Arizona, by Dr. J. Walter Fewkes.

Plates 221, 222 illustrate the forms and uses of basketry in the pueblos of northeastern Arizona before the coming of the whites. The explorations of Dr. J. Walter Fewkes in Sikyatki and Awatobi, and the Museum-Gates expedition in 1901 to examine two ruins on the Jetyto Wash, a few miles from Keams Canyon, have brought to light wicker, twilled, and coiled basketry. The wickerwork is precisely identical with the little wicker trays or plaques made in the pueblo of Oraibi and used in their religious ceremonies. The twilled work is the matting of to-day, and the coiled resembles that of the Utes or Pimas rather than the Apaches, having a foundation not of rods, but of fine material. The uses of the basketry must have been in all respects as among the Hopis of our day, but Plate 223 shows the connection of such material with the care of the dead (Catalogue No. 213074). The plate illustrates the fact that coarse wicker matting was placed in the bottom of the grave; on this was laid a matting of yucca fiber, and on this was deposited the body. In the dressing of the hair, then as now, a plaited cord of human hair was employed. A description of its discovery appears in Dr. Walter Hough's paper, Archeological Field Work in Northeastern Arizona.

Judging from the artifacts secured by the Museum-Gates expedition, these pueblos belong to the type of Awatobi and Sityatki, and, as far as appearances go, may have been contemporaneous. Dr. Fewkes regards Sityatki as one of the most ancient pueblos of the Hopi group. It is well known that Awatobi was inhabited up to the year 1700, but

---

[a] Smithsonian Report, 1896, pls. xxxii and xxxiii, after Fewkes.

there is no historical reference to the pueblos from which these specimens were derived, and there is no evidence of the Iron Age in them. It seems probable, however, that they date before the year 1700, but just how much anterior it is not possible at present to say. [a]

ATHAPASCAN BASKETRY

A summary of Athapascan basketry in its ethnic areas would include the following:

The northern Athapascans in the interior of Alaska and in the Mackenzie drainage make coiled basketry in a variety of types, the material being willow and root of the conifers. The Pacific coast group, living formerly in Washington, Oregon, and northwestern California, near the sea, of which the Hupas are the best known, excel in twined work with decoration in overlaying, but these tribes have not the versatility of the Pomo, farther south. All the weaving is of one variety, well known in the region.

The southern Athapascans, under many names, practice both coiled and twined basketry. They base their coiled work on hard stems and sew them with splints of cottonwood, mulberry, sumac, and willow or strips of yucca. They also used agave fiber.

The mescal plant (*Agave americana*), says Bourke, is to the Apache what the palm is to the East. It is baked in ovens for victuals and its juice is fermented to make a drink. For the basket maker the thorns are good needles, the fibers excellent thread material, and the flower stalk forms the frame of the carrying outfit.

The Apaches or southern Athapascan basket makers were formerly spread over eastern Arizona, western New Mexico, and in Texas along the Rio Grande, as will be seen in Powell's linguistic map. [b] They were gathered on reservations by Gen. Nelson A. Miles. Scattered bands are to be found here and there. Mr. James mentions one near Short Horn Mountains and in the neighborhood of Palomas and Agua Caliente, comprising about thirty families of basket makers. The collector or student must not be surprised, therefore, if in the hands of Apaches are seen work of other tribes. Indeed, he will frequently see the women borrowing materials, structures, forms, and even designs from outside. A large and varied collection of Apache ware is exhibited in the Free Museum of Phoenix, Arizona, collected by Messrs. Benham.

On the authority of Mrs. J. S. Newman there are five tribes on the Apache Reservation, and a few scattered members of other tribes, but five to class as basket makers. Of these the Tonto should rank first, making chiefly ollas, which require more skill than plaques or bowl shapes, and their work is universally even and good. Their

---

[a] Archeological field work in northeastern Arizona. The Museum-Gates expedition, 1901. Walter Hough, Report of the U. S. National Museum, 1901, pp. 279–358.

[b] Seventh Annual Report of the Bureau of Ethnology, 1891, pocket.

specimens are nearly always marked with the arrow point, the pattern running vertically from the center. Their proficiency is accounted for in the fact that the land allowed them on the Gila River is the least productive of any on the reservation, hence their dependence on basket making for a living.

The center or beginning of either Apache coiled bowl or olla is always wrapped with black (devil claw) and the rim finished with the same stitch as that used throughout the body of the work, both or either colors being used.

Plate 224 is a number of Apache coiled bowls belonging to the collection of J. W. Benham. The foundation is in whole stem and the sewing done with splints of white wood and martynia. A comparison of these ten pieces reveals tolerably well the genius of Apache decorations. There are discrete figures of men and beasts; there are both radial and concentric designs; in the crenelated (fig. 10) and fretted motives (figs. 5 and 9) suggestions arise which point to the Tulare area. The Apache, naturally a wanderer, has picked up here a little and there a little of design.

The White Mountain Apaches are clustered around Camp Apache, the agency, and on two of the large creeks running south from the Mogollon mesa. The art of basket making is not actively practiced at present, the younger members of the tribe finding it difficult to learn and saying that it injures their hands. Some of the old women, however, retain the ancient skill, and even superior work may be secured from the reservation. It may be said that the carrying baskets and the pitched water bottles are as frequently made as ever and are in constant use, whereas the finer bowls, which were formerly common, as among the Pueblo tribes, for storing meal, etc., are growing rarer every year and command high prices.

The baskets shown in Plate 225, Catalogue Nos. 213262 and 213268, U. S. National Museum, were secured at the agency in the summer of 1901.

Fig. 1 is a small, well-woven bowl, the design representing the sunflower.

The second figure is a modern basket with geometrical pattern, which in certain portions is quite inaccurately worked out. On the whole the design is excellent.

Plate 226 represents coiled basket bowls of the White Mountain Apache. The foundation of the upper figure is of willow, the sewing in splints of white wood and martynia in alternate rows, which are divided into four sections by V-shaped ornaments effected by changing the direction of the lines in black.

The lower figure is the same material, foundation of rods, sewing in white and black coarsely done, stitches scarcely touching. The whole surface is covered with rhomboidal figures produced by crossing of four sets of lines in pairs, passing in cycloidal curves from the bottom to the margin.   Catalogue Nos. 213264 and 213265.

The specimens were collected by Dr. Walter Hough on White Mountain Apache Reservation, 100 miles south of Holbrook, Arizona.

The symbol is that of the martynia hooks, the sharp points having been allowed to project from the inner surface in certain areas.

The shoots for basket material are gathered in the spring, tied in bundles, and put away in the houses for future use, sometimes with the bark on, at others without.   When the basket maker is ready the osiers are soaked thoroughly in water; the stems are employed whole for the foundation of the coil, and the sewing is done only with the outer layer, the inner portions being peeled off and the splints scraped. One end is held in the mouth, the other in the left hand, while the steel knife, formerly the stone knife, is used in the right hand.

The ornamentation on all this basketry is in *Martynia louisiana*, or devil's claw (Tahuate), the design itself often being the figure of the plant.   The awl used in the sewing is called by the White Mountain Indian, tsatl; the coiled bowl, tsa; the spindle-shaped water jar, tose; the carrying basket of twined work, ta tsa; the gathering scoop, pen al té, and the shoots of wood, tsin.

FIG. 192.
COILED BOWL.
Coyotero Indians, Arizona.
Collected by H. W. Read.

Fig. 192 shows the ornamentation on a coiled basket bowl of the Coyotero, on the San Carlos Agency, in southern Arizona.   The parts are in threes; the smaller design is made up of a combination of little squares and triangles, the larger design being more complicated in its elements, with its three vase-shaped parts, which terminate in the dark circle of the center.   The meaning of this design is unknown.

This specimen, Catalogue No 4428 in the U. S. National Museum, was collected on the Gila River, Arizona, by H. W. Read.

Fig. 193 is an old bottle-shaped coiled basket, made, according to Dr. Hough, long ago by the Mescalero Apache, before they adopted the present wide variety.   The foundation of the coil consists of a rigid stem overlaid with soft fiber.   The stitching passes over the foundation of the coil, under the packing of the coil underneath. The sewing is done with splints of willow or cottonwood. The ornamentation consists of six rows of coiling in brown material on the neck, a row of black material on the shoulder, with two rows of chevrons on the body. The latest Apache has only black and white in decoration; red and brown are old and rare.

This specimen, Catalogue No. 21494 in the U. S. National Museum, was collected in Arizona by Dr. J. B. White, U. S. Army.

FIG. 193.
BASKET JAR.
Apache Indians.
Collected by J. B. White.

Fig. 194 is a design on a coiled basket bowl of the Apache. The foundation of the bowl is the rod-and-splint pattern, and the sewing passes over it, under the splints of the coil below, the stitches interlocking. The design is in *Martynia louisiana*. The apparently unsystematic ornamentation is, in effect, perfectly regular. Four lines of black stitching, of the same lengths in each, proceed from a black ring around the center. From the ends of these lines the sewing is to the left in regular curves. The four radiating lines are repeated and then the curved lines until the border is reached. The suggestion of lightning or the limbs of some insect has been made out. The design has not been explained by any basket maker.

This specimen, Catalogue No. 21493 in the U. S. National Museum, was collected in Arizona by Dr. J. B. White, U. S. Army.

Plate 227 represents a jar and a plaque by the Mescalero Apache Indians of New Mexico, collected by Dr. Walter Hough, Catalogue Nos. 204651 and 204646 in the U. S. National Museum. Especial attention is directed to the width of the coils in these baskets. It will be remembered that the Fraser River tribes in British Columbia obtained an economical result of widening coils by the introduction of narrow strips of wood instead of the roots or bundles of grass for the foundation. These Apache Indians have also discovered that using two or more rods, one lying on the top of the other, would give the same result. The stitches in yucca also, instead of passing underneath another rod in the coil below, are simply interlocked with the stitches underneath. The ornamentation is produced by different colors of the same substance. The outside of the leaf is green in different shades, but the inside of the split leaf is perfectly white. By exposing the inside or the outside the angular ornamentation results. In such wide foundation the designs must be very simple. The dark lines in the lower figure are produced by using the small roots of the same plant in sewing. This fiber is very much more brittle than the leaf. Comparing these two examples with the plaques of the Hopi Indians demonstrates better than any other figures yet employed the limitations of the basket maker in the very elements of ornamentation. Each separate part of the mosaic is a long stitch, set vertically in the jar and radially on the plaque or bowl. From this the basket maker can not escape.

FIG. 194.
COILED BASKET BOWL.
Apache Indians.
Collected by J. B. White.

Fig. 195 is labeled coiled basket of the Navaho. On the authority of C. M. O'Leary, of Abbottsford Inn, Los Angeles, California, the Navaho do not manufacture baskets; but they use a ceremonial basket that is made by the Apaches and comes from Arizona. Other observers attribute these curious pieces to the Ute; but old Navaho women still understand the art.

In this example the foundation is a single rod. The body color of the bowl is that of the wood. The ornamentation is in splints of rhus dyed mahogany brown and black, and consists of four quadrants in each of which is a cross-shaped figure. The boundary of the space is black, filled in with brown. The figure is in the color of the wood and has a black border. In the sewing the stitches simply interlock with those underneath. The border of the specimen is worthy of study, being what is called elsewhere false braid. The

FIG. 195.
COILED PLAQUE.
Navaho Indians.

Apaches, on the contrary, make borders in plain coil. Catalogue No. 16510 in the United States National Musem was collected in 1873 by Governor Arny, of New Mexico.

Plate 228 is a collection of Navaho sacred basket drums belonging to C. P. Wilcomb. Baskets attributed to the Navaho are extremely uniform in every respect. On the authority of Dr. Washington Matthews the sewing material is splints of sumac (*Rhus aromatica*). Some Indians told Dr. Hough that the material was tsin, a species of willow growing along the washes. The stitches in the sewing simply interlock, and there is no attempt made to pass into the foundation of the coil underneath. The borders are in false braid

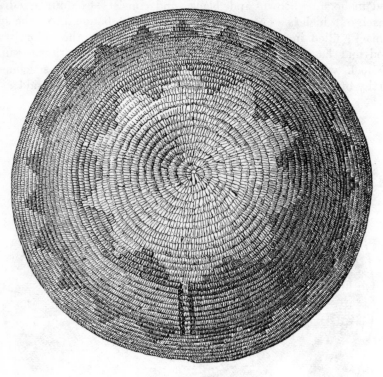

FIG. 196.
SACRED BASKET TRAY.
Navaho Indians.
Collected by Governor Arny.

passing by a "figure of eight" movement under the foundation and over the outer margin. In the ancient days a Navaho woman invented

FIG. 197.
BORDER OF FIG. 196.

this pretty border. She was seated under a juniper tree finishing her work in the old, plain way, when the god Hastseyath threw a small spray of juniper into her basket. Happy thought! She imitated the fold of the leaves on the border and the invention was complete. (Matthews.)

The decoration also of the Navaho baskets is in designs taking the form of bands for their sacred drums (fig. 196), and of crosses (fig. 195) for their sacred meal baskets. The colored bands on the drums are founded on a central stripe which may be light or dark, and from the borders project variously notched or angular figures. The one characteristic to which attention is always directed in this ware is the break in the band. It is mentioned elsewhere on the authority of Matthews that a line drawn from the center of the basket through this open pathway will end at the point where the basket was finished off, and when it is used as a drum this is the point where the hand of the medicine man must be placed in the plaque, the radial line pointing eastward. Another interpretation of this, which can not here be proven, is that this break in the ornamentation has something to do with the passing backward and forward of the spirit of the basket, as in the Pueblo pottery decoration.[a] (See figs. 196 and 197.)

Dr. Ales Hrdlicka writes that the basket work of the Hualapai and Havasupai can be studied better by having it understood that although both these peoples are associated with the Yuman family linguistically, they are decidedly one with the Apaches in physical characteristics. Their basketry, therefore, will have to be compared with that of the Apaches and not that of the Mission Indians of southern California, who are Yuman. The foundation is a solid stem with a welt. The sewing is done with splints of willow, and also now with those made from the young and tender suckers from the cottonwood tree, from 2 to 3 feet in length. The geometric ornamentation is in martynia. Among the Hualapai and Havasupai there are three kinds of baskets—that is, three forms exist, but the Havasupai are the best workwomen. The first is coarse coiled ware. When the twining is going on they leave the finished ends projecting outside and inside until the whole basket is completed and afterwards they are trimmed off all at the same time. The second is a plain coiled bowl in the shape of a caraffe, covered with pitch to make it water-tight. The third is decorated coiled work. The first is a plaque with black decoration in martynia only. The second shape is more or less cylindrical, or the rim turning in or tending toward a spherical form. In the plaque there is seldom any other decorative color than black, but the other forms, cylindrical and globose, have various colors, although mostly different shades of red. The designs are tooth-shaped or dentated, star-shaped, and crenelated. No curved lines or animal forms are used. The Hualapai also make conical carrying baskets with a head-band, the decorations being meager and consist only of lines, no geometric figures being used. Occasionally designs are painted, not woven. (See Plate 229.)

Plate 230, fig. 2, represents a Havasupai coiled basket bowl. The foundation is of rods and splints of willow and the sewing is the same. The most interesting feature is the border. It is false braid in which two rows of the coil are involved. A single splint passes down and includes

---

[a] See Washington Matthews, The Night Chant, a Navaho Ceremony. Memoirs of the American Museum Natural History, VI, pp. 1–332, New York, 1902.

both foundations, up, over, and under the upper foundation only, then back and under both to the point of beginning. This is an old specimen, had been in the possession of a family for many years. From the Sichomovi (Hopi) Pueblo, made by the Havasupai (Yuman) Indians, collected by Dr. Walter Hough.

Plate 231 represents the Havasupai basket maker at her home, which is in Cataract Canyon emptying into the Colorado River from the south, in northwestern Arizona. The most interesting feature of this plate is the association of the basket maker with her home. The steep wall of the canyon forms the back of the house, and a slight brush awning covered with grass is her shelter. So far as the house is concerned, we are as near to the lowest savage and primitive man as it is possible to get, but in the woman and her work we are on the top round of savagery. The Apache-Yuma basket makers at Palomas, Arizona, sit in front of their brush and straw shelters the same as the Pimas, hold the right side of the plaque or bowl inward, and work their sewing toward the left hand. (G. C. Simms, Field Columbian Museum.) In the previous plate the woman is making coiled basketry, but in the one here given by George Wharton James the bottle and the carrying baskets are in twilled or diagonal-twined weaving.

The Walapai, spelled often Hualapai, from Walla, tall pine, Pai, people, are also of the Yuman family and dwell near Truxton, Hackberry, and Kingman, in northern Arizona. There are less than 600 of them. They make water jars of several shapes and many sizes; household baskets and plaques, never decorated, often covered with pitch on the inside, always shallow; more or less cylindrical baskets with geometric designs in martynia, rarely painted bluish, red or white on the outside; the same with bail-like handles; great conical carrying baskets, sparingly decorated; small plaques, finer work, splints dyed; baby boards, and fanciful shapes. These are coiled on the rod and splint foundation and resemble Apache. Basketry terms are:

Wi-uat we-se-ma, prepared root of yucca, of brownish-red color.

Ma-k-tu-na, red roots of a little plant on the mountains.

K-he-é, or K-he-e-he-vah, reeds used for vertical ribs, also white or green fiber.

Ma-tha-kigh, reed for making baby boards, hoods, also for warps of baskets. An example was collected by Dr. Hrdlicka, ornamented with triangles and crenelated lines in pink and black.

The Mohave Indians (Yuman family) do not make baskets, but obtain them from other tribes, and examples will be found in every house. They obtain their rabbit-skin robes, done in twined weaving, from Paiutes (Shoshonean family) and Walapai (Yuman family). The Mohaves make constant use of the wrapped weaving. (See page 231, and Plate 17.)

The Chemehuevi are Shoshonean linguistically, and are now located on the Colorado River Agency, Arizona. They make coiled baskets. The foundation is a rod and the sewing is done with willow or other splints, maybe cottonwood. The black figures are in the pods of martynia. Only two colors are used; frequently, however, feathers are introduced under the stitches. They are the most tastefully made and the most beautiful baskets in that whole region. Catalogue No. 211028 is a Chemehuevi plaque in the National Museum collected by Captain Paul B. Carter, U. S. A. The ornamentation consists in a black center and two bands done in martynia pod. The surface is covered with a network of rhombs. Plate 232 is a collection of Chemehuevi plaques and jars in coiled weaving now in the U. S. National Museum. Especial attention is called to the purely geo metric figures on the surface, star, toothed lines, rhombs in bands, crenelated and ser rated lines in great variety. In the central figure the middle band recalls the design, a modification of which becomes the well-known flying butterfly pattern. (See Plate 195.)

FIG. 198.
GOURD IN COILED NETWORK.
Pima Indians, Arizona.
Cat. No. 76047, U.S.N.M.
Collected by Edward Palmer.

The tribes of the Piman family are in two groups, the northern, including Opata, Papago, and Pima proper; and the southern, including Cahita, Cora, Tarahumara, and Tepeguana, wholly confined to Mexico. By many scholars the Piman family would be made part of the great Uto-Aztecan.

The Piman basketry is unmistakable. The foundation is of split cat-tail stems (*Typha angustifolia*) and the sewing is with willow (*Salix nigra*) and pods of martynia, but the stitches are so fine and the work so uniform that the surface is not rugose but smooth. The Pima decoration is the exuberance of fretwork. In the National Museum are many old pieces brought home by Army officers. Edward Palmer also collected many, and recently Dr. Frank Russell has enriched the collections with material which will be the subject of a special monograph. Coiled work without foundation finds application among the Pima in the network which supports their gourd receptacles. (See fig. 198.)

It has been said that basket making was introduced among the Pima one hundred years ago, when the Maricopa sought shelter among them from the slaughter of the Yuma. At that time the Pima made pottery only. On the other hand, the Maricopa allowed basket making to fall into disuse, and now make pottery only. Both Pima and Papago make matting in twilled work, and also carrying frames covered with rude coiled lace.

They had no pails or vessels of wood, but were not slow to invent. They therefore took willows, which grow in abundance along the river, and a reed, and stripped the bark, then very adroitly split these with their teeth and wove them so closely together as to hold water. This they accomplished by means of needles or thorns of cactus, of which there are over one hundred varieties in this territory. They used these baskets while digging small ditches, the women filling them with earth and carrying them up the bank.[a]

Catalogue No. 76033, U. S. National Museum (see fig. 100), is a carrying basket (child's) of the Pima Indians, a pyramidal bag netted of the fiber of the agave; at the vertex is an opening 3 inches in diameter. The base is attached to a hoop by a string of agave fiber, with which the hoop is served; the bag is decorated with fretted work painted black and red. Two stems of the *Cereus giganteus*, 34½ inches long and one-half inch in diameter, are passed from the outside of the hoop to the inside of the bag, 10 inches apart. thence down till they pass through the opening in the vertex; at this point they cross each other at an acute angle and extend 7½ inches beyond; two other stems 14 inches long are passed into the bag, in front, in the same way, 9 inches apart, and their ends stop at the crossing of the other sticks; at this point the four are firmly lashed together and the margin of the bag at the vertex opening is fastened to the sticks.

FIG. 199.

COILED BOWL.

Pima Indians.

Collected by Edward Palmer.

Where the sticks enter the bag the hoop is tied to them by a cord of black horsehair; these also serve to tie the load in the basket. Near the bottom a small brace of wood is passed through the meshes of the bag and in front of the sticks on either side, to give it additional strength. A piece of matting of split reeds, 16 by 7 inches, is attached to the back of the basket to protect the body of the carrier; a pad of cloth is placed between the basket and matting for the same purpose.

A strong cord of twisted agave fiber, 3 feet long, is looped around the vertex; the ends passed along the posterior sticks, outside the bag, are fastened to the sticks by a loop of fiber. Above, the ends are attached to the forehead band, woven from the softened fiber of the *Yucca baccata;* it is double, and 7 inches long and 2 inches wide. The staff is of wood 21 inches long and one-half inch in diameter, painted red, ornamented at upper end with buckskin strings, and

---

[a] Isaac T. Whittemore, Among the Pimas, p. 53, Albany, N. Y., 1893.

served with agave twine; the upper end is notched. The staff is also used to support the basket in an upright position when it is unslung. (See figs. 100 and 106.) Width above, transverse, 13 inches; antero-posterior, 11 inches; depth behind, 11½ inches; front, 7¼ inches. Collected by Edward Palmer.

Fig. 199 is a coiled basket of the Pimas. The foundation is made of grass stems or cat-tail, and the sewing is done with narrow and uniform splints of cottonwood or willow, the black figures being worked in with martyn:a The puzzling and intricate ornamentation is reducible to a

FIG. 200.
COILED BOWL.
Pima Indians.
Collected by Edward Palmer.

few most simple elements and easy of construction. Four series of vertical lines start from the black bottom. At uniform distances from the beginning all the way out to the rim horizontal lines proceed to the left, terminating in small black squares. It can easily be seen that, while the vertical lines are narrow and depend upon the width of the stitches, the horizonal lines must necessarily be as wide as the rows of sewing. About two-thirds of the way from the beginning a new set of zigzags are started, and these are continued to the outer margin.

This specimen, Catalogue No. 9376 in the U. S. National Museum, was procured in Arizona by Edward Palmer, and is figured by Holmes.[a]

Fig. 200 is a coiled basket bowl of the Pima Indians. The foundation is of shredded material and the sewing is in splints of willow. The decoration is in three series, as follows: Bottom, solid black; the main portion of the body is a double row of fretwork in single lines of black; on the upper margin is a single row of fretwork. The up and down lines in this work are partly perpendicular and partly slop-

FIG. 201.
COILED BOWL.
Pima Indians.
Collected by Edward Palmer.

ing to adjust themselves to the widening of the basket. On the extreme edge, as a finish to the basket, is a false braid in black martynia.

Fig. 201 is a coiled basket bowl of the Pima Indians. The foundation is in shredded material of rush; the sewing in willow and martynia. The ornamentation consists of a black bottom, out of which rise four right-angle triangles, to which are attached a curious fret-

---

[a] Sixth Annual Report of the Bureau of Ethnology, 1888, p. 220, fig. 322.

work made up of L-shape elements. There are a number of smaller right-angle triangles worked into the figures at various points, showing that this is a constant idea in the mind of the manufacturer. Diameter, 12¼ inches; height, 4¾ inches.

This specimen, Catalogue No. 76040 in the U. S. National Museum, was collected, with many others, in Arizona by Edward Palmer. Plate 233 is a piece of the same type from the collection of C. E. Rumsey.

Plate 234 represents two Pima basket bowls in the U. S. National Museum, collections of the Bureau of Ethnology, by Dr. Frank Russell. The foundation, sewing, and border are the same as in other examples. This plate is introduced for the purpose of showing how the basket maker works out a series of concentric figures whose elements are straight lines mixed with segments of circles. The lower figure is based on a circle in black from which four points project. The concentric rings are based upon this fundamental figure absolutely. From the points segments of circles increase in length as they proceed outward. From the concave quarter of the central figure circular segments decrease in length as they proceed outward and the ends of these two sets of segments are connected by ragged straight lines. Finally the

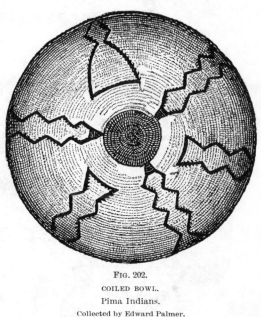

FIG. 202.
COILED BOWL.
Pima Indians.
Collected by Edward Palmer.

spaces at the four quarters on the rim are filled with small triangles in black. Could anything be more artistic than this association of the simplest elements in basket weaving?

The upper figure is on the same sort of foundation, only concentric segments alternate with series of rectangles arranged in checker patterns. These rectangles are all the same size, and are based on the four quarters projecting from the black circle. The widening of the pattern is all accomplished by the lengthening of the circular segments.[a]

Fig. 202 is a coiled basket bowl of the Pima Indians, Piman family, in southern Arizona. The foundation of the coil is in stems of finely

[a] Frank Russell, Annual Report of the Bureau of Ethnology (in preparation).

shredded fiber of cat-tail (*typha latifolia*). The sewing is in splints of willow, the stitches passing over the foundation and interlocking with those underneath. The sewing material is somewhat rigid so that the stitches are not pressed home, and the foundation shows between. Many of the stitches are split in the sewing, but it does not appear that it is systematically done for the purpose of ornamentation, as is the case with the Salish and Klikitat tribes of the farther north. The designs are in splints of martynia pod. The elements of decoration are in threes and, doubtless, have symbolic meanings, but these are not known. Diameter, 11¼ inches; height, 3½ inches.

FIG. 203.
COILED GRANARY.
Pima Indians.
Collected by Edward Palmer.

    This specimen, Catalogue No. 5548 in the U. S. National Museum, was collected in Arizona by Edward Palmer.

    Fig. 203 is a small granary of the Pima Indians, Piman family, in coiled work. The foundation is a bundle of wheat straw averaging about half an inch in diameter. The sewing is done in willow bark, the strips varying in width from a quarter to half an inch. No attempt is made to crowd the sewing material so as to hide the foundation; indeed, this would be impossible because of the width of the willow bark. The effect on the surface is to produce almost perpendicular lines from the center to the border. New rows are added as the coils enlarge.

The Pima Indians live partly on vegetable diet, the fruit of the mesquit and of other plants, and they use the granary baskets on platforms for the purpose of keeping the dried material out of the way of rodents.

To make the detail structure more clear a square inch is given in fig. 57.

This specimen, Catalogue No. 76046 in the U. S. National Museum, was collected in Arizona by Edward Palmer.

Plate 235 represents a Pima basketmaker. The Piman family have been supposed to be the connecting link between the Shoshonean of the Great Interior Basin and the Aztec or Nahuatl family of Mexico. In their present situation, however, they are cut off from the northern Shoshonean by the extension of the Yuman family.

MIDDLE AND SOUTH AMERICA

This genius [Clotho] led the souls first to cloths, and drew them within the revolution of the spindle impelled by the hand.—PLATO'S REPUBLIC.

On the border line between the Republic of Mexico and the United States is a transition between the standard forms which have hitherto been studied and the more open types of lace work and loom work. Coiled basketry of well-known varieties continues on southward, both in the lowlands and in the mountainous regions to within a few miles of the City of Mexico. Variations from these types are also in evidence, both coiled and twined, the former predominating. Foundations of grass more than an inch thick are built into immense baskets for carrying and also granaries, the sewing being done with wide strips of bark, wood, and leaves. Taking these coarse baskets for a motive, smaller and finer ones are done in better material, but still the stitches are half an inch apart. There is no occasion for surprise in this, since the linguistic families which are represented in Arizona, New Mexico, and California are also continued into the Republic of Mexico. In this area the student is clearly "within the revolution of the spindle." In addition to the coiled work just mentioned will be found coiling of the hammock type, and, interesting to know, the Chippewa on Lake Superior and the Loucheux type on the Mackenzie River are here reproduced in the carrying basket (see fig. 106). Starting out from very plain, coarse varieties of this work, it passes on into the lace-work burden baskets of the Pima, Papago, and Mohave. The figures wrought into these lace-work baskets are the same as are to be seen in the labyrinthian patterns on the basket bowls of the Pima. Quite as interesting as any of these types, the wrapped weaving before described is found in burden baskets of the Mohave. It must be recalled at this point, however, that Hudson mentions the same style of workmanship among the Pomo Indians for roof building and traps, and W. H. Holmes brought from California a framework for carrying birds in which the rods are held in place by a similar wrapping. There is also in the National Museum an old coarse mortar basket made of sticks which are bound together in the same way. A great deal of twilled and wicker work comes from the neighborhood of the City of Mexico and from Central America, and a species of coiled sewing which exists sporadically all the way from the Arctic Sea to Magellan Straits. The stitch, in addition to passing around the foundations to hold them together, also makes a wrap about the standing part between the coils. Modern coiled ware in great quantities is made up from agave fiber of fine quality, but it resembles African work more than American. A variety of forms and uses exist in baskets in Mexico; among others, the immense hats. The Caribs on the Mosquito Coast of Nicaragua are said to have plaited a pretty water-tight basket of reeds, called "patapee," but these people had been in touch with natives of Africa, who knew how to make water-tight baskets from the time of Moses at least. The Tlaxcala Indians used twined weaving in making slings. Types of work just mentioned continue on into the Central American States. No account is here made of the fine weaving and needlework, in which typical and extraordinary patterns are wrought, because they are across the boundary line and are no longer in the family of basketry made merely by hand without machinery.

Twined basketry and matting are preserved in the Peabody Museum from prehistoric burial caves in Coahuila, Mexico; among the Tlaxcala Indians (Nahuatlan family) in Central Mexico; from prehistoric graves at Ancon, Peru, and Arica, Chile; from graves at Pisaqua, Chile; from the Guatos Indians (Tapuyan family), in southern Brazil, and from the Cadioes Indians (Guaycuruan family), on the Paragua River. (C. C. Willoughby.)

Plate 236, U. S. National Museum, was brought by Frank Russell from the Yaqui Indians of northern Mexico. It is in the form of the so-called "telescope trunk," and old specimens of the National Museum were collected many years ago by Edward Palmer. The material is a kind of rush, and the weaving is in twilled work. Such baskets are employed for holding all sorts of useful articles, but especially in connection with religious practices they are the depository of charms and fetish objects.

Plate 237, in the collection of Dr. A. Hrdlicka, shows two covered baskets bandbox shaped. They are made of palm-leaf strips in twilled weaving. Hundreds of these objects are woven of various sizes, and packed in nests, and are the common receptacle for all sorts of articles among the Yaqui. Especial attention is called to the lower basket, since it is an excellent example of what has been mentioned several times in this work—namely, double weaving. Strips of palm leaf are worked in the pairs, the upper side of the leaf being outermost. At any moment, however, these strips may be separated and each member of the pair do service for warp or weft separately.

The Yaqui of Sonora, Mexico, says Palmer, split the stems of arundinaria for basketry by pounding them carefully with stones. The reeds divide along the lines of least resistance into splints of varying width, which are assorted and used in different textures. They now manufacture to order floor mats, porch screens, and the like, and sell them in Guaymas.

The Huichole Indians, living in the State of Zacatecas, Mexico, belong to the Aztecan branch of the great Shoshonean family. They have been described by Lumholtz, and are living in a state of native simplicity. They make a basket 2 or 3 feet long and only 6 inches in height with a similar cover. The material is palm leaf and the technic is twilled weaving. Similar baskets are woven by the Tarahumara (Piman), State of Chihuahua, and also by the Tepeguanos (Piman) in Durango, Sinaloa, Chihuahua, and Jalisco. These low, tray-shaped, rectangular baskets with covers are the common packing cases among these tribes mentioned of northern Mexico. (Hrdlicka.)

A wicker basket from Santa Maria del Rio, 14 leagues south of San Luis Potosi, Mexico, is Catalogue No. 76925, U. S. National Museum, made from the prepared stems of willow. The weaving is not after the fashion of the common market basket, but its parts are worked spirally in such manner that the smaller ends of the stems terminate in a braided band around the top of the body. (Compare fig. 190.) This arrangement reminds one of Dr. Matthews's Study in Butts and Tips.[a] The warp consists of groups of fine stems arranged in fours. As the bottom is oblong, five of the groups pass straight across it widthwise, while at the ends others radiate from the foci of the ellipse. The weft of the bottom is formed by means of fourteen stems, seven of which run in one direction and seven in the other, the smaller ends being fastened off on the border. The body is built up in the same way. In the ordinary wicker basket a stem is woven among the warps, and when the end is reached another stem takes its place, and so on; but in this example all the weft stems of the body begin at the very bottom and are wound in a spiral up to the upper margin. At this border the warp stems are all bent to the right for an inch and a half and then turned back again, being intertwined in a sort of openwork diagonal weaving. To form the handle seven stems on each side are thrust between the weft, and these bundles are wrapped about each other to form the twisted handle, the smaller ends being deflected so that the ends of the stems which form the body and the ends of the handle and the stems of the body are all woven together to form the braid-work at the top. Collected by Edward Palmer.

[a]American Anthropologist, Washington, V, 1892, pp. 345–350.

H. Ling Roth, in his paper on the aborigines of Hispaniola,[a] says that although none of the histories make reference to the island in which baskets were manufactured, nor even to the material out of which they are made, there is occasional mention of them, proving that formerly, as now, the Caribs and their tribes knew how to weave basket work. The Spaniards both in Hispaniola and Cuba on several occasions found men's heads cut off and sewed up with great care in small baskets. He quotes Benzoni in speaking of a feast in which baskets were adorned with roses and various flowers. Columbus found baskets in Guadeloupe full of men's bones.

A glance at the map of northern South America shows how easy it is to pass from the Windward Islands up the Orinoco and over the drainage of the Rio Negro, down to the Amazon. On this central position it is not difficult to make communication with the highlands of middle Brazil, Bolivia, eastern Peru, and Ecuador, and to pass from the Xingu River to Paraguay is easy. This explanation will clear the way for the collection of baskets now to be described.

The seventieth parallel from Greenwich may be used to divide South America into east and west basketry sub-areas. The West Indies will be counted with the eastern portions. The few widespread linguistic families serve as a bond to hold the tribes in mind. At the extreme north the Carib and the Arawak are conspicuous; the Tupi-Guarani and the Geez answer for Brazil; over the Amazon watershed, the La Plata areas, the Gran Chaco tribes follow. Patagonia and Fuegia complete the series. Over a large portion of this eastern region the types of weaving practiced in the Southern States of the Union prevail. On the western side of the continent, in the Andean valleys, the basketry is more varied and interesting, as the description and illustrations will show. The information which follows is far from complete. The little which is said will serve at least as a starting point and show that aboriginally and technically there was only one America.

Plate 238 shows an Indian woman standing in front of the agave plant—a fitting combination, since in Mexico, Central America, and northern portions of South America the agave is to the native population an enduring friend. In modern industries it has not lost its influence. The lechiguilla, ixtl, sisal, and other standard fibers are therefrom. In old times it was the substance from which receptacles, clothing, parts of household utensils and conveniences, and many other useful things were made. The figure standing in front of the plant might be called the Clotho of the agave, whose skillful fingers will turn the ideal plant into many supplies of wants.

Baskets from British Guiana are like those described by E. F. im Thurn in his work entitled Among the Indians of British Guiana.

---

[a] Journal of the Anthropological Institute of Great Britain and Ireland, XVI, p. 283.

The specimens in the National Museum are all of the twilled pattern, wrought from a brown vegetable fiber which shows the same on both sides. This twill is used with good effect in the diagonally woven cassava strainers, widely distributed, which may be contracted in length by a corresponding increase of width. When the cassava is packed into this strainer the latter is suspended and a great weight fastened to the bottom. The same device is used among us by country housewives in making curds. There is an entire lack of gaudy dyes in the Guiana baskets, the only colors being the natural hue of the wood and a jet-black varnish. The gorgeous plumage of the birds replace the dyes in ornamentation. (See Plate 239.)

The material used for basket work among the Indians of Guiana is the split stem of a kind of maranta (*Ischnosiphon*) called iturite by the Indians. For rough work other species of iturite are used, and for the roughest of all the unsplit stems of certain creepers, especially one called by the Indians mamamoorie (*Carludovica plumierii*).

The so-called pegalls (packalls) are square generally. The basket and lid are the same shape; the latter, being larger, slips over the former and entirely covers it. Many Caribs made their pegalls of an oblong shape, with gracefully curved lines, and adorn them with long strings of thick, white cotton on which are knots of colored feathers. Sometimes the true Caribs make the pegall and lid double, and between the two layers of basket work certain leaves (*Ischnosiphon*) are inserted to make the whole waterproof. Here is another example of double warp noted in several parts of North America.

Another basket, shaped like a slipper, is the suriana, for carrying heavy loads. This useful form has a wide distribution, being seen in Guatemala. The "quake," another basket, is used for storing provisions. They also serve as cages. It is made of open wicker work with a rounded bottom. Most of the baskets are manufactured in the same way and of the same material. The Nikari karus, living on the Brazilian borders, make their pegalls of the leaves of the palm (*Orbigna*), very rare in British Guiana. These are square or oblong.[a]

Plates 240 and 241 are from photographs presented by the distinguished ethnologist, Carl von den Steinen. They represent carrying baskets from eastern Brazil in the collection of the Berlin Ethnographic Museum. In order to bring the structure into comparison, baskets of the same function were selected. The following descriptions, aided by the photographs, will make plain the structure.

Plate 240, fig. 1, is a carrying basket (hasiri) of the Jamamadi Indians, living on the Rio Purus, in the collection of Paul Ehrenreich. The warp is crossed and the weft passes through the warp in regular order, so as to produce hexagonal openings. The border is formed

---

[a] E. F. im Thurn, Among the Indians of British Guiana, p. 282, London, 1883.

by simply turning over the ends of the warp and weaving them backward. The head strap is a wide strip of inner bark. Prof. J. B. Steere collected for the U. S. National Museum a fine specimen of this same type of weaving of the Jamamadi, resembling, in fact, fig. 2 of this plate. (See Plate 95, fig. 5.)

Fig. 2 is a carrying basket (shibati) of the Hypurina Indians, living on the Rio Purus, collected by Paul Ehrenreich. The warp is crossed and the weaving is done as in fig. 1, but there are twice as many weft splints, the hexagonal spaces being crossed by them. The border is formed by a hoop of wood. Strips are attached to the side of the basket for strength, and string loops at the top for attachment of the head band, which is in tough inner bark of a tree, as in No. 1.

Fig. 3 is a carrying basket (koho) from the Paressi Indians, on the upper Tapajoz River, Brazil, in the collection of Dr. Carl von den Steinen. This is an elegant piece of work and worthy of study. One-half of the warp elements are vertical and the other inclined. The weft passes through the interstices formed by the crossed warp in twos and threes. At the top a hoop is used for strengthening; the warp turned back and held firm by a single row of three-strand weaving. On the sides a rope is attached to the weft elements for loops and the headband is made, as in the other specimens, from the tough inner bark of a tree.

Fig. 4 is a children's carrying basket (mayaku) of the Bakairi Indians, on the upper Xingu River, Brazil, and fig. 5 an example for adults by the same tribe, from the collection of Dr. von den Steinen. They are made of four elongated hoops of wood. One furnishes the bed or bottom of the frame, two others the sides, and the smaller one the end. Those who are accustomed to studying utensils used in transportation will recognize in these two frames African forms. They are not basket work, either of them, in the strict sense of the word, since the webbing which fills up the hoops is true network of string; the crossings form regular knots. In both examples the headband is of bast, or the inner bark of a tree, and in the larger the binding of the bottom is in the same material.

Plate 241, fig. 1, is a carrying basket (kodrabo) of the Bororó Indians, on the Rio São Lourenço, Brazil, in the collection of Dr. von den Steinen. It is in palm leaf, in regular twilled weaving common throughout the world. The interesting portion, which ought not to be overlooked, is the border, which is the midrib of the palm leaf, with the leaflets attached. The carrying band or headband, as in other examples, is in tough inner bark of a tree.

Fig. 2 is a carrying basket of the Kabischi Indians, on the upper Xingu River, in the collection of Hermann Meyer, found in an abandoned camp. The weaving is in twilled work, forming rhomboidal patterns on the surface. The top of the basket is round and strengthened with a hoop. The bottom is square, held in shape by sticks, and carried by means of a headband of bark.

Fig. 3 is a carrying basket (*Ayacapeana guarani*) of the Kaingua Indians, on the Rio Alto Paraná, collected by Rohde Ambrosetti in southern Brazil. It is an elaborate specimen built on a framework with a round hoop at the top and two ox-bow shaped pieces of wood crossing under the bottom to give shape to the body. The upper part of the surface is in wicker work. A band around the middle in twilled weaving is ornamented with rhomboidal patterns and the lower part is also covered with wicker work. The headband is in tough bark.

Fig. 4 is a carrying basket (apoi) made by the Warrau Indians, on the Rio Orinoco-Cuyuni in Guiana. The framework and covering are interesting on account of the distribution of this peculiar form, which may be found as far north as Guatemala and around the Caribbean Sea. The work is in twilled weaving, and the border is formed by strips of wood sewed to the upper edge. The headband is in two-strand rope.

Nieuhoff describes the Brazilian basketry of his day.[a]

The baskets of the Indians of southern Brazil are made of palm-tree leaves. They call them

FIG. 204.
CARRYING NET.
Araucanian Indians.

Detail of bag.

patigua. They have also some made of reed or of cane. These are with one general name called karamemoa. They make also large broad baskets of reeds and branches twisted together. These they call panaku, and are chiefly used for the carrying of the mandioka root. In their journeys they always make use of the patigua, but the panaku is used by the slaves and negroes in the Receif for the conveniency of carriage.

The Guatos Indians in southern Brazil employ twined weaving in the manufacture of mantles and the Cadricios Indians on the Paraqua River make grass bags in the same technic.

---

[a] Voyages in Brazil, in Churchill, II, p. 132,

The figure of an Araucanian woman acting as both freight and passenger carrier is introduced from De Schryver[a] to show the extension of the buttonhole stitch technic southward. The insertion of a foundation in coiled work is not common farther north, but will be again noted at the very extremity of the continent. (See fig. 204.) The basketry of South America reaches its southern limit in the Fuegian coiled ware with slight foundation and sewing in buttonhole stitches, illustrated in fig. 59.

FIG. 205.
CARRYING NET.
Chiriqui, Colombia.

Coming over to the western side of the continent, fig. 205 is a coiled carrying bag from Chiriqui, Colombia, and is a type of an enormous amount of ware to be found in Middle America, North America, and South America. It is represented in fig. 42, and is called in this monograph coiled work without foundation. It will be seen, by looking at the detail, that the twine constituting the fabric interlocks with the stitch underneath and makes a complete revolution, catching the next stitch, and so on. Without definite information on the subject, it is believed that in making these bags some sort of a gauge is used by the weaver—a small stick which may be slipped along as the work proceeds.

The detail is shown in fig. 206, and especial attention is called to the ornamental effect of using a two-ply twine and the additional decorative feature of having the twines in different colors.

The fibers of the Middle Americans and Mexicans are of the best kind and texture, and are used in hammocks and for the most exacting labor in transportation.

FIG. 206.
DETAIL OF FIG. 205.

An interesting example of the friendly cooperation between the best material and the best workmen is to be found in the Republic of Ecuador in the manufacture of the so-called Panama hat. In Consular Report No. 821 Consul Perry M. de Leon gives the following

[a] Simon de Schryver, Royaume d'Araucanie-Patagonie, 1887.

account of it: The Manavi (Panama) hat was first made in the province of Manavi, Ecuador, about two hundred and seventy-five years ago by a native named Francisco Delgado. The present centers of the industry are Monte Cristi and Jipijapa in the province of Manavi, and Santa Elena and Cuenca in the provinces of Guayas and Azuay, respectively. They came to be known as Panama hats years ago when that city was a distributing center. Those who are familiar with them can tell by the method of beginning the work at the center of the crown the locality where the work is done. In Ecuador, Colombia, and Central America the hat is known to the natives as the Jipijapa (pronounced hipi-hapa), but as they are made elsewhere in Ecuador, principally in the province of Manavi, and as the name is easy to pronounce, it might take the place of the present misleading appellation. (See Plate 242.)

They are made from a native species of palm (*Carludovica palmata*). It is cultivated in the provinces of Manavi and Guayas and is known as "paja toquilla." In appearance it resembles very much our saw palmetto; it is fan-like in shape. Low-lying wet land is selected and the seed planted in rows during the rainy season. When the plant attains a height of 4½ or 5 feet it is cut just before ripening. The leaves are boiled in hot water and after being thoroughly sun dried are assorted and ready for use.

The material is first carefully selected, dampened to make it pliable, then very finely divided into requisite widths, the little finger and thumb nail being used for the purpose. The very finest specimens are prepared from delicate leaves that need no splitting or stiffening. The plaiting begins at the apex of the crown and is continued in circular form until the hat is finished. The story that they are made under water by candle light is untrue. The work is carried on while the atmosphere is humid, from about midnight to 7 o'clock in the morning. At night the hat is hung out in the open air so that the dew may fall upon it, and it is then in position to be worked the next day. If the strand breaks it can be replaced and so plaited so as not to affect the work nor be visible to the naked eye. The ingenious woman uses her knee for a head block. This antedates all modern appliances for giving shape to head gear. It requires from three to five months daily labor of three hours a day to make one of the finest hats. The business in its highest development is really an art, requiring patience, fine sight, and special skill—qualifications few of the natives possess. The plaiting completed, the hat is washed in clean, cold water, coated with a thin solution of gum, and polished with dry powdered sulphur. They are so pliable that they can be rolled up without injury and put in one's pocket. They will last for years and can be repeatedly cleaned.

Natives of both sexes and all ages are engaged in this work at odd times, the business being a side issue. Children make from raw, undressed straw about two of the common hats a day.

The specimen here shown is in the collection of Dr. S. O. Richey, of Washington City, and has 20 or more crossings to the linear inch. The hats vary from the ordinary form having 18 crossings or checks to the finest quality, which have twice as many. In the market they are sold at from $10 to $150. The most costly specimens are those in which there is not a break in the straw, mismatched color, or a knot showing in the work.

During the nineteenth century the cemeteries of Peru yielded the greatest abundance of relics and remains. Among the former were a mixed variety of textiles, which were types of basketry hereafter to be described. The climate of Peru is arid and almost a desert like that of Arizona or Egypt. The frail products of the textile industry that might have perished utterly in North America almost everywhere have here all been preserved. Fine specimens of old Peruvian work are to be seen in all the leading museums of the world. The Field Columbian in Chicago is especially rich in productions of this kind, gathered through the agency of the World's Columbian Exposition in 1893.

In the Peabody Museum and in the U. S. National Museum also are fine old collections brought home fifty years ago by earlier travelers and explorers in South America, and in this Peruvian basketware are to be seen not only great varieties in form and exhaustive treatment of native technical processes but adaptations to uses without number extending literally from the cradle to the grave.

The name Peru has for the ethnologist a long perspective in time, reaching through many centuries; in elevation it covers the range of habitable areas from reeking seacoasts to heights barely endurable by man. In coast line it stretches through 15 degrees of south latitude (5° to 20°). Only in width is it restricted to the narrow watershed of the Andes and a slight portion of the incline on the eastern side, reaching down to the forest line. The most celebrated of the explorations in this area have been by Reiss, Stübel, and Koppel.[a]

These authors figure the following-named types of basketry:

1. Checkerwork: In this connection should be noted a kind of openwork in which the warps are set at an angle of 45 degrees, running in two directions, forming diamond-shaped spaces. A weft passes around among these warps so as to divide the diamond-shaped spaces into triangles. Such weaving is seen in many specimens of the North Pacific area; even the Aleutian islanders practice it. It has been already described and figured in von den Steinen's plates for the eastern area.

2. Wickerwork, in Colombia and Uruguay.

3. Diagonal or twilled work, widely diffused.

4. Twined work has been recovered from prehistoric graves at Ancon, Peru, in matting, both coarse and fine, and on baskets; from

---

[a] Kultur und Industrie Südamerikanischer Völker, Berlin, 1889.

prehistoric graves at Arica, Chile, in the structure of small wallets of basketry; and from graves at Pisagua, Chile, in baskets.   On other styles of manufacture a row or two intrudes itself.

5. Coiled work without foundation is universally distributed.   With foundation of fine splints it occurs also as will be seen.[a]

In the plates of these authors the following-named technical processes will be seen:

Plate 8, fig. 1, wicker-work basket from Bogota, Colombia.

Fig. 2, crossed warp, open weaving, from Pasto, Colombia.

Fig. 3, diagonal weaving from Pasto, Colombia.

Fig. 4, twilled weaving from Panama, Colombia.

Fig. 5, wicker from Andaqui, Colombia.

Figs. 6 and 7, diagonal weaving from Otavalio, Colombia.

Fig. 8, twilled weaving from Bogota, Colombia.

FIG. 207.
ANCIENT PERUVIAN WORK BASKET.
After W. H. Holmes.

Fig. 9, coiled basketry from Copacabana, Bolivia.

Fig. 10, diagonal weaving from Quito, Ecuador.

Figs. 11 and 12, twilled weaving from Rio de Janeiro, Brazil.

Fig. 13, coarse, diagonal weaving from Guallabamba, Ecuador.

Fig. 14, open coiled basket-box from Bogota, Colombia.

Fig. 15, plaited fans from Cocamilla Indians, Peru.

Fig. 16, diagonal weaving, fan, Papayan, Colombia.

Fig. 17, checker, oblique weaving from Cocamilla Indians, Peru.

Fig. 18, wicker strainer for maté from Cerro Largo, Uruguay.

Fig. 19, diagonal weaving, tray, from Brazil.

Figs. 207 to 211 are twilled basketry found deposited with the dead in a cemetery at Ancon, Peru.   They are made of rushes and exhibit a great variety of forms, as may be seen by examining the drawings on the

[a] Compare nos. 13039, 13096 in Eleventh Annual Report of the Peabody Museum, p. 280, fig. 3; p. 292, fig. 18.

cover of fig. 207. Across the middle are two rows of ordinary over-two twilled weaving, seen also in detail in fig. 208. A noticeable feature on other specimens, however, to which attention is drawn by Holmes[a] and to which he gives the name diagonal combination, is the production of triangular figures. The weaver in going from right to left produces the effect of right-angle triangles, but in returning so regulates the decussations of the fibers as to give to the pairs of tri-

FIG. 208.

DETAIL OF FIG. 207.

After W. H. Holmes.

FIG. 209.

DETAIL OF A PERUVIAN BASKET.

After W. H. Holmes.

angles of the two rows a common hypothenuse. The effect of this combination is magical, leaving the impression of high relief. (Fig. 209.)

But the most charming effects in these Peruvian workbaskets are brought about by the use of narrow strips of wood, over which the plaiting takes place and by which broad bands of twilled work are produced. This result is manifest in figs. 210 and 211.

Another characteristic of this Peruvian work is the hinging of the cover of the basket as part of the weaving. In

FIG. 210.

DETAIL OF A PERUVIAN BASKET.

FIG. 211.

DETAIL OF A PERUVIAN BASKET.

Plate 243, evidently the workbasket of an ancient spinner in Vicuña wool, there is a single cover, but it will be seen that the modern compartment trunk has been anticipated, the basket being in three divisions, the middle one forming the cover of the lower one. The detail of the hinge as a part of the texture may be seen in the small drawings at the bottom of the plate.

Plate 244 is a twined carrying frame from the graves of Iquique, southern Peru. The framework consists of three sticks, bent in the shape of an oxbow, crossing each other at the bottom so as to give to

---

[a] W. H. Holmes, A Study in the Textile Art, Sixth Annual Report of the Bureau of American Ethnology, p. 206, figs. 297–299.

the top the form of an oblique hexagon. The ends are held in place by a stout cord of hair in natural brown color. The warp of this basket is formed by winding a white string round and round these sticks on the outside, about one-eighth of an inch apart, from the bottom to the top. The weft is a series of vertical rows of twined weaving, in some places close together and in others wide apart, for ornamental effect. The vertical stripes seen on the surface are in green, red, black, and white, twined, and in twined weaving, each block including two or more warp strands. By using two colors in the twine the patterns are variegated on the surface, first the white and then the colored strand coming into view. By comparing these specimens with the one from the Arikara Indians, fig. 125, it will be seen that in the latter two of the bows projected downward and formed the bottom, on which the basket rests. But in this case no such protection is afforded. The woman has sewed a coarse piece of woven stuff along the bottom

FIG. 212.
ANCIENT COILED BASKET FROM CHILE.

as a protection of the more delicate threads. The specimen is in the Field Columbian Museum, Chicago, and the colored plate was furnished by Dr. George A. Dorsey.

Fig. 212 is a fragment of a coiled basket from a copper mine in the district of Chuquicamata in the desert of Atacama, Chile. It was found, together with other industrial implements, associated with the body of a woman who undoubtedly met her death on the spot. From the dislocated backbone and the small stones embedded in the skin, it is supposed that she was buried by a caving in of the works. The basket of which this is a fragment, was in every respect similar to the Pima ware in southern Arizona. This fragment bears such remarkable similarity to Pima workmanship that J. W. Benham, of Arizona, who is most familiar with it, was struck with the Chilean example and wondered whether it were possible that the Pima Indians and the Chileans could have been under the same instructors.

Plates 245 to 247 are also specimens of coiled work exhibited in the Pan-American Exposition, with the mummy from Chile; the foundation of the coil of shredded material and the sewing also in soft splints. The stitches pass over the foundation and are not only interlocking but take up a portion of the foundation in its base below. These should be compared with the specimens from northern Mexico in the Peabody Museum, described by C. C. Willoughby.

Plate 248 is the side and bottom view of a coiled basket from Peru. The style is entirely modern, but it is introduced here to show two features in technic well wrought out in the northern continent. The foundation and the sewing are both in a brilliant-colored straw, species unknown. Sewing is reduced to the minimum, most of the foundation being neatly wrapped, or served with the sewing material. The stitches on the body are bifurcated most neatly, and coming one above the other give the impression of herringbone work done vertically. Finding this openwork coil and furcate stitches in Eskimo land, California, and Peru would tempt one to see the same invention arising independently in regions wide apart; but, omitting the unlimited going about in pre-Columbian times, during hundreds of years the sovereigns of Spain, France, England, and for a century Russia mixed the native tribes and their industries. Catalogue No. 150844, U. S. National Museum.

.The two areas of South America, eastern and western, unite in the Straits of Magellan. There are three linguistic families of Indians, among whom two types of basketry are found belonging to the coiled variety. They are made by women of *Juncus magellanicus*. Descriptions and figures of the stitches involved will be found in the Revue d'Ethnographie.[a] See also Lovisto.[b] The rim is made of wood veya or tshelia. The specimens in the U. S. National Museum are all of one variety, the sewing being in the buttonhole stitch, so called, and in openwork. Nothing of the kind exists in the neighborhood, so that it is within the limits of possibility that the style of technic was introduced.

In summing up what has been said on basketry in the Western Hemisphere it would seem that all the types and processes known throughout the world are to be seen here.

VIII. COLLECTORS AND COLLECTIONS

As David and the Sibyl say—THOMAS OF CELANO.

Basketry and pottery are the Sibylline leaves on which are written the thoughts and lore of our Indians. Already much has gone beyond recovery; it is for this reason that a good word is here spoken for those lovers of art who have spent time and means in redeeming the

---

a Paris, IV, p. 517.   b Guida Cora's Cosmos, October, 1884, pl. v.

more perishable of the two treasures from destruction. Pottery may be broken, but its fragments endure and bear witness. Not so basketry, made of the most perishable portions of plants, it can endure only when in contact with preservative materials, or partly reduced to ashes, or deposited in caves and other dry places, or finally, their technic but not their story may be saved by impressions left on pottery.

The following instructions are published for the great number of persons who are interested in the collection and preservation of American basketry. Besides the æsthetic elements involved and the pride of saving the best examples of a rapidly vanishing industry, there is a vast deal of culture study which ought not to be neglected.

In every collection, public or private, there are opportunities for special investigation that should not be in the possession of a single individual only. If all who are gathering baskets would preserve such information as they may be able to obtain, the bringing together of the results of all this study would be a monument for our American aboriginal women.

As pointed out in former chapters, knowledge concerning basketry seems to be illimitable, the technician, the artist, and the student of folklore finding equal pleasure in the acquisition. To begin with the manufacture, a correct knowledge of the materials includes the name of the tribe and their location, the name of the different kinds of weaving in the native tongue, and chiefly, the native name, the common name, and the scientific name of every plant or animal substance or mineral involved. The reason for this is that in order to know whether an art is indigenous or acquired, it is necessary to compare the names for definite things with those used by other tribes for the same things. Not to discourage the collector, however, it must be said that this is an ideal toward which he ought to work.

The following label of a specimen in the Hudson basketry collection, U. S. National Museum, will serve as a model to guide the collector in saving information about his specimens:

BASKET JAR of the Pomo Indians (Kulanapan family). Made from the prepared root of Kahum, or California sedge (*Carex barbarae*), throat and scalp feathers of Katátch, or woodpecker (*Melanerpes formicivorus*), breast feathers of Jucil, or meadow lark (*Sturnella neglecta*), scalp feathers of Kayán, or mallard (*Anas borchas*), plumes of Tchikáka, or crested quail (*Lophortyx californicus*), neck feathers of Tsawálu, or jay (*Cyanura stelleri*), and Káya, or prepared clam shell (*Saxidomus gracilis*), in a style of coiled sewing called Tsai, in which a single rod constitutes the basis. The sewing passes over this rod, under the preceding one, and locks in the stitch immediately underneath. Ornamentation, a row of shell disks around the margin and another row serving as a handle.

Diameter, 5 inches.

RUSSIAN RIVER, CALIFORNIA, 1896.　　　　　　　　　　　　　No. 203,415.

FROM THE BUREAU OF AMERICAN ETHNOLOGY, COLLECTED BY DR. J. W. HUDSON.

For the artistic collector there is a very important mission, to know and to foster the aboriginal patterns and motives in decoration. Many of the shapes and designs in basketry are spurious. Besides the trashy imitations of letters and common things on basketry, which mislead no one, there is an important habit springing up of getting women of one tribe to imitate the designs of another tribe. This works confusion in two ways. It confounds the student of folklore absolutely, and if there be any truth in the belief that in all art the material and the motif have in the ages adapted themselves to each other "like perfect music unto perfect words," the attempt to put Apache ornaments on Pima, or Wasco on Klikitat is discordant.

PRESERVATION OF BASKETS

The art of a people must be judged by what they need not do and yet accomplish.—A. C. HADDON.

Textiles are among the most fragile and perishable of human industrial products. Insects and rust, heat and cold, too much and too little moisture, the common accidents of life, are hastening our pretty baskets to their dissolution. Therefore, how to prolong the life of a basket is a living question with all basket lovers, and the answer will be easier if the causes of destruction are known. The three enemies of baskets are moth and rust and human fingers. By the moth are meant all destructive animals; by rust, natural decay; and in the last agency must be classed the myriad ways by which our fellow-creatures purloin and destroy our treasures. E. S. Morse tells us that the Japanese do not make of their houses bazaars for the ostentatious display of art objects, but they put them away in silk bags to bring forth when they wish to delight their friends. Those collections that have been made with a view to permanence should be kept so that they will suffer least from damage. The dust may be blown from the specimens with bellows. Those containing remnants of vegetable matter, berries, food, etc., should be carefully scrubbed with soap and water, and rubbed down with a very small portion of oil and dryer. Above all they should be poisoned with a weak solution of corrosive sublimate or arsenic dissolved in alcohol. A card catalogue giving the legend and history of each piece would add much to the value of the collection.

A list of collections of rarities in American basketry is here appended, by no means complete, but it will aid the student who wishes to prosecute his investigations further to find the material. First of all, in the great museums there are permanently in store priceless examples of basketry, and in addition many costly collections belonging to private individuals, have thus rendered a great service to this writer. It is interesting to read over the names of the men and women who long ago contributed to the great museums precious examples of uncontaminated Indian art.

AMERICAN MUSEUM OF NATURAL HISTORY OF NEW YORK. The best assemblages of American basketry are the Emmons collection from Alaska; the Teit from the Chilcotin and the Thompson Indians (Jesup expedition); the Farrand from the Quinaielt (Jesup expedition); the Farrand from the Klikitat and Oregon (gift of Mr. Henry Villard); the Dixon from northern California (Huntingdon expedition); the Briggs collection from California (gift of Mr. George Foster Peabody); the Apache collection (gift of Mr. Andrew E. Douglass); the Pepper, of ceremonial baskets of the ancient cliff dwellers (Hyde expedition); baskets from the Chukchi Peninsula collected by Messrs. Jochelson and Bogoras (Jesup expedition). If we should include birch-bark baskets, one might also mention the Stone collection from Mackenzie Basin; and the Berthold Laufer collection from the Amur River (Jesup expedition). The basketry collection has been brought together for decoration, not for technic.

ANKENY, Mrs. LEVI, Walla Walla, Washington. Salish basketry.

BARRETT, S. A., Ukiah, California. All Pomo. About 150 pieces.

BENHAM, J. W., Phoenix, Arizona. Large and rich collection of Apache ollas, rare Pimas, and other basketry from the Southwest.

BENJAMIN, Mrs. CAROLYN G., Washington City. General collection. Good in Chetimachas.

BINGHAM, Mrs. J. E., 338 Katharine street, Walla Walla, Washington.

BISHOP, Mrs. THOMAS T., 2309 Washington street, San Francisco, California. Miscellaneous.

BOGGS, Mrs. A. G., Redding, California. Principally Hat Creeks, of Shasta County, and Pit Rivers, of Modoc County. Some 200.

BRADFORD, Mrs. SIDNEY, Avery Island, Louisiana. Fine old Chetimachas.

BRIGGS, C. F., San Francisco, California. Miscellaneous. Very choice examples. Northwest coast, Pomos, Mariposan, and few fine Mission.

BRITTIN, L. H., Edgewater, New Jersey. Old Tlinkit baskets.

BRIZARD, BROUSSE, Arcata, California. Large Hupa material with illustrated catalogue.

BUCHAN, CHARLES MILTON, Tulalip Agency, Tulalip, Washington.

BUGBEE, Mrs. SUMNER W., Pasadena, California. Miscellaneous.

BURDICK, T. W., Albany, New York. Rare Tulares.

BURGESS, JOHN D., Tucson, Arizona. Pima, Maricopa, and Apache examples.

CARPENTER, Mrs. HELEN M., Ukiah, California. Pomos.

CARROLL, ANDREW W. DE LA CŒUR, Ardglass, Ireland. Good California types.

CHICAGO UNIVERSITY. Especially Mexican. See Frederick Starr.

CINCINNATI MUSEUM OF FINE ART. General collection.

COHN, A., charming specimens of Washoe baskets, Nevada.

COLE, Mrs., Pasadena, California. General collection.

COOK, Mrs. J. B., Yosemite Valley, California. About 75 examples of Mono, Washoe, and Mariposan tribes.

COVERT, FRANK M., New York. Good in Arizona basketry.

COVILLE, FREDERICK V. Fine collection from the west coast to illustrate the plants used.

CROSS, Mrs. EDWARD, Salem, Oregon.

CURTIS, WILLIAM CONWAY, Norwalk, Connecticut. The Klikitat and other basketry of Washington.

DAGGETT, JOHN, Black Bear, Siskiyou County, California. Fine collection of Yurok and Karok material. Klamath and Salmon rivers, northern California. At present on deposit in the Memorial Museum, Golden Gate Park, San Francisco, California.

DAVENPORT ACADEMY MUSEUM, Iowa. Miscellaneous collection.

DEISHER, H. K., 50 Noble street, Kutztown, Pennsylvania. Pomos and Wintuns, and a few good Maidus.

DESSEZ, Miss HENRIETTA LOUISE, Washington City.   California and Interior Basin.

EATON, the Misses, Boston, Massachusetts.   Very old California baskets.

EMMONS, G. T., Princeton, New Jersey.   Excellent old Tlinkits.

FEENEY, Miss KATHARINE, 1570 Filbert street, Oakland, California.   A fine miscellaneous collection.

FIELD COLUMBIAN MUSEUM OF CHICAGO has rich collections of basketry from all the north Pacific coast families, and especially old and beautiful specimens of Tlinkit twined ware, the gift of Mr. E. E. Ayer; from the Columbian Basin 50 Nez Percés twined wallets, many of them large and choice, and some of considerable age; 60 coiled and imbricated baskets of the Klikitats of various sizes.   The last-mentioned two collections were made by Mr. E. E. Miller.   From various parts of California, the Field Columbian possesses many choice baskets, and is especially rich in examples from tribes of the Kulanapan, Mariposan, and Moqulumnan families.   These were gathered chiefly by Dr. J. W. Hudson, but many choice examples were the gift of Mr. E. E. Ayer.   The same generous benefactor added to his gift large collections from the White Mountain, and Mescalero Apaches, and from the Pimas, made by George A. Dorsey, Charles L. Owen, and S. C. Sims added typical series from special tribes.   Dr. Dorsey's Ute collection should be mentioned, and particularly that from the Klamath tribe, numbering over 200 specimens and comprising all their forms, technical processes, and designs.

FROHMAN, Mrs. J., Portland, Oregon.   West Coast basketry and matting.

GARDNER, Mrs. GEORGE S., Laurel, Mississippi.   Tribes of Indian Territory, Georgia, and Louisiana.   Also a fair series of Pacific coast work—Alaska, British Columbia, Washington, California, and Arizona.

GRAY, Mrs. WILLIAM, Salem, Oregon.

GREBLE, Mrs. MARY D., New York City.   Rare old southern California pieces.

HALL, ROBERT C., Pittsburg, Pennsylvania.   Miscellaneous.   Good Pomos and Tulares.

HARVEY, FRED, Albuquerque, New Mexico.   Large collection from the Southwest.

HEARST, Mrs. PHEBE A., Berkeley, California.   Miscellaneous.   Very large collection. Rich in Pomos and central California tribes.   The collection is in the University of California, and exhaustive studies are being made under her generous patronage.

HUBBY, Miss ELLA S., Pasadena, California.

HUDSON, Mrs. GRACE, Ukiah, California.   Fine Pomos.   Dr. J. W. Hudson's two large collections from these tribes are in Washington and Chicago.

HYDE EXPLORING EXPEDITION, New York.   Collection of basketry from the Southwest.   Encourages the making of baskets and aids in the sale of them.

IDE, Mrs. ESTHER C., Seymour street, Syracuse, New York.   Miscellaneous.   Good Pomos and Tulares.

JACKSON, Col. JAMES, Salem, Oregon.

JAMES, GEORGE WHARTON, Pasadena, California.   Especially good in examples from California Missions.

JOHNSTON, Mrs. WILLIAM P., New Orleans, Louisiana.   Chetimaches, Choctaws, and Attacapas.

JONES, PHILIP MILLS, State University, Berkeley, California.

KEPLER, JOSEPH, Inwood on the Hudson.   General collection.

KIRKPATRICK, Mrs. I. H., Adrian, Michigan.   Fine Navahos.

LANDSBERG, FREDERICK, Victoria, British Columbia.   General collection.

LANG, Miss ANNE M., The Dalles, Oregon.   Collection of imbricated basketry.   Large and rare.

LOOSLY, Mrs. JOHN, 9 Pine street, San Francisco, California.   Miscellaneous.

LOWE, Mrs. T. S. C., Pasadena, California.   Fine, large collection.   Rich in Pomos and central California tribes.

LYNCH, Mrs. JAY, Fort Simcoe, Washington. General collection of west coast baskets.

MABLEY, Miss KATE, Detroit, Michigan.

McARTHUR, Mrs. H. K., 739 Glisan street, Portland, Oregon. Collection from Washington and Oregon.

MacGREGOR, JOHN, Hope Station, British Columbia. Thompson River basketry.

McKEE, Miss BELLE, Salem, Oregon.

McLEOD, E. L., Bakersfield, California. Large collection of baskets of Kern and Inyo tribes. A few Tulares.

McNEIL, Mrs. W. H., 1022 North Nineteenth street, St. Louis, Missouri. Miscellaneous.

MALLETT, J. H., Jr., San Francisco, California. A few fine Pomos and tribes in east-central California.

MASTERS, Mrs. W. U., Pasadena, California.

MASTICK, GEORGE H., Alameda, California. Large collection of Pomo baskets. A few good examples of Mariposan and Yokuts.

MERRIAM, C. HART, Washington City. About 1,000 examples of Western basketry, personally selected and card catalogued. A model collection.

MILLS, Mrs. ANSON G., Washington City. Select general collection.

MITCHELL, JOHN S., San Francisco, California. Miscellaneous. Good examples from Northwest coast; also Arizona.

MITCHELL, SUSMAN, Visalia, California. Excellent work of different tribes in Tulare and Kern counties, California.

MOLSON, Mrs. W. MARKLAND, Montreal, Canada. Washington Basketry.

MONTGOMERY, Mrs. J. B., Portland, Oregon.

MOSELEY, Mrs. WILLIAM H., New Haven, Connecticut. Collection on exhibition at the Peabody Museum of Yale.

NATIONAL MUSEUM.—The Museum is rich in collections of American basketry made to show all forms of technic and also to exhibit handiwork from tribes in the six areas. Beginning at the north, the collections of Ray from Point Barrow; of McFarlane and Ross at the Mackenzie mouth; the rich treasures gathered by Nelson in western Alaska; those of Dall, Turner, Applegate, and Fisher further south; and the Tlinkit ware selected by McLean, Swan, and Emmons amply illustrate the technical processes in that area.

Going southward, the Salish and other Fraser-Columbia basketry includes among others Wilkes, Swan, Eells, Shackleford, Emmons, and Willoughby collections.

The largest collections from California were made by Purcell, Ray, Stone, Powers, Hudson, Henshaw, Curtin in the north; by Holmes, Merriam, Rust, and Mead in the south.

The collections of basketry from the Interior Basin are the largest of all, being gathered by Palmer, Powell, Cushing, Stevenson, Holmes, Fewkes, Hough, Mooney, and Russell, and officers connected with the numerous surveys. Much of this is very old. From further south, from Middle and South America, the Museum is indebted to explorers and officers of various departments of the Government for typical material, the latest gathered on the Amazon by J. B. Steere.

NEWMAN, Mrs. H. W., San Carlos, Arizona. White Mountain Apache.

NICHOLSON, Miss FLORENCE, Pasadena. Choice old Californian specimens.

O'HARA, Mrs., San Francisco, California. Good pieces of Old Missions.

OWEN, Mrs. WILLIAM, Sepacuite, Panos, Alta Vera Paz, Guatemala. Fine collection of Guatemala work.

PEABODY MUSEUM OF ARCHÆOLOGY AND ETHNOLOGY, Harvard University, Cambridge, Massachusetts. Collections which ought not to be neglected by the special student. Among these should be mentioned that of Mrs. George B. Linder, of Boston, rich in California material; that of Mrs. Mary Hemenway, devoted especially to the pueblo tribes of Arizona, the Hopi, being the collection made by Thomas Keam many years ago. Dr. Edward Palmer contributed to this series also material from southern California, especially from the caves. This series contains the outfit of a society, since the baskets were accompanied also with headdresses and musical instruments.

PICHER, Miss ANNIE B., Pasadena, California. General collection.

PLATT, Mrs. ORVILLE C., Meriden, Connecticut. General collection.

PLIMPTON, F. S., San Diego, California. Miscellaneous. Very choice. Fine Pomos. Good examples of work of different tribes throughout northern, central, and southern California.

POWER, Mrs. E. B., Navada City, California. Choice Maidus.

PURDY, CARL W., Ukiah, California. Well-selected collection of Pomos.

ROBERTS, Mrs. ERNEST W., Chelsea, Massachusetts. General collection.

ROSENBERG, Mrs. ANNA M., 1605 East Madison street, Seattle, Washington. Some fine Pomos. Few good examples of Tulare and Kern tribes.

ROST, Mrs. H., Portland, Oregon.

RUMSEY, C. E., 110 Indiana avenue, Riverside, California. Miscellaneous.

RUSSELL, Mrs. GEORGE F., Portland, Oregon.

SEQUOYA LEAGUE, The. A corporation whose design is "to make better Indians." One of its objects is to revive, encourage, and provide market for such aboriginal industries as can be made profitable.

SHACKELFORD, Mrs. R. T., The Dalles, Oregon. Excellent Klikitats and Wascos.

SHARPE, Miss ELIZABETH M., Wilkesbarre, Pennsylvania. General collection.

SMITH, Mrs. EMILY A., 2226 Jackson street, San Francisco, California. Miscellaneous. A number of exceptionally fine Pomos, including several solidly feathered. Also some choice examples from Tulare, Kern, and Inyo counties, the Missions. Alaska and British Columbia, etc.

SPIEGELBERG, A. F., Santa Fe, New Mexico. Large collection of basketry from southwestern United States.

STANFORD, Mrs. JANE L. (Mrs. Leland). In her museum at Palo Alto is a good collection of Tulare baskets. Also fair representation of the Klamath River material. The latter collected by John Daggett.

STARR, FREDERICK, University of Chicago, Chicago, Illinois. Collection of basketry from southern Mexico.

STEVENS, Mrs. FREDERICK H., Buffalo, New York.

STONE, Mrs. B. W., San Francisco, California. Miscellaneous collection. Very good specimens from various tribes of central California.

TAPLEY, Mrs. LOUIS, Salem, Oregon.

TEIT, JAMES, Spences Bridge, British Columbia. Good in Thompson River. Largely in American Museum of Natural History, New York.

TEVIS, Mrs. WILLIAM, Bakersfield, California. Large collection of baskets of Kern, Inyo, and Tulare tribes. A number of very fine and rare pieces. Many old examples.

TOZIER, D. F. A very large and choice collection from southeastern Alaska, British Columbia, and Washington. On exhibition in Tacoma, Washington.

TUTTLE, E. O., 28 State street, Boston, Massachusetts. Miscellaneous. Some good Pomos and Tulares.

UNIVERSITY OF CALIFORNIA is conducting an exhaustive survey of the State, both in archeology and ethnology, under patronage of Mrs. Phebe A. Hearst.

UNIVERSITY OF PENNSYLVANIA has a large series of basketry, sandals, and other textile material from the cliff dwellers of Mancos Canyon, given by Mrs. Phebe A. Hearst.

VROMAN, A. C., Pasadena, California. Fine old Pima and Apache baskets.

WADLEIGH, W. J., Hope Station, British Columbia. Klikitats.

WANAMAKER, JOHN, Philadelphia, Pennsylvania. Miscellaneous.

WHITMORE, Mrs. W. L., Salem, Oregon.

WILCOMB, C. P., Memorial Museum, Golden Gate Park, San Francisco, California. Large and choice collection of California basketry, well identified and labeled.

WILLIAMS, H. E., Cassel. California. Fine collection of Hat Creek baskets.

IX. BIBLIOGRAPHY

And let her works praise her in the gates.—KING LEMUEL.

The following list of publications will help to follow up this study in special lines. A great awakening of interest in the processes of savage industries as the foundation of all modern machine work has stimulated the production of excellent books and papers on basketry. At the moment of going to press the author of this general treatise learns of several. Dr. P. E. Goddard, of the University of California, was so good as to lend his proof on the Hupas; Frank Russell on the Pimas had not appeared; Emmons on the Tlinkit, and Dixon and Kroeber's further studies on California basketry were not in print.

ANDERSON, ADA WOODRUFF. Last Industry of a Passing Race. Harper's Bazaar, November 11, 1899.

B., T. F. Lessons in Basket Weaving. The Papoose. New York, February and May, 1903.

BANCROFT, H. H. Native Races of the Pacific States. New York, D. Appleton & Co., 5 vols., 8 vo. Index references to basketry, weaving, and kindred topics.

BARROWS, DAVID PRESCOTT. The Ethno-botany of the Coahuilla Indians of southern California. Chicago, 1900. The University Press, 82 pp. 8 vo.

BASKET, The. A quarterly journal. Vol. 1, 1903. Pasadena, California. Edited by George Wharton James. Organ of The Basket Fraternity.

BLANCHAN, NELTJE. What the Basket means to the Indian. Everybody's Magazine, V, 1901, pp. 561–570, illustrated.

BOAS, FRANZ. The Decorative Art of the Indians of the North Pacific Coast. Bulletin American Museum of Natural History, New York, IX, 1897, 54 pp. See also the author's papers in Reports of British Association, 1889–1891.

BUREAU OF AMERICAN ETHNOLOGY. Reports, bulletins, and miscellaneous publications abound in papers discussing basketry and related matters, 1879–1903.

CARPENTER, H. M. How Indian Baskets are made. The Cosmopolitan, October, 1900.

CARR, JEANNIE C. Among the Basket Makers, California. Illustrated Magazine, October, 1892.

CHANNING, GRACE ELLERY. The Baskets of Anita. Scribner's Magazine, August, 1890.

CHESNUT, V. K. Plants used by the Indians of Mendocino County, California. Washington, 1902. Contributions to the National Herbarium, VII, pp. 295–408.

CHITTENDEN, NEWTON H. Among the Cocopahs. Land of Sunshine, Los Angeles, California, 1901, pp. 196–210, illustrated.

COLES, CLAUDIA STUART. Aboriginal Basketry in the United States. The House Beautiful, February, 1900.

COVILLE, FREDERICK V. The Panamint Indians of California. American Anthropologist, V, 1892, pp. 351–361. Washington.

———. Directions for collecting Specimens and Information illustrating the aboriginal Uses of Plants, Bulletin No. 39, Part J, U. S. National Museum.

———. Wokas—Primitive Food of the Klamath Indians. Report of the U. S. National Museum for 1902 (in preparation).

CUSHING, FRANK HAMILTON.   Pottery affected by Environment.   Fourth Annual Report of the Bureau of Ethnology. 1882, pp. 482–521, 64 figs.
DELLENBAUGH, F. S.   The North Americans of 'Yesterday. New York, 1901.
DIXON, ROLAND B.   Basketry designs of the Maidu Indians of California.   American Anthropologist, June, 1900.
——.   Basketry designs of the Indians of northern California.   (The Huntingdon California Expedition.)   Bulletin, American Museum of Natural History, New York, XVII, pp. 1–32, 37 plates.
——, and ALFRED L. KROEBER.   The native Languages of California.   American Anthropologist, Washington, N. S., V, 1903, pp. 1–26, 8 figs.
DODGE, CHARLES RICHARDS.   A Report on the leaf Fibers of the United States. Department of Agriculture, Washington, 1893.   Fiber Investigations—Report No. 5.
DOUBLEDAY, F. N.   Indian industrial Development. The Outlook, January 12, 1901.
DUBOIS, CONSTANCE GODDARD.   Manzanita Basketry, a Revival. The Papoose, June, 1903, pp. 21–27.
EMMONS, G. T.   The Basketry of the Tlingit.   Memoirs, American Museum of Natural History, New York, 1903, III, Pt. 2, 18 pls. and text figures.
FARRAND, LIVINGSTON.   Basketry Designs of the Salish Indians.   Memoirs, American Museum of Natural History, New York, 1900, II, Pt. 5, 6 pp., 3 pls., 15 figs.
FEWKES, J. WALTER.   A contribution to Ethno-botany (of Tusayan).   American Anthropologist, Washington, 1896, IX, pp. 14–22.
——.   Hopi basket dances.   Journal of American Folklore, April–June, 1899.
——.   The Snake Ceremonial at Walpi. Journal of American Ethnology and Archæology, IV.
FIRTH, ANNIE.   Cane Basket Work, 1 and 2 series.   London.
GODDARD, P. E.   Life and Culture of the Hupas.   Publications of the University of California.   First volume of the series on North American Archaeology and Ethnology, Berkeley, California.
HARSHBERGER, J. W.   Purposes of Ethno-botany.   Botanical Gazette, XXI, No. 3.
HAVARD, VICTOR.   The Food Plants of the North American Indians.   Bulletin, Torrey Botanical Club, XXII, No. 2, February; No. 3, March, 1895.
——.   Drink Plants of the North American Indians.   Bulletin, Torrey Botanical Club, XXIII, No. 2, February, 1896.
HOFFMAN, WALTER JAMES.   The Menomini Indians.   Fourteenth Annual Report of the Bureau of Ethnology, Washington, 1896, pp. 3–328, pls. I–XXIII, 54 figs.
HOLMES, WILLIAM HENRY.   Prehistoric textile Fabrics of the United States derived from impressions on Pottery.   Third Annual Report of the Bureau of Ethnology, Pt. 1, 1884, pp. 397–425, 1 pl., 55 figs; also Volume XIII, 43 pp., 9 pls., 28 figs.
——.   A Study of the textile Art in its relation to the development of Form and Ornament.   Sixth Annual Report of the Bureau of Ethnology, Washington, 1888, pp. 189–252, figs. 286 to 358.
——.   Anthropological Studies in California.   Report of the U. S. National Museum, 1900, pp. 155–187.
HOUGH, MYRTLE ZUCK (Mrs. Walter).   Plant names of the southwestern United States.   The Plant World, Washington, 1900, III, p. 137.
HOUGH, WALTER.   Primitive American Armor.   Report of the U. S. National Museum, 1893, pp. 625–651.
——.   The Hopi in relation to their plant Environment.   American Anthropologist, X, February, 1897.
——.   Environmental interrelations in Arizona.   American Anthropologist, Washington, XI, 1898, p. 133–155.
HUDSON, J. W.   Pomo Basket Makers.   Overland Monthly, San Francisco, June, 1893.
HUMBOLDT, ALEXANDER VON.   Essay on New Spain.   II, p. 297, note on California basketry.

IM THURN, E. F.   Among the Indians of British Guiana.   P. 278.   London, 1895.

JAMES, GEORGE WHARTON, Symbolism in Indian Basketry.   The Traveler, San Francisco, August, 1899.

———.   Poems in Indian Baskets.   The Evening Lamp, Chicago, September 8, 1900.

———.   Indian Basketry.   Pasadena, 1901, privately printed.   238 pp., 300 ils. 8 vo.   Third edition, 1903.

———.   The Art of Indian Basketry.   The Southern Workman, August, 1901, 10 pp., 8 figs.

———.   Basket Makers of California at Work.   Sunset, San Francisco, California, November, 1901, 12 pp., 13 figs.

KNAPP, ELIZABETH SANBORN, Raphia and Reed Weaving.   Springfield, Massachusetts, 1903.

KROEBER, ALFRED L., The Arapaho.   Bulletin, American Museum Natural History, New York, 1902, XVIII, pp. 1–150.

LUMHOLZ, CARL.   Symbolism of the Huichol Indians, Memoirs, American Museum Natural History, New York, III.   Pt. 1.

MCGEE, W J.   The Beginnings of Agriculture.   American Anthropologist.

———.   The Seri Indians.   Seventeenth Annual Report of the Bureau of Ethnology, 1892, 336 pp., 56 pls., 42 figs.

MACNAUGHTON, CLARA.   Nevada Indian Baskets and their Makers.   Out West, Los Angeles, April and May, 1903.

MASON, OTIS T.   Basketwork of the North American Aborigines.   Report U. S. National Museum, 1884, pp. 291–300, pls. I–XIV.

———.   The Ray collection from the Hupa Reservation.   Smithsonian Report, 1886, pp. 205–239, 26 plates.

———.   Primitive Travel and Transportation.   Report U. S. National Museum, 1894.

———.   Woman's Share in Primitive Culture.   New York, 1894.

———.   Types of American basketry.   Scientific American, New York, July 28, 1900.

———.   The Technique of Aboriginal American Basketry.   American Anthropologist, N. S., III, 1901, pp. 109–128, Washington, January–March, 1901.

———.   Directions for Collectors of American Basketry.   Part P, Bulletin 39 U. S. National Museum, Washington, 1902, pp. (1–31) 44 figures.

MATTHEWS, WASHINGTON.   Navaho Weavers.   Third Annual Report of the Bureau of Ethnology, 1881, pp. 371–391, 3 pls., 15 figs.

———.   A Study in Butts and Tips.   American Anthropologist, Washington, October, 1892.

———.   The Basket Drum.   American Anthropologist, Washington, 1894, VII.

———.   The Night Chant: A Navaho Ceremony.   Memoirs of the American Museum Natural History, New York, 1902, VI.

MERRIAM, C. HART.   Some little known Basket Materials.   Science, XVII, 1903, p. 826.

MINDELEFF, COSMOS.   Aboriginal remains in Verde Valley.   Thirteenth Annual Report of the Bureau of Ethnology, 1896, pp. 176–261, 40 pls., 26 figs.

MOLSON, Mrs. W. MARKLAND.   Basketry of the Pacific Coast.   Portland, Oregon, 1896.

MURDOCH, JOHN.   Ethnological Results of the Point Barrow expedition.   Ninth Annual Report of the Bureau of Ethnology, Washington, 1892.

NORDENSKJÖLD, G.   The Cliff-Dwellers of the Mesa Verde.   Stockholm, 1894.

OUT WEST, Los Angeles, California.   Monthly journal, edited by Charles F. Lummis.

PALMER, EDWARD.   Plants used by the Indians of the United States.   American Naturalist, XII, p. 653.

PAPOOSE, THE.   Monthly Journal published by the Benham Exploring Expedition. New York, 1903.

PEPPER, GEORGE H. The ancient Basket Makers of southeastern Utah. Journal American Museum of Natural History, II, Guide leaflet No. 6, New York, 1902.

PERCIVAL, OLIVE M. The lost Art of Indian Basketry. Demorest's Family Magazine, February, 1897.

POWERS, STEPHEN. Aboriginal Botany. Proceedings, California Academy of Sciences. V.

——. The Indians of California. Contributions to North American Ethnology, Washington, III, 1877.

PURDY, CARL. The Pomo Indian Baskets and their Makers. Land of Sunshine and Out West, Los Angeles, California. A series of illustrated papers of great value running through volumes XV and XVI, 1901, 1902, in that journal, with many illustrations, and also in pamphlet form.

REID, HUGO. The California Farmer, 1861. Old files for early references.

SCHUMACHER, PAUL. In Archæology of the U. S. Geological Survey west of the one hundredth Meridian, VII, pp. 239–250.

SCIDMORE, ELIZA RUHAMAH. Indian Baskets. Harpers' Bazaar, September 1, 1894.

SELLERS, GEORGE E. Markings on Pottery, of Salt Springs, Illinois. Popular Science Monthly, New York, XI, p. 573.

STARR, FREDERICK. Notes on the Ethnography of Southern Mexico. Proceedings Davenport Academy of Sciences, IX, 1902.

STEARNS, MARY WATROUS. A School without Books. Battle Creek, Michigan, 1902.

STEPHEN, A. M. The Navajo. American Anthropologist, October, 1893.

STEVENSON, JAMES. Illustrated Catalogues of Collections. Second and third Annual Reports of the Bureau of Ethnology, Washington, 1879–1881.

TEIT, JAMES. The Thompson Indians of British Columbia. Memoirs of the American Museum of Natural History, II, Pt. 4, New York, 1900, 391 pp., 7 pls., 197 figs.

WEST, ARTHUR B. University Club, Denver, Colo. Basketry photographs.

WHITE, MARY. How to Make Baskets. New York, 1902, 194 pp., ill.; also More Baskets a d How to Make Them. New York, 1903.

WILKIE, HARRIET CUSHMAN. American Basketry. The Modern Priscilla, Boston, June, 1902.

WILLOUGHBY, C. C. Hats from the Nutka Sound Region. American Naturalist, Boston, 1903, pp. 65–68, 1 pl.

PIMA BASKETRY SHOWING FRETWORK.

COLLECTION OF J. W. BENHAM.   SEE PAGE 192.

POMO FINE COILED BASKET.

COLLECTED BY J. W. HUDSON.

See page 197.

HELIOTYPE CO., BOSTON

HAZELNUT (CORYLUS CALIFORNICA). AFTER FREDERICK V. COVILE. SEE PAGE 203.

HAZELNUT (*Corylus californica*).

The main figure is a fruiting branch. Above at the left are two staminate catkins, with a pistillate flowering bud at their base, accompanied by a sectional view of a catkin scale and stamens, enlarged six times. To the right above are a terminal bud and a nut. Underneath the main figure are views of catkin scales and stamens, from front and back, six times natural size, and at the right a terminal cluster of pistillate flowers, enlarged three times. Except in the cases noted, the figures are of natural size.

Drawing by Frederick A. Walpole.

WOLF MOSS (EVERNIA VULPINA).
AFTER FREDERICK V. COVILLE SEE PAGE 205.

JULIUS BIEN & CO. LITH. N.Y.

Wolf Moss (*Evernia vulpina*).

The lichens are shown as growing on a dead branch, their usual habitat. The plant at the right is in fruit, the shallow cups (apothecia) containing the brown spore-bearing surfaces.

KLAMATH GAMBLING TRAY.

A sak-lotks′ p'a′-hlə or flexible gambling tray of the Klamath Indians of Oregon. Both warp (pa-chĭsh′) and weft (twach) are of cords of undyed twisted tule (p. 211), which are fully exposed only in the pale-brown stripe at the margin, where the ends of the warp are interlaced and bound with a strengthening cord of gray fiber from the nettle (*Urtica breweri*), slĕdsh. Every other stitch of the tray is covered by an over-laying material: the white is of reed (p. 208); the black (mok′-was) is of tule dyed in mud springs containing iron; the canary yellow is of porcupine quills (smai′-am) dyed with wolf moss (p. 205), and the brown of the ring near the center of the tray is of undyed tule.

SITKA SPRUCE (*Picea sitchensis*).

Fig. *a*, twig with staminate catkins. Fig. *b*, pistillate catkins. Fig. *c*, cones approaching maturity. Fig. *d*, mature cone. Fig. *e*, inner view of a cone scale showing the position of the two winged seeds. Fig. *f*, seeds. With the exception of fig. *e*, which is enlarged one and one-third times, the figures are reproduced eight-ninths their natural size.

THREELEAF SUMAC (*Rhus trilobata*).

The main figure is a branch in leaf and fruit. Above at the left is a single fruit enlarged one and a half times, and at the right a section of the same twice the natural size. At the left below is a flowering twig, and to the right are four views of flowers, enlarged four times, the two at the left showing the two forms of flowers, one without stamens.

Drawing by Frederick A. Walpole.

TULE (*Scirpus lacustris*).

Fig. *a*, rootstock, roots, sheathing base of the stem, summit of the stem, and inflorescence. Figs. *b* and *c*, flowers, from within, showing the scale behind. In *c* the stigmas are mature, but the stamens not yet fully developed; in *b* the stigmas have withered, the ovary enlarged, and the stamens matured. Fig. *d*, a scale, viewed from the back. Fig. *e*, a mature nutlet with its barbed bristles. Fig. *f*, a cross section of the nutlet. Fig. *a* is half natural size, figs. *b* and *c* five times enlarged, and figs. *d* to *f* ten times enlarged.

GIANT CEDAR (*Thuja plicata*).

The large figure is a branch in its natural pendent position, with full-sized but not yet opened cones. Below at the left is the apex of a twig with staminate flowers, at the right a pistillate flowering twig, and above it an end view of the same, five times enlarged. Above at the right is a mature and opened cone, one and a fourth times enlarged, and below a cone scale, from within, showing the seeds natural size, and still lower a single seed twice enlarged.

Drawing by Frederick A. Walpole.

KLIKITAT IMBRICATED BASKET.

COLLECTION OF MRS. R. S. SHACKELFORD.

See page 220.

POMO BASKETMAKER.

PHOTOGRAPHED BY H. W. HENSHAW.   SEE PAGE 222.

TLINKIT BASKETMAKER.

PHOTOGRAPHED BY G. T. EMMONS. SEE PAGE 222.

CHECKERWORK IN CEDAR BARK.

SEE PAGE 223.

CIGAR CASE IN TWILLED WEAVING.

COLLECTION OF ROBERT FLETCHER.   SEE PAGE 224.

HOPI TWILLED BASKETRY.
COLLECTED BY V. MINDELEEF AND W. HOUGH. SEE PAGE 225.

MOHAVE CARRYING BASKET.

COLLECTION OF FIELD COLUMBIAN MUSEUM.   SEE PAGE 231.

ATTU WOMEN WEAVING BASKETS.

PHOTOGRAPHED BY C. GADSDEN PORCHER.   SEE PAGE 231.

POMO TWINED BASKETS.

POMO DIAGONAL TWINED BASKETS.

COLLECTION OF C. P. WILCOMB.   SEE PAGE 234.

UTE TWINED JARS.

SEE PAGE 236.

POMO TWINED BASKETS.

FURCATED STITCHES ON COILED BASKETRY.

COLLECTION OF E. L. McLEOD.   SEE PAGE 244.

PLATE 24.

OPENWORK COILED BASKET.

COLLECTION OF C. E. RUMSEY. SEE PAGE 249.

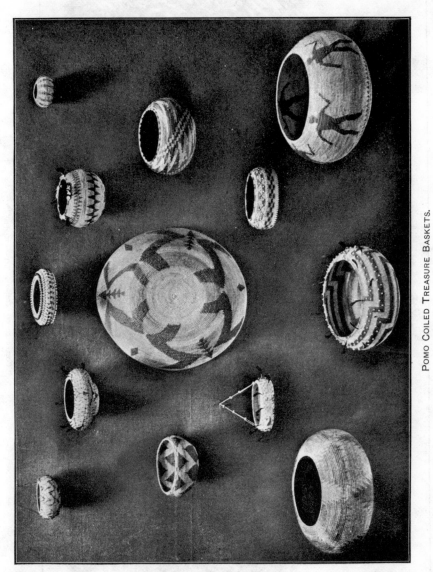

POMO COILED TREASURE BASKETS.

COLLECTION OF C. P. WILCOMB.   SEE PAGE 250.

ALASKAN ESKIMO COILED BASKET.

COLLECTED BY P. H. RAY.   SEE PAGE 251.

HOPI COILED BASKETRY.

COLLECTED BY JAMES STEVENSON AND V. MINDELEFF.

See page 252.

ZUNI OLD COILED BASKETS.

COLLECTED BY JAMES STEVENSON.

See page 253.

POMO THREE-ROD COILED BASKET.

COLLECTION OF C. P. WILCOMB.   SEE PAGE 254.

HOPI COILED PLAQUES.

COLLECTED BY JAMES MOONEY. SEE PAGE 257.

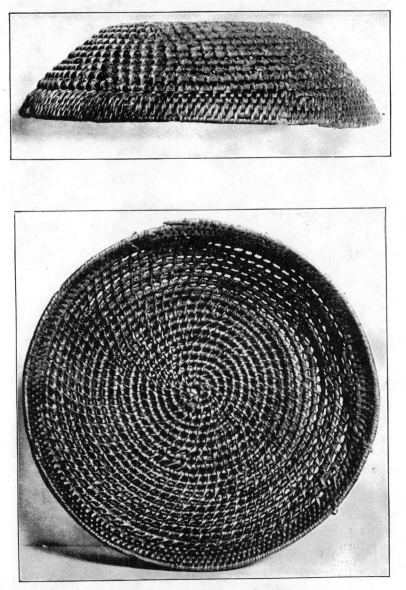

ANCIENT OPENWORK COILED BASKET.

AMERICAN MUSEUM OF NATURAL HISTORY.   SEE PAGE 257.

ANCIENT BASKET BOTTLES.

SOUTHERN INTERIOR BASIN.   SEE PAGE 258.

APACHE ANCIENT WATER JAR

COLLECTED BY WALTER HOUGH. SEE PAGE 259.

POMO THREE-STRAND BORDER.

SEE PAGE 265.

SALISH IMBRICATED BASKETS.

COLLECTED BY J. H. WILBUR AND WILKES EXPLORING EXPEDITION.

See page 274.

MISSION INDIAN COILED BOWL.

COLLECTION OF G. WHARTON JAMES.

See page 276.

TLINKIT TWINED BASKETS.

COLLECTED BY J. B. WHITE. SEE PAGE 281.

TULARE GAMBLING PLAQUES.

COLLECTION OF E. L. McLEOD.   SEE PAGE 283.

NAVAHO SACRED BASKETS.

COLLECTION OF FRED HARVEY.   SEE PAGE 283.

PLATE 40.

KERN AND TULARE HATS AND MUSH BOWLS.

COLLECTION OF E. L. McLEOD. SEE PAGE 284.

KERN AND TULARE BOTTLE-NECK BASKETS.

COLLECTION OF E. L. McLEOD.   SEE PAGE 285.

PLATE 42.

APACHE COILED OLLAS.

COLLECTION OF J. W. BENHAM, SEE PAGE 285.

SALISH AND KLIKITAT IMBRICATED BASKETS.

COLLECTION OF E. L. McLEOD.   SEE PAGE 285.

TLINKIT FALSE EMBROIDERY.

COLLECTION OF L. H. BRITTIN.   SEE PAGE 285.

OLD IMBRICATED BASKETS.

COLLECTED BY J. J. McLEAN AND WILKES EXPLORING EXPEDITION.

See page 286.

PLATE 46.

WASHOE FINE COILED BASKET.

COLLECTION OF A. COHN. SEE PAGE 287.

HOPI WICKERWORK PLAQUE.

COLLECTED BY J. W. BENHAM. SEE PAGE 289.

KLAMATH OLD TWINED BOWLS.

COLLECTED BY GEORGE GIBBS.

See page 290.

ANCIENT BASKET JARS.

PIMA BASKET BOWLS.

COLLECTION OF F. M. COVERT. SEE PAGE 296.

SKOKOMISH TWINED WALLET.

COLLECTION OF FRED HARVEY.   SEE PAGE 297.

APACHE COILED BASKET.

COLLECTION OF F. S. PLIMPTON.   SEE PAGE 297.

KERN, INYO, AND TULARE BOWLS.

COLLECTION OF C. P. WILCOMB. SEE PAGE 298.

TULARE COILED BOWLS.

COLLECTION OF F. S. PLIMPTON.   SEE PAGE 298.

SALISH IMBRICATED BASKETS.

COLLECTION OF FRED HARVEY.   SEE PAGE 299.

MAIDU COILED BASKETS.

SEE PAGE 300.

MAIDU COILED BASKETS.

SEE PAGE 300.

PIMA COILED BOWL.

COLLECTION OF FRED HARVEY.   SEE PAGE 300.

PIMA COILED BOWLS.

COLLECTION OF J. W. BENHAM.　SEE PAGE 300.

ANCIENT PIMA COILED BOWLS.

COLLECTION OF J. W. BENHAM. SEE PAGE 300.

PIMA COILED BASKET.

COLLECTION OF J. W. BENHAM.   SEE PAGE 300.

PLATE 62.

MISSION INDIAN COILED BOWLS.

COLLECTION OF G. WHARTON JAMES.

See page 300.

PIMA BASKET BOWLS.

COLLECTED BY FRANK RUSSELL.   SEE PAGE 304.

CHETIMACHA TWILLED BASKET.

COLLECTED BY C. E. WHITNEY.

TLINKIT MODERN TWINED BASKETS.

COLLECTED BY G. T. EMMONS.

See page 305.

HELIOTYPE CO., BOSTON

OREGON AND CALIFORNIA TWINED BASKETRY.

COLLECTED BY BENJAMIN AND LIVINGSTON STONE.

TLINKIT TWINED COVERED JAR.

COLLECTED BY J. J. McLEAN.

See page 309.

SALISH IMBRICATED WARE.

COLLECTION OF MISS ANNE M. LANG.   SEE PAGE 310.

POMO COILED FEATHERED BASKET.
COLLECTION OF C. P. WILCOMB. SEE PAGE 311.

JULIUS BIEN & CO. LITH. N.Y.

TULARE BOTTLE-NECK BASKET.

COLLECTION OF C. P. WILCOMB.   SEE PAGE 332.

PLATE 71.

TLINKIT TWINED WALLETS.

SEE PAGE 320.

ANCIENT TLINKIT TWINED WALLETS.

SEE PAGE 320.

TLINKIT COVERED TWINED BASKETS.

COLLECTED BY F. M. RING. AND G. T. EMMONS.

See page 320.

SYMBOLISM ON SALISH BASKETRY.

AMERICAN MUSEUM OF NATURAL HISTORY. SEE PAGE 322.

SYMBOLISM ON SALISH BASKETRY.

AMERICAN MUSEUM OF NATURAL HISTORY. SEE PAGE 323.

SYMBOLISM ON SALISH BASKETRY.

AMERICAN MUSEUM OF NATURAL HISTORY.   SEE PAGE 324.

SYMBOLISM ON SALISH BASKETRY.

AMERICAN MUSEUM OF NATURAL HISTORY.   SEE PAGE 324.

SYMBOLISM ON SALISH BASKETRY.

AMERICAN MUSEUM OF NATURAL HISTORY. SEE PAGE 326.

SYMBOLISM ON SALISH BASKETRY.

AMERICAN MUSEUM OF NATURAL HISTORY. SEE PAGE 325.

YUKI SUN BASKET.
COLLECTED BY N.J. PURCELL. SEE PAGE 326.

PLATE 81.

POMO GIFT BASKET.

SEE PAGE 330.

SYMBOLISM ON WASHOE BASKETS.

COLLECTION OF A. COHN. SEE PAGE 332.

POMO COILED FEATHERED BASKET.
COLLECTION OF C. P. WILCOMB. SEE PAGE 311.

ANCIENT CLIFF DWELLERS' BASKET.

AMERICAN MUSEUM OF NATURAL HISTORY.   SEE PAGE 333.

HOPI WICKER PLAQUE.
COLLECTED BY J. W. BENHAM. SEE PAGE 333.

HUPA BURDEN BEARER.

PHOTOGRAPHED BY A. W. ERICSON. SEE PAGE 339.

SANDALS OF ANCIENT CLIFF DWELLERS.

SEE PAGE 342.

HUPA TWINED SANDAL.

COLLECTED BY P. H. RAY.   SEE PAGE 343.

TULARE COILED CUP AND JAR.

COLLECTION OF MRS. E. GREBLE.

See page 343.

HUPA AND POMO FEATHERED BASKETS.

SEE PAGE 344.

KLIKITAT IMBRICATED BASKETS.
COLLECTED BY MRS. LEVI ANKENY. SEE PAGE 346.

HUPA FOOD BASKETS.

COLLECTED BY P. H. RAY.   SEE PAGE 346.

HOPI SACRED COILED TRAYS.

COLLECTED BY MRS. M.C. STEVENSON. SEE PAGE 346.

ORAIBI WOMAN DRYING CORN.

PHOTOGRAPHED BY GEORGE WHARTON JAMES.   SEE PAGE 346.

AMAZONIAN BASKETRY AND MATERIALS.

SEE PAGE 347.

HUPA HARVESTING BASKETS.

COLLECTED BY P. H. RAY.   SEE PAGE 349.

PLATE 97.

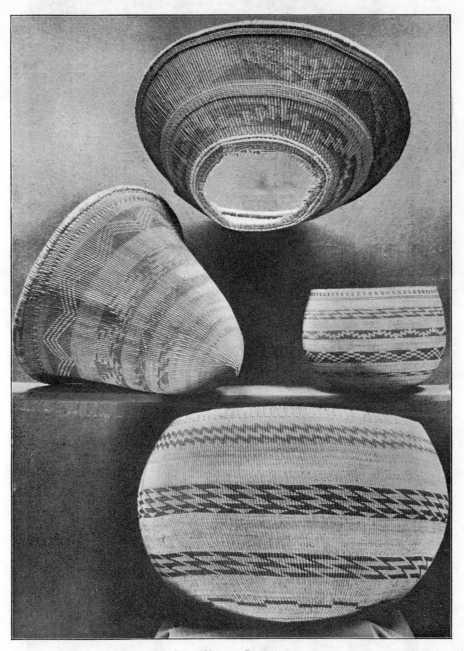

POMO MILLING BASKETS.

COLLECTION OF C. P. WILCOMB.   SEE PAGE 350.

TULARE MEAL AND MORTAR BASKETS.

COLLECTION OF C. P. WILCOMB.   SEE PAGE 351.

YOKUT WOMAN SIFTING MEAL.

PHOTOGRAPHED BY GEORGE WHARTON JAMES.   SEE PAGE 351.

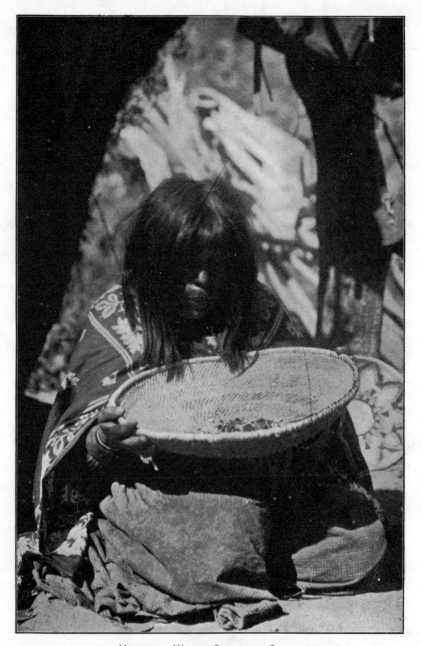

HAVASUPAI WOMAN SCREENING CORN.

PHOTOGRAPHED BY GEORGE WHARTON JAMES. SEE PAGE 351.

COAHUILLA WOMAN GRINDING ACORNS.

PHOTOGRAPHED BY GEORGE WHARTON JAMES.   SEE PAGE 351.

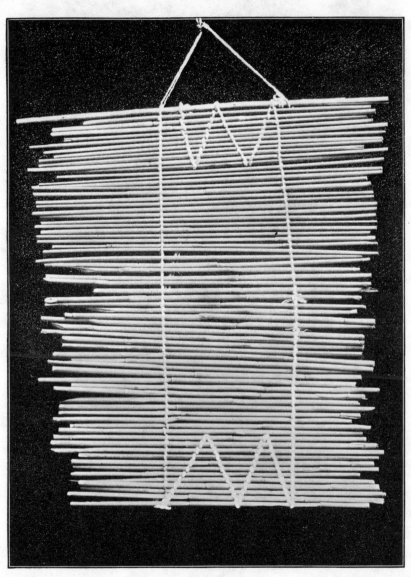

HOPI BRIDAL COSTUME CASE.

SEE PAGE 352.

ANCIENT MORTUARY BASKETS.

AMERICAN MUSEUM OF NATURAL HISTORY.　SEE PAGE 353.

ANCIENT PERUVIAN LACE WORK.

AFTER W. H. HOLMES.   SEE PAGE 353.

RELATIONSHIP BETWEEN BASKETRY AND POTTERY.

AFTER F. H. CUSHING.   SEE PAGE 354.

PLATE 107.

BASKETRY PRESERVED BY POTTERY.

AFTER W. H. HOLMES. SEE PAGE 354.

TLINKIT TWINED BASKETS.

COLLECTED BY JAMES G. SWAN. SEE PAGE 355.

TLINKIT TWINED COVERED BASKET.

COLLECTED BY J. J. McLEAN.

HOPI SACRED DANCE BASKETS.

PHOTOGRAPHED BY GEORGE WHARTON JAMES.   SEE PAGE 357.

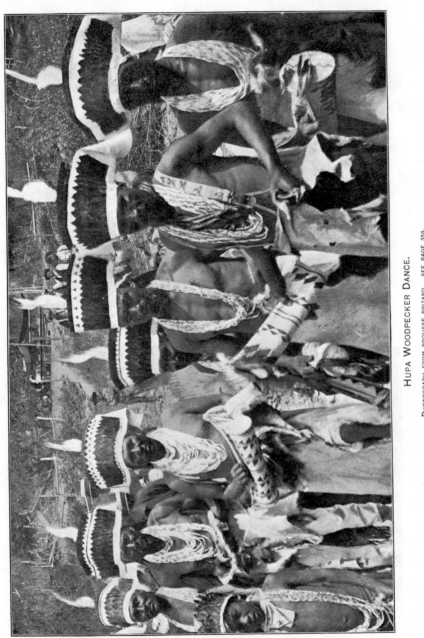

HUPA WOODPECKER DANCE.

PHOTOGRAPH FROM BROUSSE BRIZARD.   SEE PAGE 358.

POMO WEDDING BASKETS.

COLLECTION OF C. P. WILCOMB.   SEE PAGE 358.

POMO JEWEL BASKETS

COLLECTION OF C. P. WILCOMB.　　SEE PAGE 358.

POMO JEWEL BASKETS.

COLLECTION OF C. P. WILCOMB.   SEE PAGE 358.

TULARE GAMBLING TRAY AND DICE.

SEE PAGE 359.

TULARE GAMBLING TRAY AND DICE.

COLLECTION OF C. P. WILCOMB.   SEE PAGE 359.

PAIUTE BASKET BOTTLES.

SEE PAGE 361.

NAVAHO WATER CARRIERS.

PHOTOGRAPHED BY GEORGE WHARTON JAMES.　SEE PAGE 361.

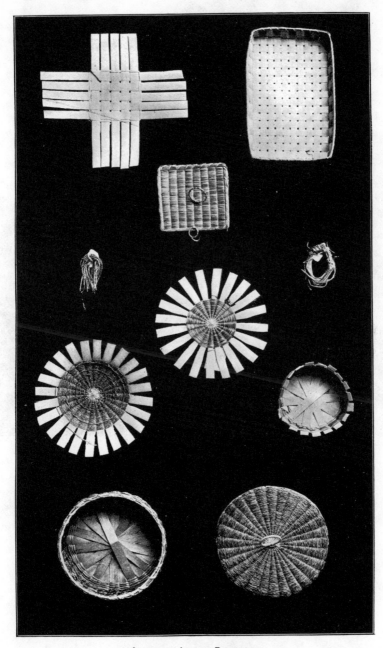

ALGONKIN INDIAN BASKETRY.

SEE PAGE 374.

ABENAKI INDIAN BASKETMAKER.

PHOTOGRAPHED BY HERBERT B. ROWLAND.   SEE PAGE 374.

CHIPPEWA INDIAN BASKETMAKERS.

PHOTOGRAPHED BY HARLAN I. SMITH.   SEE PAGE 374.

CHIPPEWA BARK MATTING.

PHOTOGRAPHED BY D. D. GAILLARD. SEE PAGE 374.

ATHAPASCAN SNOWSHOE DETAIL.

COLLECTED BY GEORGE CATLIN.   SEE PAGE 376.

OJIBWA COILED BASKETS.

PEABODY MUSEUM, MASSACHUSETTS.   SEE PAGE 377.

CENTRAL ESKIMO COILED BASKET.

COLLECTED BY C. F. HALL.   SEE PAGE 377.

CENTRAL ESKIMO COILED BASKET.

COLLECTED BY L. M. TURNER.   SEE PAGE 378

COMANCHE COILED TRAY.

SEE PAGE 378.

COILED BASKET OF PINE NEEDLES.

SEE PAGE 379.

DOG RIB INDIAN GAME BAG.

COLLECTED BY B. R. ROSS.   SEE PAGE 379.

POTSHERDS SHOWING TEXTILE IMPRESSIONS.

AFTER W. H. HOLMES. SEE PAGE 384.

OJIBWA TWINED WALLET.

AMERICAN MUSEUM OF NATURAL HISTORY.   SEE PAGE 385.

CHETIMACHA TWILLED BASKETRY.

SEE PAGE 388.

CHETIMACHA TWILLED BASKETRY.

COLLECTION OF MRS. SYDNEY BRADFORD.   SEE PAGE 388.

CHOCTAW TWILLED BASKETS.

COLLECTION OF MRS. CAROLYN G. BENJAMIN.   SEE PAGE 388.

ATTAKAPA TWILLED BASKETS.

COLLECTION OF MRS. WILLIAM P. JOHNSTON.　　SEE PAGE 388.

ALASKAN ESKIMO BASKETRY.

COLLECTED BY E. W. NELSON.   SEE PAGE 396.

ALASKAN ESKIMO TWINED WALLET.

SEE PAGE 396.

CHUKCHI TWINED WALLET.

AMERICAN MUSEUM OF NATURAL HISTORY.   SEE PAGE 397.

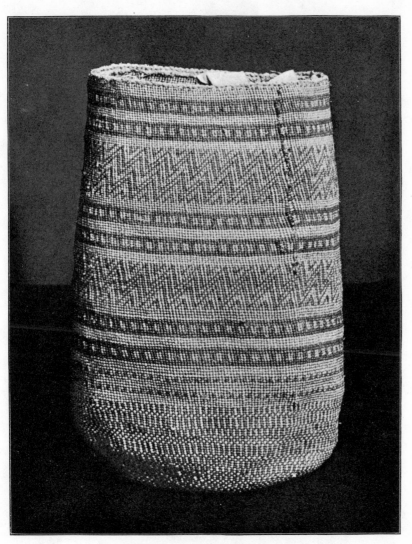

KAMCHATKAN TWINED WALLET.

AMERICAN MUSEUM OF NATURAL HISTORY.   SEE PAGE 397.

CHUKCHI COILED BASKETS.

AMERICAN MUSEUM OF NATURAL HISTORY.   SEE PAGE 402.

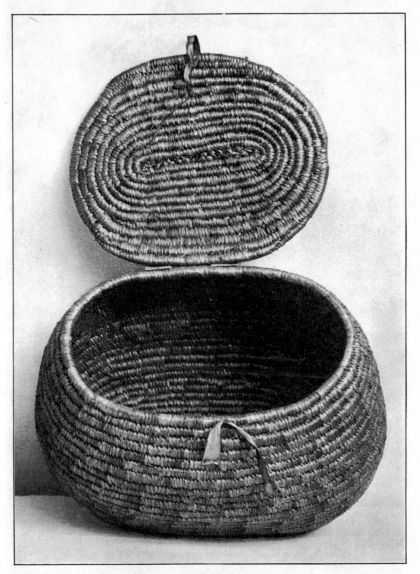

ALASKAN ESKIMO COILED BASKET.

COLLECTION OF FRED HARVEY.   SEE PAGE 402.

ALEUT TWINED BASKET.

SEE PAGE 405.

ALEUT TWINED BASKET.

COLLECTED BY L. M. TURNER.   SEE PAGE 405.

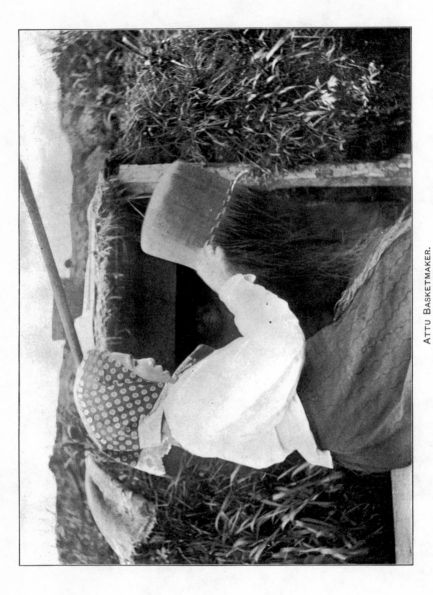

ATTU BASKETMAKER.

PHOTOGRAPHED BY C. GADSDEN PORCHER. SEE PAGE 406.

ALEUT MANUAL TRAINING.

PHOTOGRAPHED BY C. GADSDEN PORCHER. SEE PAGE 407.

PLATE 146.

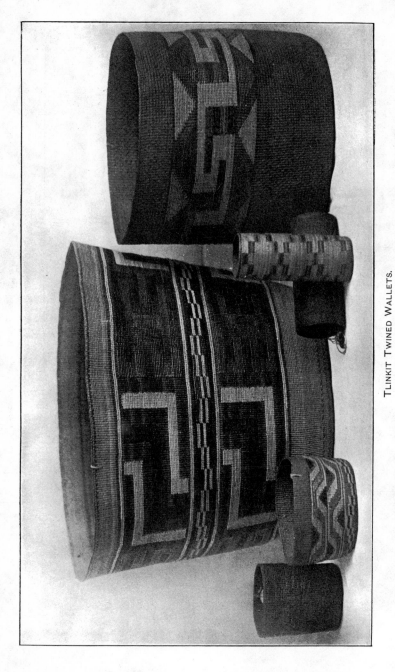

TLINKIT TWINED WALLETS.

COLLECTION OF FRED HARVEY. SEE PAGE 409.

TLINKIT BASKETMAKERS.

PHOTOGRAPHED BY G. T. EMMONS.   SEE PAGE 410.

PLATE 148.

CHILKAT CEREMONIAL BLANKET.

SEE PAGE 412.

HAIDA TWINED WALLETS.

COLLECTION OF FRED HARVEY.   SEE PAGE 416.

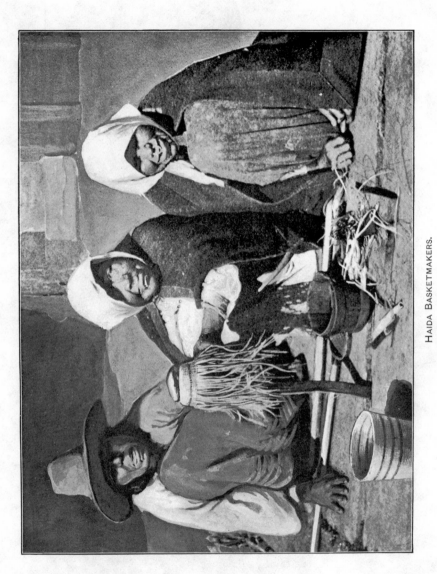

HAIDA BASKETMAKERS.

PHOTOGRAPHED BY J. G. SWAN.   SEE PAGE 416.

NUTKA INDIAN HATS.

AFTER C. C. WILLOUGHBY.   SEE PAGE 419.

SALISH TWILLED BASKET.

SEE PAGE 420.

MAKAH INDIAN BASKETMAKERS.

PHOTOGRAPHED FROM D. F. TOZIER.   SEE PAGE 420.

TYPES OF SALISH BASKETRY.

SEE PAGE 421.

TYPES OF SALISH BASKETRY.

SEE PAGE 421.

SALISH IMBRICATED BASKETS.

COLLECTION OF FRED HARVEY.   SEE PAGE 425.

SALISH IMBRICATED BASKETS.

COLLECTION OF MISS ANNE M. LANG.   SEE PAGE 425.

COWLITZ AND KLIKITAT IMBRICATED BASKETS.

COLLECTED BY CHARLES WILKES AND W. H. HOLMES.

See page 428.

KLIKITAT IMBRICATED BASKETRY (OLD FORMS).

COLLECTION OF MISS ANNE M. LANG.   SEE PAGE 429.

KLIKITAT IMBRICATED BASKETRY (MODERN FORMS).

COLLECTION OF MISS ANNE M. LANG.   SEE PAGE 429.

KLIKITAT IMBRICATED BASKET.

SEE PAGE 430.

QUINAIELT TWINED WALLETS.

COLLECTION OF MISS ANNE M. LANG.   SEE PAGE 435.

SALISH BASKETRY.

SEE PAGE 435.

CLALLAM TWINED BASKETS.

SEE PAGE 436.

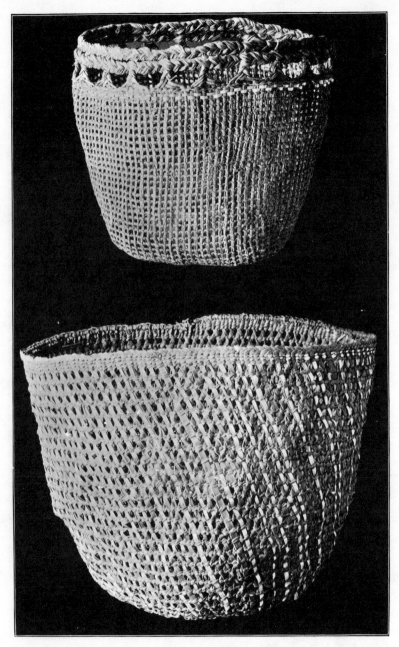

TILLAMUK AND CHINOOK TWINED WALLETS.

SEE PAGE 436.

MODOC AND NEZ PERCÉ WOMEN'S HATS.

SEE PAGE 438.

WASCO TWINED WALLETS.

SEE PAGE 439.

WASCO TWINED WALLETS.

COLLECTION OF FRED HARVEY.   SEE PAGE 439.

HUPA BASKETMAKER.

PHOTOGRAPHED BY JOHN DAGGETT. SEE PAGE 448.

KLAMATH AND WINTUN BASKETMAKERS.

PHOTOGRAPHED BY JOHN DAGGETT.   SEE PAGE 449.

POMO BASKET IN TEE WEAVE.

SEE PAGE 454.

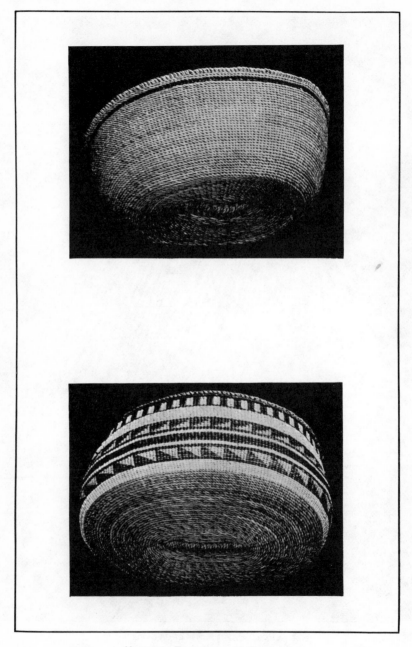

KLAMATH THREE-STRAND BASKETS.

COLLECTION OF C. HART MERRIAM.   SEE PAGE 462.

PIT RIVER TWINED BASKETS.

COLLECTED BY L. STONE AND H. F. LISTON. SEE PAGE 462.

SHASTA TWINED BASKETS.

COLLECTED BY LIVINGSTON STONE. SEE PAGE 463.

HAT CREEK INDIAN BASKETRY.

COLLECTION OF H. E. WILLIAMS. SEE PAGE 464.

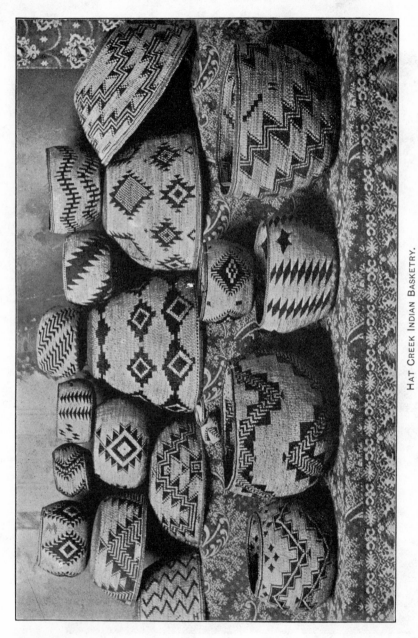

HAT CREEK INDIAN BASKETRY.

COLLECTION OF H. E. WILLIAMS.   SEE PAGE 464.

WASHOE BASKET BOWLS.

COLLECTED BY E. MEAD AND J. W. HUDSON. SEE PAGE 466.

WASHOE COILED BASKET.

COLLECTION OF A. COHN. SEE PAGE 467.

WASHOE BASKETMAKER.

PHOTOGRAPHED BY MRS. A. COHN.   SEE PAGE 467.

EASTERN CALIFORNIAN COILED BASKETS.
COLLECTED BY EUGENE MEAD. SEE PAGE 467.

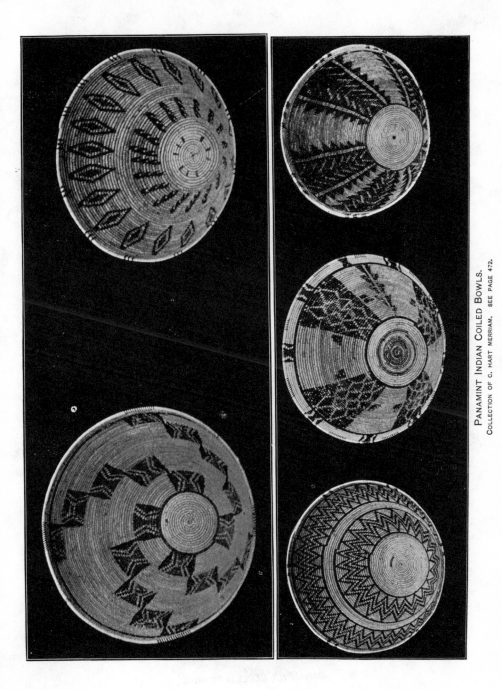

PANAMINT INDIAN COILED BOWLS.

COLLECTION OF C. HART MERRIAM.   SEE PAGE 472.

PANAMINT COILED BOWLS.

COLLECTED BY J. W. HUDSON, AND EUGENE MEAD.

See page 473.

TULARE COILED BASKETS.

SEE PAGE 474.

TULARE COILED BASKET.

TULARE COILED JARS.

COLLECTED BY STEPHEN POWERS, AND GAVIN AND LEONARD.

See page 475.

KERN AND TULARE COILED BASKETS.

COLLECTION OF E. L. MCLEOD.   SEE PAGE 476.

TULARE COILED BASKETS.

COLLECTION OF E. L. McLEOD. SEE PAGE 477.

TEJON COILED BASKETS.

COLLECTION OF E. L. MCLEOD.   SEE PAGE 477.

KERN AND TULARE COILED BASKETS.

COLLECTION OF E. L. MCLEOD.   SEE PAGE 478.

CALIENTE CREEK INDIAN BASKETS.

COLLECTION OF E. L. McLEOD.   SEE PAGE 478.

KERN COILED BASKET.

COLLECTION OF E. L. McLEOD. SEE PAGE 479.

KERN COILED BASKET.

COLLECTION OF E. L. McLEOD.   SEE PAGE 479.

PLATE 195.

KERN COILED BASKET.

COLLECTION OF E. L. McLEOD.   SEE PAGE 479.

KERN COILED BASKETS.

COLLECTION OF E. L. MCLEOD.   SEE PAGE 481.

MISSION INDIAN BASKETMAKER.

PHOTOGRAPHED BY GEORGE WHARTON JAMES.   SEE PAGE 485.

SABOBA INDIAN BASKETMAKER.

PHOTOGRAPHED BY GEORGE WHARTON JAMES.   SEE PAGE 486.

MISSION INDIAN BASKET BOWL.
COLLECTION OF GEORGE WHARTON JAMES. SEE PAGE 486.

HAVASUPAI BASKETMAKER.

PHOTOGRAPHED BY GEORGE WHARTON JAMES.   SEE PAGE 486.

ANCIENT CAVE BASKETS.

COLLECTED BY STEPHEN BOWERS. SEE PAGE 487.

ANCIENT CAVE BASKETS.

COLLECTED BY STEPHEN BOWERS.   SEE PAGE 487.

MISSION INDIAN TWINED BAG.

COLLECTED BY MISS CONSTANCE G. DUBOIS.   SEE PAGE 487.

PAIUTE WATER BOTTLES.

COLLECTED BY STEPHEN POWERS.   SEE PAGE 495.

ANCIENT BASKET MAKERS' COILED TRAYS.

AMERICAN MUSEUM OF NATURAL HISTORY.   SEE PAGE 497.

PLATE 206.

ANCIENT BASKET MAKERS' COILED WARE.

AMERICAN MUSEUM OF NATURAL HISTORY.   SEE PAGE 497.

ANCIENT BASKET MAKERS' COILED TRAY.

AMERICAN MUSEUM OF NATURAL HISTORY.   SEE PAGE 498.

ANCIENT BASKET MAKERS' COILED TRAY.

AMERICAN MUSEUM OF NATURAL HISTORY.   SEE PAGE 498.

ANCIENT BASKET MAKERS' COILED BOWLS.

AMERICAN MUSEUM OF NATURAL HISTORY.   SEE PAGE 498.

ANCIENT BASKET MAKERS' FOOD RECEPTACLES.

AMERICAN MUSEUM OF NATURAL HISTORY.   SEE PAGE 498.

ANCIENT BASKET MAKERS' HOPPER.

AMERICAN MUSEUM OF NATURAL HISTORY.   SEE PAGE 498.

SIA ANCIENT COILED BASKETS.

COLLECTED BY JAMES STEVENSON.

ANCIENT ZUÑI BASKETRY.

COLLECTED BY JAMES STEVENSON.　SEE PAGE 500.

ANCIENT PUEBLO COILED BASKETRY.

COLLECTED BY JAMES STEVENSON. SEE PAGE 501.

HOPI BASKETMAKER.

PHOTOGRAPHED BY GEORGE WHARTON JAMES.   SEE PAGE 504.

HOPI COILED PLAQUES.
COLLECTED BY JAMES MOONEY. SEE PAGE 504.

ORAIBI BASKETWEAVER.

PHOTOGRAPHED BY GEORGE WHARTON JAMES. SEE PAGE 505.

PLATE 218.

ANCIENT BASKETS FROM ORAIBI.

COLLECTED BY JAMES STEVENSON. SEE PAGE 506.

ANCIENT WICKER BASKET.

COLLECTED BY J. WALTER FEWKES.　SEE PAGE 508.

ANCIENT TWILLED AND COILED WARE.

COLLECTED BY J. WALTER FEWKES.   SEE PAGE 509.

ANCIENT PUEBLO BASKETRY.

COLLECTED BY WALTER HOUGH. SEE PAGE 509.

ANCIENT PUEBLO BASKETRY.

COLLECTED BY WALTER HOUGH. SEE PAGE 509.

ANCIENT PUEBLO BASKETRY.

COLLECTED BY WALTER HOUGH. SEE PAGE 509.

APACHE COILED BOWLS.

COLLECTION OF J. W. BENHAM. SEE PAGE 511.

APACHE COILED BOWLS.

COLLECTED BY WALTER HOUGH.

See page 511.

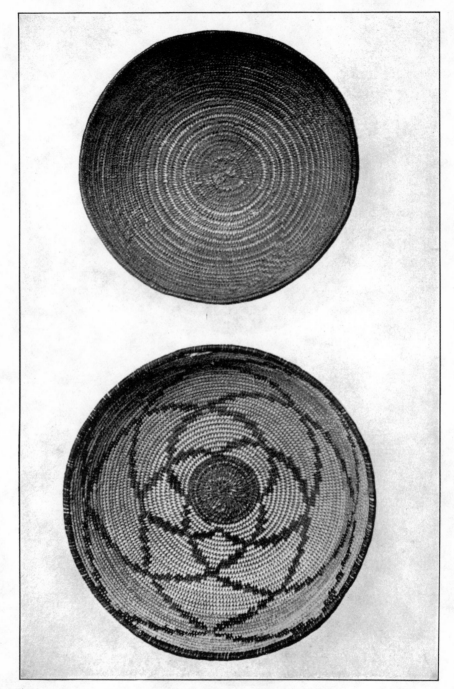

APACHE COILED BOWLS.

SEE PAGE 511.

MESCALERO COILED BASKETS

COLLECTED BY WALTER HOUGH.

NAVAHO COILED BOWLS.

PHOTOGRAPH FROM MRS. I. H. KIRKPATRICK.   SEE PAGE 515.

HAVASUPAI COILED BASKETRY.

COLLECTED BY A. HRDLICKA.   SEE PAGE 517.

HAVASUPAI COILED BOWLS.
COLLECTED BY WALTER HOUGH.

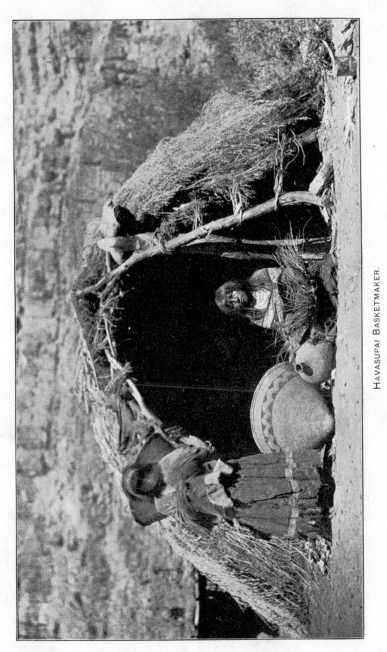

HAVASUPAI BASKETMAKER.

PHOTOGRAPHED BY GEORGE WHARTON JAMES.   SEE PAGE 518.

CHEMEHUEVI COILED BASKETS.

SEE PAGE 519.

PIMA COILED BOWL.

PIMA COILED BASKETS.

COLLECTED BY FRANK RUSSELL.   SEE PAGE 523.

PIMA BASKETMAKER.

PHOTOGRAPHED BY J. W. BENHAM.   SEE PAGE 526.

YAQUI PLUME BASKET.

COLLECTED BY FRANK RUSSELL. SEE PAGE 526.

YAQUI COVERED BASKETS.

COLLECTED BY A. HRDLICKA.　SEE PAGE 526.

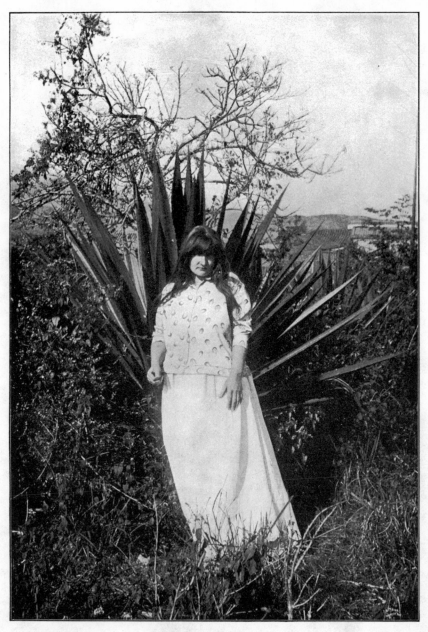

VENEZUELAN BASKETMAKER.

PHOTOGRAPHED BY R. BARTLEMAN.   SEE PAGE 528.

ARAWAK INDIAN BASKETRY.

COLLECTED BY P. FIGYELMESY.   SEE PAGE 529.

BRAZILIAN CARRYING BASKETS.

PHOTOGRAPHED BY CARL VON DEN STEINEN.　SEE PAGE 529.

BRAZILIAN CARRYING BASKETS.

PHOTOGRAPHED BY CARL VON DEN STEINEN. SEE PAGE 530.

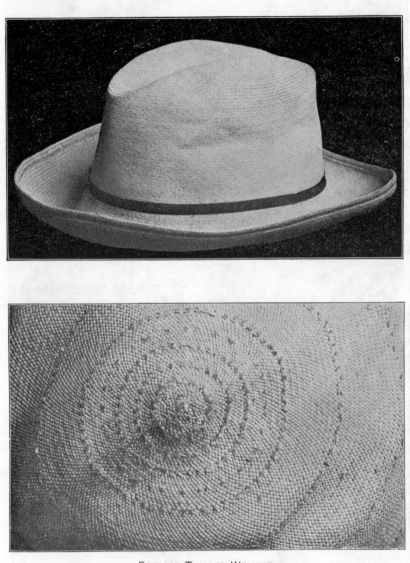

ECUADOR TWILLED WEAVING.

COLLECTED BY S. O. RICHEY.   SEE PAGE 532.

ANCIENT PERUVIAN WORKBASKET.

SEE PAGE 536.

PERUVIAN ANCIENT TWINED CARRYING FRAME.
FIELD COLUMBIAN MUSEUM. SEE PAGE 536.

ANCIENT CHILEAN COILED BASKETRY.

SEE PAGE 538.

ANCIENT CHILEAN COILED BASKETRY.

SEE PAGE 538.

ANCIENT CHILEAN COILED BASKETRY.

SEE PAGE 538.

PERUVIAN MODERN COILED BASKETRY.

SEE PAGE 538.